Kellogg on Branding in a Hyper-Connected World

KELLOGG ON BRANDING IN A HYPER-CONNECTED WORLD

Edited by
Alice M. Tybout
Tim Calkins

WILEY

For general information on our other products and services or for technical support, please contact our Customer Care Department within the United States at (800) 762-2974, outside the United States at (317) 572–3993 or fax (317) 572–4002.

Wiley publishes in a variety of print and electronic formats and by print-on-demand. Some material included with standard print versions of this book may not be included in e-books or in print-on-demand. If this book refers to media such as a CD or DVD that is not included in the version you purchased, you may download this material at http://booksupport.wiley.com. For more information about Wiley products, visit www.wiley.com.

Library of Congress Cataloging-in-Publication Data:

ISBN 9781119533184 (Hardcover)
ISBN 9781119533283 (ePDF)
ISBN 9781119533290 (ePub)

Printed in the United States of America

V10008104_021219

CONTENTS

Foreword   ix
Jim Stengel

Preface   xi
Alice M. Tybout and Tim Calkins

Acknowledgments   xvii

Introduction: The Power and Challenge of Branding   xix
Tim Calkins

Section One
THINKING STRATEGICALLY ABOUT YOUR BRAND

Chapter 1
Brand Positioning: The Foundation for Building a Strong Brand   3
Alice M. Tybout

Chapter 2
Leveraging the Power of Brand Purpose   20
Jim Stengel, Matt Carcieri, and Renée Dunn

Chapter 3
Creating a Powerful Brand Portfolio   37
Tim Calkins

Chapter 4
Competitive Brand Strategies: Creating Pioneer, Fast-Follower,
and Late-Mover Advantage   53
Gregory S. Carpenter and Kent Nakamoto

Chapter 5

Leading the Brand: Brand Strategy Orchestration and Implementation 67
  Eric Leininger

Chapter 6

The Three Keys to Building Global Brands with Soul 78
  Sanjay Khosla

Section Two
BRINGING YOUR BRAND TO LIFE

Chapter 7

Brand Design and Design Thinking 93
  Bobby J. Calder

Chapter 8

Leveraging Touchpoints in Today's Branding Environment 110
  Kevin McTigue

Chapter 9

Building Strong Connections between Brands and the Self 129
  Neal J. Roese and Wendi L. Gardner

Chapter 10

Building Strong Brands through Advertising Strategy
  in the Online Age 143
  Brian Sternthal

Chapter 11

Digital Brand Storytelling 161
  Mohanbir Sawhney

Chapter 12

Branding Services in the Digital Era 177
  Tom O'Toole

Section Three

GAINING INSIGHT ABOUT YOUR BRAND AND QUANTIFYING ITS STATURE

Chapter 13

Digital Transformation and the Evolution of Customer
   Insights in Brand Building   193
   Bridgette Braig

Chapter 14

Using Neuroscience to Assess Brands   207
   Moran Cerf

Chapter 15

Measuring Brand Relevance and Health   218
   Julie Hennessy

Chapter 16

Connecting Marketing and Finance via Brand Value   234
   Bobby J. Calder

Section Four

LESSONS FROM BRAND LEADERS

Chapter 17

Has Purpose Lost Its Purpose? McDonald's Defines
   Its Style of Marketing   249
   Silvia Lagnado and Colin Mitchell

Chapter 18

Ulta Beauty Gets a Branding Makeover   256
   Mary Dillon and Dave Kimbell

Chapter 19

Transforming a Historic Brand for a Hyper-Connected World:
The John Deere Story   263
   Denny Docherty and Mike Porter

Chapter 20
Rebranding an Organization: The Novant Health Story   271
Scott Davis and David Duvall

Chapter 21
Repositioning a Country Brand: Changing the Conversation
about Mexico   279
Gloria Guevara

Chapter 22
Managing Brand Communications in a Digital World   287
Cindy Halvorsen

Chapter 23
Customer Experience: The New Frontier of Branding   294
Sergio Pereira

Chapter 24
Brand New: Creating a Brand from Scratch   301
Paul Earle

Index   311

FOREWORD

In an age of hypercompetition, commoditization, globalization, and rapid technological obsolescence, marketers are struggling to find new conceptual bases on which to design and deliver their marketing programs.

—Philip Kotler, Professor Emeritus of Marketing, Northwestern | Kellogg

It has been 14 years since our previous edition of Kellogg's tome on branding. The quote above is from Phil Kotler's foreword to that edition. And it was written pre-iPhone, pre-Uber, pre-Twitter, pre-Alexa, pre-Instagram, and pre-Snapchat, as well as before the explosive strides in artificial intelligence and machine learning. To state the obvious: the world that Kotler described so presciently in 2005 has only become ever more challenging and bewildering for those responsible for building and managing brands.

That is why this book is essential. It is designed to help managers accelerate the growth of brands in this hyper-connected world. It is the best thinking from the most acclaimed marketing and branding school in the country; it is supplemented with wisdom from cutting-edge practitioners from companies such as Ulta, Google, John Deere, and McDonald's.

You will become a better brand builder by reading this book and putting the perspectives and frameworks to work in your business, in your research, or in your classroom. Marketing leaders will find ideas that help them create new markets and differentiate their brands from their competitors. Academics will find sparks that inspire research and guide them as they prepare the next generation of CMOs in their classrooms.

This book arrives not a moment too soon. Branding and marketing has grown in influence and importance for companies since our last edition; a recent study by Deloitte and the CMO Council revealed that CMOs are increasingly responsible for enterprise-level growth and revenue management versus communications management. And the stakes keep getting higher: since 2005, global marketing spending has increased 45 percent to approximately $585.5 billion. Yet, still too many brands are struggling to grow. Witness the sluggish growth of mature brands in categories such as food, beverage, and beauty as small, founder-led brands capture the momentum.

A word of advice on how to leverage the knowledge in this book to full advantage: treat it like a sumptuous buffet. Our book has four parts and 24 chapters, and every chapter is loaded with calories. Consume a chapter or two at a time, and let it settle. Make notes on what struck you, and how you might apply it, share it, test it. And if you approach a buffet as I do (desserts first!), you can go directly to what interests you the most. You do not need to read these chapters in sequence.

Now, get to work. The world is better when we have curious, courageous brand builders who are ready and willing to take on this very important task.

Jim Stengel

PREFACE

The world of branding has changed dramatically in the past decade, and the pace of change only seems to be accelerating. A key force driving both change and complexity is the overwhelming access to people, products, and information. In today's world, we are hyper-connected.

Consumers have an almost infinite range of products and services quite literally at their fingertips, and these options can be delivered, if not instantly, then close to it. Brand managers can connect directly with their customers, track their decision journey, and in many cases make the sale without the assistance of traditional intermediaries. The opportunities are endless for both consumers and managers, and the breadth of options has the potential to be overwhelming.

Although some argue that brands are becoming less important, we believe the opposite—that branding is becoming even more important. Brands provide differentiation, create loyalty, and even foster a sense of identity. Without a powerful, distinctive brand, firms have to rely purely on product-based differentiation, and this can be difficult to maintain.

Our goal in writing and editing this book is to help business leaders navigate this evolving landscape. We do so by drawing upon the perspectives of Kellogg's world-renowned marketing faculty, as well as those of senior executives who put theory into practice as they build and manage brands on a day-to-day basis.

This book is the latest in a series of marketing books from Kellogg, stretching back to 2001 with the publication of *Kellogg on Marketing*. Four additional books followed: *Kellogg on Integrated Marketing* (2003), *Kellogg on Branding* (2005), *Kellogg on Advertising and Media* (2008), and the second edition of *Kellogg on Marketing* (2010). These books reflect the collective wisdom of the Kellogg marketing faculty. Thousands of executives have turned to them for perspectives, frameworks, and tools when creating marketing plans and building brands.

OVERVIEW OF THE BOOK

Our introduction highlights the power and challenge of branding. The four sections that follow it focus on themes of strategy, implementation, methods, and practical applications.

Section One, "Thinking Strategically about Your Brand," covers big-picture issues. The six chapters in this section examine the intended meaning for the brand, how the brand will compete, and the vision and leadership required to create a strong brand.

Chapter 1, "Brand Positioning: The Foundation for Building a Strong Brand," provides a contemporary look at the core concept of brand positioning and describes ways to evolve a positioning strategy over time. Chapter 2, "Leveraging the Power of Brand Purpose," explains why it is important for companies and brands to articulate their purpose; that is, why they exist. Clarity about company/brand purpose has helped many companies effectively engage multiple stakeholders and in some instances is integral to brand positioning. Chapter 3, "Creating a Powerful Brand Portfolio," explores the opportunity and complexity that comes from creating a portfolio of brands.

The remaining chapters in Section One are devoted to competitive strategy, leadership, and globalization. Chapter 4, "Competitive Brand Strategies: Creating Pioneer, Fast-Follower, and Late-Mover Advantage," considers issues related to the timing of a brand's entry into a category, describing the advantages and challenges associated with being a pioneer, fast follower, or late entrant. Chapter 5, "Leading the Brand: Brand Strategy Orchestration and Implementation," highlights the importance of involvement and walking the talk at the highest level of the organization. Last, Chapter 6, "The Three Keys to Building Global Brands with Soul," details principles for managing global brands. It emphasizes the need to exert central control over a brand's essence and connection to consumers' goals, while delegating sufficient authority and responsibility to local managers to adapt the brand to cultural differences and habits.

Section Two, "Bringing Your Brand to Life," focuses on strategy implementation. Chapters in this section address the challenge of translating the intended meaning for the brand into everything that customers experience. Here is where hyper-connectivity has its greatest impact for many brands. In the pre–digital world, once the strategy was set, the execution of it followed logically. The brand positioning and research into targeted consumers' buying patterns provided clear guidance for setting the price, choosing retail outlets, developing a persuasive message, and choosing the media to deliver the message. The assumed buying process was systematic and was likened to a funnel where a consumer began by considering a set of familiar brands and narrowed the set until a "winner" emerged—the brand purchased because it best fit with the consumer's goal. Today, brands enter and exit the consideration set throughout the decision process, and the options for pricing, delivering, and communicating about brands are constantly evolving.

Chapter 7, "Brand Design and Design Thinking," begins the section by detailing how both verbal/auditory (i.e., name, sound) and visual/olfactory (i.e., shape, scent) elements significantly influence consumers' perceptions of a brand outside of their conscious awareness. Chapter 8, "Leveraging Touchpoints in Today's Brand Environment," discusses how to create a consistent and coherent brand experience at touchpoints throughout the customer decision journey.

Ultimately, brands succeed when they connect with consumers' fundamental motivations. Chapter 9, "Building Strong Connections between Brands and the Self," draws upon a wealth of academic research to describe such motivations and offer advice about how to build strong connections between a brand and the self. The next three chapters provide guidance for effectively managing brand communications (Chapter 10, "Building Strong Brands through Advertising Strategy in an Online Age," and Chapter 11, "Digital Brand Storytelling") and the service experience (Chapter 12, "Branding Services in the Digital Era").

Chapters in Section Three, "Gaining Insight about Your Brand and Quantifying Its Stature," examine methodologies for understanding consumers and evaluating brands. Chapter 13, "Digital Transformation and the Evolution of Customer Insights in Brand Building," and Chapter 14, "Using Neuroscience to Assess Brands," describe new qualitative and quantitative methods that can provide deep insight into consumers' needs and uncover perceptions of brand. Chapter 15, "Measuring Brand Relevance and Health," presents a framework for diagnosing the stage in the customer decision journey where a brand may be failing, and Chapter 16, "Connecting Marketing and Finance via Brand Value," explores how marketers and those in finance and accounting might arrive at a shared view of the monetary value of brands.

Section Four, "Lessons from Brand Leaders," reinforces the practical relevance of the concepts outlined in the previous sections with case studies and advice from people managing brands on the front line. Chapter 17, "Has Purpose Lost Its Purpose? McDonald's Defines Its Style of Marketing," looks at the challenge of finding the right balance between positioning and purpose for McDonald's. Chapter 18, "Ulta Beauty Gets a Branding Makeover," details how marketers built the Ulta Beauty brand while also supporting the numerous, well-known brands carried in its stores.

The next three chapters present case studies demonstrating that the value of strong brands and challenges associated with building them extend beyond the familiar consumer-targeted brands. Chapter 19, "Transforming a Historic Brand for a Hyper-Connected World: The John Deere Story," charts John Deere's journey from a product-focused manufacturer to a company and brand dedicated to using emerging technologies to help its core customers—farmers—optimize their yields. Chapter 20, "Rebranding an Organization: The Novant Health Story," illustrates the bold rebranding of the healthcare organization Novant Health. Chapter 21, "Repositioning a Country Brand: Changing the Conversation about Mexico," shows the power of extending the brand mindset beyond products and services, and details how public and private stakeholders came together to reposition the country of Mexico as an appealing destination for tourists from around the world.

The section concludes with guidance on creating and managing brands. Chapter 22, "Managing Brand Communications in a Digital World," presents advice on how to build brands in a hyper-connected world, with a focus on digital communications. Chapter 23, "Customer Experience: The New Frontier of Branding," outlines guidelines for managing the customer experience. And finally, Chapter 24, "Brand New: Creating a Brand from Scratch," offers some sage advice for entrepreneurs and companies seeking to create a differentiated new brand in a cluttered market.

HOW TO USE THE BOOK

This book is a collection of chapters, and each one explores a different aspect of building strong brands. The chapters are self-contained but complementary, allowing readers to use the book in a variety of ways.

The book's distinctive combination of academic frameworks and practical lessons make it appropriate for both university courses and executive reading.

An academic might assign the book for a branding course at either the MBA or executive level. For example, we use the book in our Kellogg on Branding executive education program. Chapters in the first two sections provide the basic structure for the program, and chapters from Sections Three and Four serve as additional readings that illustrate and deepen understanding of specific topics.

Students of branding not enrolled in a formal course but who seek a broad understanding of branding in today's world may wish to read the book from cover to cover. Experienced brand managers may focus their attention on contemporary concepts such as brand purpose (Chapter 2), new research methods and diagnostic tools (Section Three), and insights from their peers

(Section Four). Executives and entrepreneurs confronted with a specific challenge, such as launching a new brand, may concentrate on a subset of chapters that address decisions made during the launch period. For example, those preparing to launch a new brand might find the chapters related to brand positioning (Chapter 1), the competitive environment (Chapter 4), brand design and touchpoints (Chapters 7 and 8), and advice for creating a brand from scratch (Chapter 24) particularly relevant.

However you use this book, we hope you will find that it enhances your appreciation for brands and their continued and growing significance in our hyper-connected world.

Alice M. Tybout
Tim Calkins

Acknowledgments

We are deeply grateful to all who helped us with this book in ways big and small. It is impossible to mention everyone who helped, but a few people stand out.

We thank our colleagues in the Kellogg Marketing Department who have shared their wisdom with us throughout the years, and we are particularly grateful to those who contributed chapters to this volume. We are also indebted to the outstanding group of senior executives who support Kellogg and who made time in their busy schedules to share their wisdom. A special thanks to Eric Leininger for helping identify and recruit a number of the executive authors to the project.

Several others have been invaluable in bringing the book to completion. It was our great pleasure to work with Patty Dowd Schmitz as our copyeditor. This is the third book in the *Kellogg on* series that Patty has edited. She provided insightful feedback in a timely and diplomatic manner and the book is much stronger for her input. The book was also significantly improved by Sachin Waikar's ability to capture a powerful brand story succinctly and clearly, and by Lisa Stein's polishing of the final prose under a tight deadline. David Cohen also contributed to the editing process, and Bridgette Braig and Liz Kohler assisted in developing several of the examples included. And, a special thanks to Yvonne Kumon for figuring out how to turn exhibits into TIF files—we literally couldn't have done that without you!

Finally, we thank our editor at John Wiley & Sons, Richard Narramore, for believing in the *Kellogg on* series and trusting us to bring this book to completion. We also benefited greatly from the guidance of Vicki Adang, our Wiley project manager, throughout the project. Above all, we thank our families for their patience, support and encouragement.

Alice M. Tybout
Tim Calkins

Introduction:
The Power and Challenge of Branding

TIM CALKINS

If you want to understand the power of brands, consider Lululemon. This Canadian retailer sells fitness apparel and is best known for its yoga clothing. While it sells to both men and women, the brand particularly resonates with women. Lululemon sells good clothing; their fitness leggings perform and fit well. The items hold up after repeated use. Still, the clothing isn't completely unique. Many other retailers make similar products for use in similar settings.

Despite this, Lululemon is a remarkable business success. Revenue in fiscal year 2018 was more than $2.6 billion, with pre-tax profit of $460 million. In mid-2018, the company's market capitalization was well over $17 billion.

Lululemon does well because people are willing to pay exceptionally high prices for their products. On a recent visit to a Lululemon in Chicago, I found that leggings were selling for $98. I found a similar pair of pants at Target for $24.99.

So why are people willing to pay such a premium for Lululemon? Because of the brand. Lululemon is a special brand, one that embraces the ideas of wellness and spirituality. On social media, Lulu encourages people to live a life of balance and caring. Walking around town with a Lululemon bag makes a statement about who you are and what you believe. Buying a pair of leggings at Lululemon is completely different from buying essentially the same item at Target.

At Lululemon, you are surrounded by yoga imagery in a peaceful setting and helped by committed and engaged staff. You feel good about yourself. At Target, the aisles are often crowded with carts, families, and crying kids, and the staff is harder to find. The product is somewhat different, perhaps, but combined with the brand and the experience, there is no comparison.

If you take away the Lululemon brand, what do you have? Good clothes. There is certainly value in that, but the magic, the true value, comes from the brand. For Lululemon and many other businesses, the brand is everything.

BRANDING DEFINED

There are many different definitions of a brand floating around the business world. Some people say a brand is a promise. Other people say a brand is a set of beliefs, or a collection of equities. In the branding program at Kellogg, we define a brand in this way: a brand is a set of associations linked to the name, mark, or symbol associated with a product or service.

The key word in this definition is *associations*. A brand is all the things you think when you see a name, mark, or symbol. When you see Apple, you might think innovation, simplicity, and design. You might think of the late Steve Jobs and his distinctive black turtleneck. When you see Caterpillar, you might think tough, rugged, big, and construction.

The difference between a name and a brand is that a name doesn't have associations: it is simply a name. A name becomes a brand when people link it to other things. A brand is much like a reputation. Just like reputations, brand associations may not always be positive, however, because associations can be positive or negative. Malaysia Airlines developed associations of tragedy and danger after two tragic crashes. Facebook has developed negative associations around abuse of privacy.

Many brands have a mix of positive and negative associations. Coke has positive associations, including refreshing, tasty, and happiness, along with negative associations around health. Uber has positive associations around ease, value, and practicality, and negative associations from a sexist corporate culture.

Some brands are highly polarizing. For some people, McDonald's is a terrific option for a quick, tasty meal. For others, McDonald's isn't even an option. One of the more polarizing brands in the United States (and globally) is the Trump brand. Trump is either a positive brand associated with fresh thinking, toughness, and disruption, or a brand with a web of negative associations, such as distrust, financial corruption, and greed.

Virtually everything can become a brand: brands are not just for luxury items or consumer packaged goods. Indeed, it is difficult to come up with a product or service category in which brands don't play a role. There are hundreds of brands of water, including Évian, Perrier, Dasani, and Aquafina. Medical and pharmaceutical companies have built strong brands that have developed associations in the minds of patients and healthcare professionals; Viagra, Lipitor, and the Mayo Clinic are all brands with clear associations.

Business-to-business companies such as McKinsey, Goldman Sachs, and Baker McKenzie have developed exceptionally powerful brands. Entertainers are brands: Taylor Swift, Rhianna, and Jay-Z bring clear sets of associations. Non-profit organizations and religious groups are brands too: Save the Children, Greenpeace, the Sierra Club, Islam, and the Catholic Church.

DOES DIGITAL MEAN THE END OF BRANDS?

People are quick to question the value of brands in our hyper-connected and digital world. Do brands matter when people order many things by voice through technologies such as Amazon's Alexa? In a world in which we have instant access to vast amounts of data, do brands play a role?

These are reasonable questions. Centuries ago, brands were important because they communicated information. Marks on a piece of pottery indicated that it was from a particular craftsperson. Brand marks on a cow communicated that the animal was owned by a particular person or ranch. Today, we live in a world of almost unlimited information. So, you might think brands don't matter.

The reality is just the opposite. Brands still matter, perhaps more than ever. One reason is that brands provide differentiation. While it's easy to copy a product, it's very difficult to copy a brand. Another reason is that people today have too much information: there are millions of web pages and many of them are filled with information of debatable quality. In a world of fake news and alternative facts, what can you really trust? Brands help people distill information, simplify choices, and make decisions. Which camera is best? You can spend a few days studying all the options, or you can just trust the brand and pick a Nikon or Canon.

Brand valuation is a difficult process, but one thing all brand-valuation reports have in common is that the value of brands is fairly astonishing. In its 2018 list, "The World's Most Valuable Brands," *Forbes* listed Apple's worth at $182 billion, Google's at $132 billion, and Microsoft's at $105 billion.[1] These are not trivial numbers.

Just recently Nestlé paid $7.2 billion to license the Starbucks brand for use on coffee. Nestlé didn't pay for the technology or sourcing, nor did it receive any physical assets in the transaction. Nestlé paid for the brand.[2] Brands still matter.

HOW BRANDS ADD VALUE

A strong, appealing brand is a powerful corporate asset, and brands add value to their corporations in many different ways.

Brands Shape Perceptions

Brands have a remarkable ability to impact the way consumers view products. Consumers rarely see only a product or service; they see the product together with the brand. As a result, how they perceive the product is shaped by the brand.

Perceptions, of course, matter most. How people perceive something matters far more than the absolute truth. The question generally isn't which product or service is best; the question is which product or service people *think* is best. Is Google the best search engine in the world? Does Tesla make the finest electric cars? Does McKinsey do the best strategic thinking? Perhaps so, perhaps not. However, many people think they do, and perceptions matter most when it comes to brand value.

The presence of a well-known brand will dramatically affect how people view a product or service. If people see a premium brand name on a product, they will likely view the item as high quality, exclusive, and expensive. If people see a discount name on a product, they will probably perceive the item as low quality and cheap. In this way, brands function as prisms (see Figure I.1). How people regard a branded product is shaped both by the actual product, such as its specific features and attributes, and by the brand. The brand can elevate or diminish the product.

To demonstrate the power of a brand to shape expectations, I conducted a simple study with MBA students several years ago. I first asked a group of students what they would expect to pay for a pair of good-quality 18-karat-gold earrings with two 0.3-carat diamonds. I asked a second group of students how much they would pay for the same earrings, only this time I added the words "from Tiffany." I asked a third group the same question, but this time changed "from Tiffany" to "from Walmart."

The results were striking. The average price for the unbranded earrings was $550. With Tiffany branding, the average price increased to $873, a jump of

Figure I.1
The Branding Prism

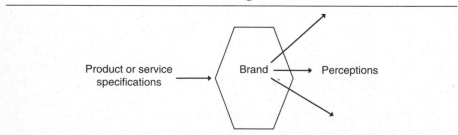

almost 60 percent. This increase was solely due to the addition of the Tiffany brand. With the Walmart branding, the price expectation fell to just $81, a decline of 85 percent from the unbranded earrings and a decline of 91 percent from the Tiffany-branded earrings.

The study highlighted the brand's power to shape perception. "Good quality," for example, means something entirely different when it comes from Tiffany versus Walmart. In addition, the experience of purchasing and wearing earrings from Tiffany is different from the experience of wearing earrings from Walmart. The distinction between the brands is not just conspicuous consumption: you can't tell a Tiffany earring from a Walmart earring from a distance.

This dynamic shows up in many settings. My colleague at Northwestern University, Brayden King, did a fascinating study with Jerry Kim of Columbia University. The two researchers evaluated the accuracy of umpires when calling balls and strikes. They found that umpires were quite accurate. However, when an All-Star pitcher was throwing, umpires tended to give the pitcher the benefit of the doubt, declaring that balls were actually strikes. The difference was quite pronounced: umpires trusted pitchers with good brands.[3] Perhaps the thinking went, "Well, that was close. With this pitcher, that must have been a strike."

Brands Differentiate Products and Services

Perhaps the most important way brands add value is by differentiating products and services. In a competitive market it is hard to succeed without differentiation. When customers realize that the offerings are all similar, they tend to focus on price. This forces companies to reduce prices (and margins) to secure market share, which reduces profits. Taken to an extreme, companies run at a break-even level, with essentially no profits at all.

Brands provide a clear basis for differentiation. With a distinctive and valuable brand, people will pay more. The entire transaction changes. People aren't dealing with a commodity product; they are dealing with something unique. It is difficult to price shop when unique brands are involved. How does an unbranded jacket compare to a Patagonia jacket? It doesn't.

Brand differentiation isn't just about perceptions—brands can change how we think about products and services. Several years ago a team of researchers used brain-scan technology to evaluate how people reacted to unbranded and branded Coca-Cola. When unbranded, people evaluated the soda in a purely sensory manner, reacting to the taste and flavor. After learning that they were drinking Coke, people reacted in a very different fashion, with the brain scans showing activation in very different parts of the brain.[4]

Brands Attract and Retain Employees

As the global economy improves, more and more firms are struggling to attract and retain the best employees. Branding plays a critical role in this process: people want to work for firms with positive brands, and they will avoid companies with weak or negative brands.

A team led by Professor Nader Tavassoli at the London Business School recently studied the impact of branding on staffing. The results were fascinating—the stronger the brand, the less executives earned. At companies with desirable brands, people accepted lower salaries. The logical explanation is that people are eager to work at companies with strong brands and are therefore more flexible when it comes to salary negotiation.[5]

There is no question that a strong brand helps when recruiting employees. People want to work for brands they like: Apple, Starbucks, Google, and Amazon have the ability to hire the best talent in the world, simply because their brands provide a sense of identity and validation.

THE MODERN CHALLENGE FOR BRANDING

While branding is exceptionally important, building a strong brand in today's hyper-connected world is an enormous challenge. Brand builders frequently mention three particular challenges: *cash*, *consistency*, and *clutter*. These are the *Three Cs* of branding.

Challenge 1: Cash

The first and perhaps most significant challenge is *cash*, or dealing with short-term financial pressures. This challenge is driven by a very simple conundrum: business executives need to deliver short-term financial results, but brands are long-term assets. Executives who hit quarterly profit targets are rewarded, and those who exceed them are often rewarded handsomely. This dynamic is true for public companies and is also true for many private companies; private equity firms are generally known for being exceptionally focused on short-term results.

While it is important to make headway on long-term initiatives such as building a strong brand in public and private firms, hitting the short-term financial targets matters most. As one of my former colleagues at Kraft Foods observed, "Good numbers don't guarantee your success. But bad numbers will get you every time."

Brands are long-term assets. If managed properly, a brand can live for decades or centuries. For example, Sony, Tata, and Veuve Clicquot were created in

1946, 1846, and 1772, respectively. All of these brands continue to be vibrant and valuable today.

Virtually all of a brand's value resides in the future; the current-year financial returns are a very small part of the total. If a brand delivers a steady stream of cash flow in perpetuity, only 5 percent of the value of the brand resides in the first year, assuming a discount rate of 5 percent.

If a manager is forced to choose between investing in a brand and missing short-term financial targets, most savvy managers will choose to hit the short-term financial returns. It's usually the career-optimizing decision. And in a supreme irony of business, a manager who boosts short-term profits while damaging the long-term health of a brand is often rewarded, while a manager who invests in a brand at the expense of short-term results is often penalized. The cost-benefit analysis on a brand-building initiative highlights the tension. The costs are quantifiable, certain, and immediate. The benefits are difficult to quantify, uncertain, and in the future.

It is astonishingly easy for brands to get caught in a so-called *branding doom loop*. The doom loop begins with an executive wrestling with weak financial results and struggling to deliver a short-term profit target. To boost sales and profits, the manager deploys programs that have a significant short-term impact, such as a price promotion or tactical digital advertising. To fund these programs, the manager reduces spending on programs with smaller short-term returns, such as brand-building programs, quality improvements, and new product development. These moves are usually successful in improving short-term results, and with better results the manager survives to fight another day.

However, the plan that was so successful in the short run may well have created long-term issues. First, the plan might prompt a competitive response. Second, customer pricing expectations may shift, as customers are now accustomed to the promoted prices. A buy-one-get-one-free offer is motivating and exciting the first time, and perhaps the second time. But eventually customers come to expect it, so companies must cut prices further to create excitement and drive sales. And third, the brand may weaken because brand-building programs were cut.

Combined, these factors put the brand in a weak position, with disappointing sales. This, of course, forces the manager to implement more short-term programs, continuing the doom loop and sending the brand into a dangerous downward spiral.

Dealing with short-term financial constraints, then, is one of the most critical challenges of branding. Managers must balance driving short-term numbers with building a long-term brand. Without understanding the challenge of cash, executives who undertake branding programs are certain to encounter trouble. They will invest in their brand without setting proper expectations, and if short-term results are weak, these managers may not survive in their positions long enough to see the benefits of their investment.

Challenge 2: Consistency

Consistency, or getting an entire organization to embrace the brand and live up to the brand promise over time, has long been a core branding challenge. Crafting the perfect brand positioning and developing the ideal brand portfolio are both noble tasks. However, if the organization doesn't understand, believe in, and *own* the brand—if the message, the brand, and the product are not consistent—the vision will remain unfulfilled.

Brands are created through a wide range of touchpoints; every time customers interact with a brand, they form associations. This means that almost everyone in a company has an impact on the brand, from the receptionist to the advertising manager to the customer service representative.

The Lululemon brand, for example, is shaped by many different elements. The clothes are important, of course, but the Lulu brand is created through the store design, shopping experience, staff, social media activity, events, packaging, pricing, and word of mouth. Traditional advertising, especially traditional TV and print advertising, is only a small part of the picture.

Many of the most powerful touchpoints are difficult for business executives to directly control. The CMO sitting in her large office at corporate headquarters simply can't be present at every point of contact. She also can't dictate employee behavior: she can't tell the cashier to smile and can't tell the phone representative to ask about an upcoming wedding.

In today's hyper-connected world, the impact of small moments can escalate. Word of mouth has always been important for brands, and there is nothing as impactful as a recommendation from a friend. The scale and power of modern communication changes the dynamics: both positive and negative behaviors can dramatically impact a brand in moments. Taylor Swift is just one example of a savvy brand builder who tapped into the positive dynamic by surprising her fans in unexpected and perfectly sharable moments.[6] But also consider how quickly the devastating stories of poor customer service at United Airlines[7] and Domino's pizza spread and damaged their brands.[8]

Consistently delivering on a brand promise is a never-ending task. Ensuring that thousands and thousands of brand moments all work together is perhaps the greatest challenge for anyone striving to build a brand. In our hyper-connected world, consistency matters more than ever.

Challenge 3: Clutter

The third great challenge facing brand executives is *clutter*. From the moment we awake until the second we drift off to sleep, we are bombarded by information, much of it trying to attract attention.

Just consider some of the numbers. The average office worker will receive more than 120 emails per day. Young people will receive and send more than 100 texts per day. A typical cell-phone user will touch his or her phone 2,617 times per day. There are 350 million photos uploaded onto Facebook each day.[9] It's hard to get anyone to pay attention to your brand, and harder still to form meaningful associations. Breaking through the clutter is a major hurdle.

There are two sides to breaking through the noise. One side is tactical excellence: anyone striving to build a brand has to be analytically savvy, deploying always-limited resources in the most effective manner possible. We now have access to remarkable data on marketing execution: we can track who sees our ads, how they respond, and whether they proceed down the purchase funnel. For many brands, we can monitor the entire journey from awareness to purchase, and focus our efforts on the key moments.

The other side is creativity. To engage with people, we have to find ways to connect to them, to give them a reason to care, a reason to interact with us. We have to find, create, and tell engaging, compelling stories.

SUMMARY

Brands are sets of associations that can add enormous value to the corporate bottom line. Most important, perhaps, brands have the ability to shape how people perceive products by elevating or diminishing a product. As a result, brands are critically important: a brand with negative associations will hurt a company, and a brand with positive associations will help.

While branding looks easy, creating and building brands is challenging. Effective brand managers must understand the challenges of cash, consistency, and clutter, and focus on overcoming the issues specific to their brand.

Above all, managers must fight for their brands. Ultimately, brands are built by people who passionately believe in them. Indeed, many of the world's best brands can be linked to a single person: Howard Schultz created Starbucks, Steve Jobs built Apple, Pleasant Roland founded the American Girl brand, Richard Branson developed Virgin, and Phil Knight was the driving force behind Nike. Brand builders understand, believe in, and devote their lives to the power of brands.

Tim Calkins is a clinical professor of marketing at Northwestern University's Kellogg School of Management, where he teaches courses that include Marketing

Strategy and Biomedical Marketing. He began his marketing career at Kraft Foods managing brands that included Miracle Whip, Parkay and Taco Bell. He is the author of several books, including Defending Your Brand: How Smart Companies Use Defensive Strategy to Deal with Competitive Attacks *and* How to Wash a Chicken: Mastering the Business Presentation. *He holds a BA from Yale and an MBA from Harvard Business School.*

NOTES

1. *Forbes* (2018), "The World's Most Valuable Brands," *Forbes*, May 23 https://www.forbes.com/powerful-brands/list.
2. Mulier, Thomas, and Corinne Gretler (2018), "Nestlé Bets $7 Billion on Starbucks to Revive Coffee Sales," Bloomberg, May 7. www.bloombergquint.com/business/nestle-enters-7-2-billion-global-coffee-alliance-with-starbucks#gs.qx=c38M.
3. Bakalar, Nicholas (2014), "Ball? Strike? It Depends: Is the Pitcher an All-Star?" *New York Times* (July 7). https://www.nytimes.com/2014/07/08/sports/baseball/study-finds-umpires-ball-strike-calls-favor-all-star-pitchers.html.
4. McClure, Samuel, Jian Li, Damon Tomlin, Kim Cypert, Latane Montague, and Read Montague (2004), "Neural Correlates to Behavioral Preference for Culturally Familiar Drinks," *Neuron* 44(2) (October), 379–387. https://www.sciencedirect.com/science/article/pii/S0896627304006129.
5. Tavassoli, Nader, Alina Sorescu, and Rajesh Chandy (2014), "Employee-Based Brand Equity: Why Firms with Strong Brands Pay Their Executives Less," *Journal of Marketing Research* 51(6) (December), 676–690.
6. Chiu, Melody (2016), "Taylor Swift Surprises Fan with a Special Performance of 'Blank Space' at His Wedding (and Gave Him a Handmade Gift)," *People*, June 4. https://people.com/celebrity/taylor-swift-surprises-fan-at-his-wedding.
7. Zdanowicz, Christina, and Emanuella Grinberg (2018), "Passenger Dragged Off Overbooked United Flight," CNN, April 10. https://www.cnn.com/2017/04/10/travel/passenger-removed-united-flight-trnd/index.html.
8. Goldman, Russell, and Jason Stine (2009), "Star of Domino's Pizza Gross-Out Video Is Sorry," ABC News, May 4. https://abcnews.go.com/GMA/Business/story?id=7500551.
9. Aslam, Salman (2018), "Facebook by the Numbers," Omnicore, January 1. www.omnicoreagency.com/facebook-statistics.

SECTION ONE

THINKING STRATEGICALLY ABOUT YOUR BRAND

CHAPTER 1

BRAND POSITIONING: THE FOUNDATION FOR BUILDING A STRONG BRAND

ALICE M. TYBOUT

In 2012, Blue Apron pioneered the meal kit concept—a "dinner in a box" for an entire family that provides a recipe and all its premeasured ingredients in a refrigerated box delivered to customers' front doors. The founders anticipated that Blue Apron would attract consumers who like to cook but who don't have time for menu planning and shopping. They also felt that their novel concept would be perfect for those who wanted to cook but lacked confidence in their ability to find tasty, easy-to-prepare recipes.

As this example illustrates, a product or service concept and a targeted group of consumers create the foundation for developing a strong brand positioning. The positioning then articulates how the company would like consumers to think about a brand. It does so by framing the brand in terms of a familiar way of achieving a goal and highlighting a basis of superiority relative to other alternatives in the frame. For example, Blue Apron might be presented as a *more efficient* alternative to shopping and preparing dinner recipes, because all the meal's ingredients are delivered to the home in exactly the right quantity. Alternatively, Blue Apron could be presented as a substitute for a takeout dinner that provides *more family fun* because family members can prepare the meal together using fresh ingredients.

As in the case of Blue Apron, a brand typically can be positioned in more than one way. The manager selects the positioning that she believes is most compelling to the target, provides a sizeable market, and is defensible in the face of competition. The Blue Apron founders chose to launch the brand as a more efficient alternative to shopping and meal prep, because they judged that saving time was important to consumers and that grocery bills provide a larger opportunity from which to "steal" food-spending dollars than takeout. Once the concept of a home-delivered meal kit was established, subsequent entrants used the meal kit category as their frame of reference and sought to differentiate their brands from Blue Apron based on greater ease of preparation (HelloFresh); superior quality and taste (Plated); or healthier, more environmentally friendly meals (Purple Carrot).

This chapter addresses the challenge of developing and sustaining a strong brand positioning in a dynamic marketplace. We begin by examining the representation of a positioning strategy in a positioning statement. Next, we explore approaches to sustaining a brand position over time. In the final section, we assess the potential for repositioning a brand and identify the circumstances in which this strategy is likely to be successful.

THE BRAND POSITIONING STATEMENT

A brand's positioning strategy can be summarized in a formal positioning statement that includes four elements: a target, a frame of reference, a point of difference, and a reason to believe. This statement is an internal document that is used to align all consumer-facing decisions related to the brand (i.e., decisions about elements of brand design, touchpoints, advertising, etc.). To illustrate the structure and content of positioning statements, consider the following statements for Apple and Lite Beer from Miller.

> For consumers who want to feel empowered by the technology they use regardless of their level of skill, Apple offers electronic devices that make you feel smarter because they incorporate leading-edge technology that is sophisticated, yet intuitive to use.
>
> For 21-to-34-year-old males with blue-collar occupations, Lite is the great-tasting beer that lets you drink more without feeling filled up because it has fewer calories than regular beer.

In the Apple example, the target is consumers with varying levels of technological skill, the frame of reference is electronic devices, the point of difference is that Apple electronics make you feel smarter than you do when using a competitor's brand, and the reason to believe is that the brand features superior technology. Similarly, in the Lite example, the target is males 21 to 34 years old, the frame of reference is beer, the point of difference is less filling, and the reason to believe is fewer calories. We begin our analysis of brand positioning by elaborating on each of these four elements of a positioning statement.

Target

The targeted customer for a brand is selected on the basis of many considerations, including the company's goals, the segments targeted by competitors, and the firm's financial resources. In the case of a new brand, the product or service may have been designed with the needs of a particular customer segment in mind. For example, the founders of Blue Apron designed their product for consumers who are interested in preparing meals at home but lack the time to plan menus and shop for ingredients. Such consumers may be distinguished from those uninterested in preparing meals at home by demographic factors (gender, age, income, family status, and geographic location) and psychographic factors (activities, interests, and opinions). For example, research might reveal that time-stressed, would-be cooks are likely to be women in dual-career households residing in urban areas who are concerned with health and nutrition. Describing a target in terms of demographic and psychographic features is useful for two reasons: first, it allows the manager to estimate the size of the targeted segment and, hence, whether it is sufficient to meet revenue goals; second, it informs pricing, distribution, and communication strategies that ultimately represent a brand's position to the target.

Note that the target description in the positioning statement need not enumerate all the features that distinguish it. The target in the Apple positioning statement is described only in terms of its behavioral characteristics (technological skill), whereas the target in the Lite positioning statement is described in terms of demographic characteristics. The objective is to describe the target in sufficient detail so that an appropriate frame of reference and point of difference can be identified.

The target description in a positioning statement often includes insight about the motivation for category and brand use. For Apple, the insight presented in the positioning statement is that the consumer's goal is to feel empowered to use technology while exerting limited effort. For Lite beer, the positioning statement represents the target's goal to be indulgent without incurring its costs—the sin without the penalty. For both brands, the consumer insight suggests a consumer pain point that is overcome by the brand. (For more discussion of consumer insight, see Chapter 13.)

It warrants mention that nontargeted consumers may also be attracted to the brand because they wish to emulate the target, or because they view the target as the expert to whom they defer judgment. For example, women seeking a high-performance razor may select the male-targeted Gillette Fusion brand because they perceive men to be more knowledgeable and concerned about shaving than they are. Conversely, men seeking a way to manage dry or frizzy hair may embrace female-targeted hair-management products such as Aquaphor because they perceive the women in their lives to have greater knowledge about hair-grooming products than they do.

Once a brand is established, its image constrains the choice of target going forward. For example, a brand that has historically attracted young, blue-collar men (regardless of whether they were the intended target) is likely to limit the brand's ability to attract, say, upscale females. We will return to this issue later in the chapter when we discuss repositioning.

Frame of Reference

The frame of reference informs consumers about the goal in using the brand. The most common way to represent a brand's frame of reference is to specify the category in which it holds membership. Stating that Lite is a beer makes it evident to most people that it is an alcoholic beverage often consumed with friends and food. Along the same lines, when the iPhone launched in 2007, the brand name and advertising focused on announcing the brand's frame of reference: a phone. This was important because at the time Apple was known for making computers, not phones (https://youtu .be/ohRQonYVcpU). It should be noted that in order to be credible when claiming membership in an established category, a brand must share key features ("points of parity") with other category members. The assertion that a new brand is a beer would be suspect if it lacked alcohol or carbonation, or if it were best consumed hot.

The frame of reference can also be conveyed by comparing the brand to a different category, as Blue Apron did when it used grocery shopping as the frame. Brands that pioneer a new category employ this approach in an effort to help consumers understand a new concept by relating it to a familiar one. Once the new concept (meal kits) becomes familiar, the pioneer—as well as later entrants, such as Plated—adopts this category as the frame of reference. Like Blue Apron, Uber used an alternative category (taxi) as a frame of reference when it pioneered the ride-hailing concept. Lyft, which followed Uber into the category, relied on consumers' understanding of ride-hailing and used that category rather than taxis as its frame of reference.

Even when a brand is not launching a new concept, it may use an alternative category because that category might more effectively specify both the brand's frame of reference and its point of difference. Along these lines, Coke Zero Sugar compares itself to the flagship Coke brand in taste, rather than the Diet Coke brand. This tells consumers that although Coke Zero Sugar's frame of reference is diet soft drinks, it is at parity with Coke in taste, implying that its point of difference is superiority in taste to other diet brands (https://youtu.be/zTZaZWkwC6E).

Finally, a frame of reference can be communicated by showing the goal that is achieved by using the brand. A humorous ad for eBay in Asia shows a man breaking an antique vase, which distresses his wife. To address this problem, he visits eBay and finds a similar vase, prompting him to celebrate by opening a bottle of champagne. His celebration quickly ends when the cork flies off the bottle and destroys the vase (https://youtu.be/26q6Pi_V6IQ).

Points of Difference and Reasons to Believe

In addition to a frame of reference, a positioning statement requires the specification of a benefit that serves as a point of difference from competition. Benefits are abstract concepts, such as *empowering, convenient*, and *safe*. The benefit selected should be important to consumers and one that the brand can own. The choice of benefit depends on a brand's rank in a category: leaders select the benefit that reflects the main reason for using the category (e.g., Tide cleans best), whereas follower brands reflect a niche benefit (Gain makes clothes smell fresh). A brand's ownership of a benefit is enhanced when it is supported by a reason to believe, which is concrete proof that gives credence to the claim that a brand has the benefit. The reason to believe that Apple will make the consumer smarter is the series of cutting-edge products the company has produced—iPod, iPhone, iPad, and Macintosh computers. Similarly, the reason to believe that Harry's bread delivers the benefit "nice and soft" is the image of a child napping with her head on the bread (see Figure 1.1).

One way to present a brand's reason to believe is to feature an attribute. This might entail specifying ingredients: Jif tastes better than other peanut butters because it is made with fresh-roasted peanuts. Or, the attribute might relate to a brand's equity: Louis Vuitton's luggage is superior because of the brand's travel heritage. In addition, for some positionings, country of origin provides an attribute reason to believe: Perrier is the most refreshing sparkling mineral water because it comes from a spring in Vergèze, France.

The other type of reason to believe involves the presentation of an image—that is, the people involved and occasions when the brand is used. This might entail using a spokesperson with an established and favorable personal brand. Stephen Curry, who is recognized as a professional basketball superstar, serves as a spokesperson for Under Armour basketball shoes, which is a personification of the reason to believe Under Armour's superior performance point of difference.

Figure 1.1
Reason to Believe

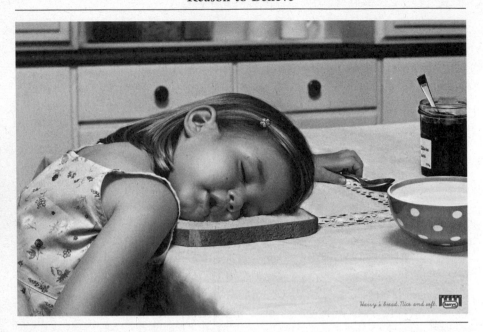

Harry's bread. Nice and soft.

In selecting a reason to believe, attributes that are important to consumers are generally considered first, because they are the most compelling way to provide evidence that a brand possesses the claimed benefit. Sales of the Instant Pot programmable pressure cooker grew rapidly because it provided a means of cooking foods more quickly, reliably, and safely than other pressure cookers, due to its programmable feature. The challenge in developing an attribute reason to believe is that in most instances it is imitable. Thus, there is often a small window of opportunity to achieve scale before an attribute point of difference is matched by a competitor, making it into a point of parity. For example, in response to Instant Pot's success, a number of competitors have entered the programmable pressure cooker category, including Ninja, All-Clad, and Phillips.

The difficulty in sustaining an attribute reason to believe in the face of competition prompts the choice of an image reason to believe in the majority of instances. This approach allows the brand to own the reason to believe by frequently advertising people and/or occasions of product use. Moreover, the choice of an appropriate image can induce substantial growth in sales. Along these lines, the promotion of Dos Equis beer by "the most interesting man in the world" (who did not always drink beer, but when he did, he drank Dos Equis) grew brand sales by 34.8 percent between 2007 and 2015.[1]

Representing a Point of Difference in Terms of Value

A brand's point of difference is often represented by the value it provides consumers, which can be assessed in terms of the following conceptual equation:

$$\text{Value} = \frac{\text{Benefits (Physical} \pm \text{Emotional)}}{\text{Costs (Monetary} + \text{Time)}}$$

The numerator of the equation represents benefits in terms of the brand's physical quality and the emotional response it evokes, whereas the denominator presents the costs in terms of both monetary and time expenditures associated with acquiring and using the brand.

Brands often compete on value in either the numerator or denominator. For example, in the coffee shop category, Starbucks competes in the numerator with superior-tasting coffee (physical) and offering a comfortable destination (emotional). By contrast, McDonald's and Dunkin' compete in the denominator: these brands offer coffee quickly and inexpensively for people on the go. The elements of value that are not the basis for differentiation serve as points of parity with other brands in the competitive frame. Thus, Starbucks must avoid the perception that waiting times are inordinately long or that the brand is too expensive, and McDonald's and Dunkin' must have good enough tasting coffee and pleasant enough stores lest consumers reject them as options when purchasing a cup of coffee.

Some brands compete on all the benefits represented in the value equation. For example, GEICO's positioning highlights the insurance brand's superior quality that consumers can trust (numerator of the value equation), and announces that consumers can save money in as little as the 15 minutes it takes to sign up (denominator). This strategy has the advantage of framing the brand as all-inclusive, which implies that other brands are deficient on some benefit. However, consumers who want to maximize one benefit, say price or quality, may be attracted to a GEICO competitor that emphasizes only what they seek. Thus, a potential liability of the "does it all" strategy is that it may result in other brands dominating on specific elements in the value equation. Even when the claim that the brand "does it all" is warranted, consumers may perceive the claim lacks credibility because it runs afoul of their lay theories about the way the world works ("You get what you pay for").

A virtue of the value equation in developing a brand's position is that it links the position to the marketing mix. The physical quality is determined by the brand's product or service characteristics, the emotional benefits are derived from the consumption experience and the brand image, time costs are linked with the channel of distribution, and monetary costs are determined by the price charged.

Orchestrating the Frame of Reference and Point of Difference

An effective brand positioning strategy requires that the frame of reference, point of difference, and reason to believe are aligned in a way that maximizes demand. Consider Bounty, the paper towel brand that attempted to enhance its growth by adding strength as a benefit to the brand's greater absorbency equity. The reason to believe was that Bounty was not only effective for quickly cleaning up spills, but also for scrubbing pots and pans and cleaning fish tanks. However, presenting these applications as reasons to believe Bounty's strength changed Bounty's frame of reference from paper towels to sponges, which put Bounty in competition with brands such as Scotch-Brite sponges. The sponge category frame of reference is characterized by absorbency and durability, characteristics on which it would be difficult for Bounty to compete. Bounty does dominate Scotch-Brite on the hygienic dimension, in that a Bounty paper towel is a one-use disposable and a sponge is not. However, this point of difference is a point of parity with other paper towels, and it risks undermining Bounty's absorbency point of difference in relation to other paper towel brands if strength were associated with a lack of absorbency.

The Bounty example illustrates that a brand should select the frame of reference that will attract the most substantial demand for the brand while also providing it with a defensible point of difference. Bounty's effort to broaden its frame of reference resulted in a different frame becoming salient, which, in turn, obscured Bounty's point of difference in relation to other paper towels.

Another alignment issue pertains to the fit between the frame of reference and the reason to believe a point of difference. In the positioning statement for Lite beer presented earlier, the brand was represented as tasting great (a way of presenting the beer frame of reference) and as having fewer calories (the reason to believe "less filling"). Here, consideration should be given to whether "fewer calories" is negatively correlated with great taste. If it is, the credibility of the great taste claim is likely to be undermined by the fewer calories reason to believe, which is used to support the less filling benefit.

Testing Your Brand Positioning Statement

Once you have developed a positioning statement, it is useful to check it for *clarity*, *credibility*, and *distinctiveness*. First, show it to people outside the company. For many consumer products and services, friends and family will work well. However, when products require special expertise, targeted customers should be sought. Ask these individuals to read the positioning statement and to indicate the situations in which the brand would be used, why it is claimed to be superior to other options, and whether they believe these claims. If people outside your company cannot grasp the positioning from the statement, it lacks clarity. If they do not believe the statement, it lacks credibility. Second, replace your brand name in the positioning statement with that of a competitor. If the statement still seems reasonable, it lacks distinctiveness. Failing either test indicates that additional work on the statement is warranted.

SUSTAINING A BRAND POSITION

Once a brand's position gains traction, in most instances the goal is to sustain that position over time. Some brands have a position that is timeless, and thus sustaining it is straightforward. For many years, Marlboro cigarettes were represented by cowboys, which implied that the brand was for independent individuals who empowered themselves to reach their goals. This campaign was run in the United States for about 50 years. However, for many, additional strategies are needed to sustain a position. Here we discuss several of the more frequently used approaches.

Modern Instantiation

Modern instantiation sustains a position by focusing on the same brand benefit over time, but depicting it in a contemporary context. For example, since its introduction in 1898, the Grape-Nuts cereal brand has been positioned as the natural, ready-to-eat cereal that contributes to health and well-being. However, the context in which this benefit is presented has changed over time to reflect consumers' view of the meaning of health. In the early 1970s, Grape-Nuts promoted health and well-being with TV advertising featuring naturalist Euell Gibbons as a spokesperson. This reflected consumers' interest in communing with nature at that time. In the mid-1980s, the context for Grape-Nuts advertising was a consumer's country house, which mirrored the aspirations and lifestyle of the me generation. In 2013, Grape-Nuts represented health with TV advertising that featured Sir Edmund Hillary—the first person to climb Mount Everest—consuming the brand during a break in a climb, paralleling consumers' interest in extreme sports as a way of achieving health and well-being.

Switching from Attribute to Image Reasons to Believe

Another means of sustaining a position is to switch from an attribute reason to believe that is no longer news to consumers to an image reason to believe a brand benefit. For example, Extra gum initially promoted its long-lasting flavor, which prompted users to chew it longer, which in turn reduced acid in the mouth, thereby providing some protection against cavities (https:// youtu.be/PeTS0sWFSLE). More recently, the brand extended this equity through the characters Sarah and Juan, where Juan used the Extra wrapper and pen to create art, including a drawing of himself asking Sarah to marry him, which she saw exhibited in a gallery (https://youtu.be/upsrMt-JMzA). Thus, Extra's long-lasting attribute was extended by an image campaign presenting a long-lasting relationship. In the process, the focus changed from personal hygiene to community and sharing.

Laddering

A brand's point of difference benefit can also be sustained by a laddering-down or laddering-up strategy. Laddering down involves starting with an abstract benefit and enumerating multiple attribute reasons to believe, which are con-crete. For example, Volvo used a laddering-down strategy by introducing a variety of attributes, including antilock brakes, a collision warning system, and a blind-spot warning system, all of which serve as reasons to believe the functional benefit of enhanced protection for the driver and passengers. The presentation of various reasons to believe a point of difference benefit sustains news about the brand.

Laddering up involves a more complicated process. First, the brand presents an attribute reason to believe, which is concrete. This attribute implies a func-tional benefit of that attribute, which in turn implies an emotional benefit, which serves as the basis for the brand's essence. Volvo employed a laddering-up strategy when it presented the safety attributes noted earlier to support the functional benefit of enhanced protection, which in turn implied the emotional benefit of peace of mind. This emotional benefit was the basis for implying the brand's essence, which is "Volvo is the brand for people who embrace life."

Laddering up sustains interest by relating the brand to increasingly abstract and enduring consumer goals. Along these lines, Volvo's laddering up suggested a contemporary way to express the brand's commitment to safety. The company noted that 19,000 cyclists in the United Kingdom are involved in accidents every year, and many of these accidents occurred at night when bikers are difficult to see. Further, many luxury car owners (Volvo's target) also cycle as a hobby. These observations motivated the company to create LifePaint, a paint that is invisible during the day but reflective in the dark, making it easy for drivers to see bicycles painted with it. LifePaint provided news about Volvo's commitment to safety and preserving lives, and its sale at dealerships resulted in a sales increase of more than 1,000 cars.[2]

Brand Purpose

A brand *positioning* statement answers the question, "How do we want targeted consumers to think about the brand in relation to other brands?" A brand *purpose* statement answers the question, "Why does the brand exist (beyond the goal of financial gain)?" The answer to the "why" question reflects the beliefs and values of the organization. As such, it goes beyond the positioning statement's focus on a particular target and addresses the concerns that encompass other stakeholders, such as employees and investors. Chapter 2 provides a detailed discussion of brand purpose and its importance. Here, we offer a few observations about the relationship between brand positioning and brand purpose.

In some instances, a brand's purpose is front and center in the positioning, serving as the basis for differentiation or the reason to believe. Title Nine is a women's athletic-wear company that follows this approach to positioning. The company develops products specifically for women's bodies. It began in the 1990s with a line of sports bras for runners and expanded its offerings to include a range of women-specific gear well before Athleta, Lululemon, and others entered the market. Arguably, the availability of Title Nine clothing contributed to more women and girls participating in and succeeding at sports. Named for the landmark Title IX legislation from 1972, which stipulated gender equality and prohibited gender discrimination in education, the brand highlights the value-based goal that the brand established for itself—more girls and women would transform their lives through the achievement and attendant esteem benefits that sports provide. As founder Missy Park noted, "We were working to build a business around the idea that we would change the world, if we could just get our workout in."[3]

For other brands, the role of brand purpose is apparent only as a company considers the implications of a brand's point of difference and reasons to believe. Always is a brand of feminine hygiene pads and panty liners produced by Procter & Gamble. These categories (rather than tampons) are often the ones used by young women when they begin menstruating. The Always brand claims to provide a leak-free, comfortable fit. It supports this claim by featuring demonstrations of absorbency and showing the curved shape of its products in advertising. These attributes provide the emotional benefit of enabling young women to feel confident in coping with the new experience of menstruation. In recent years, Always has extended this equity to present the brand's purpose—helping young women feel confident in dealing with the stereotypes they face (https://www.youtube.com/watch?v=VhB3l1gCz2E).

As the Always example suggests, a brand's positioning that is abstracted to a higher purpose can engage consumers about issues that matter to them. This is especially important in today's always-on digital world, because brands generate limited news. Yes, a new feature may be added to a brand or an existing one enhanced, but such improvements are infrequent and thus not sufficient to sustain engagement. The outdoor sportswear company Patagonia does a good job of engaging its customers through its brand purpose. The brand sells technical gear and apparel for "silent sports," which are those that do not have motors but instead connect people with the natural world. Patagonia's point of difference is its commitment to the highest-quality minimalism in all of its products, with a do-no-harm mentality in both the manufacturing and use of its products. The reasons to believe this point of difference include not only the technical performance aspects of its designs, but also its pioneering use of organic cotton and innovation in using recycled plastic bottles to create synthetic fibers.

The higher purpose of the brand is to facilitate access to and participation in "wild and beautiful places," and to play an active role in protecting these places. To support this commitment, the company offers grants to climate, environmental, and sustainability groups and uses its web site to promote opportunities to volunteer or otherwise engage with such groups. Recently, Patagonia founder Yvon Chouinard led lobbying and advocacy efforts against reducing the size of Bear Ears National Monument in Utah. Further, the company has sued the U.S. federal government to reverse the decision to reduce the park's size. The purpose of these initiatives is to provide the opportunity to deepen Patagonia's connection to its customers around shared goals.

Even brands that might seem to lack an obvious link to brand purpose may uncover one with reflection. Honey Maid graham crackers are positioned as a nutritious snack because they are made with wholesome ingredients, including whole grains and real honey. Honey Maid's brand purpose is linked to its equity by elevating "wholesome" to celebrate and honor families of all stripes, colors, and definitions. Honey Maid uses social, digital, and traditional media to showcase LGBTQ and racial inclusivity in specifying what it means to be a wholesome family. Honey Maid even turned the anti-gay response to its TV ad featuring gay dads and biracial families into digital content (coupled with the hashtag #thisiswholesome) that transformed hate into love (https://www .youtube.com/watch?v=cBC-pRFt9OM).[4]

Authenticity in walking the talk proved critical in making Honey Maid's brand purpose more than just an assertion. The company's actions spoke to the authenticity of its elevated version of what wholesome means. However, when positioning at the level of purpose, a brand should recognize that it will be held to the standard espoused, and that all employees must walk the talk. Starbucks, a firm committed to social justice, was taken to task in spring 2018 when an employee at a Philadelphia store acted in a manner suggesting racial bias.[5] Had the same deplorable incident occurred at say, 7-Eleven or Dunkin', one suspects it would have received less attention in the press and provoked less outrage by customers.

REPOSITIONING A BRAND

When a brand position is developed, the goal is to sustain it over time. However, certain circumstances may require the repositioning of a brand, which may involve changing the frame of reference or reframing. This typically is necessary when a brand is the first entrant in a category.

Consider the introduction of Miller Lite, which was the first successful light beer in the United States. Its frame of reference was regular beer, which had great taste, and its point of difference was less filling, which was supported by fewer calories than other beers as the reason to believe. The entry of Bud Light resulted in consumers changing their perception of the frame of reference from regular beer to light beer. This new frame changed Miller Lite's point of difference—less filling—to a point of parity and thus part of the frame of reference. To differentiate the brand, Lite had to develop a new point of difference. Bud Light beat Miller Lite to the punch by promoting its superior taste, which was supported by the fact that Budweiser's base brand was the "King of Beers." By focusing on its superior taste, Budweiser adopted the point of difference that is a key determinant of beer choice, leaving Lite to find a niche benefit. Blue Apron faces a similar challenge with the emergence of other brands in the meal kit category.

Repositioning is also warranted when a brand's position is too broad to be supported by the reason to believe. For example, Aleve was positioned as a convenient analgesic that effectively relieved pain and only needed to be taken every 12 hours. However, this broad frame of reference did not fit with the brand's reason to believe. In fact, for consumers, 12-hour dosing implied slow acting rather than convenient. To align the reason to believe with the frame of reference, Aleve was repositioned as the brand that relieves arthritis pain. Narrowing the position in this way made the convenience of infrequent dosing a compelling reason to believe for those suffering chronic pain. Although this frame narrowed the number of people being targeted, Aleve was relevant to the 40 million people in the United States who suffer with arthritis. Moreover, it set Aleve apart from Advil and Tylenol, which require more frequent dosing to sustain pain relief.

Another situation in which repositioning can be achieved readily occurs when the initial position failed to gain traction. For example, Apple introduced its first-generation watch as a fashion item whose band could be changed to accommodate different wearing occasions (see Figure 1.2a). This position was changed a year later when the watch was reframed as a functional device for those interested in health and fitness (see Figure 1.2b). This repositioning was successful because the Apple Watch never gained traction as a fashion accessory but was relevant for monitoring health and fitness.

Changing or sharpening a position may also be appropriate and feasible when the original positioning has been diluted due to licensing or other growth-motivated activities, or the brand has been "hijacked" by consumers who are not the desired target. Such was the case for Burberry in the early 2000s. Loose control over licensing deals resulted in the brand name appearing on a wide range of products (including chocolate) at price points that varied dramatically. Further, football (soccer) hooligans ("chav") had embraced the brand and sported caps and umbrellas with the distinctive plaid pattern (often counterfeit) at games where brawls in the stands were common.

The repositioning of the Burberry brand, which was led by Christopher Baily and Angela Ahrendts, involved regaining control of licensing and distribution, dialing back the use of the Burberry plaid in the apparel, stepping up innovation in design, using supermodel Kate Moss and other celebrities in advertising, and creating a strong online presence. These activities drove sales growth for a decade and reestablished Burberry as a luxury brand that blends fashion and function in a uniquely British way. In late 2017, the new CEO, Marco Gobbetti, who was recruited from Céline, announced his plan to reposition Burberry as a super luxe brand, similar to Dior, Hermès, and Gucci. The jury is out as to whether this repositioning will succeed, but the brand's heritage in functional outdoor attire may limit how far upscale it can move. At a minimum, Old Navy's experience serves as a cautionary tale about the difficulty in moving a brand up to a higher fashion or luxury tier.

Figure 1.2
Apple Watch Initial (a) and Revised (b) Positioning

(a)

(b)

Old Navy was a brand for value-oriented families interested in purchasing casual clothing. Old Navy's reason to believe was the unusually wide selection of T-shirts, jeans, khakis, and other casual attire. When a new chief marketing officer was hired, a line of trendy but inexpensive clothing was introduced with the goal of appealing to young, fashion-conscious women. However, the space allocated to the trendy items reduced the breadth of selection that was central to Old Navy's position and frustrated its core consumers. Old Navy sales declined dramatically—over 20 percent in several months. Similar, equally disastrous results occurred when new CEOs at JCPenney and Lands' End attempted to reposition those brands as more fashion-forward. Existing customers were not impressed, and not enough new customers were attracted to offset the defecting old customers.

In sum, once a brand has traction in its current position, repositioning is a strategy of last resort, as it is likely to alienate the brand's core users. It may also conflict with the prior brand position and thus confuse consumers. And even if these issues do not arise, repositioning typically takes considerable time and financial resources. Nevertheless, modest changes in a position are sometimes warranted to better align a brand's frame of reference with its point of difference and reason to believe, as was described for Aleve. Moreover, when a brand is the first entrant in a category where the frame of reference is typically another category, repositioning is generally required, as we noted for Lite beer and Blue Apron. Finally, when a brand has not gained traction in a position, adopting a new frame of reference may be warranted, as was the case for Apple Watch. However, consideration should first be given to the strategies for sustaining a position discussed earlier.

SUMMARY

A brand's positioning serves as the foundation for all brand-building activities. It is summarized in a statement that captures the target, frame of reference, point of difference, and reason to believe the point of difference. This statement is a succinct summary of how the brand will compete in the marketplace and guides all decisions related to the marketing mix. Ideally, the positioning endures over decades, though changes will be needed to maintain relevance to new generations of the target and to maintain customer engagement. A variety of strategies are available to help achieve this goal, including modern instantiation, laddering, and brand purpose. Nevertheless, repositioning is sometimes necessary. This is likely to be the case when a new category is being established and the initial frame of reference is, of necessity, an alternative category. Repositioning may also be necessary when a brand position has been diluted or abandoned through undisciplined tactics or the market opportunity for the current position is limited. However, repositioning an established brand is always a challenge, because consumers' perceptions of it are slow to change. Repositioning failures outnumber the successes, which highlights the importance of getting things right the first time!

Alice M. Tybout is the Harold T. Martin Professor of Marketing and a past chairperson of the Marketing Department at the Kellogg School of Management. She is also co-director of the Kellogg on Branding Program and director of the Kellogg on Consumer Marketing Strategy Program at the James L. Allen Center. She is co-editor of two previous Wiley books, Kellogg on Branding *(John Wiley & Sons, 2005) and* Kellogg on Marketing, *2nd ed. (John Wiley & Sons, 2010). She received her BS and MS from Ohio State University and her PhD from Northwestern University.*

NOTES

1. Avery, Tom (2009), "Jonathan Goldsmith, Dos Equis to Part Ways," dbtechno. com, March 10, 2016, http://www.dbtechno.com/entertainment/2016/03/10/ jonathan-goldsmith-dos-equis-to-part-ways.
2. Gladstone, Matthew, and Wiktor Scoog (2016), "'Or By': How Two Little Words Made Volvo's Safety Matter Again," WARC, IPA Effectiveness Awards.
3. "In the Beginning" (n.d.), Title Nine web site. https://www.titlenine.com/ category/company-info/t9-history.do.
4. "Honey Maid: Love" (2014), YouTube, April 3. https://www.youtube.com/ watch?v=cBC-pRFt9OM.
5. Stewart, Emily (2018), "Starbucks Says Everyone's a Customer after Philadelphia Bias Incident," Vox.com, May 19. https://www.vox.com/identities/2018/5/ 19/17372164/starbucks-incident-bias-bathroom-policy-philadelphia. In addition to Chapter 5, also see Vila, Rodrigues, and Sundar Bharadwaj (2017), "Competing on Social Purpose," *Harvard Business Review*, September–October.

CHAPTER 2

LEVERAGING THE POWER OF BRAND PURPOSE

JIM STENGEL with MATT CARCIERI and RENÉE DUNN

In the 1980s, Procter & Gamble (P&G) was the Amazon of its day. It was an innovative market leader with aggressive growth goals. John Smale was its CEO at the time, and while he had a very different profile from Amazon CEO Jeff Bezos, the men share two common characteristics: a healthy disdain for the short-term perspective of Wall Street and a drive to expand their businesses and dominate their markets through better products and services.

Smale, like Bezos, also believed in hiring the absolute best people, training them like no other company, and giving them early responsibility and accountability.

But P&G in the 1980s, unlike Amazon today, strongly believed in standard processes and rituals. Every brand at P&G had an annual budget meeting using the same format. Each brand used a similar approach to packaging design, trade promotion, and advertising strategies. One mandate was that each brand would have a "copy strategy"—P&G believed that all great advertising began with great language, or copy. That strategy had to be one sentence long and focus on one benefit. It was always a functional benefit and usually a product superiority benefit. All communication about the brand had to emanate from this one sentence. It was sacrosanct and only changed as a result of deep and inarguable consumer research.

A few examples of what a P&G copy strategy looked like in the 1980s:

- Tide Plus Bleach makes clothes whiter than any name-brand competitor.
- Dawn cuts grease faster than the other leading brand.
- Jif provides more fresh-roasted peanut taste than any national brand.

20

In 1984, an infamous year in the annals of advertising thanks to Apple's "1984" ad, P&G was beginning to lead a revolution in how the company practiced brand building. At the time, P&G was encouraging its marketing and R&D people to find ever-more creative ways to understand consumers, ranging from in-home visits to town-hall meetings to sit-downs with influencers. The brand management team of Jif Peanut Butter (chapter author Jim Stengel was a member) seized those opportunities and began to have different kinds of conversations. Jif was already a trusted product that was in millions of households, and it was available in thousands of stores. But was that enough? Could the team have a greater impact by focusing on what young mothers cared about? Could they do that in a way that made sense for the Jif brand? How could the team switch its mindset to be a service-plus-product brand versus just a product brand?

The Jif brand managers at P&G did not consciously know it at the time, but they were expanding their view of how to build a brand. They were moving from an approach centered on copy strategy to a *purpose-centered* approach. Asking a simple question—"How can Jif make a bigger difference in the lives of our consumers in a way that makes sense coming from this brand?"—changed everything. The team began publishing content on nutrition, made the packaging safer, and rallied everyone who worked on Jif—including the technicians at the plants in Kentucky and Virginia—to brainstorm how to make lives better for Jif's consumers. (For a related discussion, see "laddering" in Chapter 1.)

One initiative that emerged from this work was a program to help PTAs at local schools across the country. Jif's brand managers linked funding of local PTAs to purchases of Jif in their neighborhoods, a rough precursor to the TOMS shoes model of buying a pair of shoes to help someone else.

Jif's business momentum accelerated, and it became an inspiration for other brands within P&G. The brand team was asked to tell their success story at several high-profile management meetings, including the all-employee annual meeting, so the company could learn what was special about this group.

Over time, P&G further advanced its thinking on how to grow a brand behind a purpose-inspired strategy, and eventually the company formalized its approach, reinventing its brand-building framework to start with *purpose*.

THE CASE FOR PURPOSE

"Purpose" as a central concept in business and society is as old as the hills and therefore has many definitions or interpretations. Most practitioners of purpose in business see it as a brand or company's higher-order mission: an articulation of why a company or brand exists. It is sometimes referred to as a "brand ideal," as it is usually so aspirational that it will never be fully realized.

In the 1890s William Hesketh Lever, founder of Lever Brothers, wrote this about the purpose of his fledgling company: "To make cleanliness commonplace; to lessen work for women; to foster health and contribute to personal attractiveness, that life may be more enjoyable and rewarding for the people who use our products." One hundred thirty years later, Unilever is still operating on its purpose—with revenue of $64 billion—and ranks among the most sought-after employers.

Similarly, Walt Disney started his company in 1923 to "bring happiness to millions." Robert Wood Johnson started Johnson & Johnson in 1886 "to alleviate pain and disease." These companies are still true to their purpose today.

The Business Case for Purpose

The quantitative business case for purpose has also been building for decades:

- In their 1994 classic *Built to Last*, authors Jim Collins and Jerry Porras identified a set of breakout companies that, as a central element of their success, had a "sense of purpose beyond just making money." Collectively, they outperformed the financial markets 15 to 1.[1]
- In 2007, the Wharton-published book *Firms of Endearment* by authors David Wolfe, Jagdish Sheth, and Rajendra Sisodia examined 28 companies operating with purpose. Over a 10-year period, these companies beat the S&P by an 8-to-1 margin.[2]
- In the 2012 book *Grow: How Ideals Power Growth and Profit at the World's Greatest Companies*, the author (Jim Stengel) worked with research partner Millward Brown Optimor on a study using the Brand Z database of 50,000 brands. They studied the financial and consumer results of these brands over 10 years, finding that the majority of leading companies were purpose driven and that they grew three times faster than the competition.[3]
- Academic research published in 2016 that used data from the Great Places to Work Institute found that firms "exhibiting both high purpose and clarity" had systematically higher stock market performance.[4]
- An Insights2020 study sponsored by several organizations, including the Advertising Research Foundation, found that 80 percent of companies that overperform on revenue growth link everything they do to purpose.[5]
- A Korn Ferry study found that purpose-driven consumer products firms grew their topline by more than nearly 10 percent from 2011 to 2015, while their peers grew from 2 to 4 percent.[6]

More recently, the business case for purpose has extended to employee recruitment and engagement. It's no secret that employee engagement is more challenging than ever. Gallup's most recent *State of the Global Workplace* study shows a shocking result: 85 percent of employees are disengaged or actively disengaged at work.[7]

Purpose is perhaps the strongest antidote to this disease. Studies from two of the world's largest consulting groups provide strong evidence:

- In its 2016 *Putting Purpose to Work* report, PricewaterhouseCoopers (PwC) found that 83 percent of employees say that purpose in the workplace adds meaning to day-to-day work, and 53 percent say it energizes them.[8]
- In a similar study, Deloitte found that 73 percent of employees who report working for a purpose-driven company say they are engaged in their work.[9]

Author Daniel Pink, in his runaway bestseller *Drive*, found "that the most deeply motivated people—not to mention those who are the most productive and satisfied—hitch their desires to a cause larger than themselves."

The Purpose Perfect Storm

Every so often in the business world a symbolic event signals a sea change, and we never forget it. The first iPhone launch changed the world in 2007. Tesla changed the car-buying and driving experience in 2009 when it released its first model. And on the darker side, we remember the fall of Enron in 2001 and the 2008 financial crisis.

The purpose sea-change event happened in January 2018, when Larry Fink, the CEO of BlackRock, the largest asset manager in the world, sent a letter to shareholders with this message: "Society is demanding that companies, both public and private, serve a social purpose. . . . To prosper over time, every company must not only deliver financial performance, but also show how it makes a positive contribution to society. Companies must benefit all of their stakeholders, including shareholders, employees, customers, and the communities in which they operate." Fink's letter accelerated the purpose conversation in every boardroom, and it added lightning, thunder, and high winds to what was already the perfect purpose storm.

While purpose has been an organizing concept in business for centuries (consider the Banca Monte dei Paschi di Siena, founded in 1472 with a purpose to help those in need with low-interest loans), the urgency to reorient business principles and processes around a company's unique purpose has never been more intense. The reason is that we are experiencing the single largest shift in a workforce in the history of our planet: the influx of millennials and Gen Zers, the first digitally native employees.

The impact of this cannot be overstated. Since the authors of this chapter left P&G in the late 2000s, we and our colleagues have personally visited with 400 companies; we found that among every company's top three challenges is how to create a culture that brings out the best in the new workforce. Purpose is far more important to this generation than to their older colleagues: PwC found that millennials are five times more likely to stay with a company when they have a strong connection to its purpose, versus nonmillennials who are about two times more likely to stay.[10]

The change in workforce is the most powerful catalyst in the purpose perfect storm, but there are others. Faith and trust in government to lead positive change has never been lower. People are looking for businesses to pick up the slack, and consumers seem willing to reward them for it. According to a 2015 Nielsen study, 66 percent of consumers would pay more for products from more socially responsible companies.[11]

Many of the heroes and role models in our culture now are global business leaders, and the ones who rise to the top are deeply purpose oriented. *Business Insider* annually ranks the top global business leaders for their results and also indicates how they achieved them. Here is *Business Insider* CEO Henry Blodget's perspective on its recent rankings:

> The more money you make, the implication is the better and more successful you are. We believe this cheapens the mission and sense of purpose that many great business leaders bring to their companies and products. And it certainly undersells their inspiring accomplishments.[12]

Some of the leaders who have appeared in the *Business Insider* rankings include Bill and Melinda Gates, Marc Benioff of Salesforce, Salman Khan of Khan Academy, Anne Wojcicki of 23andMe, Jack Ma of Alibaba, and Mary Barra of General Motors.

The perfect storm is raging. Sixty-four million millennials and Gen Zers are working today, versus 41 million baby boomers. The largest fund manager in the world is changing his investment criteria. Governments across the world are more inept than ever. Our business heroes are explicitly purpose oriented.

Now what? How does an organization truly lead with purpose? How does it become a way of working versus a slogan? Is there a new model of brand building?

Figure 2.1
Purpose Path to Growth Model

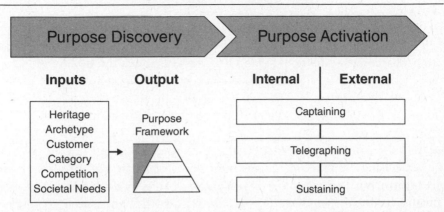

The Purpose Path to Growth Model

The genesis of the purpose path to growth model began when this chapter's authors were at P&G. Matt Carcieri began purpose pilots with a handful of P&G brands in the late 1990s and 2000s. Renée Dunn, with her human resources background, tackled the organizational transitions required to become purpose oriented, and Jim helped champion and scale the work as the global head of marketing for P&G. We left P&G to pursue development of the new model with 100 percent of our effort, joined by other like-minded colleagues. We have worked, refined, and improved this model in more than 80 companies, and this chapter reflects those lessons.

The high-level overview of this model is illustrated in Figure 2.1. Once business leaders are convinced that the business case for purpose is strong and relevant, the model is designed to help leadership teams work in two phases:

- Phase 1: Discover (or rediscover) their purpose through a deep, exploratory journey, with the output being a "purpose framework" for their brand or their company.
- Phase 2: Activate their purpose across their internal and external ecosystems.

Phase 1 involves mining the brand's heritage, determining the underlying archetype that governs the brand, assessing customers' deep motivations, taking stock of category and cultural trends, and identifying relevant "needs of the world." Through a facilitated choice-making process, we build a purpose framework, which is shown in Figure 2.2.

Figure 2.2
Purpose Framework

The framework answers four critical identity questions: Whom does the brand seek to attract? Why does the brand exist? What does the brand promise? And, how does the brand come to life in the marketplace (i.e., tonality of advertising, packaging, logo)? Each question leads to specific, interrelated choices: an articulation of the high-order purpose, as well as the supporting belief system, promise, and personality. A purpose statement alone is insufficient; these additional elements form the template for effective activation.

Note that although we've referred to "brand" throughout this section, the same inputs and outputs apply to a corporate enterprise as well. In many cases, a brand and company are one and the same: Apple and Twitter are good examples. But in other cases, such as P&G and Berkshire Hathaway, the enterprise comprises dozens of individual brands. While some minor modifications are required, the general process to develop an enterprise or a brand purpose is the same, and the model holds for all types of business and social entities. We have found that a primary motivator for developing an enterprise purpose is to attract and retain talented people, while the reason many brands pursue purpose is to make a bigger difference in the lives of their customers.

Phase 2 begins with internal activation, which is a critical precursor to activating the purpose in market. For a purpose to be authentic in its execution, it must be lived inside. Whether the impetus to take the purpose journey begins from inside forces (such as employee disengagement) or outside forces (such as customer apathy), the early and relentless focus must be on the company's employees. Atlanta-based SunTrust bank began its purpose journey to instill financial confidence in its millions of customers; SunTrust's leaders quickly realized that two-thirds of their employees did not feel confident in their own financial health. The bank embarked upon a multiyear effort to address its employees' financial confidence before taking its purpose activation to external customers.

In the implementation of purpose—both internally and externally—there are three major activity systems. We call the first one "captaining," and it encompasses all the behaviors and communications that are required of leadership. The second plank is "telegraphing," which reflects a variety of signaling activities—demonstrative acts that show the organization is "walking the talk." The last plank involves a host of internal and external "sustaining" initiatives, which serve to reinforce and perpetuate the focus on purpose with employees and drive new activations in the market.

We have no shortage of frameworks and models in the branding and marketing world. Many of them are based on sound data, and most of them improve over time with experience and continual learning. This model is no different, with one key exception: the process and output of this model must be owned by the CEO. Purpose is not owned by any one discipline—it absolutely must be endorsed and championed by the CEO.

We have found that when these two steps are done with commitment and perseverance, a team finds new energy, more creativity, more vitality, and ultimately, growth in their business. The process works whether the challenge is an enterprise purpose or a single-brand purpose.

KEYS TO MAKING THE MODEL WORK

Five underlying principles enable the purpose path to growth model to help leaders grow their business.

Common Understanding of the Case for Purpose

The case for change needs to be compelling and shared by all. We have learned that diagnostic questions such as the ones below are the critical underpinnings to a productive purpose journey. Engaging with thought leaders in the organization—using the probative questions below to guide the dialogue—is a necessary first step to establish the business case for change.

What is your motivation for change?
- What is driving your interest in establishing/evolving your brand purpose?
- Why engage in this work *now*?
- What impact do you expect the purpose path to growth process to have on your business and organization? What does success look like as an outcome?
- What is the rallying cry or burning platform for this change effort?

What are the business drivers for change?
- How would you describe your business's growth over the past five years?
- How would you describe your industry's growth over the past five years?
- What is your brand's performance against your company's key measures?
- How does your brand/product/service compare to that of your primary competitors?
- What new consumer/customer expectations and needs do you anticipate will impact your brand within the next three years? Five years?
- What new technological disruptions or innovations that may impact your business do you see on the horizon?

What is the state of your purpose?
- If it exists, what is your current purpose statement or concept?
- How do you measure and track brand health? What is your brand's performance against these measures?
- To what extent is your brand's purpose rooted in a clear understanding of your core beliefs and brand heritage?
- To what extent does your brand's purpose capture values that are shared with the brand's customers? How so?
- To what extent does your brand's purpose motivate employees? How so?

Shared Leadership and Advocacy

While the CEO must own the output and implications, other influential leaders from the organization can lead the process. In our experience with a global beauty company, the head of corporate communications led the process. In a similarly sized consumer products company, the head of strategy led the work. We are also believers in the power of a small, empowered, multifunctional coalition of leaders who serve as the stewards for the purpose journey. This group will be critical to sustaining focus, ensuring momentum, and providing oversight for monitoring the impact of purpose on the business and organization.

Top-Down and Bottom-Up Engagement

The process must be inclusive without bogging down due to consensus decision-making. By the time the purpose is broadly shared by the CEO in whatever manner she or he deems appropriate, a large swath of the employee base should already feel engaged in the purpose and its potential ramifications.

For example, a large, Italian-based multinational decided to gain input from all major regions via employee video interviews before public deployment. These interviews were then used as part of the launch of the company purpose, which the CEO led.

Integrate. Integrate. Integrate.

Begin with the end in mind, which is a sustainable, dynamic, differentiating business model with its foundation in purpose. That means the model needs to be baked into the organization's business rituals, goals, and behaviors. Leaders need to implement the purpose into metrics, policies, and daily work once they have internalized the purpose for themselves and inspired their teams to rethink their work based on the purpose. One home-improvement firm realized the power of its purpose when it resulted in a different kind of work being valued in its stores: work that better enabled employees to assist customers to accomplish projects that were important to them.

It's Emotional, and That's Okay

The process of discovering (or rediscovering) and activating a brand or company purpose gets to the heart of a business, and also gets to the heart of people. Be prepared for joy, tears, memories, anguish, exhilaration, and even life changes. A large real-estate development firm had small-group meetings where its associates told stories of their purpose coming to life, and many had trouble finishing their stories. That is when you know you are tapping into a purpose that is deep, authentic, and sustainable.

THE PURPOSE PATH TO GROWTH MODEL IN ACTION

Every team's journey through this model is different, because every team, business, and culture is different. Here, we show two case studies of companies who have fully embraced the model, with purpose at the center of the way they will grow and seize competitive advantage.

Pharmavite: Bringing the Gift of Health to Life

Founded in 1971 by pharmacist Barry Pressman and entrepreneur Henry Burdick, Pharmavite was built on a heritage of integrating science with quality nutrients and minerals, in order to make good nutrition more accessible for consumers via vitamins and dietary supplements. After decades of growth in a highly competitive category, and after the company had expanded through acquisitions, the leadership concluded that the company needed a step change in its strategic direction. They were in search of a clear purpose around which to galvanize the business leaders and provide a unifying rallying cry for all Pharmavite employees: its higher purpose.

The Pharmavite leadership reached out to us for help in their journey to reorient their business toward a purpose-centric approach. Our engagement in the Pharmavite purpose discovery process began in earnest with an immersion into the company and its brands (including the flagship Nature Made brand), the culture of the organization, the company's heritage, and its inherent purpose. The insights gained from our immersion were rich and informed the design of facilitated purpose discovery workshops we conducted for the C-suite team and the extended leadership team.

Through the purpose discovery workshops, we determined that Pharmavite isn't just in the vitamin business; it's in the vitality business. It's in the business of supporting consumers in living the energetic, strong, and active lives that they desire. This was an important distinction that created meaning well beyond what's "in the bottle." Our work led to several beliefs closely held by company leaders, including those who had been with the company for decades. Previously unarticulated, these beliefs were resoundingly embraced by employees as representing the essence of Pharmavite's worldview. Key beliefs included:

- Energy and vitality fuel the pursuit of happiness.
- Our world of plenty is creating a poverty of health.
- Good health should be within reach for all.
- Complete nutrition is not about quick fixes.
- You can't have trust without truth.

Rooted in the company's heritage and upheld by strongly held beliefs and values, the discovery journey culminated in a simple and relevant purpose statement: *We exist to bring the gift of health to life.*

On multiple levels, this statement resonated with the company leadership. It spoke to their reverence for life. It spoke to the role that health plays in the quality of how people live. It harkened back to the intent of the founders to bring the basics of good nutrition and essential nutrients and minerals to consumers. It spoke to their hearts and their minds.

Armed with this newly articulated purpose, we focused on internal activation. Everything we know about driving organizational change is underscored by the fact that leading from the top is unquestionably important. However, identifying and empowering a small, multifunctional team of stewards, who keep the momentum moving forward and engage the organization, can make the difference between a purpose journey that stalls and one that gains momentum and is sustained over time. Pharmavite's CEO Jeff Boutelle appointed such a team.

Charged with shepherding the internal activation of the Pharmavite purpose, the purpose activation team brought the passion, commitment, and sense of accountability necessary to breathe life into the purpose and lead the actions necessary to engage the company's 1,400 employees. Within weeks of completing the executive work on the purpose discovery stage, the team created a two-year activation plan. Informed by the newly minted purpose discovery work and the team's perspective on the business, culture, and successes and failures of previous organizational change efforts, we created a road map for engaging employees and embedding the purpose into the culture of the organization.

The activation plan included key elements designed to signal to employees that the commitment to purpose was real and would become a sustainable part of the company. Leadership-readiness initiatives over several months provided the top 150 leaders with the tools to develop their own individual connection to the purpose before deploying it to employees. Telegraphing leadership's commitment during the year one activation of the new purpose began at employee "road shows" at every company site, with passionate messaging from site leaders, purpose-centric engagement activities, and changes in the physical workspace. In fact, following his attendance at a road-show event, an inspired warehouse employee stated, "Now I understand that I'm not just here to help Pharmavite make money. . . . I'm here to help people be healthy."

Company leaders understood that in order to truly bring the gift of health to consumers, they needed to start with Pharmavite's employees. The company launched a number of initiatives among employees, including weekly deliveries of fresh fruit, free vitamins, and a program of in-depth wellness screenings that gave employees a snapshot of their overall health and potential health risks, coupled with one-on-one coaching from registered dietitians.

Another manifestation of the company's purpose was in the design of the new corporate headquarters. What began as a typical office relocation became an opportunity for fundamental change in the company's work environment. Drawing inspiration from the purpose and the healthy lifestyle associated with its California roots, the company created a purpose-centric work environment. Key features of the new space included open collaboration areas, meditation rooms, and ergonomically designed personal work areas. Close proximity to a fitness center and an outdoor campus area conducive to group walks and other healthy activities also reinforced its health focus with employees on a daily basis.

To begin to bridge the company's purpose to the external community and to support the belief that good health should be within reach for all, Pharmavite began a three-year partnership with Feed the Children, a nonprofit organization focused on alleviating childhood hunger. This program distributes millions of Nature Made children's vitamins at multiple events across the country and gives employees an opportunity to volunteer their time to bring relief to thousands of families in need.

Pharmavite's foundational corporate growth strategy is being built from the ground up based on purpose, and all company brands have developed brand strategies and a purpose that roll up to the top. Longer-term initiatives to reinforce and align the organization to its purpose include a multifunctional exploration of how purpose informs changes to its business objectives and tactics as well as its systems and work streams, including a revamping of the recruiting and performance management processes, and a launch of a new employee rewards and recognition programs.

The purpose story is still being written at Pharmavite, but it's an inspirational case of the power of committed leadership and a mindful approach to the internal activation of a purpose authentically tied to the DNA and heritage of the company.

Airbnb: Creating a World Where Everyone Can "Belong Anywhere"

Another example of the purpose path to growth model in practice is Airbnb. In 2007, founders Joe Gebbia and Brian Chesky had an idea to make a little extra cash by renting an air mattress on the floor of their San Francisco apartment. A decade later, their $3 billion business has completely disrupted the hospitality industry, and purpose has been a major driver.

A few years into the company's young life, Douglas Atkin, the global head of community, embarked on a quest to make explicit Airbnb's purpose. The output of that process was captured in a two-minute video, which stated:

> The world is full of cities and towns, constantly growing larger.
> But the people within them are less connected.
> Yet we are all yearning for a sense of place.
> We are all seeking to belong.
> We all want to connect and share, to feel accepted and feel safe.
> Imagine having that anywhere.
> Airbnb stands for something much bigger than travel.
> We imagine a world where you can belong anywhere.

On the company's web site, co-founder and CEO Chesky writes, "At the heart of our mission is the idea that people are fundamentally good and every community is a place where you can belong." The company's stated purpose is to "create a world where everyone can belong anywhere."

As the purpose path to growth model prescribes, internal activation at Airbnb started under the guidance of Chesky. In 2017, when U.S. president Donald Trump issued a travel ban against citizens from majority-Muslim countries, Chesky took a high-profile stance in opposition to the measure. In response, he offered free housing to refugees caught in limbo. He told *Fortune*, "The notion that you wouldn't accept somebody from a country because of who they are is just in complete violation of all the values that we believe."

Internally, Airbnb takes robust steps to telegraph the ideal of *belonging* to its employees. Meeting rooms in the company's San Francisco offices are designed to have the look and feel of rooms in a home. Each conference room is a representation of an actual host property, and a spate of "landing zones" (instead of offices) aims to ensure that employees can "belong anywhere" within the headquarters. Diversity and inclusion are core values of the "Airfam"—as the company calls its workforce—and everyone stays connected through biweekly, live-streamed world meetings and an annual, all-company conference called "One Airbnb." In each of the regional offices, a "ground control" team makes sure employees regularly connect around birthday celebrations and holiday events.

The company's conviction about belonging shapes the external experience of the brand as well. The company's looped, love-infused logo (which it calls the "Bélo") is a symbol of belonging, and its corporate tagline is "Belong Anywhere." Asserting its commitment to inclusion, the company requires all of its hosts and users to sign a pledge against discrimination.

In the purpose path to growth model, a key element of external telegraphing is a disruptive act that strongly conveys the brand's purpose. Following the 2017 Trump travel ban, Airbnb fielded such an act. The company crafted an ad called "We Accept" and aired it during the Super Bowl. Featuring a montage of multicultural faces, it proclaimed, "We believe no matter who you are, where you're from, who you love or who you worship, we all belong." Its hashtag—#weaccept—topped the trending list during the Super Bowl, and while not without some political controversy, the ad earned the brand a net bump in customer goodwill.

Today, the company continues to drive its business "on purpose." Inspired by a world where people can belong anywhere, it has expanded its offerings beyond "homes for hire" to include "experiences to acquire." Airbnb customers can participate in a French cheese tasting in Paris or a sacred tattoo ceremony in Bangkok. Through a partnership with Resy (a restaurant reservation app), Airbnb users can also research and reserve places to eat during their travels.

PURPOSE 2.0: WHAT NEEDS TO BE DONE

Essentially being a for-profit creates opportunity for doing greater good. And financial success as a for-profit with a social conscience carries greater credibility with your peers, potentially influencing actions of other businesses.

—Brian Walker, former CEO, Herman Miller

The blind pursuit of profit at all costs is untenable. It is essential that we make money the right way. After all, if communities suffer as a result of a company's actions, those returns are not sustainable.

—Indra K. Nooyi, former chairman and CEO, PepsiCo

These quotes from the leaders of two iconic companies underscore what still needs to be done for purpose to be adopted as the platform for brand building in the future.

Brian Walker from Herman Miller highlights the need for more examples, more cases, and more storytelling about purpose as the foundation for growth and vitality. Human beings are compelled to act through powerful stories, and we simply do not have enough stories or cases about leaders shifting their business models toward purpose. We hope that this chapter, with its brief exploration of Airbnb and Pharmavite's journeys with purpose, is a small step in that direction.

Indra Nooyi speaks to the sustainability of results and to the importance of making money the right way. Larry Fink of BlackRock is also challenging industry norms to gravitate toward a new framework for decision-making. We believe that an evolution of current key performance indicators is needed, which would go beyond the income statements and balance sheets that currently measure leadership performance in every company. What should corporate boards be evaluating? What questions should they be asking? What does corporate governance look like for a purposeful approach to business?

Empirical research on the financial benefits of a purpose-centered management approach is still in its infancy. Several prominent academics have begun the work, including Raj Sisodia at Babson College, Philip Kotler at Northwestern

University's Kellogg School of Management, and Michael Porter at Harvard Business School. But there is still room for more growth in this area. Perhaps one day there will be entire journals devoted to the field of purpose, just as there are now to the field of advertising.

To this end, we need progress toward an industry standard for assessing a company's performance versus best practices: a "purpose audit." Every accountant studies and eventually masters the generally accepted accounting principles (GAAP) as they work in the field. They have a framework upon which to judge a firm's financial statements. What is our analog for purpose? Can we research and develop a GAAP for a purpose-centric approach to business? Imagine the power of such a framework to help achieve the vision Fink so magnificently laid out in his 2018 letter to shareholders: "To prosper over time, every company must not only deliver financial performance, but also show how it makes a positive contribution to society."

SUMMARY

Purpose as the central organizing concept for a business has been around for centuries, and the case for purpose as the foundation of a thriving brand or enterprise has only gathered momentum in the intervening centuries. But the case has gotten more urgent as customers and employees are expecting more from the brands they support and the brands that hire them.

Business leaders who ground their strategies in a purpose that inspires employees and impacts customers are winning. They are raising the standards for others. Yet, these leaders are still the exception and not the rule. Frameworks such as the purpose path to growth model provide road maps for those who wish to take this journey. As we continue to learn and gather additional empirical data via industry and academic studies, there is no doubt that the focus on purpose will also continue to shift and evolve, inspiring both today's and tomorrow's leaders who aspire to build growing sustainable businesses.

Jim Stengel is president and CEO of The Jim Stengel Company. He is a former global marketing officer for Procter & Gamble. A prolific writer, speaker, and advisor, Jim is the author of Grow: How Ideals Power Growth and Profit at the World's Greatest Companies, *and* Unleashing the Innovators: How Mature Companies Find New Life with Startups. *Jim is also a senior fellow and adjunct professor at the Kellogg Markets and Customers Initiative.*

Matt Carcieri is a brand strategist at The Jim Stengel Company. Prior to joining the company Matt spent 15 years in brand leadership positions at Procter

& Gamble, where he worked on brands such as Pringles, Folgers, and Pantene. He has an MBA from Georgetown University.

Renée Dunn is a growth consultant at The Jim Stengel Company. Before consulting with Jim, Renée spent 25 years with Procter & Gamble as a human resources executive. Known as a strategic HR business partner and for asking the tough questions, she led and implemented HR initiatives impacting multiple functions, geographies, and business units across the company. Renée is a Kellogg Graduate School of Management ('83) alumna.

Notes

1. Collins, James C., and Jerry I. Porras (1994), *Built to Last: Successful Habits of Visionary Companies*, New York: HarperCollins.
2. Sisodia, Raj, Jag Sheth, and David B. Wolfe (2007), *Firms of Endearment: How World-Class Companies Profit from Passion and Purpose*, Upper Saddle River, NJ: Wharton School Publishing.
3. Stengel, Jim (2011), *Grow: How Ideals Power Growth and Profit at the World's Greatest Companies*, New York: Crown Business.
4. Gartenberg, Claudine, Andrea Prat, and George Serafeim (2016), "Corporate Purpose and Financial Performance," Working Paper #17–023, Harvard Business School (September).
5. Kantar Vermeer, ESOMAR, ARF, LinkedIn, and Korn Ferry, (2014), "Driving Customer-Centric Growth," Insights2020 white paper.
6. Pearlman, Russell (2018), "Profit vs. Purpose: The Duel Begins," Korn Ferry Institute (May 15).
7. Gallup (2017), *State of the Global Workplace*, New York: Gallup Press.
8. PwC (2016), "Putting Purpose to Work: A Study of Purpose in the Workplace," PwC (June).
9. Deloitte (2014), "Culture of Purpose: Building Business Confidence; Driving Growth: 2014 Core Beliefs and Culture Survey," Deloitte Development LLC.
10. PwC (2016), "Putting Purpose to Work: A Study of Purpose in the Workplace," PwC (June).
11. Nielsen (2015), "The Sustainability Imperative," Nielsen (October 12).
12. Blodget, Henry (2016), "Henry Blodget: Introducing the BI 100: The Creators, Celebrating a Better Capitalism," businessinsider.com, June 13.

CHAPTER 3

CREATING A POWERFUL BRAND PORTFOLIO

TIM CALKINS

In 2014, executives at investment banking giant Goldman Sachs identified a promising new growth opportunity: consumer lending. The firm had long focused on high–net worth individuals and business clients, but the outlook for these businesses was somewhat troubled. Expanding into a new segment, consumer lending, could provide incremental growth.[1]

The problem, however, was that the Goldman Sachs brand was not ideal for consumer banking. Dustin Cohn, head of brand management and communications, explained the problem: "When you called it 'Goldman Sachs,' consumers said, 'Well, I've heard of Goldman Sachs, but that's not for me—that's for wealthy people and institutions.'"[2] The other problem was that offering small consumer loans might damage the Goldman Sachs brand's reputation as a partner for wealthy families and corporate titans.

Goldman resolved this issue by introducing a new brand, Marcus, to offer personal loans and savings accounts to individuals. The firm used a brand endorsement structure, calling the new firm Marcus by Goldman Sachs to tap into the power of the Goldman brand. Since the launch in 2016, Marcus has grown rapidly; by 2018 Marcus had more than 1.5 million customers and had made $3 billion in loans.[3]

Goldman's move to introduce a new endorsed brand is a perfect example of a brand portfolio decision. These portfolio moves are complicated and important. In some respects, managing a portfolio is branding's greatest challenge.

Building a single brand is a hard, especially in our hyper-connected world. Determining the correct positioning, optimizing the design, and managing the various touchpoints—all while developing and executing business initiatives that deliver profits—is a difficult undertaking. Indeed, most of this book is devoted to the topic.

Managing a brand portfolio, or a collection of brands, takes the challenge to another level. When dealing with a brand portfolio, the challenge is building a collection of brands, each with different meaning. Decisions that are optimal for one brand might not be optimal for another; building a successful brand portfolio requires trade-offs and tough choices.

Brand portfolio strategy focuses on questions such as: Should we launch a new brand or sub-brand? Should we acquire a new brand? How do we prioritize our brands? Do we have too many brands? Should we discontinue some of our brands?

Every organization needs to consider its brand portfolio. Even if a company has only one brand, it may decide to launch or acquire a new brand, or introduce a sub-brand or branded service. All of these moves impact the broader brand portfolio.

This chapter highlights how brand portfolios can drive profitable growth, explains why portfolios, if not managed well, can become major problems, and provides five keys to success.

Brand Portfolio Strategy Definitions

Before proceeding too far in a discussion of brand portfolios, it is important to cover a few key definitions.

Primary Brand

The *primary brand* is the main name on a product or service. This is generally the largest branding element on a product package or in a piece of communication. This is also what people refer to when they talk about the brand. Facebook, Apple, and Lufthansa are all primary brands.

By definition, every brand has a primary brand. The very simplest branding structures have just a primary brand and product description. Brands such as McDonald's restaurants, Starbucks coffee, Northwestern University, and Google search engine are all examples of a primary brand followed by a product description.

Sub-Brand

Sub-brands are secondary brands that fall below the primary brand in prominence. In most cases, the sub-brand will be more prominent than the descriptor that follows it. The key distinction is that the primary brand continues to be the most important branding element. For example, Honda uses a sub-brand system for many of its vehicles. The Honda Civic compact car has a primary brand (Honda), a sub-brand (Civic), and a descriptor (compact car).

Sub-brands are usually employed to distinguish a group of products or service offerings that differs in some meaningful way from the primary brand. The Toyota Highlander SUV is a Toyota, with all of the positive associations that the brand brings. The Highlander sub-brand is a group of large SUVs that are both rugged and family friendly.

Sub-brands can vary substantially in prominence, but there is a limit to how important the sub-brand can become; if the sub-brand becomes more prominent than the primary brand, then the sub-brand is actually the primary brand. Ram, for example, was at one point a sub-brand underneath the Dodge brand. Eventually, executives realized that for truck buyers, Ram was actually more powerful than Dodge, and they made Ram the primary brand.

Hyatt Corporation used a sub-brand structure when it launched Hyatt Centric in 2015, a new line of hotels targeting millennial travelers. Hyatt was eager to reach young, digitally savvy travelers, a segment it called "modern explorers." As Kristine Rose, vice president of brands at Hyatt, noted, "The modern explorers are truly a savvy, curious group. Their expectations are simple, but their standards are high and they want their experience to be intuitive and smart. They want all the options and must-haves from a full-service hotel, but without any fuss or complications."[4] With a sub-brand structure, Hyatt hoped to capitalize on positive associations with the Hyatt brand, while also indicating that this new line of properties was somewhat different and unique—and targeted to a very specific demographic.

Endorser Brand

Companies will use an endorsement branding strategy to highlight a connection to another brand. Marcus by Goldman Sachs is a perfect example of an endorsement strategy: Marcus is a distinct brand, but it is associated with Goldman Sachs. It is different but shares some characteristics. Steinway Corporation used a similar approach when it entered the mid-tier piano market. The company introduced a new brand, Boston, but included an endorsement from Steinway. The Boston by Steinway line of pianos is not the top-of-the-line Steinway, but it has some connection.

Endorsers can vary substantially in visual and verbal prominence, conveying everything from a very slight to a very strong endorsement. Like sub-brands, endorser brands can never exceed the prominence of the primary brand; if the endorser brand is the largest branding element, then it is actually the primary brand, not an endorser.

Marriott Corporation makes extensive use of endorser brands in its portfolio. The company's brand portfolio includes Residence Inn by Marriott, Courtyard by Marriott, AC Hotels by Marriott, Protea Hotels by Marriott, and many other brands that carry a Marriott endorsement.[5] The goal of this approach is to let people know that the different brands have a connection to Marriott, which means travelers can count on a certain level of quality and reliability as well as a common rewards program.

Ingredient and Service Brands

Companies can brand ingredients and ancillary services in addition to branding the core product or service offering.

Ingredient branding is commonly used to differentiate from competitors. If a company can brand one of its ingredients, it becomes a point of differentiation. A vague phrase, such as "heavy duty" or "high quality," is easy for competitors to copy. A branded ingredient or service is different because it is legally protected, so it cannot be copied by competitors. A branded ingredient or service can become an enduring point of differentiation. A competitor could create its own ingredient brand, but it can't use the same one. Unlike a patent, a branded ingredient can last forever.

This is a fairly common approach to differentiation. For example, Glad trash bags employed this strategy by adding a fragrance to its bags and creating a branded ingredient, OdorShield. The brand OdorShield wasn't part of the product name, but it was prominently featured on the package. Similarly, Chrysler created an ingredient brand around an engine, the Hemi, to indicate a high level of performance. In hotels, Westin introduced the Heavenly Bed.

Service brands are similar to ingredient brands but are used for particular service offerings. Air France-KLM created a new brand for its rewards program, Flying Blue. Lufthansa used a similar approach with the Miles & More brand.

THE POWER OF BRAND PORTFOLIOS

Building a portfolio of strong brands is a classic strategy for driving revenue and profit growth. A collection of powerful brands can reach different customer segments and capitalize on shifts in the market.

The strategic thinking behind brand portfolios isn't complicated. Start with the core challenge: growth. Firms today are under constant pressure to generate incremental revenue and profit. If you are a public company, growth is essential to keep investors happy: people don't line up to invest in a company that isn't growing. Private companies also have to grow, as private equity managers are not known for their patience. Family companies have to grow, too, because there are usually more and more family members to support as the years go by.

Stretching the Brand

So how do you grow? One way is to stretch your brand and broaden its appeal. Sometimes a company will extend a brand into new categories. Other times a firm will reach new target groups within the same category. Porsche, for example, has stretched its brand to multiple segments of the auto industry. For many years the core of its brand was small, high-performance, expensive cars. This was distinctive but also limiting: the world doesn't need many tiny, super-fast cars. So over the past 15 years, Porsche has stretched its brand. In 2002, the company launched the Cayenne, a large SUV, in an effort to reach families. Later, Porsche introduced a four-door sedan, the Panamera, and then a smaller SUV, the Macan. In the process, Porsche drove significant growth. The Cayenne is now its best-seller.

Danish design firm Vipp has grown by stretching its brand to new categories. The company's core product was a durable, stylish trash can. In 1996, the brand introduced its second product, a toilet brush. From there, the brand expanded into furniture, lighting, kitchens, homes, and even a line of hotels. Vipp's solid, durable, and expensive product has become something of an icon, leading Vipp to enter different parts of the household industry. As CEO Kasper Egelund explained, "We were a trash-can brand. Then we became a bathroom brand, then a kitchen and bathroom brand, and now we're what you call a lifestyle brand. But is that it? There's no rule that says this is where it ends. You have to have a dream and then pursue it like hell."[6]

The challenge with stretching a brand is that it only works to a certain degree. If a company stretches its brand too far, it can become less distinct. Great brands stand for something specific—you can't be all things to all people. The more you stretch a brand, the closer you get to the "all things to all people" dilemma. Some brands simply can't stretch very far. As Andy Palmer, CEO of luxury British automaker Aston Martin observed, "This is not a car company that is ever going to be selling a lot of cars. Part of its mystique is the exclusivity."[7]

Fashion giant Ralph Lauren Corporation illustrates what can happen when a brand expands too far. The brand, founded by Ralph Lauren in 1968, started as an upscale fashion brand with a distinctive sense of style. Over time the firm expanded and launched dozens of new product lines, including Polo Ralph Lauren, Double RL, Ralph by Ralph Lauren, RL Restaurant, and Ralph's Coffee Shop. The new lines drove significant growth, with sales reaching $7.6 billion in fiscal year 2015. The expansion also weakened the Ralph Lauren brand. Industry analyst Neil Saunders observed, "The Ralph Lauren flagship on New York's Upper East Side is a world away from the selection of random Polo sweaters thrown onto a fixture at Macy's. It is becoming increasingly difficult for the two to coexist without causing brand confusion."[8] Sales slumped in 2016, and in 2017 the company lost almost $100 million.

Expanding the Brand Portfolio

An alternative approach to growth is to create a portfolio of brands so a company has different brands reaching different segments of customers. With a brand portfolio, a corporate parent will have multiple brands in the market. One brand might target families while another brand targets young, single people. In many cases, customers are not aware of the ownership structure. In several research studies, I've found that people generally have no idea who actually owns many of the brands they use every day.

A portfolio provides many advantages. First, it lets a company capitalize on opportunities in the market. If there is a compelling segment or opportunity, the firm can create a brand to address it. Second, a portfolio provides flexibility. It is possible to launch, acquire, spin off, and discontinue brands. Third, a portfolio reduces risk. If one brand encounters trouble, the other brands in the portfolio may be fine—or even benefit as people look for alternatives.

Facebook, for example, has a portfolio of brands in the market. The core of the company is the Facebook network, where people post and share photos, videos, and comments. The firm also acquired Instagram in 2012, a network where people primarily share images. Many people are unaware that Facebook now owns Instagram.

Some organizations have vast portfolios. Marriott Corporation has more than 25 brands, brewing giant AB InBev owns more than 400 brands, and Coca-Cola Corporation owns more than 500 different brands.

The Characteristics of Strong Brand Portfolios

Strong brand portfolios have several characteristics. First, each brand within the corporate portfolio has clear associations and a distinct customer advantage. The brand meaning is clear, and the brand creates value. Customers understand and value the brand.

Second, there is little overlap. The best brand portfolios have distinct brands, with each brand going after different segments of the market. Overlap is almost always a concern; the more overlap, the more difficult the different brands are to manage. Redundant brands create confusion and conflict.

Third, a strong brand portfolio has a manageable number of brands. Each brand requires attention and support: a company must have the resources to monitor quality, field customer complaints, engage on social media, and optimize production and pricing for each brand.

Portfolio Problems

Without care and attention, a brand portfolio can quickly become a problem: instead of being a key driver of growth and profit, the portfolio creates complexity, inefficiency, and conflict. Key portfolio problems include weak brands, redundant brands, and too many brands.

General Motors Corporation provides a vivid example of what can happen if a portfolio is not managed well. For many years, GM was one of the leading corporations in the world. It was the dominant auto manufacturer and also one of the top manufacturers in the world. GM's brand portfolio drove much of this growth; the company had different brands, each aimed at a distinct customer segment. In the U.S. market, the Chevrolet brand was positioned for young people starting out who were looking for a practical, reliable car. Pontiac had a bit more flash and performance for people making progress in their careers and earning a bit more money. Buick was a family car—safe and reliable. Oldsmobile provided comfort and a touch of luxury for more mature buyers. And Cadillac was the ultimate sign of luxury. If you drove a Cadillac, your ship had clearly come in.

As GM expanded, however, the firm started to manage the brands more and more independently. The company put someone in charge of Chevrolet and told that person to drive growth, then put someone else in charge of Pontiac who was told to drive growth, too. So the managers did what they were told to do: grow. A logical way to grow is to expand the product line. The Chevrolet manager started introducing slightly bigger and snazzier cars, hoping to keep people in the Chevrolet franchise. The Pontiac manager grew the brand also, with a similar approach. The Cadillac manager employed a similar strategy.

Eventually, the operations team at GM observed that each brand was now selling a similar car, so there was money to be saved by embracing a platform manufacturing process. GM started selling variations of essentially the same car under the different brands. This was efficient from a production standpoint but weakened each individual brand.

With weakening brands, GM decided to add new, distinctive brands. It bought the Saab brand to anchor the high-end consumer market. GM also acquired the Hummer brand and then launched the new Saturn brand to compete on the low end.

Eventually, GM ended up with a vast collection of overlapping brands in the U.S. market: Saturn, Chevrolet, Pontiac, Buick, Oldsmobile, Cadillac, Saab, Hummer, GMC, and GM. This was a disaster: inefficient, confusing, weak. The problematic portfolio is one reason GM went bankrupt in 2009.

An important lesson from the GM example is this: it isn't enough to optimize each brand on its own. A parent company must consider and effectively manage the overall portfolio in its entirety.

MAKING PORTFOLIO DECISIONS

Portfolio decisions are some of the most important and challenging a business leader will face. One reason is that portfolio decisions are long term. When you launch a new brand, you have to manage it for many, many years. When you kill a brand, it is gone.

Portfolio decisions also usually require trade-offs among brands. Building all of the brands simultaneously and maximizing the total portfolio are often very different things: often the best way to build a portfolio is to focus on some brands at the expense of others.

The decisions can become emotional. The team leading a brand is often very attached to it; the brand may even give the team a sense of identity, just as some brands give their customers a sense of identity. As a result, people working on a brand will often fight very hard to defend it, lobbying for resources and attention even when the moves might not be right for the company as a whole.

Most challenging, perhaps, is the fact that there is rarely a clear answer to a portfolio decision, and in most situations there are no analyses that will conclusively prove that one decision is right and another is wrong. Portfolio decisions are affected by many variables, making it difficult to construct a financial model that will clearly indicate which path will lead to the most long-term profitability. The results depend on the assumptions that go into the analysis. You can do various analyses—concept tests and financial modeling—but none of the analyses will decisively determine the "right" answer.

While portfolio questions are challenging, they cannot be ignored. Every company must address brand portfolio questions. Each time a company launches a new product, it makes a portfolio decision. Similarly, each time a company sets financial targets and allocates resources, it makes a portfolio decision.

Optimizing each individual brand in the absence of a broader perspective is a bit like worrying about each particular color in a painting: the individual colors may be nice, but they must work together to create a beautiful piece.

BRAND PORTFOLIO MODELS

There are two basic models for brand portfolios: "house of brands" and "branded house." Companies employ both models widely, and both have strengths and weaknesses.

House of Brands

The classic and most powerful model for a brand portfolio is the house of brands. With this model, a company will own a number of different brands, possibly with several different brands in the same category. Each brand exists on its own. The company minimizes cannibalization and redundancy by creating a distinct positioning for each brand.

In a particular category, for example, one brand may target price-sensitive customers and compete on low prices, while another brand may target performance-oriented customers and compete on technical features. Companies employing the house of brands model often use a distinct corporate name. As a result, consumers are often unaware that a company's brands are all owned by the same parent.

Procter & Gamble is a classic example of a company employing a house of brands approach. The company owns dozens of different brands, including Dawn, Crest, Charmin, Bounty, Gillette, and Always. Each brand is distinct: the P&G brand is not used in a meaningful way on any of the products. Indeed, the only way a customer would know the brands are owned by P&G is by studying the fine print on the back of the label or spending some time on Google.

LVMH group is another example of a company embracing the house of brands model. LVMH owns more than 70 different luxury brands across categories that include fashion, wines and spirits, and watches. LVMH brands include Louis Vuitton, Chandon, Krug, Hennessy, Marc Jacobs, Berluti, Fresh, Hublot, Zenith, and Sephora. Each brand is distinct; LVMH owns and manages the brands but plays no role in each product's branding. There is no LVMH store, no LVMH credit card, and no LVMH frequent buyer program. The corporation capitalizes on synergies. There are common HR policies, for example, and a centralized real estate group to manage retail properties. Customers have no idea that the brands are all owned by the same firm.

The house of brands structure has a number of compelling advantages. The most obvious is that each brand can be precisely targeted to a group of consumers with a distinct product offering and positioning. There is no need to stretch a brand beyond its positioning: if an opportunity is compelling but the existing brands in the portfolio are not appropriate, the company can acquire or launch a new brand. When PepsiCo saw a need for a carbonated drink to compete with LaCroix sparkling water, for example, it expanded its portfolio in 2018 by launching a new brand, Bubbly, targeted precisely at the opportunity. This made perfect sense: extending the Pepsi brand itself into carbonated water would have created confusion about the new product and confusion about Pepsi.

Similarly, a house of brands strategy makes it easy to build a global business, because brands can play in the countries where they are most relevant. If a brand is not meaningful in one country, for example, the parent company can acquire or launch another brand that is.

The house of brands approach does have downsides, the biggest being that it can be a challenge to manage. Each brand needs to make decisions about pricing, new products, advertising, and other matters. If a company doesn't have an entrepreneurial culture, a house of brands approach can lead to debilitating complexity. It can also be inefficient. If a company pursuing a house of brands model isn't careful, it can end up with a large number of small brands, each one lacking the scale needed to drive substantial profits. Supporting the corporate brand—important for investors, business partners, and employees—requires additional spending.

Branded House

The opposite brand portfolio strategy is the branded house. In this model, a company takes a single primary brand across multiple products and categories. Purely executed, all the products a company produces are sold under a single brand name. Most often the corporation has the same name as the primary brand.

Uber is an example of a branded house. The company, founded by Travis Kalanick and Garrett Camp in 2008, operates solely under the Uber brand. In a bid to drive growth, Uber has expanded its product offerings, providing food delivery and unique experiences. It continues to leverage the Uber brand name.

Virgin Group is another example of a branded house. British business leader Richard Branson created the brand in 1971. The company first operated a music store in London, then gradually expanded into new businesses: airlines, telecommunications, financial services, soft drinks, wine, and many more. The Virgin brand is used across almost all of these categories, making Virgin one of the most broadly applied brands in the world.

The branded house drives focus on the brand. Because there is just one brand, it receives an enormous amount of senior management attention. Branson is very focused on the Virgin brand; he doesn't get distracted managing a dozen different ones. It is also efficient, because all the company's marketing efforts support the primary brand, which builds scale. Sponsoring an event such as the World Cup or the Olympics requires enormous investment, putting it out of reach for small brands.

Perhaps the biggest challenge with a branded house model is that the brand can become diluted as it spreads across different product categories. Virgin is unique because it successfully plays in disparate markets, unified by the popular and dynamic Branson. Other companies have more difficulty. The Hewlett Packard brand, for example, is used in different categories (and now by different companies) and has lost much of its distinction.

The branded house model can also constrain innovation and growth. If all ideas must fit under the one primary brand name, a company may not pursue good ideas simply because they don't fit under the brand's umbrella.

KEYS TO SUCCESS

There is no one magic formula for creating a strong brand portfolio. Each company and situation is unique, with dynamics that require a deep strategic assessment of the particular situation. What works in one situation will not necessarily work in the next. There are, however, some best practices.

Key to Success #1: Build and Extend Core Brands

The first and most important lesson in portfolio strategy is that it is always best to start with the core. If a company doesn't have a strong foundation, it will be impossible to invest in new brands. As a result, establishing a strong base is priority number one. This means that if you have a new idea that fits with your existing brand, put it there. The innovation will help the existing brand, and the existing brand will help the innovation.

Keep in mind that it is possible to go too far: extensions can weaken a brand, creating confusion and dilution. Extending the Gerber brand into beer, for example, would weaken the meaning of the baby-food brand. As Jack Trout writes in *Differentiate or Die*, "The more things you try to become and the more you lose focus, the more difficult it is to differentiate your product."[9]

It is useful to ask three questions about any line extension. First, will the existing brand help the new product? The existing brand must be an asset for the new product, but this is not always the case—as noted above, existing brands can sometimes diminish the appeal of a new product. Using the Clorox brand on a new line of salad dressings, for example, will not help sales of the new product. The Clorox brand is associated with bleach, which is obviously not a positive in the world of salad dressing. Similarly, using Kikkoman, a well-known brand of soy sauce, to launch an airline will simply create confusion.

Second, will the new product help the existing brand? The new product must be positive for the base brand. Damaging a strong brand by launching a poor-quality or confusing extension makes little sense.

Third, is the new product a good business idea? It may be possible to extend a brand into a new category, but the idea must make good business sense. Simply because a product can expand into a new category doesn't mean it should. Entering an existing, well-established category with a nondifferentiated item is not likely to be successful, regardless of how compelling the brand is.

Apple illustrates the power of focusing on the core brand. The company consistently uses the Apple brand on all of its new products. This creates two positive dynamics: the new products help the Apple brand, demonstrating its innovative and contemporary nature, and Apple helps the new products through its positive associations of excellence in design and customer experience.

Key to Success #2: Add Brands to the Portfolio to Address Major Opportunities

It is important to be open to launching new brands. One of the most obvious times to launch a new brand is when the company is going after a new market—either a new segment of an existing category or an entirely new category. If the brands currently in the portfolio are not well aligned with the opportunity, it may make sense to add a new brand to the portfolio rather than extend a current brand.

There are even times when it makes sense to launch the same product under different brand names, if the product is positioned against different uses. In the pharmaceutical industry, for example, compounds are occasionally introduced under different brand names to address different needs. Amgen introduced its biologic compound denosumab under the Prolia brand name to treat osteoporosis in older people and under the Xgeva brand to prevent bone fractures in oncology patients.

When a company has a breakthrough technology or new product idea, it should carefully consider whether it is best to extend an existing brand or to introduce a new brand. Launching the new product idea under an existing brand will give the product a set of initial associations, and this may actually limit its long-term appeal. As Harvard marketing professor John Quelch noted, "By bringing important new products to market as line extensions, many companies leave money on the table. Some product ideas are big enough to warrant a new brand."[10]

By contrast, using the opportunity to introduce a new brand could drive high levels of incremental volume and lead to long-term growth. Importantly, a new brand can create its own identity. This is particularly important when the existing brands have limited appeal.

Of course, launching a new brand is costly, and if technology changes, the new brand's point of difference could become irrelevant. Sanka, for example, was a line of decaffeinated coffee. When the decaffeinated alternative was adopted across the coffee category, the benefit of Sanka vanished. Today, Sanka is a weak, fading brand.

When evaluating whether to add a brand to the portfolio, a company must do three important things: it must ensure that the new brand is distinct from the existing brands in the portfolio; it must be sure that the financial returns are positive; and it must ensure that the organization has the resources to manage the new brand.

Key to Success #3: Proactively Prune Weak and Redundant Brands

Just as pruning dead flowers from a plant ensures that the remaining buds will grow and flourish more abundantly, pruning is an essential part of managing the brand portfolio. Pruning weak brands will ensure that the remaining brands will continue to grow and thrive.

Brand portfolios tend to expand over time due to acquisitions and new product introductions. Few companies deliberately set out to create unwieldy brand portfolios, but often it is the natural result of expansion. Complex and unwieldy portfolios are difficult to manage, as each piece of the puzzle requires attention.

Redundant brands are a particularly difficult problem for companies: it is exceptionally hard to manage multiple brands in the same market space. Trading sales between brands, often at great cost, is not a good way to do business. Inevitably, redundant brands also create internal conflicts. Each management team, likely motivated by the need to deliver strong business results, will fight for sales attention, marketing spending, and new product ideas.

Retail giant Macy's has dramatically pruned its portfolio in recent years, taking dozens of regional department stores and bringing them together under just two brands: Macy's and Bloomingdale's. The company combined iconic local brands such as Marshall Field's (Illinois); Dayton's (Minnesota); Robinson's (California and Arizona); and Lazarus (Ohio). In the process, Macy's increased efficiency and built scale.

Pruning a portfolio has two benefits. First, it helps promising brands grow, enabling management to focus its time, attention, and resources on its most profitable brands. Second, it eliminates brands that will likely never play a meaningful role in the company portfolio.

Unfortunately, managers often have few incentives to prune the brand portfolio. Pruning is not glamorous work. At most companies, the rewards go to people who launch new initiatives and create new brands, not to people who identify and prune the deadwood.

Pruning is a difficult decision. It is final, absolute, and, for those who have come to have an emotional connection with the brand, very sad. Decisions to prune a portfolio should be made with care, as it is hard to reverse the decision, and eliminating a brand means disposing of a key company asset.

Once a decision has been made to prune a brand, there are several ways to accomplish the task. First, brands can be divested, or sold to another company. This likely maximizes the value of the brand, but it could create a new competitor. Second, brands can be harvested, or managed solely for short-term profits. Third, brands can simply be discontinued, or pulled off the market. This needs to be done carefully to ensure that another company does not pick up the trademarks.

P&G, for example, lost control of its bathroom tissue brand White Cloud when in 1993 the company discontinued the old brand in order to focus its efforts on its primary bathroom tissue brand, Charmin. Tony Gelbart, an enterprising marketer, noticed P&G's move and applied for the White Cloud trademark, declaring that it was an abandoned mark. After years of legal fights, Gelbart secured ownership of White Cloud and relaunched it as a premium brand at Walmart. P&G tried to kill White Cloud but ended up competing against it.[11]

Finally, brands can be combined. In this scenario, brands are gradually brought together, with the company transitioning customers over time. For example, Nestlé folded its Contadina line of refrigerated pastas into the Buitoni brand. Nestlé made the change very gradually, first adding Buitoni to the package as an endorser, then making Buitoni the primary brand and Contadina the sub-brand, and finally dropping the Contadina name entirely. Nestlé maintained category leadership during the transition.

Key to Success #4: Keep Things Simple

In business, too much complexity is almost always a problem. In branding, this is particularly true, as a complex brand portfolio is a challenge to manage. Every brand in a corporate structure must be managed and tracked, so each bit of complexity makes it harder to develop and execute business plans.

Every branding element requires investment. Introducing a sub-brand that is meaningless to customers, for example, creates needless complexity. A company must invest in creating meaning around a branding element; otherwise it should simply use a product descriptor.

In an effort to capture the best of all worlds, managers have an incentive to introduce many sub-brands and endorsers. The result, though, is that customers sometimes have no idea what any brand stands for. A good rule of thumb: if you can't explain a brand structure in a sentence or two, it is too complex.

Key to Success #5: Involve Senior Management

In order to achieve the best results, brand portfolio decisions should be made at the very highest levels of an organization, for three reasons. First, as discussed earlier, portfolio decisions are enormously important; few will have as important an impact as a brand portfolio decision.

Second, portfolio decisions require a long-term perspective. Managers charged with delivering short-term financial targets obviously have an incentive to maximize short-term results. However, short-term thinking shouldn't drive a portfolio decision.

Third, portfolio decisions often require trade-offs among brands. The goal in managing a portfolio is to maximize the whole, not the parts. The managers responsible for delivering results for a particular brand aren't usually interested in hurting their own brand's results to help another brand; thus, senior management must be the decision maker. Nicolas Hayek, the former CEO of Swatch Group, managed a wide range of brands. He observed, "Each brand is different, so each message is different. But each brand has a message. My job is to sit in the bunker with a machine gun defending the distinct messages of all my brands."[12]

SUMMARY

Managing brand portfolios is one of the great challenges in branding. As hard as it is to build a strong brand, it is even harder to build a portfolio of great brands. The answers are seldom clear, and the trade-offs are significant. Still, a company must focus on the portfolio challenge in order to prosper. Great results don't come from strong brands—they come from strong portfolios of brands.

To build a strong portfolio, firms should build the core, add brands to address compelling new opportunities, proactively prune weak brands, keep things simple, and involve senior management.

Tim Calkins is a clinical professor of marketing at Northwestern University's Kellogg School of Management, where he teaches courses that include Marketing Strategy and Biomedical Marketing. He began his marketing career at Kraft Foods managing brands that included Miracle Whip, Parkay, and Taco Bell. He is the author of several books, including Defending Your Brand: How Smart Companies Use Defensive Strategy to Deal with Competitive Attacks *and* How to Wash a Chicken: Mastering the Business Presentation. *He holds a BA from Yale and an MBA from Harvard Business School.*

NOTES

1. Hoffman, Liz, and Peter Rudegeair (2018), "Goldman Sachs, Adviser to the Elite, Wants to Be Your Local Bank," *Wall Street Journal* (February 27). https://www.wsj.com/articles/goldman-sachs-adviser-to-the-elite-wants-to-be-your-main-street-banker-1519745369.
2. Wolf, Janine (2018), "What's in a Name? $ucceSS," *Chicago Tribune* (June 20), 4.
3. Faux, Zeke, and Shahien Nasiripour (2018), "Why Goldman Sachs Is Lending to the Middle Class," *Bloomberg Businessweek*, June 29. https://www.bloomberg.com/news/articles/2018-06-29/why-goldman-sachs-is-lending-to-the-middle-class.
4. Trejos, Nancy (2015), "Hyatt Creates New Brand for Modern Travelers," *USA Today* (January 27). www.usatoday.com/story/travel/hotels/2015/01/27/hyatt-new-brand-centric/22388513.
5. "Explore Our Brands" (n.d.), Marriott Corporation web site. http://www.marriott.com/marriott-brands.mi.
6. Rachlin, Natalie (2018), "Vipp Smart," *Wall Street Journal Magazine* (March 5), 72.
7. Boston, William (2015), "Porsche Taps the Brake as Sales Surge," *Wall Street Journal* (March 21), B3.
8. Abrams, Rachel, and Vanessa Friedman (2017), "Tensions Between New and Old, Played Out at Ralph Lauren," *New York Times* (February 2). https://www.nytimes.com/2017/02/02/business/ralph-lauren-ceo-stefan-larsson.html.
9. Trout, Jack (2000), *Differentiate or Die*, New York: John Wiley & Sons, 171.
10. Quelch, John A., and David Kenny (1994), "Extend Profits, Not Product Lines," *Harvard Business Review*, September–October, 155.
11. Neff, Jack (2017), "Started from the Bottom," *Ad Age* (November 13), 28.
12. Taylor, William (1993), "Message and Muscle: An Interview with Swatch Titan Nicolas Hayek," *Harvard Business Review*, March.

CHAPTER 4

COMPETITIVE BRAND STRATEGIES: CREATING PIONEER, FAST-FOLLOWER, AND LATE-MOVER ADVANTAGE

GREGORY S. CARPENTER and KENT NAKAMOTO

Brands achieve remarkable success using very different strategies. Some brands pioneer new markets, as Intuitive Surgical did when it launched the first robotic surgery system, or when Louis Roederer produced Cristal, the first prestige champagne cuvée. Other firms enter an established market soon after the pioneer with a fast-follower strategy. General Electric and Samsung have used this approach with great success. Still other brands challenge established market leaders by entering long after the pioneer. Consider Apple, which launched the iPhone a full 34 years after Motorola invented the mobile phone.

Firms debate when to enter a market. Is it better to pioneer a market, better to be a fast follower, or best to wait and enter as a late mover? For some firms, the debate rests on the assumption that competition is like a game. Firms study the technology and structure of the market, and they conduct market research hoping to discover the rules of the game. These market-driven firms succeed by playing the game and meeting customer needs better, faster, or cheaper than rivals. The ideal timing of entry, however, is difficult to determine before the game begins.[1] Without the ability to predict the timing and strategies of future entrants, firms often rely on simple rules or approaches that have proven successful.

Rather than simply seeking to understand the game, market-driving firms see competition as an evolving game and they seek to influence it.[2] Amazon and Netflix do so using technological disruptions, but other firms (such as Starbucks and De Beers) use social influence. For example, De Beers transformed 175-million-year-old carbon crystals into symbols of love and devotion, creating a $50 billion market. For market-driving firms, competition is a battle for influence. Brands that win influence shape consumers' language, brand perceptions, and even the amount consumers will pay for a brand.[3] Brands with influence shape the competitive game, gaining competitive advantage regardless of when they enter the market. From this perspective, pioneering, fast following, and late moving are simply different strategies to influence consumer learning. In this chapter, we'll explore how pioneers, fast followers, and later entrants influence consumer learning and shape the rules of the competitive game for enduring advantage.

PIONEERING ADVANTAGE

Intuitive Surgical launched the first robotic surgery system in 2000. Compared to traditional surgery, Intuitive Surgical's da Vinci Surgical System enables minimally invasive procedures with smaller incisions, while surgeons operate with greater precision and dexterity. Patients typically suffer less pain, lose less blood, and recover more quickly with shorter hospital stays and fewer complications. Although robotic systems are used in a limited number of procedures, Intuitive Surgical estimates that almost half of the 20 million inpatient surgeries performed in the United States could be performed robotically. Such a large opportunity attracts the attention of Medtronic, Johnson & Johnson, and Verb Surgical, among others. Challenging Intuitive Surgical, however, will not be easy. Since 2000, Intuitive Surgical has sold over 4,000 da Vinci systems and has introduced three new generations of technology. Thousands of surgeons now have experience using its robotic system. According to one analysis, "Intuitive Surgical reigns as the undisputed leader in surgical robots."[4]

Successful pioneers are tempting targets for competitors. Coca-Cola, Cristal, eBay, Levi Strauss & Company, Red Bull, Intel—all pioneers—have attracted countless challengers. Although pioneers do indeed fail (and some are overtaken), research over the past 30 years demonstrates that successful pioneers outsell later entrants in a broad range of industries. Some do so for years or even decades.[5] Figure 4.1 shows data from one study of brand-entry timing on the average market share in consumer-goods markets earned by brands based on their order of entry relative to the pioneer.[6] Compared to the pioneer, the second entrant earns, on average, 71 percent of the market share of the pioneer; the third entrant receives 58 percent; and so on up to the sixth entrant, which earns less than half the market share of the pioneer. Market share tallies are

Figure 4.1
Estimated Market Share Based on Order of Brand Entry Relative to the Pioneer's Market Share

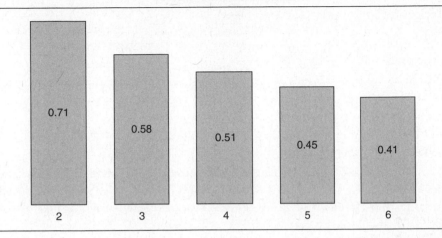

statistically adjusted to control for differences in positioning, pricing, advertising, and distribution. Thus, the sixth entrant receives less than half the share of the pioneer after adjusting for differences in marketing strategy.

The consumer behavior that creates a pioneering advantage contradicts our intuition. Consumers should be indifferent when considering two equivalent alternatives. The evidence, however, suggests that consumers systematically favor a pioneer over an otherwise equivalent later entrant. To match the pioneer's market share, a later entrant must make itself *more* attractive—by spending more on advertising, for example, or by pricing below the pioneer. The need for later entrants to spend more or charge less creates a systematic advantage for the pioneer. Understanding the factors that produce advantage for the pioneer over later entrants provides valuable insight for pioneers and later entrants alike.

A Pioneer Is a Low-Risk Choice

A pioneer's advantage rests on consumers' experience with it. When the pioneer launches its product, it is entirely novel, and consumers may be skeptical. Through experience, they learn whether the product works or fails. If the pioneer works, consumer demand increases, attracting new rivals. Even if the later entrants copy the pioneer *perfectly and adopt identical strategies*, they are untried, and as such they carry greater risk. To overcome the risk, later entrants offer consumers some additional benefit. For example, later entrants commonly price below the pioneer or spend more on advertising to induce trial. Thus, consumers' experience with the pioneer imposes a burden on later entrants and creates an advantage for the pioneer.[7]

Consumers Remember Pioneers

Before the pioneer enters, consumers have no awareness of any brands in the category. The market simply does not exist. Through trial and experience, consumers learn about the pioneer. Other brands enter the newly created market, and consumers learn about them as well. Through this process, consumers develop thoughts and memories associated with different brands. Consumers have more experience with some brands than others, which means that consumers recall some brands more easily than others. If asked to name all the brands of energy drinks, for example, we might think first of Red Bull and Monster, but we might struggle to recall others, such as Burn or Zevia.

What makes a brand more memorable? Many factors, of course, but studies show that one factor is the order in which consumers learn about brands. In a series of experiments, researchers varied the order in which consumers experienced the same set of brands. After learning about all the brands, consumers rated the brands, noting the brands' positive and negative features. The result: consumers recalled more positive features of brands they learned about first. This effect appears to stem from the following process: as brands successively enter the market, consumers learn that each brand has unique features as well as shared features. As more brands enter, the novelty of each new entrant diminishes, so consumer learning diminishes. As a result, consumers typically devote more thought to learning about the pioneer as compared to later entrants. Knowing more about the pioneer enables consumers to recall it more easily, which means that pioneers are more frequently in the choice set and therefore are more likely to be chosen.[8]

A Pioneer Sets Category Standards

Traditional approaches to marketing strategy assume that customers know what they want. According to this logic, consumers understand brand attributes or features, know how to value brands, and have a clear logic for choosing among alternatives. But before a pioneer creates a market, none of this knowledge exists. With the exception of preferring sweet to bitter foods, most human preferences are learned. Realizing this fact leads to a very different approach to market pioneering. Rather than seeking to *discover* what consumers want, pioneers *influence* what consumers want. As Steve Jobs famously argued, "Some people say, 'Give the customers what they want.' But that's not my approach. Our job is to figure out what they're going to want before they do."[9] According to this logic, the pioneer has a unique opportunity to create the knowledge that guides consumer behavior. Moreover, before other brands enter, the pioneer's influence is unchallenged.

The pioneer influences two critical aspects of consumer thinking. First, the pioneer can become uniquely linked or even synonymous with the product category. Psychologists describe such brands as *prototypical*. Coca-Cola, Google, and Uber offer examples. Each is strongly linked in the minds of buyers to soft drinks, Internet searches, and ride-sharing services, respectively. Consumers recall highly prototypical brands more easily, and this contributes to their more frequent consideration and choice of pioneering brands. Later entrants, being less prototypical, are simply considered less often and, therefore, chosen less often.

Second, the pioneer influences consumer preferences. Based on experience with the pioneer's brand, consumers learn how to value features and attributes. For example, in one experiment researchers designed six brands of software that differed along two attributes. Participants first saw a description of one of two brands from that set alone and then learned about the remaining five brands. The results show that subjects strongly preferred the brand they learned about first. Subjects described its combination of attributes as more ideal than the combination of attributes available from other brands. In other words, the pioneer influences the preferences that consumers learn, so that consumers prefer the pioneer.[10]

By shaping preferences, the pioneer sets the standard that consumers use to judge all brands. Surgeons will compare other robotic surgery systems to the da Vinci system. But the comparison process produces some unexpected judgments. Being different from the pioneer, later entrants lack something important. By being different, later entrants fail to meet the standard.[11] Brands that are similar to the pioneer suffer in comparison. Challengers to Red Bull who claim to be like Red Bull are simply not Red Bull. Challenging a successful market pioneer can even benefit the pioneer.[12] In the legendary battle between Coca-Cola and Pepsi, Pepsi advertised that consumers preferred Pepsi to Coke in blind taste tests. Pepsi's market share rose, but Coca-Cola's market share rose more. By comparing itself to Coca-Cola, Pepsi acknowledged that Coca-Cola is the standard, reinforcing its advantage over Pepsi.

FAST FOLLOWING: A DIFFERENT PATH TO SUCCESS

Although pioneers enjoy valuable advantages, fast followers can overtake pioneers. Facebook followed but quickly surpassed MySpace and Friendster in social networking. After Häagen-Dazs pioneered super-premium ice cream in the United States, Unilever quickly launched the super-premium ice cream brand Magnum in Europe and Asia, creating a leading global brand. In technology, fast following has led to some remarkable successes. General Electric overtook EMI, the pioneer in CT scanners, by entering quickly after EMI created the market.

Samsung has pursued fast following with a zeal matched by few others. The company has built a remarkable track record as a fast follower by using a copycat approach: imitating the market leader quickly at a lower price. Copycats typically fail when attacking long-established pioneers, as Pepsi's experience illustrates. However, copying a market leader quickly, before the pioneer becomes well established, can be effective. Samsung demonstrated this first in the television market when it copied RCA's technology and drove the leader from the market. Hoping to avoid the same fate, Apple designed the iPhone to make imitation difficult. Nevertheless, today Samsung leads Apple in global sales of smartphones. Apple's CEO remarked in frustration that the "copycats had done it again." Apple is a more valuable company, but by being the ultimate fast follower, Samsung has devoured competitors and helped lift South Korea out of poverty.[13]

The Fast-Follower Advantage

The success of Samsung is not unique. Golder and Tellis examined fast followers in a historical analysis of 50 product categories, including frequently purchased consumer goods, consumer durables, and industrial products.[14] They categorized brands based on their timing of entry as *market pioneer, early followers,* and *later entrants.* Golder and Tellis found that market pioneers, on average, fare less well than might be imagined from the research and experience highlighted in the first section of this chapter. The typical pioneer retained its leadership position for five years. Early followers, however, led the markets they entered in 53 percent of the markets examined. These results suggest that fast followers can overcome a pioneer's lead.

Golder and Tellis did not explore how fast followers overtake pioneers, but subsequent researchers have taken up this question. Shankar, Carpenter, and Krishnamurthi examined how timing of entry affects the sales of pioneers, fast followers, and later entrants. In one study, they examined ethical pharmaceuticals.[15] Over time, 29 brands entered six markets as pioneers, fast followers, or late entrants. The researchers modeled each brand's sales as a function of the brand's timing of entry (pioneer, fast follower, or later entrant), the marketing activities of each brand, and the cumulative previous sales of the brand and those of its rivals. The pattern of sales showed that fast followers enjoyed advantages compared to other entrants: they grew faster and generated more sales from each marketing dollar spent.

Catching the Wave: Growth-Stage Entrants

Fast followers grow faster throughout the lifespan of the market than other entrants. Pioneers, in fact, grow most slowly over the entire life of a market. This may occur because they bear the burden of building the category, which can take years or decades of slow growth. This process may have long-term consequences for the pioneer. AOL founder Steve Case has said that the pioneering Internet-access company was "an overnight success 10 years in the making" because of the work and investment that went into creating a mainstream market for network access. Fast followers, by definition, enter as the category is accelerating rapidly and are able to ride the growth wave for the long run. By contrast, later entrants grow faster on average than pioneers, but slower than fast followers. Late entrants, however, are disadvantaged: they top out at a lower sales level than other entrants, and they reach their top sales level more slowly than others.[16]

A key factor that can help a fast follower overtake a pioneer is superior access to talent and capital. Pioneers may create a new game but lack the experience or resources to win it. With too few resources, the pioneer will not be able to thoroughly influence preference formation, establish its product as the category standard, gain high brand awareness, and become viewed by consumers as the low-risk choice. Fast followers do bear risks, of course, but they do not bear the same risks as the pioneer.

LATE MOVERS: DIFFERENT BUT NOT DISRUPTIVE

Unlike fast followers, some firms enter long after a market emerges. Cialis followed Viagra by six years, Google followed Netscape by eight years, and Toyota sold its first cars in the United States decades after Ford and GM did. These late entrants faced well-known pioneers and well-established rules of competition. Consumers are aware of brands and have well-established preferences and comfortable choice routines, which define competition among brands. These existing rules tend to favor established brands, and many later entrants do fail, but some nonetheless succeed. How do later entrants overtake market leaders when so many fail?

Overlooked Value

One successful strategy for late movers is differentiation, a classic approach that focuses on identifying important, overlooked sources of value. After Henry Ford began mass-producing cars and overtook pioneer Mercedes-Benz (which built cars by hand), GM famously differentiated from Ford by offering different colors and brands, creating the most valuable company in the 20th century for two decades. After entering the U.S. market in the 1950s, Toyota became the most valuable company in its industry by offering high-quality, fuel-efficient cars. More recently, cloud-storage firm Dropbox seeks to distinguish itself from Apple's iCloud, Lyft seeks to highlight differences with Uber, and Perrier and San Pellegrino remind us of the difference between French and Italian sparkling water. Each of these firms has identified something valuable to consumers that rivals have overlooked. A critical question, however, remains: What prevents the market leader from simply imitating the challenger, wiping out its potential advantage?

One study offers insight into the type of late-entrant differentiation that is difficult for the market leader (whether a pioneer or fast follower) to imitate successfully.[17] Experimenters showed participants a set of brand-product combinations for two product categories: automobiles and soft drinks. The autos included SUVs and sports cars; the soft drinks included colas and lemon-lime flavors. Participants saw the same product features associated with either a pioneering or highly prototypical brand (e.g., Jeep or Porsche in automobiles and Coca-Cola or 7Up in soft drinks) or a less prototypical brand name (e.g., Mitsubishi for automobiles and Hanssens for soft drinks). They then rated the attractiveness of all the product-brand combinations as well as their perceived similarity. The researchers used these ratings to estimate the individuals' preferences for the original product-brand combination (e.g., Jeep SUV) and the extension of that brand (Jeep sports car).

The results were interesting. For products that were similar to the pioneer, participants strongly preferred the pioneering brand to a less prototypical brand with the same attributes (e.g., a Jeep SUV was preferred to a Mitsubishi SUV). If the product was an extension that differed from the pioneering version of the product, the pioneer was still strongly preferred (e.g., a two-wheel-drive Jeep SUV was preferred to a two-wheel-drive Mitsubishi SUV). When the product was highly dissimilar from the pioneer, however, the less proto-typical brand was preferred to the pioneer. For example, subjects preferred a Mitsubishi sports car to a Jeep sports car, and a Hanssens lemon–lime soft drink to a lemon–lime version of Coca-Cola. These results suggest that the pioneer has a strong advantage close to its original position, but it has a *disadvantage* as it moves further away from that original position.

Just Different Enough

These findings suggest a late-entry strategy. Close to its original position, the pioneer has an advantage over other brands. If a late entrant encroaches on the pioneer's position, the pioneer can simply imitate the late entrant with devastat-ing effect. For example, Coca-Cola quickly overtook smaller rivals that launched caffeine-free and diet cola. Further from the pioneer's original position, the pio-neer is at a disadvantage relative to other brands. For example, after launching its pioneering SUV, Jeep's attempt to launch a sports car, Jeepster, failed. A Jeep sports car was simply too inconsistent with consumer perceptions of Jeep, which had become strongly associated with rugged, off-road vehicles. If a later entrant chooses a position sufficiently far from the pioneer's original position, the pio-neer cannot effectively imitate its challenger. In that case, consumers will favor the later entrant over the pioneer. For example, when launching its luxury vehi-cle, Toyota positioned its Lexus brand as similar enough to Mercedes-Benz to be attractive to consumers, yet far enough away so that Mercedes-Benz could not easily imitate the Japanese competitor's excellent service.

Thus, the key to differentiation for a late entrant is to *position as close as pos-sible to the pioneer, while still remaining far enough from the pioneer to limit devastating imitation.* This strategy rests on the fundamental notion that consumers per-ceive the pioneer's and later-entrant's brands differently. Pioneers have power-ful brands, but with that power comes inflexibility. Later entrants have weaker but more flexible brands. By positioning just far enough from the pioneer, a later entrant can exploit the pioneer's weakness and gain advantage through differentiation.

LATE MOVERS: THE POWER OF INNOVATION

When *Business Insider* published its list of the 10 most valuable brands in 2018, Amazon, Apple, and Google topped the list, reflecting the power of innovation to create valuable brands.[18] Each of these companies achieved great success and created valuable brands by *building* something great—like a market pioneer—but also by *replacing* something great.[19]

Amazon sought to redefine retailing and create, in the words of Jeff Bezos, "Earth's most customer-centric company." Similarly, Apple challenged IBM in computers, even though at the time many considered IBM one of the world's best-managed and largest companies. Google entered the market after nine other firms, including Yahoo!, AltaVista, and a host of others. Like Amazon and Apple, Google challenged the status quo and reshaped consumer thinking. By doing this successfully, these firms have created enormously valuable brands.

The Innovation Challenge

An innovative late mover faces many of the same risks as a pioneer. Like a pioneer, an innovative late mover is offering something entirely new and untested. Consumers are unaware of the brand, but the late mover is entering a category in which it is likely to be judged by the standards established by earlier entrants. Furthermore, an innovative late entrant faces established rivals. Before Apple entered the personal computer business, IBM was the safe choice and global market leader. Furthermore, well-established firms have resources to challenge newer entrants. How does a late mover like Apple overcome all those disadvantages?

Evidence suggests that innovation creates advantages for late movers that established firms simply cannot match.[20] One study focused on 13 brands of ethical pharmaceuticals launched in two different markets. Pioneers created each market, and no firms chose to enter as fast followers. Multiple brands, however, entered once the market was well established. Some of these late entrants were innovative, others were not. Innovative late movers overtook pioneers in both markets.

What enabled these late movers to be successful? In the markets studied, innovative late movers created larger potential markets than the pioneer or other later entrants. Their customers were more loyal than those of the pioneer or other late entrants. With larger potential markets and greater brand loyalty, the innovative later entrants grew faster than their rivals. Thus, brands that entered late with a meaningful innovation enjoyed an *advantage* over the pioneer and other rivals. By contrast, brands that entered late without any sort of meaningful innovation served fewer potential customers, their promotional spending was less effective at generating sales, their buyers were less loyal, and, as competition grew, they suffered most in terms of lost sales. Noninnovative late entrants quite simply struggled.

The entry of an innovative late mover affects the success of other brands as well. In the two markets examined, as the past sales of the innovative late entrant increased, the sales growth of the pioneer *decreased*. In fact, the success of the innovative late mover coincided with *reduced* future success of the pioneers. Furthermore, greater past success of the innovative late mover was associated with a reduced effectiveness of the pioneer's marketing spending. Success of an innovative late entrant can, in other words, diminish the advantages associated with pioneering. By contrast, greater past success of noninnovative later entrants had no such effect on the pioneer. In essence, innovation by late entrants enables a brand to impose costs on its rivals, creating an advantage associated with late entry and a disadvantage associated with pioneering.

Successful, innovative late movers enjoy powerful competitive advantages, similar to those enjoyed by successful pioneers. Google offers a vivid illustration. Entering after nine other firms, Google offered a far simpler concept for search compared to the portal concept advanced by Yahoo!. Google has become synonymous with search, just as Coca-Cola and Red Bull are synonymous with the product categories they created. Google has enormous awareness advantages over other entrants; it has become the safe choice for search, establishing a new standard against which other search engines are judged. The rapid growth of Google creates a disadvantage for other late entrants. In 2015, consumers used Google for 69 percent of Internet searches, but by 2017, a mere two years later, consumers used Google for 75 percent of their Internet searches.[21] By comparison, fewer than 10 percent of consumers use Microsoft's Bing, despite the dominance of Microsoft in operating systems and its massive resources.

Strategic Innovation

Although high-tech innovative late movers command our attention, technology is not essential for innovation. Starbucks provides an excellent illustration. Humans have consumed coffee in one form or another for 1,500 years, making it the world's oldest traded commodity. The first coffee house, Kiva Han, opened in Istanbul in the sixteenth century. Starbucks appeared in 1971, long after the retail sales of roast and ground coffee had eclipsed coffee house revenues. Two brands dominated the U.S. coffee market—Folgers and Maxwell House—which roasted, ground, and vacuum-packed inexpensive coffee in cans sold in grocery stores for home brewing. Seeing little differentiation between the two brands, consumers often chose based on price, and retailers used coffee as a loss leader, advertising low prices to attract customers to their stores. As prices fell, producers lowered quality.

Starbucks's groundbreaking approach, which offered high-quality, high-priced coffee and a unique experience, challenged Folgers and Maxwell House by reinventing a concept pioneered by Kiva Han. For an innovative late mover like Starbucks, education is critical. As former chairman Howard Schultz explained: "Don't just give the customers what they ask for. If you offer them something so far superior that it takes a while to develop their palates, you can create a sense of discovery and excitement and loyalty that will bond them to you."[22] Despite opening its doors four centuries after the pioneer, Starbucks enjoys many of the advantages associated with market pioneering. As a well-known and trusted choice strongly associated with coffee, Starbucks has set a new standard for coffee and consumer experience.

SUMMARY

Though market pioneering, fast following, and late entry are distinct strategies, the success of all three approaches depends upon the same consumer learning process to create a competitive advantage. The strategies differ in that they respond to different stages in the development of a market. But the general approach of shaping the consumer learning process through competitive strategy holds across all three.

All three approaches use brands to define the rules of the competitive game and create competitive advantage in the process. Pioneers have the obvious opportunity to establish the rules of the game. With sufficient skill, resources, and insight, a pioneer can create a category, become strongly associated with it, and create a distinctive brand that is relatively insulated from its rivals. When pioneers falter, however—whether due to insufficient resources, unrefined technology, or another reason—fast followers can pounce and gain advantage.

Entering a mature market with established players can be challenging, so the opportunity for late movers is less obvious. Established market leaders have many advantages, which often include the resources to react aggressively and with devastating impact. And the same process that creates success for a pioneer also creates opportunity for late entrants. A later entrant that differentiates through innovation can exploit the pioneer's relative inflexibility. Innovative late entrants can restart the learning process, overtaking the pioneer and placing it in the unfamiliar role of follower.

These differing strategies reveal new insights about brand competition. Brand strategy is often viewed as a game where the rules are defined by consumers who dictate which product categories and which attributes are valued. Consumers reward brands according to their preferences, bestowing competitive advantage on the winners.

The strategies outlined in this chapter suggest a different mode of brand competition. Rather than trying to win consumers by understanding their preferences, brands can succeed by shaping the rules of the game: by helping customers understand what they want. By shaping consumer preferences, brands shape the competitive game, increasing the odds of enduring success.

Gregory S. Carpenter is the James Farley/Booz Allen Hamilton Professor of Marketing Strategy, Director of the Center for Market Leadership, and faculty director, Kellogg Markets and Customers Initiative (KMCI) at the Kellogg School of Management, Northwestern University. He holds a BA from Ohio Wesleyan University and an MBA, MPhil, and PhD from Columbia University.

Kent Nakamoto is the R.B. Pamplin Professor of Marketing, Pamplin College of Business, Virginia Polytechnic Institute and State University. He holds a BS from the California Institute of Technology, an MS from the University of Wisconsin, Madison, and a PhD from Stanford University.

NOTES

1. For a discussion of conditions favoring late entry, see Shankar, Venkatesh, and Gregory S. Carpenter (2012), "Late Mover Strategy." In *Handbook of Marketing Strategy*, Eds. V. Shankar and G. Carpenter, Gloucestershire, U.K.: Edward Elgar.
2. For a discussion of the differences between market-driven and market-driving firms, see Jaworski, Bernard J., Ajay K. Kohli, and Arvind Sahay (2000), "Market-Driven Versus Driving Markets," *Journal of the Academy of Marketing Science* 28(1), 45–54.
3. For an analysis of market-driving firms, see Humphreys, Ashlee, and Gregory S. Carpenter (2018), "Status Games: Market Driving through Social Influence in the U.S. Wine Industry," *Journal of Marketing*.
4. Speights, Keith (2016), "Better Buy: Intuitive Surgical, Inc. vs. Johnson & Johnson," The Motley Fool, October 16. www.fool.com/investing/2018/08/26/better-buy-intuitive-surgical-inc-vs-johnson-johns.aspx.
5. See Lieberman, Marvin B., and David B. Montgomery (2012), "First Mover/Pioneer Strategies." In *Handbook of Marketing Strategy*, Eds. V. Shankar and G. Carpenter, Gloucestershire, U.K.: Edward Elgar.
6. Calculated using estimates from Urban, Glen L., Theresa Carter, Steve Gaskin, and Zofia Mucha (1986), "Market Share Rewards to Pioneering Brands: Empirical Analysis and Strategic Implications," *Management Science* 32, 645–659.
7. Schmalensee, Richard (1982), "Product Differentiation Advantages of Pioneering Brands," *American Economic Review* 72, 340–365.
8. Kardes, Frank R., and Gurumurthy Kalyanaram (1992), "Order-of-Entry Effects on Consumer Memory and Judgment: An Information Integration Perspective," *Journal of Marketing Research* 29, 343–357.
9. Isaacson, Walter (2011), *Steve Jobs*, New York: Simon & Schuster.

10. Carpenter, Gregory S., and Kent Nakamoto (1989), "Consumer Preference Formation and Pioneering Advantage," *Journal of Marketing Research* 26(3) (August), 285–298.

11. Carpenter, Gregory S., and Kent Nakamoto (1990), "Competitive Strategies for Late Entry into a Market with a Dominant Brand," *Management Science* 36(10) (October), 268–278.

12. Carpenter, Gregory S., and Kent Nakamoto (1989), "Consumer Preference Formation and Pioneering Advantage," *Journal of Marketing Research* 26(3) (August), 285–298.

13. Oliver, Christian (2012), "Fast Follower Leads the Way," *Financial Times* (March 20).

14. Golder, Peter N., and Gerard J. Tellis (1993), "Pioneering Advantage: Marketing Logic or Marketing Legend?" *Journal of Marketing Research* 30, 158–170.

15. Shankar, Venkatesh, Gregory S. Carpenter, and Lakshman Krishnamurthi (1999), "The Advantages of Entry in the Growth Stage of the Product Life Cycle: An Empirical Analysis," *Journal of Marketing Research* 36(2) (May), 269–276.

16. Shankar, Venkatesh, Gregory S. Carpenter, and Lakshman Krishnamurthi (1999), "The Advantages of Entry in the Growth Stage of the Product Life Cycle: An Empirical Analysis," *Journal of Marketing Research* 36(2) (May), 269–276.

17. Carpenter, Gregory S., Donald R. Lehmann, Kent Nakamoto, and Suzanne Walchli (1993), "Pioneering Disadvantage: Consumer Response to Differentiated Entry and Defensive Imitation," Working Paper, Kellogg School of Management, Northwestern University.

18. Tyler, Jessica (2018), "The 10 Most Valuable Brands in 2018," *Business Insider*, August. https://www.businessinsider.com/most-valuable-brands-in-the-world-for-2018-brand-finance-2018-2.

19. An innovative late entrant can be viewed as a pioneer, depending on your perspective. For example, as a retailer, Amazon is an innovative late mover in a long-established industry. As an e-commerce firm, Amazon is pioneering a new market.

20. Shankar, Venkatesh, (1998), Gregory S. Carpenter, and Lakshman Krishnamurthi, "Late Mover Advantage: How Innovative Late Entrants Outsell Pioneers," *Journal of Marketing Research* 35(1) (February), 54–70.

21. Mangles, Carolanne (2018), "Search Engine Statistics 2018," smartinsights.com, January 30. https://www.smartinsights.com/search-engine-marketing/search-engine-statistics.

22. Schultz, Howard, and Dori Jones Yang (1997), *Pour Your Heart Into It: How Starbucks Built a Company One Cup at a Time*, New York: Hyperion, 35.

CHAPTER 5

LEADING THE BRAND: BRAND STRATEGY ORCHESTRATION AND IMPLEMENTATION

ERIC LEININGER

The previous chapters in this book are devoted to the discipline and creativity required to strategically position a brand and a portfolio of brands for success in a rapidly changing and hyper-connected marketing ecosystem.

It is equally critical to apply the same level of discipline and creativity to the orchestration and implementation of the brand platform. As Phil Marineau, former CEO of Levi's, taught his teams, "You will be more successful if you get the strategy 80 percent correct and the execution 100 percent correct than getting the strategy perfect and executing at only 80 percent."[1]

This chapter will focus on why strong leadership of brand implementation is so important. We will look at pitfalls to avoid and consider a framework for driving brand implementation.

LEADERSHIP, IMPLEMENTATION, AND BRANDING

A company cannot sustain a strong brand image, let alone be agile in the marketplace, unless marketing leaders focus on and anticipate potential implementation issues during the development of brand strategy. Senior leaders must communicate an implementation-friendly strategy that inspires cross-functional collaboration. Too many strategies are overly elegant and complex, which can deprive the initiative of focus. This in turn can lead to unwieldy and suboptimal execution. Simply put, if employees across the organization don't understand the brand positioning, it will be impossible to bring it to life.

Many brand impressions are created by the actions of frontline employees, who often have the greatest impact on defining a brand. The absence of strong implementation practices can result in frontline actions that create consumer confusion, or worse yet, negatively impact brand equity. Even the greatest brands experience brand implementation and orchestration issues.

Starbucks is one such example. The company is regarded by many as one of the great brands of our time. In April 2018, however, a Starbucks employee called the police when two African-American men refused to leave the store (they were waiting to meet a friend). The police eventually arrested the two men, who were indeed just waiting for a friend. The incident received wide coverage in the media, and people pointed to it as an example of racism in the United States. A video of the scene was viewed on social media more than 10 million times.[2] While Starbucks executives strived to create a brand built on inclusiveness and progressive values, the actions of one employee did enormous damage.

Although a great deal was written about how Starbucks managed this crisis, very little was written about how the brand was being governed, or not governed, when the store manager made the decisions that prompted the crisis. Despite the fact that the brand was firmly established as a "third place" to work (in addition to home and the workplace) or enjoy leisure time, decisions about whether noncustomers could use the seating and restrooms without making a purchase were left up to store managers. On one hand, this was a laudable commitment to delegation and trust in frontline management. On the other hand, it was an inherently risky business practice for the brand.

Of course, this begs the question of what organizational function, and what level of that function, should have been responsible for anticipating a potential implementation issue such as this. Clearly, many internal stakeholders had a role in this situation and might claim ownership of issues ranging from store operations to social responsibility to marketing, and potentially more. In the end, this was a brand implementation and orchestration issue well before it was a crisis. The lesson is that the chief branding officer in an organization (most likely the CMO) must be tightly aligned with operations on the brand promise and how that promise should play out in customer interactions.

United Airlines was dealt a similar blow when employees summoned police to remove a passenger from a plane. Video clips of the incident, where the man was literally dragged from his seat and was injured in the process, were shocking.[3] Domino's faced a similar crisis when bored store workers filmed a video showing them putting cheese up their nose and putting nasal mucus on a pizza.[4] Of course, implementation isn't always a problem. At times, employees dramatically enhance a brand with efforts that go above and beyond normal expectations.

Internal implementation is all too often overlooked in the branding process, as agencies and executives craft a strategy for positioning a product and then declare the branding challenges solved. The subject has certainly received scant academic attention. The Harvard Business Review Press search engine returned only 67 citations for brand strategy implementation, but 1,720 citations for brand strategy creation.

So why doesn't implementation receive the attention it deserves? Formulating strategy can highlight original and often brilliant ideas that are inspiring and instructive. Implementation, done well, is often the result of an organization doing what it knows how to do in an aligned and sequenced orchestration. Implementation reflects "how we get things done around here," and is more likely the result of observational learning and oral history, supported by established mechanisms to bridge functional silos. Institutional memory, in other words, is presumed to carry the day. It is therefore easy but incorrect for implementation to be seen as entirely idiosyncratic to an organization as opposed to a generalizable, transferable skill.

PITFALLS IN BRAND STRATEGY IMPLEMENTATION

Several common pitfalls can hinder brand strategy orchestration and implementation.

First, senior management's commitment is a must. If senior executives are not fully on board, it will be hard or impossible to bring a brand strategy to life. Implementation will inevitably consume significant resources and will very likely require a struggle against ingrained practices and organizational inertia. Brand strategy implementation is by definition a cross-functional, enterprise-wide effort. Senior management support will be necessary to help align the organization to sustain a strategy across all customer touchpoints in an organization.

Second, the brand strategy must be implementation friendly. All too often, brand leaders create elaborate, complex frameworks that are difficult or impossible for frontline employees to understand. If a brand platform isn't clear and direct, it won't be implemented. Marketing language sometimes plays a bigger role than customer and employee language, which inevitably leads to problems.

Third, it is critical to address company culture. Formal guidelines and rules can be helpful, but without efforts to embed the brand in company culture, the brand experience won't come to life for consumers. The formal implementation process must be supported by the informal organization.

Fully inculcating a brand strategy across an organization is not for the faint of heart. As Kellogg professor Ed Zajac observed, "While everyone is familiar with the saying 'culture eats strategy for breakfast,' that presumes that culture and strategy are at odds with each other. When the two are aligned, however, I say that 'culture feeds strategy.'"

Ideally, your company culture and values support the brand, and employees feel that taking personal ownership of animating a strategy is everyone's responsibility. Yet, it is more likely that you will encounter resistance and will need to have the relationships and support in place to influence many people over whom you have no direct control.

Fourth, companies are often populated with functional silos that don't agree on the path forward. Even within marketing, silos can appear, as subspecialties fragment the marketing function. As one CMO recently said to me, "I have 45 people in my marketing department. If I lined them all up and asked them to write down what we are trying to accomplish with the brand, the core message will become diffused as it is viewed through the lens of each specialist. Keeping the specialists inside and outside the company focused on the big picture is a huge challenge."

Fifth, the right measurement tools need to be in place. It is tempting to measure *inside-out* process metrics instead of *outside-in* brand health metrics. Successful brand strategy efforts are grounded in the organization's external factors—customers, competitors, categories, and context. Implementation efforts begin with the end goal in mind and work back to what the organization must achieve, rather than beginning with internal roles and responsibilities charts that describe what the organization is accustomed to doing. The adoption of an enterprise-wide *consumer journey* methodology is an essential tool that needs to be done correctly in order to identify the most valuable metrics.

Sixth, and finally, any brand implementation plan must be dynamic and able to manage the inevitable trade-offs that arise. It is critically important to create initial wins to build momentum. You do not want your management team asking, "When will something wonderful happen?"

A Framework for Brand Strategy Orchestration and Implementation

To understand the challenge of brand orchestration and implementation, I conducted in-depth interviews with senior marketing leaders at 15 companies across a range of business models: consumer packaged goods, technology services, insurance, homes, and marketing services.

Figure 5.1
Brand Strategy Implementation Model

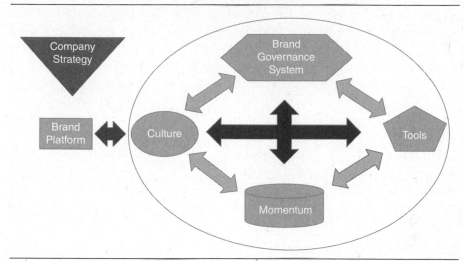

An underlying pattern of behavior guiding brand strategy implementation emerged from these interviews. The model has six elements, all of which are important if an organization is going to build and embrace strong brands: company strategy, brand platform, culture, tools, brand governance system, and momentum (See Figure 5.1).

The framework is designed to help organizations assess the quality of their orchestration and implementation practices. Ultimately, those practices support the ability to make smart decisions and deal with the trade-offs that are sometimes required to maintain a great brand. Sometimes a company needs to sacrifice short-term profitability in order to maintain brand quality, perhaps skipping a short-term promotion in order to maintain brand value. Luxury watch producer Richemont, for example, recently decided to buy back inventory from retailers in order to prevent discounting and gray-market sales that might damage the brand. Finance director Burkhart Grund explained the move this way: "We don't believe that having our inventory in the gray market will help long-term brand equity, so that's why we bought it back. That's what the story is all about."[5]

Company Strategy

Branding must be tightly linked to the overall company strategy. As a result, the first element is a statement of company strategy. How will the firm create value and drive results? How important are brands in this approach? If brands are not seen as a prime economic driver for the company, there is a risk that branding initiatives will lack support and fail to take hold. An organization focused on winning with a purely low-price strategy, for example, is not likely to invest heavily in brand building.

Brand Platform

The foundation of a brand is the branding platform—a clear definition of the desired brand associations. This includes brand positioning, brand character, and brand purpose.

It is impossible to lead a brand-building effort if you are not clear on what the brand should stand for. As Shelley Haus, senior vice president of brand marketing at Ulta Beauty, observed, "The lack of a great, clear brand strategy is the kryptonite to great brand strategy implementation."

It is important to remember that a brand platform is bigger than a creative brief, which is usually held within the province of the line marketing organization. A brand platform needs to play across functions. It is the starting point for myriad touchpoints across the organization. It distills unifying points of alignment.

Marketing leaders cannot wait until the strategy is fully developed to design implementation and execution plans. The most important issues must be anticipated at the outset, and they need to be considered while the strategy is being developed. Leading marketers think in terms of an *implementation-friendly brand strategy that inspires cross-functional collaboration*.

One way to determine if a brand platform is implementation friendly is to consider three guidelines:

1. It should be easily understood by everyone in the organization.
2. Everyone in the organization should be able to see how their jobs relate to the brand.
3. It should provide a rallying cry to motivate employees and help them identify initiatives that will add value to the brand.

Other chapters in this book discuss the different elements of the platform. The purpose of this chapter is to help you establish a brand platform and be certain that it is implementation friendly.

Culture

If the culture, both formally and informally, does not value and support brand building, it won't happen. *Branding should be brought to life in everyone's area of responsibility*.

This means that brand leaders need to have the relationships and support in place to influence many people over whom they do not have any direct control. This is particularly true in organizations with multiple independent but interdependent power nodes, such as global companies and franchisee and dealership organizations. The only solution to this challenge is to commit the time to listen, engage, and solicit support from cross-functional and frontline employees that drive important brand impressions.

A company's culture also needs to be able to value the different skills required for brand-building implementation. The core implementation skills are generalizable, but knowledge of a specific industry domain and of a particular organizational culture is also critical. Jim Skinner, former CEO of McDonald's, observed, "Anyone can write a strategy. The real work is bringing that strategy to life in the context of the McDonald's business system and operating culture."

Company culture is certainly affected by senior leadership, so it is essential that the senior team model certain behaviors; they need to demonstrate a deep understanding of customers and the role of the brand in customers' lives. A. G. Lafley, former CEO at Procter & Gamble, set this tone. He personally engaged with customers during in-home interviews and famously identified the three moments of truth for all P&G brands:

- At the point of purchase: Why would the consumer choose our product?
- At the moment of use: Does the product do what the consumer expects it to do?
- At the moment of social media: Would the consumer say good things or bad things?

Although Lafley's three moments of truth were created in the world of consumer packaged goods, any company should be able to identify a similar short list of moments of truth in its industry. Lafley used his consumer and market visits to teach, train, and empower team members—not just tell them what to do.

Senior leadership guidance alone won't bring a brand to life: training, processes, and incentives have to help employees throughout the organization understand the brand strategy and how they impact it. Employees also need the tools and ability to deliver outstanding service and bring the brand to life every day.

Brand Governance System

Brand implementation becomes more difficult as organizations grow. In particular, global organizations face special challenges, as their customer touchpoints occur all over the world. In addition, our hyper-connected world means that timing is compressed; brand leaders can't spend days or weeks debating the proper way to respond to a customer issue. In many cases, every second counts.

All of this makes brand governance critically important. How are decisions about the brand addressed? Who creates key policies? Who makes brand decisions?

The commonly heard advice is that "global sets strategy and local executes strategy." Use extreme caution with this guidance; employees who implement will be more committed and more effective if they are part of the strategy formulation. Those who set strategy need to be committed to building implementation-friendly strategies.

The best practice is to convene a brand council with a clear leader who absorbs all of the issues and perspectives. The brand council is usually not a voting group or a completely consensus-driven group; it is a forum to gain input and generate alignment. As Larry Light and Joan Kiddon argue in their book *New Brand Leadership*, creating "freedom within the framework" is a compelling approach to ensure that brand leadership principles are in place and that local creativity will enrich the brand locally. The creativity is focused by the framework, thereby building the brand.

A brand council will generally meet quarterly or semiannually to review and share best practices, and identify situations where freedom has been extended beyond the framework and needs to be checked on a continuing basis.

Tools

Brand leaders can use a range of tools to guide brand growth. Certainly, it is critical to have a clear strategy. At a minimum, two tools are needed to guide and measure implementation. The exact content of these tools will depend on the nature of the business, but generic outlines can be adapted by any business.

First, a brand leader needs to create clear brand guidelines. People won't follow guidelines if they don't know what they are or can't locate them. This means that a brand leader's first task is to create an easy-to-use platform that employees can access. Often, this will be a web site that includes the strategy and best practices, and templates to execute the strategy.

Second, a brand and business-balanced scorecard is essential to evaluate overall progress and to ensure that brand metrics are considered in the context of overall financial metrics. Almost all businesses run on their financial key performance indicators (KPIs). It is important to have brand- and customer-oriented KPIs, too.

Most businesses have either too many or too few brand-oriented KPIs. These metrics proliferate when there is not a clear view of the relationship of those metrics to the short-term and long-term health of the business.

There are three types of KPIs. Criteria measures include things such as Net Promoter Score (NPS) and customer satisfaction metrics. These are useful for continuous improvement monitoring, but they tell us *what* and *how high*—not *why*. Execution KPIs, such as service levels and response times, are also useful, but often these measures get buried in the middle level of the organization. Capability KPIs, such as employee and process development, are the most overlooked metrics.

I am often asked how to identify the right short list of consumer and customer KPIs. This should include, but not be restricted to, a quantitative exercise that identifies leading indicators and contra-indicators of business performance. However, that analysis might not yield measures that reflect new goals or new external conditions.

We need to focus KPIs on the actions that will ensure success with our customers. The consumer journey is an analytic tool to help us identify the most critical success factors. However, proponents of the consumer journey often exaggerate the case by establishing an absolute requirement to understand and maximize every consumer touchpoint. The fact is that not every interaction point has equal value, nor do we always have funds to make every moment as fully enriched as a customer might desire. As a consequence, consumer and customer metrics proliferate.

Laura Barry, senior director of marketing services at AbbVie, mobilized AbbVie marketers with the phrase "moments of meaning." After mapping the entire patient journey, Barry and her team identified the moments that carry the most importance from a patient perspective and financial value for the brand, and then created KPIs around those moments.

Momentum

Momentum is a critical—and often overlooked—part of brand implementation. The core challenge is that many branding efforts take a long time to play out. Perceptions of a well-established brand tend to change slowly and only when strong actions are taken. Strengthening a brand sometimes involves narrowing the target definition. But this does not always produce short-term results.

However, some marketing efforts work quickly. You can get on Facebook, place well-targeted and meaningful ads, and watch your traffic increase in just a few minutes. But brand-building efforts are usually not like this.

For this reason, if you aren't careful, senior management might only see costs and expenses from the branding initiative (all downside) and not the benefit (the upside). (See Chapter 16).

As a result, it is important to ensure that there are quick wins that create initial momentum and can be used to justify a long-term commitment to the strategy. In designing brand implementation, momentum is a critical factor. You need to start with visible wins and use this momentum to proceed farther down the road.

Two Critical Roles

It is important to note the two critical roles in a branding journey. The first is the CEO's. If top executives in companies believe in the power of brands and understand how strong brands will drive results, they will support branding efforts. This is critical, because building strong brands takes resources, and there are always trade-offs to be made. When a team debates quality and margin, which will prevail? With a brand-driven CEO, there is the possibility that quality may be a key consideration of brand building.

The second critical role is that of the brand leader—the person who champions the brand and manages it on a day-to-day basis. A CEO will not have the time to create and enforce brand design standards. Someone else in the firm needs to be responsible for the health of the brand.

The role of brand leader can reside in different places. In traditional fast-moving consumer goods firms, the brand manager often played the role of brand champion. In recent years, more and more firms, including P&G, Uber, and Noodles & Company, have created a chief brand officer position responsible for building and monitoring brand health. This role elevates the brand and addresses the cross-functional challenges, especially when human interactions are a critical driver of brand impressions.

At many firms, the role of brand leader falls to the chief marketing officer. This is a logical decision, but it can be a challenge because the CMO needs to play multiple roles and sometimes has a narrow span of control. If a company isn't careful, people will think that brand building is the job of the marketing department. For a CMO to be a successful brand leader, the role must be broadly defined.

SUMMARY

Ultimately, great brands come from committed organizations. Getting the brand strategy right is key, but it is just the first step. A brand flourishes when the organization embraces the direction and brings it to life, inside and outside the organization.

Eric Leininger is a clinical professor of executive education at Northwestern University's Kellogg School of Management, where he co-leads the Kellogg Chief Marketing Officer Program and teaches in numerous executive education programs. Prior to joining Kellogg, he was senior vice president at McDonald's as well as Kraft Foods. He received his BA from the University of Pennsylvania and MBA from the University of Michigan's Ross School of Business.

NOTES

1. Interview with Phil Marineau, September 9, 2018.
2. Hauser, Christine (2018), "Starbucks Employee Who Called Police on Black Men No Longer Works There, Company Says," *The New York Times* (April 16). https://www.nytimes.com/2018/04/16/us/starbucks-philadelphia-arrest.html?action=click&module=RelatedCoverage&pgtype=Article&region=Footer.
3. Victor, Daniel, and Matt Stevens (2017), "United Airlines Passenger Is Dragged from Overbooked Flight," *The New York Times* (April 10). https://www.nytimes.com/2017/04/10/business/united-flight-passenger-dragged.html.
4. Clifford, Stephanie (2009), "Video Prank at Domino's Taints Brand," *The New York Times* (April 15), https://www.nytimes.com/2009/04/16/business/media/16dominos.html.
5. Atkins, Ralph (2018), "Richemont Profits Hit by €200M Watches Buyback," *Financial Times* (May 18). https://www.ft.com/content/aadf6c6c-5a7b-11e8-bdb7-f6677d2e1ce8.

CHAPTER 6

THE THREE KEYS TO BUILDING GLOBAL BRANDS WITH SOUL

SANJAY KHOSLA

The quick-cut video shoots rapid-fire questions at young men: "Is it okay to be skinny?" "Is it okay to not like sports?" "Is it okay for guys to be nervous?" Finally a voice directs the viewer to go ask Google. When the viewer obliges, Google turns up singer-songwriter John Legend, who advises, "Guys are searching for answers, but there's no one way to 'be a man.'"

The sentiment and the digital platforms are all of the moment. Though artfully made, the only startling thing about the promotional package is the name behind it: Axe, the men's grooming brand that made its mark around the world by promising to turn teenage boys into girl magnets via high-testosterone, racy ads. Surely Axe wasn't going soft with this new campaign?

No, says Axe, the brand hasn't made a sharp left turn from its sex-obsessed past. Rather, brand managers say, they are simply responding to more enlightened, modern attitudes about masculinity. At heart, Axe (a brand of the Anglo-Dutch giant Unilever) is tapping into the same core emotion: young people everywhere want to be attractive to other young people.

This example illustrates how Axe has turned itself into a world-wide juggernaut by following three converging principles for building a global brand: (1) finding the common threads among people's needs and emotions by focusing on similarities that cross borders; (2) getting the right balance between global and local, with the vision and resources coming from company headquarters and the savvy and insight from frontline operators (going "glocal"); and (3) staying nimble and orchestrating rollouts under a robust business plan with maximum agility.

Below, we examine these principles in more detail.

FINDING THE COMMON THREADS: WINNING WITH GLOBAL INSIGHTS

Going global starts with the search for common threads across boundaries. First, start by looking for similarities between your brand's market and others, then segment according to common habits and needs. Finding local managers to tailor the product to local tastes, then monitoring the introduction and making adjustments, can help fine-tune the offering.

Find the Common Thread

Some of the most powerful global brands grow from powerful, universal desires—desires that have passports, so to speak. In the Axe example, is there a teenage boy anywhere in the world who doesn't have his mind on sex? This simple concept crosses all boundaries and can be leveraged.

Similarly, Nike has led the global running shoe market by recognizing that everyone wants to be an athlete. Uber disrupted the taxi business worldwide by answering the universal call for user-friendly, cost-efficient urban transportation. And Airbnb created a new home-sharing market by recognizing the need for a more affordable and flexible way to book lodging. These are all common threads that can be used to build a global brand.

Segment across Habits and Needs

Not every brand has the potential for such a broad reach, but with today's explosion of data disclosing the lives of consumers, it's possible to isolate more targeted markets. Indeed, companies are recognizing that national boundaries make only crude groupings of people. It's far more effective to segment people according to their habits and needs. Not South Koreans, but new South Korean mothers, for example. Not Italians, but retired Italian couples. Not Mexicans, but Mexican car enthusiasts. Data that allows for this kind of segmenting is now available virtually anywhere in the world.

L'Oréal, the French cosmetics company, has skillfully mined data to develop relationships with its customers in more than 130 countries. Among other things, the company created an app that adopts virtual technology to allow customers to try on L'Oréal makeup using their smartphones. As of 2017, more than 20 million people had downloaded the app, providing L'Oréal with information about the interests and needs of its customers. L'Oréal uses the data to help maintain its place as the world's largest cosmetics company.

Enlist Local Managers

Finding similarities across borders is only the preliminary step in entering a global market. A brand must have people on the ground who know the nuances of the culture and the market and can manage the operation. That often means bringing top-notch local people onto the team. Sometimes a mixture of the native born with company veterans works well. For example, Kraft's Oreo cookie initially floundered in China, in part because the company assumed that what is good for the United States is good for China.

Local managers are necessary to supply the knowledge to tune the product to local tastes and habits, while maneuvering through issues of presentation, pricing, distribution, and competition. Marketers can't simply assume that a good idea travels well. Kellogg's, the multinational food manufacturing company, attempted to crack the Indian market by introducing Corn Flakes. But cereal is essentially an American breakfast staple, typically served with cold milk. Many Indians didn't know what to make of Corn Flakes. What's more, milk in India tends to be warm, which turned the Corn Flakes into a soggy clump.

Test and Adjust

When a target spot in the market is identified, start small. Test and learn. See how the product introduction goes. If it goes well, scale up quickly. If it fails or falters, figure out why—failure can be a terrific teacher.

With some testing and learning, Airbnb found that automatically translating its web site for international travelers was not always effective. While these travelers search for lodging in their native language, automatic translation often led travelers to assume that their host spoke that language. To avoid confusion, Airbnb has opted for displaying host pages in the host's native language with the option to translate.

No metric covers all cases, but managers need to monitor carefully the success of an introduction (or lack of it). Careful testing and learning helped turn Tang, the legendary powdered drink, from a $500 million product outside the United States to a $1 billion global titan in five years. The owner, Kraft Foods, had grown frustrated with Tang's steady but slow growth in the half century since it was created as a nutritious, lightweight drink for astronauts. In 2007 a glocal team tackled the problem and proposed a number of innovative solutions. For one, the team considered lowering the price point by producing Tang in single-serving sachets, which could be dropped into a child's lunch box, for example. But producing the sachets was complicated and could be expensive. So Kraft tested the idea in Brazil alone. Only after the sachets proved a hit there did the company scale production and introduce the new packaging around the globe.

GOING GLOCAL: GETTING THE RIGHT BALANCE OF GLOBAL AND LOCAL

A company operating internationally needs to rely on collaborative networks, balancing the resources and vision of the global managers with the market savvy of local managers. In many companies, the silos remain standing, and they have to come down if the brand is to succeed on a global scale. Success is based on hitting the right balance between hopelessly local and mindlessly global. What's important, though, is that within the collaborative network the lines of responsibility are clearly drawn from the start. Who is responsible for this decision, who for that? The issue can become especially acute when deciding how far to go in mixing the global and local elements in marketing. And finally, a brand must understand its core essence.

Decentralize to Find the Right Balance

For a company such as Airbnb, finding the right glocal balance is imperative and relies on effective decentralization to shift the balance locally when needed. While things such as cleanliness standards are global, international markets bring new challenges. For example, Airbnb must be local when it comes to sign-up methods and currency. In the United States, it's easy to create an Airbnb profile by linking a Facebook account to the site, but this type of sign-up would be impossible in places such as China, where Facebook is inaccessible. Instead, Airbnb must decentralize enough to tap local knowledge and create sign-up methods through channels such as WeChat.

Airbnb also must take into account local payment options. Before the 2016 Summer Olympics in Rio de Janeiro, Airbnb accepted only U.S. dollars as the Brazilian payment method. In the year leading up to the Olympics, Airbnb made arrangements to start accepting payments in the real, the Brazilian currency, through credit cards and other methods.

Draw Clear Lines of Global/Local Responsibility among Collaborative Networks

In the late 1990s, Kraft tried to introduce America's most popular cookie brand—Oreo—to countries abroad. Kraft had high expectations for the introduction, but for the most part the world couldn't have cared less. After a decade, the cookie was only nudging into foreign markets, and the company was ready to shut the effort down. But after Kraft named Oreo one of its 10 priority brands, the cookie got one last push.

Kraft set up a collaborative network of teams that included managers in the United States and in local countries. The network listed the drivers of growth and laid out responsibility—global or local—for each. In China, for example, the local managers suspected that the cookie's traditional pack sizes made it too expense for the typical family. So Kraft started offering Oreos in smaller units in China, going from 14 cookies in a package to seven. The local managers also knew that Chinese tastes weren't necessarily American tastes. They arranged to produce Oreos in special Chinese flavors, such as green tea and strawberry, as well as in a version that was less sweet than the American cookie.

The collaborative network also drew strict lines of responsibility when it came to marketing. It would have been efficient to stay global, with one basic ad everywhere. But in China the local managers wanted to feature the Chinese NBA star Yao Ming in a commercial. Those managers knew the market, and they made the right call. At the same time, the global managers knew that the general content of the ads had to follow global guidelines, maintaining the brand's focus on the emotional connection between parent and child.

Understand the Core Essence of the Brand

Kraft also faced an interesting puzzle in trying to decide what to do with an American Oreo tradition—the iconic "twist, lick, dunk" ritual of eating the famous cookie. Would the tradition travel beyond its home? Research offered no help. "Twist, lick, dunk" was unheard of in other countries. What's more, Americans dunk in milk, and milk is far less prevalent in the Middle East, Asia, and South America. Still, the ritual underscores the uniqueness of the Oreo cookie, and it connects directly to an essential element of Oreo's identity—the bond between parent and child. Should Kraft go global or local?

The team argued over it. Eventually, the local Chinese team said, "Okay, the ritual means nothing here, but we're willing to give it a try, as long as we can feature Yao Ming." On the other hand, the French said, "No way." One French manager even went so far as to utter, "We are not lickers in France. Americans lick. We don't."

In the end, Kraft had to make a judgment call. "Twist, lick, dunk" is at the heart of Oreo. The team decided to go with the ritual everywhere and take the chance that it would catch on.

The decision paid off, and Oreo's business grew worldwide. In developing markets, Oreo revenues increased fivefold in six years, turning into a billion-dollar operation. And equally important, Oreo's profitability in these markets was higher than the average.

Nike offers another example. In 2017, the company was hailed for its inclusivity by producing a hijab for Muslim female athletes. The company launched the light, airy product on an extremely local level through video campaigns in the Middle East featuring famous female athletes from the region. Yet, even though the Nike Pro Hijab is a niche product, it stays true to Nike's global brand. The garment—for now, only available in black—features the iconic Nike swoosh. The design mimics Nike's basic advertising, and the idea follows the company's global insight that everyone wants to be an athlete. The Nike Pro Hijab helps women to "Just Do It," as the slogan states.

With Axe, the overriding brand essential was the promise that these products would turn a teenage boy into a sex object. Though the marketing varied around the world and has evolved in the past few years, it always revolved around that promise.

In the case of Tang, the glocal team came to an insight—perhaps obvious in retrospect—that the drink's best asset in today's world was its sustainability advantage. Tang is lightweight, requires only water, and is environmentally friendly. The team used that insight to push back against sodas and other rivals in the beverage category, and found great success partnering with environmentally conscious children's groups. Starting in Brazil, Tang developed a series of lively commercials that later were adapted for broadcast in other countries, including Mexico and Argentina.

Apple presents an interesting case, in which its choice of a core essential has inhibited a product's success internationally. The company decided that its identity was indelibly linked to its design, and as such Apple wouldn't fundamentally change the product, regardless of where it was introduced. But that means the iPhone remains expensive throughout the world. As a result, Apple has had a difficult time expanding in India, for example, which trails only China as the largest smart-phone market in the world. The Indian market features lots of low-cost competition—a quarter or less the cost of an iPhone—and the powerful Apple brand has little cachet there. As a result, despite various initiatives, iPhone penetration in India has lagged—well below the iPhone's penetration in China, for example.

By contrast, Uber has held to its core essential of efficient, low-cost urban transportation but has added a variety of local twists. In response to competition, for example, Uber offers a motorized rickshaw service in India and Pakistan, and a water taxi in Istanbul.

As these brand expansions illustrate, marketers entering a global market must know the brand's core essentials—the qualities so linked to the brand's identity that they should remain constant around the world. Obviously, a key task in successfully building an international presence is identifying those core essentials. They belong on the global side of the glocal mix, regardless of the local market. They should be articulated specifically and turned into positioning guidelines that are clear to all. Even as the local marketing varies according to the country and culture, the guidelines should keep the brand consistent.

ORCHESTRATING A GLOBAL ROLLOUT

The business model for going global should offer a pathway beyond a successful introduction. Brand managers must create a strategy to grow over time through expansion, innovation, and efficiencies. To do that in a digital world, staying nimble is imperative—a company must be capable of responding and adjusting quickly. Brands must also educate the new international markets they enter and must be careful not to expand too quickly: start small and scale thoughtfully.

Stay Nimble and Create Agility

The simple principle in glocal is to be agile and decide what needs to be done globally and locally based on where you can get competitive advantage. Moving into an international market gobbles time and resources. Worse, it usually adds complexity to the overall business—and complexity can be a hobgoblin in global brand introduction.

Over the last decade or so, many small startups have successfully wedged their way into markets, often stealing customers from large, cumbersome operations. Big companies can effectively compete globally in today's environment, but they have to reorganize themselves to adopt the agility necessary to stay nimble. Several of the principles that we've already discussed push the organization in that direction: forming collaborative teams; clarifying responsibility; and starting small, then testing, learning, and scaling up when the results justify it. In general, a company that wants to go global must streamline or shed many of the rules and hierarchies that slow it down.

Educate New Markets

If a company is introducing a product or brand that is new to a country or culture—in other words, opening up a new category—consumers need to be taught to use the product, which can take time. Also, the not-invented-here syndrome occasionally raises its head and can disrupt glocal management.

For example, when Unilever (based in London) was ready to roll out Axe worldwide, the North American team had little interest in taking on the product. The members said the aerosol deodorant market didn't exist in the

United States and the advertising was too erotic. The London-based team told them the category would grow and the commercials could be toned down. They argued that 14-year-old American boys, like boys everywhere, dream of seducing girls. Still no go. As a result, it was several years before Axe was introduced in the United States—years that the product could have been earning tremendous profits for Unilever.

Start Small and Scale Thoughtfully

Even if a product sells well in a new market, scaling it up across multiple markets must be done thoughtfully and with precise orchestration. Simply put, the reason to go global is to grow the business. There are any number of subsidiary advantages—tapping expertise from different environments, improving channeling of resources, encouraging investor enthusiasm, and so on. But the drive for growth is behind them all. And in order to achieve growth, companies have to know what makes the product work and then program the expansion by relying on the principles of glocal management: creating a business model that starts small and scales thoughtfully.

For example, the consumer electronics company Best Buy stumbled when it moved rapidly across markets before realizing that for various reasons the big-box concept—huge stores filled with many categories of products—didn't have the appropriate business model for markets outside of the United States. In the past five years, the company has substantially dialed back overseas operations while refocusing American operations, in particular emphasizing price and service. Best Buy's stock price rebounded more than sixfold between the end of 2012 and late 2017.

When you have a good idea that clearly crosses borders, there's a natural eagerness to expand quickly, particularly as potential rivals spring up. Speed is important, but it carries risks; a company must be careful not to lose sight of its values in the rush. Uber offers a prime example. From its founding in San Francisco in 2009, the company expanded at a breakneck rate, operating in more than 80 countries by the first quarter of 2018. But as board member Arianna Huffington has said, that culture of hyper-growth has had serious costs. Internally it contributed to a range of management issues, including abuse and sexual harassment charges. As Uber expanded around the world, the company has also faced an array of external crises, from strikes to legal battles to a threatened ban. While bookings were still growing in 2017, the company continued to lose money and competition has intensified. "The world has changed," Huffington told a *Time-Fortune* conference not long after founder and CEO Travis Kalanick stepped down in June 2017. "What happens now in the culture of a company affects the business metrics."

Airbnb faced its own problems when the company expanded too rapidly in Paris, Berlin, and Barcelona. Because the business category was new, the cities were unsure how to characterize homes being rented through Airbnb. Nonetheless, the company rushed forward, sometimes completely disregarding local regulations. This resulted in fines. Barcelona, for example, charged Airbnb 600,000 euros in November 2017 for advertising unlicensed properties.

The risks of careless expansion come at two levels. One has to do with oversight. The basics of any business—safety, compliance, hygiene, law—get lost as companies cut corners in their eagerness to grow. The second, higher-level risk goes directly to the values of the company: What's the purpose? Why are we here? How do we operate successfully and retain our integrity? Nike, which for many years outsourced its manufacturing without worrying terribly about local factories, has struggled for years to shed the impression that it relies on child labor. Walmart has spent years and hundreds of thousands of dollars working through charges of bribery to speed the opening of stores in Mexico and other foreign countries.

In the global environment, the argument that you're not responsible for the behavior of your overseas vendors or that you were simply following local practices doesn't work anymore. Your values start at home and must transcend international borders.

SUCCESS STORIES AND CHALLENGES

How do you decide when to take a brand global? Though the process may start with a gut feeling—a eureka moment, a sudden inspiration, or insights based on research—none of those events suffice. You may have built a nifty new widget that's tearing up the American markets, but that's no guarantee that your charmed product will be loved by consumers in Germany or Malaysia or Brazil. Similarly, you don't go global simply because you see a huge market out there—plenty of companies have floundered after being enticed by the lure of more than a billion consumers in India and China.

Rather, what it takes to succeed globally is a smart and disciplined business model that's hardwired into commercial reality and the right glocal mix. Let's take a look at several brands that have faced these challenges.

Axe

In the early 1980s, Unilever was looking to push into the growing field of grooming for men. The company wanted to create a body spray—a combo deodorant-cologne—targeted to young men, particularly shy types who could be persuaded that a few spritzes from the right body spray would bring the girls flocking.

Thus was born Axe, a relatively inexpensive product that Unilever introduced in France in 1983. There was little magic in the concoction's chemical formula. The magic came with the marketing that unabashedly, though with an overlay of wit, focused on sex.

Axe turned into a French hit, and Unilever realized that because it had created a brand based on a universal truth—adolescent boys want to score with girls—Axe had global potential. In the ensuing years, Unilever successfully rolled out Axe in numerous countries around the world. The marketing was tuned to the local culture (as noted above, American commercials weren't as erotic as those presented in France, for example). But the promise that Axe would help attract girls stayed consistent. In a typical offering, one commercial showed a cheerleader tackling and starting to undress a football player, presumably because he was wearing Axe.

Over the years, Unilever continued to add men's fragrances, shampoos, and so on under the Axe brand. And as the world of digital and social media opened up, the marketing of Axe moved with the times. The portfolio featured, among other highlights, a lively Facebook account, postings on news feeds where young men were likely to linger, sponsorships of Web comedy shows, and Web commercials far racier than standard TV fare. Axe even created a digital game. Recently, however, as attitudes about masculinity and what's attractive in men have changed, the marketing of Axe products has followed the curve, with campaigns valuing individuality and self-discovery, such as the "Is it okay for guys to . . ." campaign.

The Axe example shows that tapping into a fundamental desire and staying agile can pay off handsomely. In fact, the brand serves as a good case study in the fundamentals—and occasional perils—of building a global brand. The essentials behind smart branding are the same whether you are staying within the United States or going abroad. Do you have a good idea, do people want what you are selling, can your product (or service) establish an emotional connection in the market, is your message consistent through all available platforms? The basic concepts prevail. That remains true even as marketing changes dramatically in the new digital age and entry barriers fall. Small, fast-moving local operators pose a greater threat than ever before, but that simply underlines the need for larger players to stay quick on their feet.

Gillette and Chesebrough-Pond's

As we have discussed, the real art to succeeding internationally lies in figuring out the global-local balance: What should be managed centrally and what should be handled by the local managers? Where should brand managers rely on global expertise and where should they rely on local knowledge?

Getting the glocal balance right is delicate, and Gillette got it wrong when it first introduced its low-cost razors in India in the early years of the 21st century. The Boston-based mothership didn't understand the local marketplace. Much of rural India lacks ready access to running water, and as a result, shaving cream clogged the razors, a problem that even the best marketing plan could not have overcome. The introduction flopped because it was "mindlessly global."

On the local side of the flop ledger, Unilever acquired the American skin-cream company Chesebrough-Pond's, which already sold its products around the world. As it expanded over the years, Pond's had represented its brand with a sweet little tulip that appeared in ads and on packaging. The problem was that local operations had been allowed to draw their own versions of the flower, and thus Pond's was represented by more than 50 different tulips. That's "hopelessly local."

The lesson here is that global and local need to work in tandem, drawing on their respective strengths. The formula will vary, but typically global expertise relates to elements of the business that cross borders—the fundamentals of technology, R&D, the company's safety concerns and basic values, and, importantly in this context, the overall positioning of the brand. Managers at company headquarters, with a gaze that looks over the product in all its local appearances, should have the best vantage to ensure that the essence of the product remains consistent, along with the message supporting it.

Folks at the local level—the people closest to the ground—should have the best insight about the context and the culture. They should know the ins and outs of the marketplace: the tastes and customs of consumers, the pricing and distribution particulars, the potential competitors. The local team's knowledge should hold sway when those ground-level factors are an issue.

McDonald's

The glocal mix plays out in different ways depending on the product. McDonald's has enjoyed enormous international success in large part because it maintains a consistency in offerings, presentation, style, and look. But the company couldn't possibly sell its signature hamburger in India, where Hindus revere cows and a significant part of the population is vegetarian. So McDonald's caters to local tastes with food such as the Chicken Maharaja Mac (a double chicken patty) and the McAloo Tikki (a burger made with Indian spices in a potato-and-peas patty).

At the same time, McDonald's has stayed consistent with its emphasis on global elements, which are the essentials of the McDonald's brand. The Indian business retains the signature McDonald's naming devices and even the style and look of the altered product. The in-store presentation—fast and clean—is the same. Marketing across Indian media holds to the traditional company theme that a McDonald's meal is fun: eat there and happiness follows. And, of course, all marketing carries the iconic golden arches. A McDonald's ad in India would be identifiable virtually anywhere in the world as part of the McDonald's empire.

SUMMARY

Today, almost all areas of the world have entered the connected age, in which consumers everywhere have information and people at their fingertips, often on two or more screens at the same time. That means that marketing needs to be always on at both the global and local levels, engaging constantly with consumers across various platforms and through assorted programs. This is becoming the standard operating procedure for marketing, and today it pertains to almost anywhere in the world.

If the need for glocal management wasn't obvious before, the advance of digital news sites, blogs, and social media should make it so now. To communicate effectively, a marketer must know the twists and turns of local culture, and of course speak the local language. At the same time, the back and forth between consumers and company representatives risks shattering the brand's identity into many pieces. Headquarters—the team with the global outlook—has to ensure that the core essentials endure.

It's almost a sure bet that technological innovations and changing attitudes will continue to roil the business of building brands. *But the fundamentals persist.* Anyone who remembers an Axe commercial from a decade ago—with an Army of bikini-clad women chasing down a thrilled young man—would probably be startled to see an Axe promotion today, with its gentler notions of what it means to be a man. But Axe has remained on top by recognizing a universal desire, applying balanced glocal management, and staying agile behind a solid business plan. That's the way to build a global brand with soul in a changing world.

Sanjay Khosla is a senior fellow at the Kellogg School of Management, CEO of Bunnik, a management consulting and leadership coaching firm, and a senior advisor at the Boston Consulting Group. He is currently on the board of Zoetis *(an animal-health company) and was also on the board of Best Buy. Previously, he was president, developing markets of Kraft Foods (now Mondelēz), where he built the business from $5 billion to $16 billion in six years while dramatically improving profitability. Before that, he enjoyed a successful 27-year career with Unilever and a few years at Fonterra. Khosla is the co-author of the book* Fewer, Bigger, Bolder: From Mindless Expansion to Focused Growth.

SECTION TWO

BRINGING YOUR BRAND TO LIFE

CHAPTER 7

BRAND DESIGN AND DESIGN THINKING

BOBBY J. CALDER

Modern brands as we know them first emerged in the mid-1800s. As companies began to understand the ways in which creating a "brand identity" for a product could increase the product's success in the marketplace, brand design began to take shape as an important tool in forming the product's identity. Crafting an identity is essentially an act of design—it is making a product into something that is immediately recognized in a certain way by consumers.

The Cadbury brand, which originated in England, was one of the first modern brands, and the company used innovative brand design to create a unique brand identity. The Cadburys—father and sons—began by selling drinking chocolate at retail stores and then moved into manufacturing. In 1866 they acquired equipment that enabled them to remove cocoa butter, which until then had degraded the taste of the drink, from the cocoa beans. They launched the brand "Cocoa Essence," selecting that name because it conveyed *purity* to consumers and positioned the brand as a pure, unadulterated chocolate drink. They added Cadbury to the brand name to give an identity to the maker of the drink. They also used the signature line "Absolutely Pure Therefore Best" to encourage association with *high quality*, and often used a picture of a young girl on the product to emphasize purity.

By 1905 Cadbury had designed a logo using a script version of its name with the last letter extending upward from the loop of the "y" as a stylized cacao tree (see Figure 7.1). In what came to be the parlance of marketing, the company had by then created a strong identity for the brand. In Cadbury's case, the perception was, "It's not just chocolate, it's pure, high-quality chocolate."

93

Figure 7.1
First Cadbury Logo

CADBURY Brothers, Limited.

The term "brand identity" is still in use today. Creating a brand identity continues to be central to branding and should be distinguished from advertising and other forms of marketing communication. Today, a better term for identity is "brand design."[1] Companies are increasingly realizing the importance of design and of embracing "design thinking." Fundamentally, design is about making something. Engineers make products, architects make buildings, and graphic artists make stylized objects.

The design movement is about approaching any problem in the mode of "show, don't tell." It emphasizes empathy with users, creating by prototyping, and testing. Its strength lies in its engagement with people outside of traditional design disciplines, such as engineering, in the design process. For marketers there is nothing new in the idea of empathetic insight and testing. And, dressed up in the language of the Stanford d.school, the rhetoric of design thinking can be off-putting. Yet design thinking is valuable in that it licenses nondesigners to think in "making mode." The implication for brand design is that marketers should be active participants in the design process, not just passive recipients of something created by a designer based on a loose brief.

Today, marketers often feel unable to engage with the brand design process. In fact, many managers literally freeze when given a Sharpie and asked to think in making mode. Marketers who can talk conceptually about a brand's positioning or analyze a pricing problem can barely bring themselves to try to create a brand name by making a prototype of one on a flip chart. This stems from their inability to apply their marketing expertise in making mode, and it is why brand design is often left primarily to nonmarketers, with marketers relegated to an "I like that one" role.

In this chapter we will use a systematic approach to illustrate how marketers can think in making mode to create a brand design.

A Design-Thinking Process for Developing a Brand Design

The key to brand design lies in an understanding of the psychology of branding. First, it's important to understand that good brand design mainly influences consumers on an unconscious level. In this vein, Nobel Laureate Daniel Kahneman refers to System 1 (unconscious) and System 2 (conscious) thinking.[2] Let's take a look at these concepts in closer detail.

System 1 and System 2 Thinking

For our purposes, System 1 thinking involves the unconscious associations triggered by a brand design. By contrast, System 2 thinking is slow, conscious, deliberative thought. Consumers who pay conscious attention to an advertisement's content are engaged in System 2 thinking. When consumers see the word "pure" as part of a brand design, they typically process this through System 1. In System 1, both verbal and visual cues along with other cues trigger associations that form a perception that can influence behavior without any conscious realization. And these associations may shape subsequent System 2 conscious reflection as well.

Consumers might or might not spend time consciously thinking about a brand in a System 2 way. Yet it's important to note that successful brand design is not predicated on this. A marketer approaching brand design in making mode must understand that the goal of the design is to create the desired System 1 associations at an unconscious level; an effective brand design is one in which all of the design elements cue the intended System 1 associations. Establishing associations in the consumer's mind that lead the consumer to recognize and interpret the brand without cognitive effort creates a perception that is consistent and supportive of the brand's positioning concept.

To this end, the brand design should begin with a clear vision of the associations that the brand design is intended to create. With these associations clearly identified, you can then prototype (make a preliminary version of) the design cues. It is very difficult to accomplish this in the usual "tell" mode of marketers. But a design-thinking marketer can participate in making cues by working in tandem alongside the designer, who contributes the technical skill of creating and polishing the design.

Coca-Cola: An Example of System 1 and Brand Design

Let's use an example of a very familiar brand to illustrate the process. At this writing, the brand positioning of Coca-Cola for targeted consumers is something like this: Coca-Cola is a thirst-quenching cola with a refreshing taste that brings joy to everyone. The company uses both advertising and content marketing to try to get consumers to think about (System 2) the concept that "Coke brings joy." Yet, considerable resources are devoted to brand design as well. The goal is to create System 1 associations that support the concept. The associations are depicted in a perceptual mind map (see Figure 7.2) of Coca-Cola's traditional identity equities: that it is *refreshing* and *timeless*. It has always been enjoyed by people all over the world. But it is also culturally in tune with contemporary associations about time. Currently Coca-Cola connects to consumers who associate themselves with a *fast-moving lifestyle* in which there is little time for personal enjoyment. Coca-Cola is about taking the time to enjoy a *celebratory moment*.

The key to brand design is having a clear view of the associations that are the design objectives. Because System 1 is automatic, fast, and nonverbal, there is no need for a long brief, such as those used for advertising. Identifying

Figure 7.2
Illustrative Perceptual Mind Map for Coca-Cola Brand Design

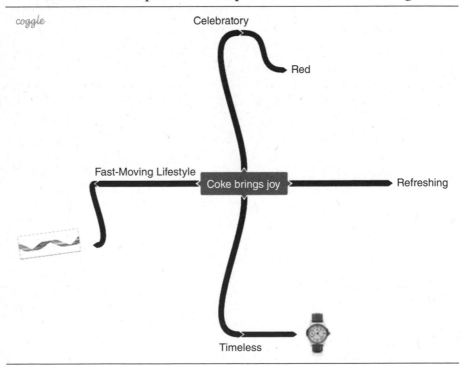

and focusing on three or four key associations is usually enough to guide the design effort. Using a perceptual mind map to show the desired associations (as in Figure 7.2) is a good way to remind the design team that the design should be intended to cue the consumer to make a few fast System 1 connections, which together lead to a strong perception of the brand. Visuals can help make the desired associations even more clear. Designers often find visual representations of design intent, or mood boards, especially useful.

The classic watch in Figure 7.2 visually conveys the intended timeless association of Coca-Cola. The flowing ribbon likewise captures the dynamically changing quality of a fast-moving lifestyle. The key point is that the design should concentrate on triggering associations. Continuously checking the brand design against the perceptual mind map helps maintain this focus. Any other criteria, such as functionality, competitive differentiation, or design aesthetics, should ordinarily be secondary considerations. A good design will produce a few strong associations that cause consumers to recognize the brand and interpret it perceptually as intended. A design that fails to do this is a bad brand design.

The next time you encounter a Coca-Cola touchpoint (a store display, someone drinking a Coke, a soda machine), think about the design in terms of the associations pictured in Figure 7.2. Notice that every aspect of the design relates to the associations. The flowing Spenserian script of the name cues both timelessness and movement. This is reinforced by the dynamic contour ribbon that mimics the shape of the bottle laid on its side. The basic red color is celebratory. Clearly picturing the associations and attendant perceptual meanings has allowed marketers (and designers) to make sure that each component of the design does its job.

THE COMPONENTS OF BRAND DESIGN

Figure 7.3 presents a systematic way of thinking about the various components of a brand design. Consider it a template or checklist tool. Each element cues the intended associations in a different way. The first two columns are verbal/auditory cues, while the second two are different modalities: visual and olfactory cues. If each element does its job, all of them will contribute and blend together in a harmonious consumer perception. Sound and scent are less commonly used, but are increasingly important to consider because they are experiential, and experiences are increasingly important to branding. Any brand designer should at least explore using all 12 elements, as shown in Figure 7.3 and described below.

Figure 7.3
Brand Design Template

Verbal/Auditory Modality		Visual and Olfactory Modality	
Brand Naming	Category Naming	Illustration	Color Palette
Corporate Identity	Brand Lexicon	Brand Symbols	Shape
Signature Lines	Sound	Corporate Symbols	Scent

Brand Naming

Every brand has a name. Even a no-name, generic product has a brand name—the "no name" brand. Names can be descriptive or evocative, but either way, a brand name is an important tool for cueing associations. When the ride-sharing service Uber was launched in 2010, the original positioning concept was an affordable luxury black car service. Or more precisely, Uber was a way for CEO Travis Kalanick and his friends to "roll around San Francisco like ballers."[3] The name selected was "UberCab." In naming the brand, the obvious associations to target were *approachable luxury* and *high status*. Of course, "uber" means an outstanding example of something, in this case an outstanding cab. But associations with "cab" are at odds with the intended associations. Luckily for Uber, the word "cab" caused political problems with city governments, so the name was shortened to "Uber" and rendered as shown in Figure 7.4. This gave the new brand the intended association.

By 2016 the Uber brand concept had evolved into "everyday routine convenience." Consumers had come to think of the brand as a transportation utility. Associations to the old name became counterproductive. So in 2016 the company developed a new brand design around the intended associations of *efficient*, *convenient*, and *ordinary*. The name itself had too much identity equity to change, but the way it was rendered was altered to cue the new associations, as shown in Figure 7.5. In this version the name is blocky, straight, and more

Figure 7.4
Original Uber Logo

Figure 7.5
Repositioned Uber Logo

UBER

ordinary looking. The shared slant of the ends of the "E" and the "R" ties them together, and the word becomes more of a descriptive noun, as in "driver."

Coming up with a brand name that evokes strong associations might seem easy. History, however, suggests how easy it is for companies to go astray. In its day, the BlackBerry smartphone was technologically advanced in terms of its reliability and security. But the company's engineering prowess was not matched by its approach to brand naming. Originally the company favored the name "PocketLink," to suggest that it was more than a regular phone. As with other candidate names—AirWire, Banjo, Banter, Photon, Tailwind, and TelTop—associations were either weak or nonsensical. The naming firm, Lexicon, eventually created the name "BlackBerry" by arguing that it would be associated with connectivity.[4] The association eventually became so strong that consumers used the term "crackberry" to describe people who used the phone to stay in constant touch. Notice the phonetic rhythm and alliteration of the "BB" softer consonants in "BlackBerry." This associated the phone with high touch rather than high tech. Although wildly successful, BlackBerry eventually failed to keep up with the rise of touchscreens. Too late, BlackBerry (which had changed its corporate name from Research in Motion) introduced an Android phone with a slide screen. It did not help that this phone was named "Priv." The thought was that this would reference the company's strength in privacy technology, but the name evoked no associations. Sadly, such tales are all too common.

Similarly, a car manufacturer named one of its models "Nova," leading to an unfortunate association for Spanish speakers: "nova" translates to "no go" in Spanish. Another example of a poor brand name choice occurred when a leading hospital chain near Chicago decided to end its affiliation with a university teaching hospital and stop using the university's name. Rather than be locked into any new partnership by using the partner's name, the hospital chain decided to identify itself only as a university hospital. Because it was located on Chicago's North Shore, it adapted the name NorthShore University HealthSystem. A smart move from a business point of view, but not so smart as a brand name. Consumers associated the system with a university that they had never heard of—because there was no NorthShore University.

A point to keep in mind is that consumers don't have to be aware of associations with names and might well deny having them. It is unlikely that many consumers would realize that the brand name "Tiffany" originates from the Latin word meaning "manifestation of God," but the association with "heavenly" is still there. Nor would consumers know that the phonemes that compose the name—ti.fa.ni—are mastered late in childhood speech acquisition, and because of this people associate them with things that are less common.[5] Similarly, "sharp" names (such as "Jax") are associated with sourness, and round names (such as "Berry") are associated with sweetness. Names that use front-of-the-tongue vowels, such as "Priv," are perceived as smaller than names using back vowels. In general, names that are more fluent (easier because they are shorter or more pronounceable) are preferred, even by investors making supposedly rational decisions.[6] System 1 associates fluency with familiarity and having a positive attitude toward a brand.[7] One does not have to be a linguist to intuitively feel such subtle associations.

Keep in mind that design can be faddish in terms of naming as well as other cues. Recently some brands have adapted first names of people as a way of making their brands *friendlier* in online environments: there is "Casper" the mattress brand, "Marcus" the financial brand, and "Oscar" the health insurance brand. Once a design fashion catches on, however, it gets overused, and consumers consciously begin to notice the overuse, weakening the desired associations. Unfortunately, companies may opt for a design fad without even considering associations.

Corporate Identity

Company names by definition convey identity. A Disney brand can have its own brand name, but "Disney" brings its own associations and can influence associations to the brand name. Federal Express is another good example. Originally the company positioned its overnight delivery service around the concept of "reliability you can count on," because the company owns its own planes. As the industry matured, consumers came to expect reliability from all providers. Federal Express had to differentiate more on speed, with delivery times shorter than 24 hours. As part of this repositioning, they adapted the brand name "FedEx." The name became more of a verb, with an association with *fast action*. This allowed Federal Express to remain the name of the company that provided the brand FedEx. This corporate identity was associated with *technology* and *owning a fleet of planes*, thus supporting and adding to the brand name.

Although some companies lean to a "house of brands" approach, in which a collection of brands is only very minimally identified with a shared corporate identity, it has become increasingly common for companies seeking to support their brands with a highly visible corporate identity to take a "branded house" approach. Federal Express provides one example (see Chapter 3 for a more detailed discussion of the house of brands and the branded house approaches). Indeed, this has become standard practice in many industries. For example, "Marriott" serves as a corporate identity for the brand "Courtyard by Marriott." "Courtyard" is associated with *not-a-traditional hotel* while "Marriott" suggests *familiarity*.

Sometimes the company name and brand name are the same, such as the "Marriott" brand hotel. In an interesting twist, Ford created the "Lincoln Motor Company" as a corporate identity for the Lincoln brand, which was previously a Ford brand. But again, the trend is to use corporate names and brand names synergistically. Johnson & Johnson, the company, originally sold dental floss using the brand name "Johnson & Johnson." This served to give the brand a *medical* association. The company wanted to associate the brand more with *convenience*, so it changed the brand name to "Reach," with "Johnson & Johnson" becoming a corporate identity. Notice in Figure 7.6 how the company name adds a *medical* association to the brand name. It should be noted, however, that a company must have an identity before a corporate name can support a brand name. Compare Johnson & Johnson to made-up names such as Diageo and Mondelēz International. Again, both the corporate identity name and the brand name will ideally contribute to the desired associations.

Signature Lines

Although often thought of as part of ads, signature lines are short slogans that express the brand positioning concept in a single sentence. While these lines function as a memory aide in advertising, they can serve as an associative cue in brand designs. Consider the McDonald's line, "I'm loving it." The line appears on store windows, menus, and other brand design touchpoints. It has very

Figure 7.6
Corporate plus Brand Name Identity

little literal meaning but is rich in associative value: *nostalgia, warmth, friendliness*. Another example is the Ball Park brand of hot dogs, which is positioned as the quintessential American hot dog. The name is rendered using the script associated with *baseball*, the quintessential *American* game. Its signature line, "So American you can taste it," reinforces the association with *American*.

Signature lines do not have to be particularly creative to be used as an associative cue; a good line often leads to just one strong association. "Good to the last drop" associates coffee with a drink that still *tastes as good at the end as it did at the start*. "A diamond is forever" links De Beers to *enduring love*.

In fact, requiring consumers to think in a System 2 way can actually undermine the value of a signature line. Rhode Island attempted to brand itself with the line "Cooler and Warmer." You might be able to figure out what was intended if you work hard enough, but associations to warm and cool are inconsistent—in fact, they fight each other. Then there are lines such as "Nothing else is a Subaru." It does not associate Subaru with anything. Signature lines should not require System 2 thinking. In a good brand design, signature lines contribute to the desired System 1 associative meaning.

Category Naming

The product category to which a brand belongs is a source of identity. It provides a frame of reference for associations to other similar products. But companies often take the category as a given, with the category being defined either by common knowledge or industry definition. Pepsi belongs to the cola category; Rust-Oleum, in industry speak, belongs to the coatings category. As a matter of brand design, however, the category identification should not be treated as a given; it should be chosen for design purposes. For instance, at one point the soft drink 7 Up chose to identify the brand as belonging to the "uncola" category in order to weaken the association to other cola brands and be perceived as different. Similarly, Uber decided that the brand belonged to the ride-sharing category, rather than the taxi category. The name "smart phone" was a brand design decision, not a definition.

Chobani created a successful new brand of yogurt largely by associating it with a new category: Greek yogurt. This brand design decision both disassociated the brand from competitive yogurt brands and associated it with *Greek heritage*. As the category grew at the expense of traditional yogurts, General Mills, the maker of Yoplait, was forced to introduce its own Greek yogurt, considering brand names such as Ygéia! and Yoganos in an attempt to strongly link to Greek heritage.[8] Yet these brand names did not test well: Chobani owned the category association. Eventually General Mills introduced

Figure 7.7   Category Name Emphasis

the brand "Yoplait Greek." The brand name and category associations weakened each other, and the product failed. Finally, General Mills successfully introduced "Oui by Yoplait," identifying the category as "French-style yogurt," which strengthened the brand name and category associations.

Category names can be created entirely for brand design purposes. In pioneering automotive navigation systems, Motorola created the category name "Telematics" to associate its offering in the minds of automotive engineers with *communications* rather than *electronics*, which would have favored the competition. Firms can actually create categories in this way. In Figure 7.7, note the prominence of the category name "vitaminwater," which links the brand to *healthy*. Associations to the brand name followed from the strong category association.

Brand Lexicon

While naming is a critical tool for brand design, brand managers should also think of verbal cues more generally. A brand can develop a set of words or phrases that are repeated over time and add to associative meaning. Think of how McDonald's uses menu terms. The menu could be just descriptive names, such as double-decker hamburger. Instead, the terms "Big Mac" and "Big Breakfast" connote *belly-full satisfaction*. The children's meal is a "Happy Meal," reinforcing associations to *warmth* and *friendliness* even for customers without a child. The "Maharaja Mac" in India (double chicken patties) and the "Tamago Double Mac" in Japan (two beef patties and a fried egg) associate sandwiches with local tastes. Every brand should have a veritable lexicon of brand design words and phrases. The Oreo brand lexicon always features "lick, twist, dunk" to connect the brand to *fun*. Burger King never misses the chance to use "flame grilled" to associate the brand with *cooking on the grill*.

Sound

Aural brand design entails using a short sound or a musical stimulus to trigger a brand association. As with all design elements, the association can be inherent in the stimulus or it can derive from associations created by other elements. A classic example of the former is the roar of the lion at the beginning of Metro Goldwyn Mayer (MGM) movies. The trademark roar immediately triggers an association with *being alert*. The Yahoo! yodel did much the same thing.[9] One of the most successful uses of sound in a brand design was Intel's incorporation of a musical whishing sound as an audio logo for the "Intel Inside" brand name for its computer chips. Retailers such as Starbucks and Williams-Sonoma extend this concept by selling music CDs carefully curated to strengthen brand associations.

All the cues discussed so far use the verbal/auditory modality, and we have seen that visual modality also comes into play with the way words are rendered. But the visual mode is important in its own right. Much of the brain is wired primarily for visual cues, to which we now turn.

Illustration

Visual cues are harder for marketers (versus designers) to appreciate, but they are just as important for an effective brand design as verbal and auditory cues. A picture or drawing can sharpen and enrich a desired association.

Campbell's launch of "Chunky" soup is an example of the power of visual illustration. The positioning concept for the Chunky brand was "the soup you can eat like a meal." It reflected the insight that consumers were increasingly having soup as a meal, rather than as an appetizer. But many male consumers felt that soup might not be substantial enough for a full meal; hence the positioning and the brand name "Chunky." Originally, the product was introduced with just the name "Chunky" featured on the can. It was initially unsuccessful. The addition of a simple illustration of a spoon loaded with chunks of food (see Figure 7.8) was sufficient to get consumers to make the desired associations. The illustration has been improved over time, and the brand continues to be successful.

One of the first companies to recognize the power of visual illustration was Gerber, the baby food company. The picture of a baby on the Gerber brand cemented the association *cares about babies* (see Figure 7.9). The picture was so powerful that it became culturally iconic. Interestingly, Gerber was also one of the first companies to recognize that younger adult consumers, especially those eating by themselves, were receptive to simple, one-dish meals. Unfortunately, in introducing its one-dish brand, "Singles," it incorporated into the brand design the Gerber name, which held a strong connection to the baby illustration (see Figures 7.9a and 7.9b). Think about the associations this created for Singles. What young adult wants to associate his or her dinner with *baby food*,

Figure 7.8
Chunky Soup Illustration over Time

Figure 7.9
Gerber Baby Illustration (a) and Singles Brand (b)

(a)   (b)

much less *being single* and *eating alone from a jar*? Illustrations can make a brand design, and they can also break a brand design.

Brand Symbols

Visual brand design cues can be representational or symbolic. Brand symbols can cue associations just as strongly as illustrations (think modern art versus realistic art). These symbols can be incorporated into the brand name or stand alone. When Walmart wanted to reposition itself around not only the concept of "saving money," but also "living better," it created the abstract sunburst symbol (yellow lines radiating out from a circle) to create the association to *life* and *pleasure*. UPS is positioned as a basic service on the order of the fire or police department. Its symbol thus takes the form of a shield bearing the lowercase letters *ups* to associate the brand with *being official* and *routine*.

Corporate Symbols

Of course, symbols can also be used to cue corporate identity. Automotive badges, such as the distinctive rendering of the Ford name or the nested VW symbol, are good examples. Associations to these are largely derivative and develop over time. But the Ford badge certainly conjures associations to a brand such as the F-150 truck.

All too often, however, company logos are designed with little attention to brand design considerations. Amusingly, a British B2B firm, RJMetrics, used an internal hackathon to come up with a new visual identity. The resulting logo took the form of a complex geometric figure called a dodecahedron, which is five times more complex than a tetrahedron. The rationale for the logo was that it showed that the firm dealt with complexity. The firm was quite surprised that the new look was greeted by a barrage of tweets asking, "Why is your new logo a pair of Y fronts?"—underpants commonly known to U.K. customers."[10] Needless to say, the association was not good for the brand.

Color Palette

Just as a brand should have a brand lexicon of words and phrases, it should also use a palette of a few colors selected for their associative value. UPS uses the color brown to reinforce the associations to *basic* and *routine*. The brown trucks and uniforms cue the desired associations.

Even when color is not intended to have associative meaning, it can make the brand distinctive and acquire derivative value. Originally Pepsi used the colors red and blue only to differentiate itself from Coca-Cola, but the colors have come to be associated with Pepsi. Indeed, one only has to think of the colors in flags to appreciate the symbolic importance that a palette can acquire in conjunction with other associations. The app Color Hunt has examples of effective palettes.[11]

Shape

The three-dimensional shape or form of a product can be another potent symbolic cue. Think of McDonald's French fries container. It is designed to frame and showcase an overflowing number of fries. In fact, the tool used to fill the container is designed to put so many fries into the container that some actually fall out, only to be discovered at the bottom of the bag once all the fries are thought to be gone. All this creates associations to *caring* and *friendliness*.

Similarly, the shape of bottles can strongly affect perceptions of wine brands. Compare something as basic as the shape of the typical Bordeaux bottle, with its squared-off high shoulders, to the more rounded Burgundy bottle. The difference might originally have been functional, having to do with sediment differences, but each shape now has its own associations.

Scent

The use of scent (or olfaction) as a brand design element is increasingly common. Everyone is familiar with the scent of a newly purchased automobile and the associations it brings. Similarly, food smells can elicit strong associations. Olfaction is, in fact, wired much more directly to the brain than other senses, which accounts for the strong associative power of smells.

Perhaps the leading example of scent branding is the hotel industry. Holiday Inns use the same scent worldwide in their lobbies. W hotels use a signature fragrance with lemon and lime notes; Westin hotels use one with cedar and vanilla notes. Hyatt Place uses its Seamless scent, which connects the brand to "welcoming elegance and calm through a blend of fresh blueberries and light florals on a base of warm vanilla and musk."[12]

Sometimes scent is used, as with sound, simply to differentiate. Then, of course, there is Cinnabon, the cinnamon roll company frequently found in shopping malls. The company locates its ovens so as to maximize the smell of warm cinnamon rolls for passersby in order to cue associations with *comforting* and *satisfying*. Rolls are made often, and extra brown sugar and cinnamon are put in the oven to boost the smell. The use of scent in brand design will continue to grow, extending to environments such as airline departure lounges, with scents associated with different destinations.

HOLISTIC DESIGN

We have stressed the importance of understanding and implementing the basic elements of brand design to ensure that marketers consider—and if possible incorporate—all of the available tools from the standpoint of desired associations into the brand design. Ultimately, of course, the design has to come together so that the whole is more than the constituent elements. All the cues must consistently link to the same associations and reinforce each other.

At the same time it is difficult to separate out the individual elements in a complete prototype or finished design, so the brand design template (Figure 7.2) provides a useful check on the holistic design. Fill in each space with the implementation of that particular design element. You should be able to see that each element is designed to trigger the associations called for in the perceptual mind map and contributes to the holistic design.

By focusing on the brand design template, marketers and designers can truly work together. The role of the marketer is to specify the associations in the perceptual mind map and to evaluate whether each cue triggers the intended associations. The role of the designer is to prototype design ideas for each cue. By having a common focus on a set of associations as the end goal of the process, marketers and designers can communicate more effectively and be more completely involved in the brand design process.

SUMMARY

Brand design is a powerful marketing tool. Unlike advertising, it does not seek to persuade consumers to consciously think in a certain way about the benefit of a brand. Effective brand designs provide cues that lead to unconscious associations in the consumer's mind. These associations can directly affect consumer behavior and make consumers more receptive to advertising appeals. In this chapter we have seen that 12 types of cues can be effectively used to create associations. Focusing on each cue separately can optimize design effectiveness. And, by focusing overall on the same associations, the resulting design can have a holistic quality that enhances its impact. With this approach marketers can use design thinking in a systematic way to create brand designs that can make a major contribution to the success of any brand.

Bobby J. Calder is Charles H. Kellstadt Professor Emeritus of Marketing at the Kellogg School of Management and a professor of journalism, media, and integrated marketing communications at Northwestern University. He has been a consultant to numerous companies, as well as to government and not-for-profit organizations. He also served as editor or co-editor for three books published in the Kellogg on *book series. He received his BA, MA, and PhD degrees from the University of North Carolina at Chapel Hill.*

NOTES

1. Calder, Bobby J., and Steven DuPuis (2011), "Packaging and Brand Design." In *Wiley International Encyclopedia of Marketing*, Eds. N. J. Sheth and N. Malhotra, Hoboken, NJ: John Wiley & Sons.
2. Kahneman, Daniel (2011), *Thinking, Fast and Slow*, New York: Farrar, Straus and Giroux.
3. Hempel, Jessi (2016), "The Inside Story of Uber's Radical Rebranding," *Wired*, February 2. www.wired.com/2016/02/the-inside-story-behind-ubers-colorful-redesign.
4. Colapinto, John (2011), "Famous Names," *The New Yorker*, October 3. www.newyorker.com/magazine/2011/10/03/famous-names.
5. Pathak, Abhishek, Gemma Calvert, and Carlos Veasco (2017), "Evaluating the Impact of Early- and Late-Acquired Phonemes on the Luxury Appeal of Brand Names," *Journal of Brand Management* 24, 522–545.
6. Green, T. Clifton, and Russell Jame (2013), "Company Name Fluency, Investor Recognition, and Firm Value," *Journal of Financial Economics* 109, 813–834.
7. Lee, Angela Y., and Aparna A. Labroo (2004), "The Effect of Conceptual and Perceptual Fluency on Brand Evaluation, *Journal of Marketing Research* 41(2), 151–165.
8. Duhigg, Charles (2017), "Yoplait Learns to Manufacture Authenticity to Go with Its Yogurt," *The New York Times* (June 26). www.nytimes.com/2017/06/26/business/yoplait-learns-to-manufacture-authenticity-to-go-with-its-yogurt.html.
9. www.youtube.com/watch?v=iC1a8xXQQDo.
10. Moore, Robert J. (2013), "Our Logo Looks Like Underpants: A Case Study in Internationalization," blog.rjmetrics.com, October 9. https://blog.rjmetrics.com/2013/10/09/our-logo-looks-like-underpants-a-case-study-in-internationalization.
11. https://colorhunt.co/popular.
12. Minsky, Laurence, Colleen Fahey, and Caroline Fabrigas (2018), "Inside the Invisible but Influential World of Scent Branding," *Harvard Business Review*, April 11. https://hbr.org/2018/04/inside-the-invisible-but-influential-world-of-scent-branding.

CHAPTER 8

LEVERAGING TOUCHPOINTS IN TODAY'S BRANDING ENVIRONMENT

KEVIN McTIGUE

One of the greatest struggles in modern marketing and branding is staying current with the rapid evolution of channels, marketing vehicles, and technologies. Should our brand be on Instagram? How about Facebook? What content do we need to provide on LinkedIn? Should we allow customers to interact with us on Twitter?

Across B2C and B2B, marketers are racing to keep up with the rapid consumer adoption of new digital tools and channels. Some are entirely new, such as voice-activated technology, as popularized by Amazon's Alexa. More frequently, new opportunities to interact with customers—*touchpoints*—come in the form of new features available on popular existing platforms such as Facebook and Google. It seems that every week a new window of opportunity opens for brands to connect with their customers. At the same time, marketers are dealing with scarce dollars, time, and personnel resources to allocate to the most important touchpoints.

To those responsible for ROI, critical questions emerge: Which channels and touchpoints are most important? Which ones drive actual business value? And, most important, how do we bring our brand to life across these touchpoints to create a valuable and differentiating experience?

Given the pace of technological evolution, we could answer these questions today, but by the time you read this chapter, the answers would be wrong. So we won't discuss what channels and touchpoints are "right" right now; instead, we will outline an approach that will help marketers consistently and effectively answer these questions for their brands over time.

In this chapter, we'll try to answer these four common questions:

1. How can we identify the right touchpoints?
2. How can we prioritize among them?
3. How can we ensure that we are using them to create value for our customer and our business?
4. How can we practically execute consistently across all these touchpoints?

WHAT IS A BRAND TOUCHPOINT?

Brand touchpoints are any point where your brand intersects with the consumer. They are the multiple places you see, hear, touch, speak with, and experience a brand.

Let's use a car brand—any brand—as an example. A touchpoint is the ad you recently saw for the brand's newest introduction. It is the ad you remember from 10 years ago, the Instagram post of your friend's similar car, the rental car you experienced a couple years ago. It is your brother's 1995 model and your friend's comment about his car. It is also the car review site, the manufacturer's online car configurator tool, and your recent visit to the brand's dealership for service, as well as the salesperson you talked with, the dealership decor, and the receptionist's friendly (or unfriendly) greeting. It's even the type of coffee the dealership served while you were there. It's easy to go on and on—and that's just for one brand.

Whether large or small, every single interaction is collected by your brain consciously or unconsciously to help you form a brand image. Brands are the assembled meaning of consumers' interpretations of all the brand-related touchpoints they experience.[1]

Marketers purposefully design touchpoint intersections to create a specific brand meaning that aligns with their positioning. When touchpoints are managed well, marketers can drive not just differentiation and choice, but the ability to charge a premium, increase loyalty, and create a platform for future line extensions—all the wonderful things that strong brands bring to their firms.

Let's take a look at Starbucks, one of the most famous brands in the world. The coffee company has become an iconic brand directly because of the detailed attention it pays to every customer touchpoint, and as a result, the Starbucks brand has widely extended to mean much more than just coffee. The company's complex and successful touchpoint system includes advertising and social media, of course, but these marketing functions support the experience touchpoints as well, including the service of the baristas, the pioneering smartphone payment platform, the loyalty program, and the unique in-store experience. Every aspect of the Starbucks ecosystem is a deliberate touchpoint, and together these touchpoints work in concert to create a valuable and differentiating experience for the Starbucks customer, which adds up to a unique brand image that has tremendous value.

THE CHALLENGE: EXPONENTIAL GROWTH OF TOUCHPOINTS

Over the past 50 years the consumer brand experience has evolved from a handful of media choices paired with an in-person sales experience to an almost limitless array of touchpoint possibilities. The great challenge that marketers face is the exponential growth of these touchpoints.

Recently the consulting firm BCG joined with consumer information company IRI and the Grocery Marketers Association to examine the online and offline touchpoints for a relatively low-involvement category: consumer packaged goods (CPG).[2] Common sense would suggest that the purchase path for a CPG product such as soap would be easy to predict and easy to manage. But common sense proved to be wrong. In fact, the study identified over 50 potential touchpoints in a typical purchase path. For higher-involvement decisions in industries such as auto, travel, or B2B, the complexity of touchpoints is nearly overwhelming.

The rapid growth of options has made it ever more difficult to identify what touchpoints our customers are using. Over half of the most popular digital properties—Facebook, YouTube, Messenger, WeChat, Line, Instagram, Pinterest, Spotify—did not exist just 15 years ago. The mobile platform rose to prominence in 2007 with the iPhone, and many still considered it a niche as recently as 2013. Voice-enabled technology and augmented reality (technologies that use computer-generated images overlaid on a user's real-life view of the world) are being touted as the next major touchpoint enablers. Will they be? As platforms rise and fall in popularity at the pace of popular music, marketers struggle to understand and keep up with their customers' continually changing behaviors.

In addition, this speed of change makes it hard to understand the value of different touchpoints. Historically, when firms explored a new channel opportunity, benchmarks were used to help assess value. With the recent rapidity of change, benchmarks do not always hold true from one month to the next, from one company to the next, or even between brands or products within a company.

Compounding the challenge is the fact that consumer expectations for how brands behave across touchpoints are growing as well. Consumers have been trained to expect much more from their user experience, thanks to industry disrupters such as Uber, Amazon, and Airbnb. A consumer-driven lens that prioritizes customer value with high levels of responsiveness and customer care was once a differentiator, but is now simply the cost of entry. This is occurring across B2C and B2B, and frequently customer expectations within a category are being set by experiences outside that category.

Matt Watkinson and Will Sansom from the marketing think tank Contagious have argued this point in their theory of "transference of experience expectations."[3] It's no longer enough to be the best in your industry and expect customers to give you a pass on the type of experience you create for them. As leading and disruptive firms continually up the ante, new normals rapidly emerge that make it imperative for all companies to catch up in ways that are right for their businesses and their customers.

So, the key question is: How do companies decide what touchpoints are most important for their brand?

THE CUSTOMER JOURNEY

To make these decisions, marketers don't need a list of the best touchpoints; such a list can easily change monthly. What marketers really need is a mechanism to consistently identify and prioritize the right channels, and the right role of those channels to create value. Specifically, marketers need to:

1. Identify the most relevant touchpoints at any time and understand the role that these channels play for consumers.
2. Identify the most important business goals served by those touchpoints.
3. Focus organizational resources on the most important touchpoints.

To assist marketers in this process, we reference a model that has been in existence for over a century: the *customer journey* construct. But we interpret it in new ways for the modern age.

The Customer Journey Model

The customer journey model is generally credited to Frank Dukesmith, who in 1904 introduced the basic idea of a multistep sales process. This helped salespeople, and eventually marketers, think of the purchase process as a path and not a single action. Marketers used this concept throughout the 20th century with tweaks and variations to help plan tactics for distinct purchase phases and to move consumers "through the funnel." The model was generally brought to life as *AIDA*: the phases of awareness, interest, desire, and action.

In 2009, consulting firm McKinsey & Company evolved the concept, bringing several key ideas to the mainstream business consciousness.[4] McKinsey described the previously linear journey as a loop in which the customer was always evaluating. It popularized the idea that customers diverge into different paths postpurchase, with some going back into the consideration phase while others shortcut the path through loyalty. And importantly, McKinsey added the idea of a *trigger*, or inflection point, when some type of catalyst begins the active purchase process.

Today, we use journeys to help identify and prioritize touchpoints. As the complexity of the digital experience has grown, user experience experts have created elaborate journeys to help define user stories. These maps identify critical paths and potential friction points at which customers experience difficulties. This process allows user experience designers to match the right features and functionality of their product or service to specific stages of a digital experience journey.

From Company-centric to Consumer-centric: A New Take on an Old Framework

At the core of the modern model is a change from a company-centric to a consumer-centric approach. Historically, funnel models focused on company goals first: that is, moving consumers from awareness to interest to purchase to loyalty and so on. But in the modern age, marketers must flip the model to focus on consumers. What do they want? What needs do they have? What are their habits? In doing so, a company can obtain a more accurate and helpful view that better allows it to serve the customer's needs—and achieve the company's goals in the process.

While the bones of this approach have been around in some form for 100 years, it's important to note that the application of its principles in new ways is more valuable than ever before. Understanding the 21st century customer journey can help us manage tactical complexity. Furthermore, as the promise of big data becomes a reality, increased visibility about customer behaviors through data makes establishing an organizing framework all the more critical.

A TOUCHPOINT-SPECIFIC APPROACH

The model discussed in this chapter is built on the shoulders of the existing frameworks and aims to comprehensively help identify and prioritize brand touchpoints. At the same time, experience has shown that in order for the

Figure 8.1
The Customer Journey

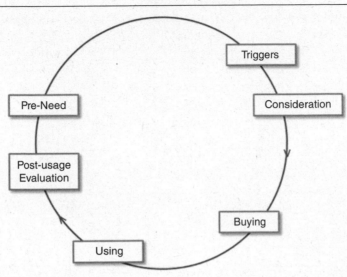

model to be practical and usable across organizations, it must be fundamentally simple. Complexity can always be added, but at its core, the model must be simple enough to achieve unilateral adoption within firms and not be the sole domain of high-priced consultants.

Fundamentally, the modern customer journey follows a basic circular path that progresses through the common buying phases (see Figure 8.1). Again, significant variations can be added at any stage, but at a high level these simple core stages adapt to fit most industries and purchases.

The model begins with the pre-need phase, the point at which the customer is not actively involved in the category. At some point in the customer's journey, a trigger event starts the active evaluation period, which may stretch from short to long depending on the buying complexities of the category, the individual, and his or her past experience. An omni-channel buying process follows, with multiple paths to purchase. The final phases move through usage of the product or service and evaluation of the experience.

Pre-need

Interestingly, the pre-need phase is not part of the actual buying process, but is the stage where 99 percent of customers exist in any category (see Figure 8.2).

Figure 8.2
Typical Customer Distribution

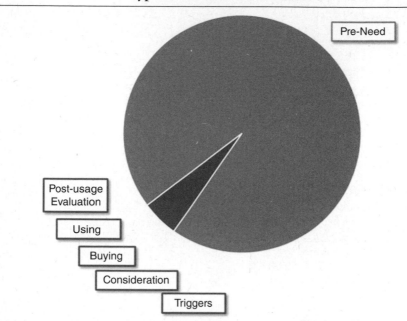

A customer may have purchased shoes, but 99 percent of customers are not thinking about their next shoe purchase until a trigger event occurs. Most relevant for businesses, the pre-need phase is usually where companies direct the most advertising dollars in trying to reach this 99 percent—their potential customers. One of the benefits of isolating this time frame is understanding how to best interact with customers who are not specifically looking to interact with your brand.

For B2B companies, this pre-need stage usually identifies key stakeholders who have a simple need to stay current about trends and products in their industry. This leads to behaviors such as reading industry publications and newsletters and attending conferences. B2B marketers at this stage are generally seeking to build awareness of their solutions and establish credibility. For example, on its digital site 99U, software provider Adobe provides its target customers with useful content that drives interaction (and data collection) but holds off on the hard sell.

For B2C, we frequently find companies advertising broadly to consumers at the pre-need stage, who are likely not actively interested in their product category. Advertising to the uninterested is not necessarily wrong, as it has been shown that building high levels of brand awareness has an oversized impact in low-involvement categories. However, reaching this group of consumers does require advertising communications teams to work harder to break through the clutter.

An example is Starwood, the parent company of numerous hotel brands. The company is a frequent poster on photograph-heavy Instagram. Its social posts typically focus on beautiful imagery of enticing vacation locales. The images are intentionally not heavily branded advertisements or promotions for last-second deals. In using the journey construct, Starwood likely found that many of its target customers at the pre-need stage were on Instagram and were interacting with travel imagery.

This type of content is exactly in line with Starwood's target customers' needs and their behavior on this platform at this stage. We can also assume that these posts are driving some awareness of Starwood's properties and are thus working toward its business goal to help consumers find Starwood hotels when they are ready to book their vacations.

Trigger

At some point in the customer journey there is a trigger, or inflection point, that shifts the model and consumer behavior from passive to active. Your lease on a car is coming due, a machine is starting to break down at your factory, your hair gets too long, you expand your family with a new child, or you simply run out of gum.

Google calls this "ZMOT," for zero moment of truth. It's the moment when you grab your laptop, mobile phone, or some other wired device and start learning about a product or service you're thinking about trying or buying.[5] In other words, a customer has identified a need and begins the process of looking for a solution. These trigger points are incredibly valuable to marketers because brand relevance peaks as the buying process begins. Money spent reaching someone at the trigger point will motivate action at much higher levels than someone in pre-need.

Across both B2B and B2C companies, increasing spending at the trigger point of the journey is becoming a common tactic to prioritize messaging, as this money is spent at the exact time when a customer's purchase process begins. For instance, searching "vacations in Mexico" on Google is a beacon to advertisers that a customer has moved from pre-need into active category participation. The most obvious touchpoint for advertisers is the paid search results. Beyond search results, that search for vacations is now data that becomes part of the user's digital profile. This means that advertisers can then buy across the digital landscape from banners to videos to sponsored social posts. While competition can drive up pricing for the precious touchpoints associated with these triggers, it is essential that firms learn the most relevant triggers for their offerings.

Consideration and Evaluation

The consideration and evaluation phase has become dominated by the idea of content marketing, or inbound marketing. The basic premise is that as consumers research a choice, a firm should provide the answers their customers seek and even establish itself as the authority on a given topic in order to help positively influence the purchase.

This strategy has been driven by a dramatic shift to self-guided research in the Internet age. A 2017 Forrester report found that "68 percent of B2B buyers prefer to research online on their own, up from 53 percent in 2015 . . . and they considered gathering information online on their own superior to interacting with a sales representative by a margin of 53 percent to 17 percent."[6] B2B firms are spending significant resources on aligning both the content (white papers, product videos) and the functionality (comparison tools, ROI calculators) that their disparate customers seek.

For B2C, the level of evaluation can be almost negligible, but in many categories it is still important, particularly for first-time purchasers. Consumers researching running shoes may start by asking friends, reading a running blog for recommendations, and even checking out reviews on Amazon. In some categories, companies are tracking consumers' digital behaviors along this path to better understand how they are making decisions. For example, automakers are beginning to use sophisticated digital journeys based on real-time consumer behavioral data to understand what behaviors are occurring at what points of the car-buying phase. Using a mixture of first-party data (from their own data gathering) combined with third-party data from other sources, marketers are stitching together the most common paths and the most important components of the path that lead to purchase.

For instance, a potential customer goes to tesla.com to look at the models and signs up for a newsletter, in the process agreeing to the web site's cookie policy. Then the customer goes to autotrader.com, edmunds.com, and audiusa.com. Later he or she responds to a Tesla newsletter by clicking through to a financing offer, making an appointment online, and coming in for a test drive. All of the actions taken on this day can be collected and then aggregated to build out a model of what comprises the key parts of the consideration and research phase.

Buying

Omni-channel commerce is a current marketing buzzword. Simply put, it consists of matching a company's purchase options with a customer's preferences to purchase. Like other phases, the buying phase is rapidly changing territory, as digital buying options have proliferated in recent years to challenge on-site purchases at physical locations.

The tendency is to think of multichannel buying as simply enabling e-commerce or mobile commerce alongside sales from physical locations, but it is more complicated. E-commerce darling Warby Parker, an eyewear company, attributes more than half its sales to physical stores, but founder Dave Gilboa notes that "about 75 percent of our customers who shop in our stores have been to our web site first."[7] The future of commerce will not likely be a binary choice between offline and online, but an integration of the two.

In recent years, U.S. grocery stores have been scrambling to fight Amazon, learning from their European counterparts that have been leaders in enabling digitally driven options, such as Waitrose and Sainsbury's. Companies are intensely studying consumers' buying behaviors and their underlying needs, and matching those to their particular store's unique capabilities. This process is driving success in the online/offline pairing of click-and-collect shopping, whereby customers purchase online but pick up their products at a physical location. Understanding the buying needs that drive customers enables firms to create the purchase path that best meets the needs of their shoppers—and the best pairing of off- and online.

Usage

The usage phase is traditionally defined as the experience that a customer has with a product or service once it has been purchased. Overall satisfaction with the offering is paramount, but a deeper understanding of usage can unlock insights for future communications and even innovation.

It's also important to understand how the other phases work together to create an overall user experience. For example, by deep-diving into the usage stage, a large floral-delivery company was able to prioritize the critical pain points in its postpurchase usage stage. The product was the delivery of flowers to the receiver. But the driving need for the giver was not simply making sure that the flowers arrived at their destination. Instead, the consumer was most driven by being able to create a moment of surprise and joy for the intended recipient. The flowers were simply a vehicle for the *expression of care*. This led to differentiating usage improvements in the delivery process, as well as additional offerings and services that addressed this core need.

Post-usage Evaluation

In the post-usage evaluation phase (see Figure 8.3), customer behavior will diverge. In past customer journey models, marketers would hope for users to progress to a loyalty phase or an advocate phase, where they would turn to social media with abounding praise for their product or service. These are the desired *business* goals from this phase, but they are not a customer-centric approach to understanding this phase. As McKinsey suggested with its loyalty loop, everyone does not "restart" the journey in the same way.[8] In the model (Figure 8.3), there are multiple paths in the post-usage evaluation phase: rejecters, price-driven switchers, loyalists (who return with a predilection for repurchase), and even the coveted evangelists, who would never think of purchasing any other brand.

Critically, understanding which customers diverge where and why will inform a marketer's future actions. Marketers must look for the types of people and the types of experiences that drive loyalty, and use that knowledge to focus their future actions. For example, a large CPG company recently explored a segmentation process that examined past buyers' data in order to understand the telltale traits of those who are predisposed to becoming loyalists versus those who buy primarily on price, as well as those who become brand rejecters. This knowledge enables the company to deliver different messages and

Figure 8.3
Post-usage Evaluation

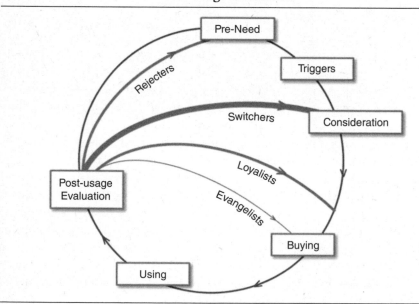

promotions to the two former groups and eliminate the likely brand rejecters from the media buy.

At a simpler level, the post-usage evaluation phase allows marketers to understand the likelihood of advocacy behavior and manage that proactively. All brands would love social media influencers to widely praise their offerings, and as such, they frequently try to promote this behavior. While expecting all customers to become evangelists may be impossible, all brands must actively manage their online reputation in some fashion, as the growing power of ratings and reviews becomes a key influencer for consumers.

CREATING A CUSTOMER JOURNEY

For a company, creating an effective and positive customer journey is an exercise in prioritization. This section outlines the practical actions marketers can take to start this process and create a valuable journey model that will help them make sound decisions. This process involves defining the brand's most important customer targets, determining each segment's primary path to purchase, and then mapping marketing efforts to this knowledge. Along the way, it is important to realize that we may not always have all the data we need (but we should begin the process anyway!), and that customer journeys are always evolving—just like our approach.

Who Are Our *Most* Important Targets?

A fundamental premise of modern marketing is prioritizing the allocation of marketing resources to a distinct target segment rather than a broad population. Traditionally, market segments have been defined as distinct populations of customers who share a set of driving needs within a category. Marketers choose to focus their resources on a target segment for whom they can create more value than the competition. And in turn, that target segment will respond by purchasing from the company and driving value for the firm. This process of segmentation and targeting is a means to focus limited budget and time on the activities that will drive the most value.

In practice, it is difficult to narrow to a single target segment. A company with multiple brands will have multiple target segments, and a large brand will frequently choose to target several segments. For example, McDonald's targets multiple segments for different product lines and times of the day. This complexity is compounded in B2B situations in which a single product line can have multiple distinct buyers and also multiple key decision makers who influence purchase.

As a result, identifying the right target segments for whom to create a customer journey can be complex, but the complexity should not hinder companies from taking on the challenge. Mapping a customer journey for distinct segments will provide significant guidance to firms looking to focus their marketing dollars for the greatest return.

The tool is most useful when focused on a distinct segment. If not, the needs, attitudes, and activities become watered down and less useful. As such, it's important to force prioritization: For which segment would this understanding create the most value? As their acumen grows, marketers can add more segments as the firm's needs and resources dictate. Start with the segments that are likely to create the most value and then scale.

What Is the *Primary* Path for This Segment?

Once a target segment (or segment) has been identified, the marketer must then identify that segment's *primary* path to purchase. Even one target segment could include millions of individuals with millions of different paths. Consider the visual metaphor of a large, grassy city park, such as Hyde Park in London. Millions pass through the park every day, often choosing a different path. But when we look down from above, we see the well-worn trails of the most frequent paths. The key here is to *prioritize* and choose the most well-worn path. Typically it follows the basic flow shown in Figure 8.4.

To identify the most frequently used paths, companies rely upon a variety of sources, such as internal customer data, external data, and larger-scale research. (See the "Finding the Data to Craft the Journey" section below for more details.)

Once the primary path has been identified, marketers must ask three questions *at each stage* of the journey (see Figure 8.5):

1. What are your target customers' *most important* needs at each stage? What is the goal they are striving for?
2. What are your customers thinking? What are their key attitudes, drivers, friction points, and challenges? What do they think about your brand? What *delights* them?

Figure 8.4
Typical Customer Path

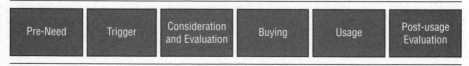

| Pre-Need | Trigger | Consideration and Evaluation | Buying | Usage | Post-usage Evaluation |

Figure 8.5
Key Questions by Stage in the Customer Journey

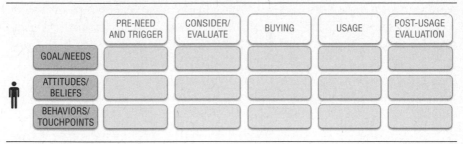

3. What do your customers do (and where do they do it)? What are your customers' *most relevant* behaviors by stage, and what are their *most frequented* touchpoints?

Using this model paints a picture of the consumer's journey from *his or her* perspective. This is important because we have described consumers not as we wish they were, but how they actually are. That perspective allows marketers to plan their interactions with them in ways that are most relevant to them and thus most efficient for the company.

Figure 8.6 presents an illustrative model constructed for a vacation company.

Figure 8.6
Illustrative Vacation Planning Customer Journey

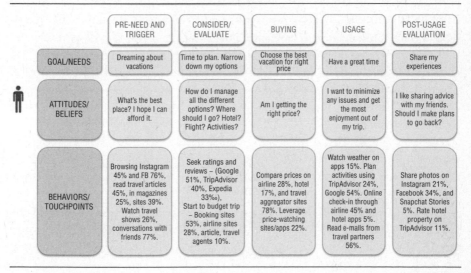

Figure 8.7
Mapping Business Goals and Key Performance Indicators

	PRE-NEED AND TRIGGER	CONSIDER/ EVALUATE	BUYING	USAGE	POST-USAGE EVALUATION
GOAL/NEEDS					
ATTITUDES/ BELIEFS					
BEHAVIORS/ TOUCHPOINTS					
GOAL					
KPIs					

What Business Goals Do We Need to Achieve?

At this stage, the lens shifts from the consumer to the business (see Figure 8.7). Marketers must ask, "What is the ideal outcome for our firm at each part of the customer journey?" In the pre-need phase, that outcome might be a certain level of awareness. For example, a luxury automaker with high awareness might have the express goal of changing long-set attitudes about its brand in the pre-need phase.

In the consider/evaluate phase, marketers evaluate where the segment is learning the most about their product: from third-party consultants, from in-depth online research, or simply from the front of the package? In the buying phase, how are they buying now? Are they purchasing differently from competitors? The usage phase examines whether the customer is having a frictionless experience and identifies potential opportunities for improvement. In the post-usage evaluation, marketers must determine whether customers are sharing feedback online or through other methods.

After establishing the goals, marketers must consider how they will measure success against these goals. What are the key performance indicators (KPIs) that will help benchmark your progress? Is there a brand-attitude tracking study in place? Is there a Net Promoter Score (NPS) mechanism to understand usage satisfaction? Or, if social sharing of user-generated content is the goal, then you will need social listening tools to measure efforts. The vacation company example showcases the kinds of goals and associated KPIs that might be considered (see Figure 8.8).

Figure 8.8
Illustrative Vacation Planning Journey with Goals and KPIs

	PRE-NEED & TRIGGER	CONSIDER/ EVALUATE	BUYING	USAGE	POST-USAGE EVALUATION
GOAL/NEEDS					
ATTITUDES/ BELIEFS					
BEHAVIORS/ TOUCHPOINTS					
GOAL	Make her aware of COMPANY vacations.	Make COMPANY vacations one option	Sell 5K vacations monthly digitally	Ensure experience is positive	Increase loyalty Drive referrals
KPIs	Awareness to 45%	In top 3 brands considered Site traffic to 15K	Conversion of 3.5%	NPS of 4.2	Rebook rates to 40% Social listening metrics

Finding the Data to Craft the Journey

In almost every scenario, companies will likely lack all the information they need to create a perfected journey map. However, it's important not to postpone the exercise due to lack of complete data. At worst, marketers will have a more instructive framework than they had before, and at best they will have a fairly accurate depiction of the company's most important customer journeys. Frequently, the initial journey helps identify the specific research that would be most valuable to pursue.

To gather the data you need, you may want to turn to variety of sources, including:

- *Your internal team.* A small team of experienced internal resources can craft a fairly usable journey in just a few hours.
- *Existing research.* Many companies are awash in studies done by various groups over the years. The journey model can create meaningful value by simply having the disparate research studies aggregated into a single framework.
- *Secondary research.* While secondary sources may not provide an exact match to your target, data on "CPG shopper" or "B2B buyer" behavior can help to fill in the blanks.
- *Primary research.* Qualitative research can be used to uncover new information. Do your B2B customers engage with Twitter? How are they using it? Are they following industry leaders? More in-depth quantitative

studies also help you understand the scope and scale. What percentage of the customer base is using this channel? Is it more common with certain segments? This data gathering can be as low fidelity as a phone call with a customer or a quick survey. In addition, digitally based diaries in which customers use a mobile app to note their feelings and activities during a purchase path can be used to help identify touchpoints. These are particularly helpful for capturing offline touchpoints.

- *Online data.* The most recent progression of journey mapping is tracking the online behaviors of the customer base throughout the journey. By matching customer data to third-party data providers, marketers can stitch together an aggregate view of the most important touchpoints that critically tie back to sales. As data capabilities grow, marketers can increase their understanding of the evolving customer journey.

How to Best Leverage Journeys

Now that you have a map that covers your target customers at the distinct phases of their journey and that maps their needs onto your organizational goals, you have the key elements for a tactical plan and can methodically allocate resources to the phases with the most opportunity (see Figure 8.9).

Figure 8.9
Illustrative Complete Vacation Planning Journey Analysis

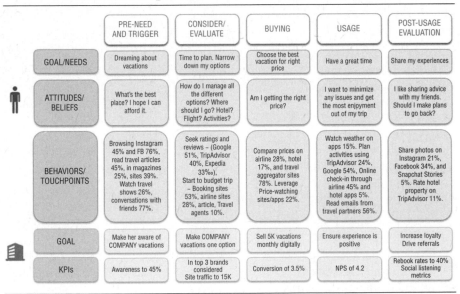

	PRE-NEED AND TRIGGER	CONSIDER/ EVALUATE	BUYING	USAGE	POST-USAGE EVALUATION
GOAL/NEEDS	Dreaming about vacations	Time to plan. Narrow down my options	Choose the best vacation for right price	Have a great time	Share my experiences
ATTITUDES/ BELIEFS	What's the best place? I hope I can afford it.	How do I manage all the different options? Where should I go? Hotel? Flight? Activities?	Am I getting the right price?	I want to minimize any issues and get the most enjoyment out of my trip	I like sharing advice with my friends. Should I make plans to go back?
BEHAVIORS/ TOUCHPOINTS	Browsing Instagram 45% and FB 76%, read travel articles 45%, in magazines 25%, sites 39%. Watch travel shows 26%, conversations with friends 77%.	Seek ratings and reviews – (Google 51%, TripAdvisor 40%, Expedia 33‰), Start to budget trip – Booking sites 53%, airline sites 28%, article, Travel agents 10%.	Compare prices on airline 28%, hotel 17%, and travel aggregator sites 78%. Leverage Price-watching sites/apps 22%.	Watch weather on apps 15%. Plan activities using TripAdvisor 24%, Google 54%, Online check-in through airline 45% and hotel apps 5%. Read emails from travel partners 56%.	Share photos on Instagram 21%, Facebook 34%, and Snapchat Stories 5%. Rate hotel property on TripAdvisor 11%.
GOAL	Make her aware of COMPANY vacations	Make COMPANY vacations one option	Sell 5K vacations monthly digitally	Ensure experience is positive	Increase loyalty Drive referrals
KPIs	Awareness to 45%	In top 3 brands considered Site traffic to 15K	Conversion of 3.5%	NPS of 4.2	Rebook rates to 40% Social listening metrics

For example, when your B2B salesperson says, "We need more content on the web site," you'll have an idea of how many customers are coming to the site for information in the consider/evaluate phase, and what information is most important to solving their needs at this stage. Should you be enabled on Google Home or Amazon Alexa? You'll know if your target is likely using the platform, and if so, at which stage of the journey. Your marketing team can ask, "How should we drive awareness on this platform? How might we increase product satisfaction at this stage?" You'll have a strategic framework and a blueprint to begin these discussions with information and data that is grounded in your customers' behavior and in your business goals.

SUMMARY

Marketers will always need to connect with their customers, but where and how those connections occur will inevitably change. The relative importance of the connection points will be different for various customers, categories, and products. But by systematically mapping touchpoints and creating a customer journey based on your target customers' behavior, marketers will be able to understand where to prioritize and focus, which is the key to ROI. This process will allow a firm to create differentiated value by meeting the distinct needs of its customers over time. Congratulations—the touchpoints are bound to change next month! But now you have a model to make sense of this changing marketing world.

Kevin McTigue is a clinical associate professor of marketing at Northwestern University's Kellogg School of Management, where he teaches a variety of marketing courses. Prior to joining the Kellogg faculty he worked in the consulting practice at SapientRazorfish. Earlier in his career he spent seven years at Hillshire Brands/Sara Lee managing a wide range of brands. He received his BS from Miami University and his MBA from Kellogg.

NOTES

1. Iacobucci, Dawn, and Bobby J. Calder (2003), *Kellogg on Integrated Marketing*, Hoboken, NJ: John Wiley & Sons.
2. Hadlock, Patricia, Shankar Raja, Bob Black, Jeff Gell, Paul Gormley, Ben Sprecher, Krishnakumar S. Davey, and Jamil Satchu (2014), *The Digital Future: A Game Plan for Consumer Packaged Goods*, GMA (August). http://www.gmaonline. org/file-manager/IRI%20BCG%20Google%20eCommerce%20Cobranded_ FINAL2.pdf.

3. Wakinson, Matt, and Will Sansom (2015), Now/Next/Why 2015 (conference presentation), Chicago, IL.

4. Court, David, Dave Elzinga, Susan Mulder, and Ole Jørgen Vetvik (2009), "The Consumer Decision Journey," *McKinsey Quarterly* (June). 2009, https://www.mckinsey.com/business-functions/marketing-and-sales/our-insights/the-consumer-decision-journey.

5. Lecinski, Jim (2011). *ZMOT: Winning the Zero Moment of Truth* (vook). https://www.thinkwithgoogle.com/marketing-resources/micro-moments/2011-winning-zmot-ebook.

6. Hoar, Andy (2017), *Death of a (B2B) Salesman: Two Years Later*, Forrester report (March 29), 2017, https://www.forrester.com/report/Death±Of±A±B2B±Salesman±Two±Years±Later/-/E-RES126861#figure1.

7. Thompson, Derek (2017), "The 4 Reasons Why 2017 Is a Tipping Point for Retail," *Atlantic*, November 16.

8. Court et al. (2009), see Note 4.

CHAPTER 9

BUILDING STRONG CONNECTIONS BETWEEN BRANDS AND THE SELF

NEAL J. ROESE and WENDI L. GARDNER

INTRODUCTION

Marketers have long known that connecting a brand to the consumer's sense of self can bring powerful rewards in loyalty and profitability. Great brands from Coca-Cola to Harley-Davidson and Amazon to Apple have succeeded not only by offering superior products and services but also by affording the opportunity to clarify and enhance the consumer's sense of who she is and how she fits into society. At the extreme, customers emblazon brand logos throughout their homes (a Coca-Cola–themed kitchen) and even onto their bodies (a Harley-Davidson tattoo), powerfully testifying to an enduring connection between the self and the brand. But building such self-expressive brands is not easy, and misunderstandings of the psychology of the self can result in costly mistakes.

Psychologists conceptualize *the self* as a knowledge structure in human memory that motivates individual behavior, including purchasing and consumption. This chapter provides an overview of the current psychological understanding of the self to provide a guide to smart branding decisions in the hyper-connected era.

THE SELF

Psychologists define the self as a component of human memory. The self is one *knowledge structure* among many that resides in human memory. A knowledge structure is a network of related information linked together by shared meaning. Knowledge structures consist of discrete bits of information that vary in their levels of activation (or tendency to be used in decisions and actions). Activation can come from a current situation, such as hearing news of the World Series, which reminds a person about ideas relating to baseball that had already been stored in memory. Higher activation can come from the frequency of prior activation; sometimes a concept is so frequently activated that it is said to be chronically activated. Let's say John is a fervent baseball fan and thinks about baseball all the time. John doesn't need to hear news about the World Series to be reminded of baseball. He thinks about baseball on his own all the time anyway. Co-activation of concepts forges associations in memory. If John eats hot dogs every time he attends a baseball game, eventually the mere sight of a hot dog will activate thoughts of baseball for him. Associations in memory are the raw ingredients of what are called *self-brand connections*, defined as associations between the self-concept and the brand.[1] But what is the self-concept?

The Self-Concept

The *self-concept* is a particularly vast knowledge structure that embraces such information as preferences, memories of past experiences, group memberships, and details about close relationships.[2] In our hyper-connected world, people are increasingly connected to others at the touch of a finger, yet only those connections linked to the self-concept in memory will be of much consequence. Because the self is so vast and the capacity to consider information is limited, comparatively little of it is active at any one point in time.

The *working self-concept* describes aspects of the self that are active at any given point in time. If someone were to ask you right now, "Tell me about yourself," the answers that would immediately come to mind would reflect this working self-concept. Some of the working self-concept will involve momentarily active aspects; others will be chronically activated. For some, being a Chicago Cubs fan is a chronically active part of their identity and is likely to be acted upon with correspondingly greater frequency. Indeed, chronically activated self-knowledge tends also to be more central to who we are. And what is more central is more likely to drive purchase and loyalty.[3]

Brands may also be knowledge structures. *Brand image* is the term typically used to describe the network of associations in any one consumer's mind that encompasses all that is known and felt about the brand. Great brands such as Harley-Davidson, Montblanc, and Apple have complex and varied brand images that consist of numerous interlocking nuggets of information. As large as the knowledge structures of such great brands may be, however, they are dwarfed in scale by the self-concept.

Self-Concept Clarity

People differ in their certainty of who they are. People high in *self-concept clarity* are chronically certain of their core identity and are generally happier as a result.[4] The brand that can connect to a consumer high in self-concept clarity will enjoy powerful brand loyalty. A committed long-distance runner, deeply sure of her runner identity, will potentially remain highly loyal to Nike. Her self-concept clarity affords the luxury of exploring entirely new identities. Because she finds it appealing to add new aspects to the self, she may adopt new and varied brands that embody self-aspects she lacks. By contrast, those low in self-concept clarity show wider variation over time in what they see as important aspects of themselves. Such people also resist additions to the self-concept until they feel "stabilized," and so react negatively to novelty.[5] Accordingly, brands that position on innovation or variety seeking are more effectively targeted at those high in self-concept clarity.

Self-concept clarity increases with age because people learn about themselves through experience and observation of themselves. In the same way that a person can watch a friend's actions over time and infer an outgoing personality trait, that same person might look inward, ponder memories of their actions over time, and reach a similar inference of outgoingness. This process is termed self-perception. Brands may join this process to expand self-brand connections. For example, Joan notes that she regularly drinks Brisk iced tea and so infers that she is a "Brisk drinker."

Mere possession is enough to start the process of self-brand connection. An object that is owned carries greater intrinsic value to the individual than the same object that is not owned, a pattern termed the *endowment effect*.[6] Consumers will pay more to keep from losing an owned object than they would pay to acquire the same thing in the first place. Importantly, mere ownership initiates shifts in the associative structure of memory that create new self-brand connections.[7] Because most people view themselves favorably, possessions take on this positive halo. Whatever becomes associated with the self in memory becomes more valuable.

LINKING THE BRAND TO THE SELF

Successful brands connect to consumers by linking to primary motives that drive consumer behavior. Here we discuss three such primary motives: *coherence* (the need for clarity and certainty about the self), *agency* (the need for individual competence and achievement), and *communion* (the need for social acceptance).[8]

Motive 1: Coherence

Coherence reflects a need for clarity and certainty about the self. People seek assurances of who they are at various stages of their lives, and one way to gain such assurance is by buying a particular brand. For example, uncertainty about the self and thus the need for coherence is especially prevalent in teenagers as they transition from childhood to adulthood, The same is true for individuals transitioning into parenthood, in and out of relationships, and out of the workforce and into retirement. Throughout the lifespan, people look for ways to confirm what they already believe about themselves and seek out verification from others. For example, Connor has always seen himself as rebellious, but after a recent promotion with new responsibilities, he tries to reaffirm that rebellious nature by buying brands—such as Harley-Davidson—that symbolize rebelliousness and thus verifies this aspect of his self-concept to himself and to others.

Motive 2: Agency

Agency reflects a need for individual competence and achievement. People like to feel that they are capable and effective. In part, this motive reflects a desire for unique individuality. People look for ways to demonstrate their abilities and achievements, and it feels good to bask in past glories and to show off in front of others. For example, Patrick thinks of himself as a talented swimmer and enjoys displaying medals from past competitions in his bedroom. Patrick buys the Speedo brand's premium line of swim goggles for casual use at the beach in order to signal his achievements in competitive swimming.

Motive 3: Communion

Communion reflects a need for social acceptance and belonging that includes close relationships and memberships in organizations. People seek acceptance and approval from close others, such as friends and romantic partners, and they seek security through fitting in with larger groups. For example, Sherry is a fan of the Chicago Cubs. She benefited from the camaraderie and shared joy in the team's 2016 World Series victory. Sherry buys Chicago Cubs apparel to signal her allegiance with this team and its fan base.

The Inward versus Outward Focus

We have seen how three distinct motives can drive brand purchase. Each of these motives may be directed either inward or outward. The inward focus is

introspective, with thoughts and actions centering on individual-level characteristics. For example, Tom buys an Omega watch because James Bond wore
this brand in various films over the course of the 007 franchise's history. In
buying Omega, Tom highlights connections between himself and James Bond.
The brand helps him to see himself in the same light as the confident, sophisticated British superspy.

The outward focus is exemplified by Erica, who buys a ModCloth shirt
because her immediate circle of friends also favors this brand. For Erica, the
purchase helps to secure social acceptance by signaling aspects of the brand
image, such as a quirky and upbeat style, which is valued by her friends.
Whereas the audience for Tom's brand purchase is himself, the audience for
Erica's brand purchase is a social group.

Consumers generally want to display to others exactly who they are, but
they vary greatly in when they do so, and how. Momentary goals can amplify
the outward focus, as when striving to make a good impression at a job interview. Also, people may try to compensate for perceived threats to their public
image. Recall the earlier example of Connor, who buys Harley-Davidson. He
is especially likely to wear his Harley-branded jacket in front of new colleagues
who might otherwise assume him to be a conformist simply because of his
new job.

PULLING IT TOGETHER: THE MOTIVE MATRIX

To map out how customers might relate to a brand, we have designed a tool
called the motive matrix. Uniting the three primary motives with the inward
versus outward focus into a 3×2 grid, the motive matrix contains six cells
that specify the unique ways that a consumer can use a brand to achieve
self-fulfillment (see Figure 9.1). Smart branding decisions begin with an
understanding of which of these six cells will form the basis of brand design
and communications.

The inward focus is introspective, with thoughts and actions centering on
individual-level characteristics. In essence, consumers sometimes buy brands
with an internal audience in mind. Any of the three motives may target this
inner audience. For coherence, a person might make an anonymous charitable
donation in order to clarify her moral identity. For agency, a person might
download a productivity app to highlight his competence. For communion,
a person might wear a silver keepsake under her clothing as a secret symbol
of her connection to a loved one. In each case, a distinct motive drives consumption that signals to an internal audience something important about the
self-concept.

Figure 9.1
The Motive Matrix

MOTIVE FOCUS	Coherence Need for clarity about identity	Agency Need for competence and achievement	Communion Need for social acceptance
Inward The individual is the audience	Brand used privately to clarify identity *Example:* Connor buys Harley-Davidson brand to affirm identity as a rebel	Brand used privately to affirm competence *Example:* Tom buys Omega brand because wearing what James Bond wore makes him feel sophisticated	Brand used privately to affirm social ties *Example:* Martha adorns her Christmas tree with Coca-Cola souvenirs, just like her family did
Outward Other people are the audience	Brand used publicly to clarify identity *Example:* Laura buys the Montblanc brand to project new identity as senior manager	Brand used publicly to signal competence *Example:* Patrick buys the Speedo brand to signal competitive swimming achievements	Brand used publicly to signal social ties *Example:* Sherry buys a Chicago Clubs hat to signal her allegiance with other Cubs fans

The outward focus is public, centering on how the self is seen by others. A consumer may buy a brand with an external audience along with any one of the three motivations in mind. For coherence, a person might publicly donate to the Red Cross to confirm his identity of social responsibility. For agency, a person might buy DeWalt tools to signal her do-it-yourself skills. For communion, a person might wear a Chicago Cubs cap to emphasize his team allegiance.

SEVEN PRINCIPLES FOR BUILDING STRONG SELF-BRAND CONNECTIONS

The motive matrix is a tool for clarifying and sharpening decisions about brand design and communications, with the end goal of building strong self-brand connections. To use the motive matrix effectively, follow the following seven principles.

Principle 1: Target One Motive

Building strong self-brand connections begins with identifying which motive to target and with what focus (see Figure 9.1). The most basic principle is to target just one motive. To target more than one motive risks difficult complexity for the company and confusion among consumers. Most brands benefit from the clarity of targeting only one motive.

Dove's "Real Beauty" ad campaign celebrates women's naturally unique, individual characteristics. "Real Beauty Sketches" was a 2013 entry in the campaign that enjoyed viral success with its emphasis on inner sources of beauty (https://www.youtube.com/watch?v=XpaOjMXyJGk). The campaign's success owes much to its laser-like focus on the agency motive (with an inward focus). Many fashion brands also target the agency motive to help customers express their individuality and aesthetic preferences. Recall our earlier example of Tom, who buys the Omega brand to emphasize aspects of his ideal self (again, with an inner focus). Other fashion brands emphasize the communion motive, as in our earlier example of Erica, whose outward focus prompts her to buy the ModCloth brand in order to fit in with a group. ModCloth encourages communion through the sharing of design ideas that are then approved by the brand community before going into production (e.g., "Be the buyer" and "Make the cut" programs) and through ads that feature ModCloth employees having fun together.

New brands will especially benefit from the rigor of targeting just one motive. Trying to appeal to more than one motive risks diluting the brand image. Only mature brands that command a deeper set of associations within their brand image can attempt to target more than one motive. Harley-Davidson, a 100-year-old brand with a powerfully resonant brand image, fulfills both agency and communion motives with its emphasis on rebellious individuality alongside brotherhood among fellow brand aficionados. Chrysler is another mature brand with deep roots in America. Chrysler's 2011 "Born of Fire" ad (https://www.youtube.com/watch?v=DEk5LpUT_vo) tapped into all three motives: coherence by emphasizing Detroit citizens' self-concept as scrappy Midwesterners able to rise from the ashes of the Great Recession, agency by way of a comeback story, and communion by emphasizing the common ground that unites Americans.

These two examples are exceptions to the more general rule. They reveal how challenging it can be to target more than one motive. For most brands, the best practice is to target just one primary motive.

Principle 2: Target Life Transitions for Powerful Self-Brand Connections

The self-concept changes over time, often slowly but sometimes sharply as a result of key life transitions, such as moving to a new city, marrying or divorcing, losing or gaining a job, having children, and the like. Such life transitions usually involve incorporating new identities into the self-concept. For example, the birth of a first child requires integration of a "parent" identity into the self-concept, threatening the coherence motive with both an inward focus (pondering the new "me") and outward focus (conveying the new identity to friends and family).[9]

Some life transitions require de-emphasizing an old identity (e.g., the new retiree) and others require establishing a new identity (e.g., the new parent). These challenges alter consumers' preferences in predictable ways during common rites of passage. Trading in the sports sedan for the minivan upon the birth of a child is not only practical but also announces to oneself and the world the new identity of fatherhood. The freshman arriving at college experiences shifts to the self-concept along all three motives. In coherence, the transition to adulthood involves fundamental changes in identity. In agency, past academic achievement meets far more demanding challenges. And with communion, old friends are left behind as the search for new inclusion begins. As a result, freshmen buy products that symbolize their new role (college-branded T-shirts, calculators), while also displaying symbols of their former childhood (stuffed animals) and recent friendships (high school photos, a grandmother's ring).

Major life transitions are "major" precisely because they alter the way all three primary motives unfold. In these momentous periods, consumers are particularly open to embracing new brands, regardless of whether the life change is positive or negative. Brands become more meaningful when they assist in these transitions. The opportunity peaks within six months to a year post-transition, during which time consumers are maximally open to new brands. In the hyper-connected age, marketers enjoy increasingly informative data streams enabling the identification of specific consumers undergoing specific life transitions. For example, social media posts reveal imminent weddings, births, retirements, and so on. Deft brands will locate these life transitions to become part of the consumer's new identity. The hyper-connected era significantly accelerates the traditional point-of-entry targeting (such as reaching out to first-time parents with diaper offers) with hyper-targeting. Rather than offering the same product to all first-time moms, hyper-targeting brings a much more specific product with a specific message to a specific consumer.

Principle 3: Use the Brand to Bridge Self-Concept Conflicts

Major life transitions are one driver of self-concept change, but another is psychological conflict. The coherence motive underlies this when two or more important aspects of identity are in conflict. Each person has multiple identities, that is, woman, wife, Korean, software engineer, and so on. In this example, "woman" and "wife" are compatible, because they overlap in several aspects (e.g., empathic), whereas "software engineer" is less compatible because it is a male-dominated profession. Accordingly, the "woman" identity conflicts with the "software engineer" identity, resulting in an unpleasant feeling that may be resolved through changes to the self-concept.

One kind of self-concept change is integration, which can happen if two identities are co-activated. Recall the example of the baseball fan who came to associate hot dogs with baseball through the experience of eating them at baseball games. In a similar fashion, two identities that are experienced simultaneously will become more highly associated and integrated. An integrated "working mother" identity is forged by both individual experiences (such as holding a sleeping infant while sending work-related e-mails from home) and institutional experiences ("Take our daughters to work" days).

Brands can help to resolve identity conflicts. The feminine and stylish software engineer, for example, may be drawn to the feminine-themed office product brand See Jane Work. Using a rose gold paperclip, for example, is a small flourish unlikely to be noticed by colleagues, yet it brings a moment of joy by bridging (and celebrating) two identities that might otherwise be in conflict. Similarly, our earlier example of Connor, an office worker who identifies as rebellious, might sip from his Harley-Davidson mug while at work, gratified by bridging two identities. Brands may find success in extending into categories in which the brand offers a highly specific salve to identity conflict. At first glance, a Patagonia branded briefcase (available for purchase at the time of writing) might seem odd, but is appealing to environmentally aware outdoor enthusiasts (the brand's core target) who nevertheless spend their days in an office environment.

Principle 4. Use the Brand to Compensate for Threats to the Self-Concept

Like a household thermostat, the self-concept is actively regulated around a person's view of him- or herself as informed by the motives of coherence, agency, and communion. When the self-concept is threatened by bad experiences or personal challenges, gaps are exposed between the actual versus ideal way the consumer sees herself. Such gaps feel unpleasant and motivate a search for ways to compensate in order to restore the desired self-concept.[10] Brands offer one such way to compensate. In one scholarly study, consumers whose agency self-view (e.g., intelligence) was threatened subsequently chose products more reflective of intelligence (e.g., a fine writing instrument) as a way of compensating for the perceived shortcoming.[11] In another such study, consumers who made an embarrassing purchase (such as *The Complete Idiot's Guide to Improving Your IQ*) later gravitated toward products that counteracted the embarrassing impression that was created by the initial purchase (such as *Scientific American*).[12]

Brands can help consumers to repair their sense of self by amplifying an already stable aspect of the self or building connections to a new aspect of self. Further, brands can offer both direct as well as indirect forms of compensation. That is, compensation may work on a symbolic level, and brands may offer many ways for consumers to repair and preserve their preferred way of seeing themselves. For example, the newly unemployed worker might well prefer products that enhance his sense of competence outside the workplace, such as those highlighted in Home Depot's "More Doing" ad campaign. Similarly, Lean Cuisine's "Weigh This" ad campaign pivoted away from the self-threat of obesity to connect the brand to customers' agency motive in terms of inner strength. In one Lean Cuisine ad, various women stand near a scale but instead of weighing themselves, they weigh their personal accomplishments.

Strong self-brand connections benefit the company not only by driving purchase, but also by protecting the company in a time of crisis. The most ardent followers will stay loyal and actively defend the brand, just as they would a close friend who runs into trouble.[13] In the aftermath of Samsung's exploding battery crisis in 2016, passionate smartphone customers defended the brand on social media and advocated faith in the brand's engineering prowess, in no small way contributing to the success of the 2017 follow-on smartphone that fixed the battery problem.

Principle 5: Design Distinct and Exclusive Brand Communities

To achieve communion, the ideal brand community is distinct, exclusive, and intermediate in size. That is, the brand community has clear boundaries to accentuate both within-group belonging and between-group distinctiveness, and is neither too small nor too large. To be sure, brand growth is nearly always the primary business goal, but a brand community that becomes too large fails to meet consumers' need for distinctiveness (agency). In fact, the strongest brand communities—those that propel the fiercest loyalty—are relatively small.

Basic psychological research shows that groups that are numerical minorities foster greater group identification among members than do majority groups. However, groups that are too small will fail to deliver the benefits of belonging. Thus, the ideal brand community shows a U-shaped relationship between group size and brand engagement, with a group that is neither too small nor too large delivering the greatest engagement. The key insight is that agency and communion sit in a state of dynamic tension. To quote a recent scholarly summary: "As group membership becomes more and more inclusive, the need for inclusion is satisfied, but the need for differentiation is activated; conversely, as inclusiveness decreases, the differentiation need is reduced but the need for inclusion is activated."[14]

Along these lines, a scholarly study by Abrams found that the greatest engagement among music fan communities occurred with music genres that were neither too mainstream nor too niche, but instead featured an intermediate level of exclusivity.[15]

In addition, the strongest brand communities have a brand foil—a competitor that clearly defines what the brand is *not*. Consider the Harley-Davidson brand community in the 1950s and 1960s. The rugged, masculine, counterculture aspects of the brand image represented an in-group that was both small and clearly positioned against a majority out-group comprising conformist, middle-class society. Similarly, the Apple brand community in the 1980s and 1990s was small yet positioned prominently against IBM and Microsoft. These earlier eras were arguably the halcyon days of passion among the Harley-Davidson and Apple brand communities. Brands that go on to become market leaders face a correspondingly more difficult time delineating and maintaining a brand community, not only because calling out competitors is anathema (Coca-Cola never mentions Pepsi in its brand communications), but also because the very size of the brand community fails to deliver on the individual distinctiveness side. The Apple brand currently exemplifies this situation of being a victim of its own success. With market leadership comes a weakening of the brand community, as Apple has seen in recent years.

Principle 6: Use Multifaceted Brand Storytelling

Because human memory is constantly changing in terms of what is currently activated, and because the self-concept is a vastly larger knowledge structure than the brand image, any effort to insert the brand into the self-concept requires a sustained effort. Put simply, the brand is easily crowded out of memory. One way to address this problem is frequent advertising, a tried-and-true tactic that is already widely used. Another way to strengthen and enlarge connections in memory is to use more varied content in brand communications, which widens the range of associations between the self-concept and the brand image. Apple powerfully broadened its brand image with its "Think Different" campaign in 1997, which featured over two dozen iconoclastic personalities, among them Einstein, Gandhi, and Picasso (https://www.youtube.com/watch?v=cFEarBzelBs). Because knowledge of these colorfully complex individuals was widespread, connecting them to the Apple brand image resulted in a substantial widening of potential insertion points into consumers' memory. Moreover, by leveraging consumers' admiration of such creative geniuses, Apple tapped into consumers' aspiration to elevate their own self-concept to the level of creative genius.

Because stories are powerfully memorable (lists of information are more easily recalled when couched in story form), storytelling remains a time-tested way of inserting brands into consumer memory (see Chapter 11 for more on the impact of storytelling). Chrysler's "Born of Fire" ad, mentioned earlier, told a "who we are" story of the struggles, scrappiness, and solidarity of the citizens of Detroit, emphasizing a resilient spirit that was inspirational in the aftermath of the Great Recession. Smart brands increasingly use social media for storytelling that over time injects fresh content and complexity into the brand image. The more distinct ways a brand image can connect to the self-concept, the bigger the impact on sales, in part because the brand is less likely to be forgotten or crowded out by competing self-expressive brands.

Principle 7: Incentivize Brand Usage

Because the self-concept grows through passive observation of one's own behavior, mere brand usage becomes a powerful tool for building self-brand connections. It can be very effective to incentivize usage as opposed to mere purchase. Digital applications of loyalty programs such as the Starbucks mobile app, which makes usage more fun, can enhance the perceived self-relevance of the brand simply through passive observation of oneself. The prominent placement of the brand logo, along with incentives to use the app, further drives self-brand connections.

Digital apps have also made it much simpler to offer free trials, which can start the process of self-brand connection through initial usage. For example, a music-streaming service offering a one-month free subscription will lay the groundwork for the consumer to identify with the service. Even before any monetary transaction has been made, using the free service results in passive observation and strengthens self-brand connections in memory, which ultimately drives purchase. The practice of auto-enrollment with opt out for an online subscription is yet another way to build self-brand connections usage. When consumers are automatically signed up for a service, they are more likely to use it at least once before deciding whether to opt out without purchasing, again laying the groundwork for self-brand connections.

SUMMARY

In our hyper-connected world, brands must confront an ever-changing array of challenges. Yet, new opportunities are also emerging. A particularly compelling opportunity centers on making powerful emotional connections to consumers by understanding the psychology of the self. The motive matrix is a new tool rooted in contemporary psychological science. Brands both big and small may benefit from the rigor of motive matrix to guide smart branding decisions.

Neal Roese is the SC Johnson Chair in Global Marketing, Kellogg School of Management, and professor of psychology (courtesy), Weinberg College of Arts and Sciences, both at Northwestern University. His research examines cognitive processes underlying choice, focusing on how people think about decision options, make predictions about the future, and revise understandings of the past. He holds a PhD in social psychology from the University of Western Ontario (Canada).

Wendi Gardner is an associate professor of psychology and associate professor of learning science, Weinberg College of Arts and Sciences, Northwestern University. Her research focuses on the centrality of social inclusion to the self. She holds a PhD in social psychology from Ohio State University.

NOTES

1. Harrigan, P., U. Evers, M. P. Morgan, and T. Daly (2018), "Customer Engagement and the Relationship between Involvement, Engagement, Self-brand Connection and Brand Usage Intent," *Journal of Business Research* 88, 388–396. https://doi.org/10.1016/j.jbusres.2017.11.046.
2. Greenwald, A. G., and M. R. Banaji (1989), "The Self as a Memory System: Powerful, but Ordinary," *Journal of Personality and Social Psychology* 57(1), 41–54. http://dx.doi.org/10.1037/0022-3514.57.1.41.
3. Verplanken, B., and R. W. Holland (2002), "Motivated Decision Making: Effects of Activation and Self-Centrality of Values on Choices and Behavior," *Journal of Personality and Social Psychology* 82(3), 434–447. http://dx.doi.org/10.1037/0022-3514.82.3.434.
4. Mittal, B. (2015), "Self-Concept Clarity: Exploring Its Role in Consumer Behavior," *Journal of Economic Psychology* 46, 98–110. https://doi.org/10.1016/j.joep.2014.11.003.
5. Emery, L. F., C. Walsh, and E. B. Slotter (2015), "Knowing Who You Are and Adding to It: Reduced Self-Concept Clarity Predicts Reduced Self-Expansion," *Social Psychological and Personality Science* 6(3), 259–266. http://dx.doi.org/10.1177/1948550614555029.

6. Morewedge, C. K., and C. E. Giblin (2015), "Explanations of the Endowment Effect: An Integrative Review," *Trends in Cognitive Sciences* 19(6), 339–348. https://doi.org/10.1016/j.tics.2015.04.004.

7. Gawronski, B., G. V. Bodenhausen, and A. P. Becker (2007), "I Like It, Because I Like Myself: Associative Self-Anchoring and Post-decisional Change of Implicit Evaluations," *Journal of Experimental Social Psychology* 43(2), 221–232. https://doi.org/10.1016/j.jesp.2006.04.001.

8. Swann Jr., W. B., and J. Bosson (2010), "Self and Identity." In *Handbook of Social Psychology*, 5th edition, Eds. S. T. Fiske, D. T. Gilbert, and G. Lindzey, New York: McGraw-Hill, 589–628.

9. A. Mathur, G. P. Moschis, and E. Lee (2006), "Life Events and Brand Preference Changes," *Journal of Consumer Behaviour* 3(2), 129–148. https://doi.org/10.1002/cb.128.

10. Mandel, N., D. D. Rucker, J. Levav, and A. D. Galinsky (2017), "The Compensatory Consumer Behavior Model: How Self-Discrepancies Drive Consumer Behavior," *Journal of Consumer Psychology* 27(1), 133–146. https://doi.org/10.1016/j.jcps.2016.05.003.

11. Gao, L. S., S. C. Wheeler, and B. Shiv (2009), "The 'Shaken Self': Product Choices as a Means of Restoring Self-View Confidence," *Journal of Consumer Research* 36(1), 29–38. www.jstor.org/stable/10.1086/596028.

12. Blair, S., and N. J. Roese (2013), "Balancing the Basket: The Role of Shopping Basket Composition in Embarrassment," *Journal of Consumer Research* 40(40), 676–691. https://www.jstor.org/stable/10.1086/671761.

13. Lisjak, M., A. Y. Lee, and W. L. Gardner (2012), "When a Threat to the Brand Is a Threat to the Self: The Importance of Brand Identification and Implicit Self-Esteem in Predicting Defensiveness," *Personality and Social Psychology Bulletin* 38(9), 1120–1132. https://doi.org/10.1177/0146167212445300.

14. Leonardelli, G. L., C. L. Pickett, and M. B. Brewer (2010), "Optimal Distinctiveness Theory: A Framework for Social Identity, Social Cognition, and Intergroup Relations," *Advances in Experimental Social Psychology* 43, 63–113. https://doi.org/10.1016/S0065-2601(10)43002-6. https://doi.org/10.1016/S0065-2601(10)43002-6

15. Abrams, D. (2009), "Social Identity on a National Scale: Optimal Distinctiveness and Young People's Self-Expression through Musical Preference," *Group Processes and Intergroup Relations* 12(3), 303–317. https://doi.org/10.1177/1368430209102841.

CHAPTER 10

BUILDING STRONG BRANDS THROUGH ADVERTISING STRATEGY IN THE ONLINE AGE

BRIAN STERNTHAL

Brand building often entails a significant investment in advertising. In the United States, media advertising is expected to grow from $195 billion in 2016 to $245.6 billion in 2020,[1] and worldwide it is expected to increase from $550 billion to $724 billion.[2] Advertising spending online is particularly noteworthy—it has increased from about $21.2 billion to over $88 billion in the past decade,[3] and in 2017 it surpassed TV as the leading advertising medium.[4] The expectation is that search will continue to be the dominant online medium, with a predicted 43 percent share of advertising revenue in 2020, followed by banner advertising with about half that revenue, and with social media coming in third.[5]

In addition, the forecast is for programmatic advertising to increase in the United States from $25.48 billion in 2016 to $45.72 billion in 2019.[6] This type of advertising involves real-time bidding for digital advertising space served to consumers whom advertisers have targeted based on their online behavior. By contrast, TV ad spending is expected to remain the same or drop slightly in the next several years, reflecting a loss of viewership among those under 35 years of age, a demographic coveted by many advertisers.[7]

These trends raise a number of issues regarding the role of advertising strategies and institutions in building brands. One pertains to the function of advertising agencies. The four major advertising houses—WPP, Publicis, Omnicom, and Interpublic—have reported that organic growth is flat. Advertisers complain that agencies are not nimble enough to produce the timely, micro-targeted online messages needed to create a positive short-term return on investment. Another issue relates to the growing use of online advertising, and particularly programmatic advertising, which typically focuses on brand attributes. This approach presents a problem for major brands that often are at parity in terms of product attributes and compete on nuanced insights about how a brand and category fits into consumers' lives. Finally, there is a growing concern about the transparency of online advertising buying. Juniper Research estimates that in 2018 advertisers spent about $19 billion for ads that were never seen by consumers.[8] The absence of a reliable way to confirm online ad placements and exposures has prompted advertisers to concentrate their advertising expenditures with trusted media (Google and Facebook), and to explore the use of blockchain applications, which provide a permanent, decentralized, and shared digital ledger that continuously updates transactions across a network.[9]

In this chapter, we examine three issues related to advertising and brand building in the online age. First, we discuss consumer insight that is the basis for advertising strategy. Next, we assess the use of insight in designing creative executions. Finally, we examine how media are used strategically to transmit advertising messages.

CONSUMER INSIGHT

Consumer insight involves the consideration of three distinct types of analysis. One pertains to the motivational factors that prompt the purchase and consumption of categories and brands. A second type of insight depicts the process by which consumers use advertising information to make brand judgments. Finally, consumer insight entails an analysis of the diffusion process by which consumers share brand information.

Understanding Fundamental Motivations

Consider advertising for three brands of chocolate candy. Advertising for Snickers shows an unproductive individual resolving a problem by eating a Snickers bar, which pertains to competence (https://www.youtube.com/watch?v=fKkMLc5qVsY). Hershey's Kisses depicts people sharing the brand, which implies it enhances community (https://youtu.be/AbOd-fcl6Rw). And Reese's presents a close-up of the brand where bites are taken to expose the peanut butter filling, emphasizing contentment (https://www.youtube.com/watch?v=VZSsgLl978E). We refer to these fundamental motivations as the 3C framework (see Chapter 9 for a related discussion).

Competence refers to consumers' ability to achieve their goals. A brand can enhance consumers' feeling of competence when it promotes self-efficacy:

that is, consumers' belief that they are capable of achieving their goals. Snickers' advertising suggests that consuming the brand will enhance self-efficacy among hungry consumers. Another approach that brands use to engender a feeling of competence is self-validation. A good example is GoldieBlox, a construction toy that validates preteen girls' ability to apply science, technology, engineering, and math principles (https://www.youtube.com/watch?v= QvOmco5FEoQ&feature=youtu.be). Finally, competence can involve the perception of control, which reminds consumers that they have discretion in making consumption choices. Control is the basis for Burger King's "Have it your way" campaign.

A second fundamental motivation is *community*, which involves collaboration or affiliation with others in achieving a goal. Tough Mudder is an obstacle course event where the primary goal is not only to complete the course, but also to help others do the same. Competence is a less salient motivation because participants' performance is not timed.

A third fundamental motivation is *contentment*, which refers to the desire to experience the positive feelings that result from using a product or service. Häagen-Dazs ice cream promises contentment by promoting the ingredients that make the taste of the product exceptional, and Ben & Jerry's ice cream promotes contentment by describing its unique flavors.

Although brands typically focus on a fundamental motivation, other motivations may also be relevant. Finishing the obstacle course also engenders a feeling of competence for Tough Mudder participants, and successfully completing a GoldieBlox construction task also results in a feeling of contentment.

Understanding these fundamental motivations provides a way to align a brand's content strategy with consumers' motivation for using the brand. Consider the light ice cream produced by Häagen-Dazs. It was produced using a special technology to break up the butterfat, so that less was needed to make the light version taste as good as regular Häagen-Dazs with fewer calories per pint. By contrast, Halo Top is high-protein, low-sugar ice cream that has 360 or fewer calories per pint—far less than that of Häagen-Dazs or Ben & Jerry's. In 2017, Halo Top became the pint leader in supermarkets, whereas Häagen-Dazs light did not attract substantial demand.

One explanation for this disparity relates to the alignment of the brands' position with consumers' fundamental motivation for consuming it. Halo Top satisfies consumers' desire for competence (fitness) by enabling them to consume an entire pint that is packed with protein but has relatively few calories. By contrast, consumption of Häagen-Dazs was motivated by contentment. Producing a light version of the brand—even one that tasted as good as the flagship product—was perceived as undermining contentment. The successful introduction of Häagen-Dazs Five, which was positioned as containing only milk, cream, sugar, eggs, and cocoa, supports this view. These natural ingredients framed "healthful" in a manner that was consistent with contentment for this brand.

Processing Advertising Messages and Brand Judgments

Another type of insight pertains to the process through which consumers learn about brands from advertising, and how they use this knowledge to make brand judgments. For example, an ad for Hanes boxer brief underwear (Figure 10.1) supports the claim of exceptional comfort by featuring lightweight mesh material that is breathable and does not ride up. This appeal is likely to be effective if consumers value comfort and find reasons to believe this benefit is compelling. However, consumers, and especially those with significant prior knowledge about the category and brand, might engage in a more detailed evaluation of the information presented in the message by assessing its content in relation to what they know. This analysis might cause them to question the ad's assertions based on their prior knowledge, possibly by expressing skepticism that a mesh fabric would be comfortable. This suggests that persuasion

Figure 10.1
Hanes Boxer Brief Ad

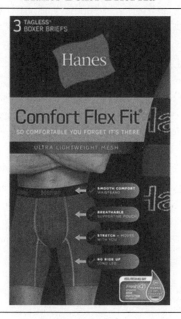

in response to advertising often involves some degree of self-persuasion: the impact of an ad depends on the extent to which information about a brand resonates with and enhances consumers' prior knowledge.

The premise that the persuasive impact of advertising is often attributable to self-persuasion implies that prompting consumers to advocate for a brand or category is an effective means of persuasion. Consider an anti-smoking public service ad aired in Thailand, which showed young kids walking up to adults who are smoking in public and asking them for a light (https://youtu.be/YC8ANzimf_Q). The smokers typically rejected this request and presented reasons why kids should not smoke. Later, the kids handed the smokers a note asking them why they worried about kids smoking but not their own habit. All smokers kept the note, and many threw away the cigarette they were smoking. Inquiries about how to stop smoking increased 40 percent in response to this campaign.[10] Prompting consumers to rehearse their own counterattitudinal thoughts induced a reconsideration of their prior attitudes and behavior.

The impact of advertising messages on consumers' brand evaluations depends not only on the message content and consumers' response to that content, but also by how that content is framed. One approach to framing involves matching the consumer's motivation to achieve competence, community, or contentment with the manner in which the brand benefit is presented. Consider two commercials for Tampax tampons. One shows a man and a woman boating when the boat begins to leak. The woman cleverly uses a tampon to plug the hole (https://youtu.be/8a3sbk9BE9o). The other Tampax commercial shows a woman in a white dress opening the medicine cabinet and taking a Tampax tampon from a carton. In the next scene, she walks rapidly to work, without taking notice of those around her who are signaling that her skirt is caught in her underwear, exposing her panties. When she arrives, she glances in a mirror, notices the problem, and confidently deals with it (https://youtu.be/KszJ3FEkWq8).

Both commercials reflect consumers' motivation to achieve competence related to control. Deciding which of these messages is likely to prompt a more favorable opinion about Tampax requires a knowledge of consumers' orientation in achieving control. When the consumer adopts a safety orientation, referred to as "prevention," the boat commercial is more effective: Tampax tampons plug leaks, which keeps the user safe. By contrast, when consumers' orientation is accomplishment, referred to as "promotion," wearing a white dress and moving quickly are actions that offer a better fit because they reflect rapid and successful progress toward achieving confidence.

Fit between consumers' orientation and a message frame creates a positive feeling that is transferred to the evaluation of the brand.[11] Thus, for those who view tampons primarily as a way to feel safe, the message frame used in the Tampax boat commercial fits with this goal, producing a positive feeling. This feeling is transferred to the brand and enhances its evaluation. Similarly, for those who view tampons as a way to enable them to confidently accomplish their tasks, the white dress commercial would provide the better fit and thus enhance evaluations.

The view that both message content and framing can influence brand evaluation raises the question of when each process is dominant. Consumers typically base their brand evaluations primarily on the message content and their prior opinions, unless this prompts them to be uncertain about their evaluations. When this occurs, they rely on their feelings about how they made the judgment in evaluating the brand.[12] This observation suggests that a greater reliance on feelings about how brand judgments were made occurs for online advertising than for advertising vetted by traditional media.

A third process consumers use to make brand evaluations involves perceptual processing (see Chapter 7, "Brand Design and Design Thinking," for a detailed discussion). This occurs when the brand choice is habitual or when consumers have low involvement in a product category. In these instances, consumers rely on perceptual cues to make a judgment with minimal processing of the message or retrieval of prior knowledge. Consider Tropicana orange juice, which many consumers purchased based on a few perceptual cues, such as package color and visuals. When the brand changed the packaging to make it more contemporary (Figure 10.2), sales fell about 20 percent within six weeks.[13] Some consumers did not recognize the Tropicana packaging in brand advertising or in-store. Others felt it was not the product they were familiar with, which reduced their desire to purchase the brand.

Diffusion, Community, and Sharing of Information

Consumers sometimes share their brand knowledge and preferences with others, a process referred to as "diffusion." Research suggests that most sharing of information both on- and offline occurs among a relatively small number of groups that include family members, co-workers, college friends, and neighbors. Within these groups, the vast majority of people have close ties with 5 to 10 people; in fact, about 80 percent of their communications are with these individuals. As a result, the number of *cascades*—instances in which one person shares with another—is very low. For Yahoo, Facebook, and many other social media sites, 96 percent of cascades involve no sharing, or sharing with one or two people, and 99 percent of cascades involve fewer than seven.[14]

Figure 10.2
Tropicana Packaging Change

BEFORE   AFTER

If sharing is limited, how does information go viral? How has the "Gangnam Style" video achieved over three billion views since 2012? How did the Dollar Shave Club's (DSC) initial YouTube video register over 25 million views? Current evidence suggests that diffusion of information in most cases involves an advertiser exposing information to many consumers using broadcast (i.e., one-to-many), who then share this information with several others. The rapid diffusion of the "Gangnam Style" video is likely to have occurred because it was presented on broadcast media, including YouTube, talk shows, and news programs. The DSC video presented a message that resonated with consumers (less costly blades and razors) in a sufficiently entertaining and novel way to achieve notice on Reddit, an online news aggregator, which exposed a substantial number of Reddit's 400 million unique visitors to the DSC video (https://www.youtube.com/watch?v=ZUG9qYTJMsI).

Although this analysis suggests that broadcast is essential for the rapid diffusion of a brand message, there are conditions when the use of social media is sufficient for diffusion. This occurs when there is a community in place, as is the case for political parties, online gamers, and runners. In these situations, the number of cascades is substantial, as there are close-knit community ties among a group of people with similar interests. At some point, sustaining growth may require firms to attract individuals who are not part of the community. In these instances, broadcast media such as TV or advocacy by an individual with a large number of followers (for example, on Twitter) is needed to sustain brand growth.

For the first six years of its existence, Tough Mudder grew participation in its obstacle-course events using only Facebook, because the organization knew there was a community of potential participants who engaged in extreme physical activity in a community context, including military personnel, firefighters, and police. These individuals had a wide network of other people with whom they communicated regularly. However, once the core participant communities had been tapped, Tough Mudder developed TV programs, commercials, and other broadcast media to recruit additional participants.

CREATIVE STRATEGY: USING INSIGHT TO DESIGN PERSUASIVE MESSAGING

Now that we understand more about consumer insight, we turn our attention to creative strategy. The first step is the creative brief, which includes a statement of a brand's position (target, insight, position; see Chapter 1 for more details) and provides guidance about executing that position in advertising (tonality, mandatories, equities). Following is an illustration of a creative brief for Burger King:

> *Ad Objective:* To grow the frequency of consumers' visits to Burger King.
>
> *Consumer Target:* Men ages 18–34.
>
> *Consumer Insight:* Target individuals feel that they have little control over their lives. They appreciate when they can specify their preferences and have them satisfied.
>
> *Position:* Burger King is the quick-serve restaurant with great-tasting food that is the most satisfying because Burger King's large portions and tasty options empower you to have it your way.
>
> *Brand Personality:* Fun, irreverent.
>
> *Mandatories:* Food visuals with appetite appeal.
>
> *Equities:* Have it your way, self-absorbed spokespeople.

In designing creative strategy, we consider three strategic elements: gaining consumers' attention to a commercial's content, stimulating consumers to elaborate or amplify the message content, and ensuring the linkage between the brand name and its benefit.

Gaining Attention

The initial focus in designing an ad is to develop a creative execution that draws attention to information in the message. Presenting information that is novel, or presenting it in a surprising and unexpected manner, is often used to gain attention. Humor can serve this purpose. For example, Le Trèfle, a French brand of toilet paper, attempted to stem the decline in category use by showing that despite the replacement of paper with a tablet computer for many tasks, paper still has an important role in the bathroom (https://youtu. be/SxOdSysbxwM). The campaign generated 25 million YouTube views in 10 days, and Le Trèfle's sales increased by 130 percent.[15] Humor successfully drew attention to the fact that the brand marketed toilet paper.

Threat appeals provide another means of gaining attention. Threat is often employed to focus people's attention on the dire consequences of not complying with the message advocacy. For example, anti-smoking ads often depict the blackened lungs and shortened life that result from smoking. The concern in using this approach is that consumers might engage in fear control, which involves activating idiosyncratic ways of managing fear. For example, some smokers might light a cigarette as a means of calming the fear induced by an anti-smoking ad. A more compelling use of threat is to focus the message on the danger and then provide an effective means of overcoming it. For example, an Allstate ad shows a couple enjoying ice-skating at an outdoor rink. When one of them falls against the building, the impact dislodges snow from the roof above where their car is parked, damaging it. The commercial then announces how Allstate solves this problem (https://www.youtube.com/watch?v=VSOlzbK27-8&feature=youtu.be).

Amplification

Paying attention to an ad is not sufficient for advertising to be persuasive in most situations. Message recipients must also be able to relate the advertising message to their prior knowledge about the category and brand, as well as to their goals. This process is called "amplification," or elaboration. We describe a variety of commonly used approaches to prompt amplification of a message and identify the situations in which each is appropriate.

Announce the Brand Benefit   When a brand has a benefit that offers a point of difference from the competition and is important to consumers, the task is simply to link the brand to that benefit. This approach, termed "hard-sell advertising" by the Ted Bates ad agency that popularized it, is illustrated by advertising that states, "Buy this brand, get this benefit." Famous campaigns using this approach include "Rolaids spells relief" and M&M's "Melt in your mouth, not in your hand."

Amplify the Benefit   For many brands, the benefit requires amplification to be persuasive. The nature of the amplification depends on whether the brand benefit is framed to fit with a promotion or prevention orientation. Rent the Runway provides a way to rent rather than buy designer clothing for a variety of occasions. To illustrate this benefit, Rent the Runway used print advertising that framed the benefit in terms of accomplishment desired by those with a promotion orientation: the brand enabled users to convert their closets into an office that could be used to launch a startup. Presenting this less obvious benefit might prompt consumers to think about Rent the Runway's more obvious benefits, such as accommodating changes in taste and fashion economically. By contrast, DSC advertised its benefit in terms of safety that fits with a prevention orientation: the brand helps consumers save time and money when buying razors, blades, and other bathroom products (https:// youtu.be/FGF8ccvFZ-8).

Provide Proof of a Brand Benefit by Presenting an Attribute Reason to Believe It
In most instances, a reason to believe the claimed benefit helps persuade consumers about a brand's benefit. Along these lines, Grainger developed a radio advertising campaign to inform consumers who work in the areas of maintenance, repair, and operations (MRO) that Grainger has their back because of the breadth of MRO products it inventories and its expert service. Separate ads describe different products and services, all implying Grainger provides reliable support for those engaged in MRO.

Clarify the Superiority of a Brand Benefit by Comparing It to Other Brands
Another means of amplifying a brand's benefit is to compare a brand to its alternatives. Typically, such comparison involves a follower brand comparing its benefits to a category leader. Thus, Surface Pro 3 tablet compared itself to the MacBook Air by describing features it had that the MacBook Air did not: a touchscreen, a detachable screen, and a pen (https://www.youtube. com/watch?v=DsJijtU4Lxc&feature=youtu.be). Leading brands also compare themselves to followers. This occurs when consumers are well aware of a brand's competitors, and as such comparison offers the clearest means of communicating brand superiority. Finally, comparison can be used to convey product improvement. This entails showing how a brand outperforms its prior model. Duracell followed this strategy by claiming superior longevity of its new battery by comparing it to the performance of its predecessor.

Illustrate Brand Performance When It Cannot Be Demonstrated: Analogy
Another approach to comparison involves the use of analogies. This device is
typically used to inform consumers of a feature they are not familiar with by
comparing it to something that is understood. Along these lines, the Hanes
men's boxer brief campaign described earlier included a commercial that drew
attention to how Hanes provides protection and comfort by using an analogy showing a female kangaroo protecting her young offspring in her pouch
(https://youtu.be/7zHVzFBsSs0).

Provide a Reason to Believe a Brand Benefit: Spokespeople   Under Armour
grew its basketball shoe sales using advertising that featured star player Stephen
Curry, and Nike was highly successful when Michael Jordan promoted its brand.
Although spokespeople can enhance the effectiveness of advertising, they can also
undermine it. The effectiveness of spokespeople is diluted when they advertise for
many brands. Many consumers mistakenly attributed a McDonald's Super Bowl
ad featuring Michael Jordan and Larry Bird to Nike, which was especially problematic because Bird was a spokesperson for Converse basketball shoes. Spokespeople can defect, as Paul Marcarelli did when he became the spokesperson for
Sprint after years of advocating for Verizon by asking, "Can you hear me now?"
Spokespeople can discredit the brand, as Subway sandwiches spokesperson Jared
Fogle did when he was convicted of child molestation. Finally, spokespeople can
die, leaving the brand without an important link to its equity, as occurred when
Smith Barney's long-time spokesperson John Houseman passed unexpectedly.

Demonstrate a Performance Benefit: Story Grammar   For some brands, the
reason to believe a benefit requires proof of brand performance. Story grammar provides a way to present this proof. It entails identifying a problem and
showing how the brand successfully overcomes the problem. For example,
Mercedes-Benz aired an ad documenting its superior handling in snow by
showing a dad driving his son to a movie in a Mercedes sedan during a snowstorm. There are no cars on the road, but the son keeps repeating that his date
will meet him at the theatre. When they arrive, neither his date nor anyone else
is there. As they are about to leave, a Mercedes SUV arrives with the boy's date,
proving that Mercedes can make it through a snowstorm while other vehicles
cannot (https://youtu.be/Uwo_E7GFd-A).

Brand Linkage

Even when consumers pay attention to a commercial and amplify the message content, the absence of a link between the brand and its benefit can

undermine a message's persuasiveness. One factor that weakens brand linkage is the late identification (ID) of the category and brand. Late ID invites viewers to think about things other than the advertised brand or category. Consider an ad showing a preteen boy winning several points while taking a tennis lesson from an instructor. This prompts the instructor to go all-out to win a point, which he celebrates as the boy's parents—tennis greats Andre Agassi and Steffi Graf—arrive to pick up their son. The ad closes with a voiceover saying, "The right genes make all the difference," as the slogan "Genworth Financial, built on GE heritage" appears. Although viewers often remember the story, almost none recall the brand (https://youtu.be/o1o81K6J1g0).

Another factor that undermines linkage of the brand to the benefit presented in an ad is creative execution that may be too similar to that used in other ads in the category. Ads for upscale hotels often show the lobby, the restaurant, or a guest room with views, as illustrated in the ads for the Ritz-Carlton and the Four Seasons hotels shown in Figure 10.3. If anything, such undifferentiated ads build demand for the upscale hotel category rather than a particular brand.

The failure to link a brand to the benefit presented in advertising is less of a problem than it was a decade ago. This is because consumers whose attention has been attracted to some element in an ad can usually use this information to find it on YouTube or another online site, thus providing a means of linking a brand and benefit. Allstate's "Mayhem" commercials, which illustrate the danger people face when driving, feature a late ID of the brand. This did not undermine brand linkage because there were over 20 million views on YouTube during the first year of airing.

Figure 10.3
Print Ads for the Ritz-Carlton and the Four Seasons Hotels

THE 4MS OF MEDIA STRATEGY: TRANSMITTING MESSAGE CONTENT

Media strategy involves reaching the brand's target using vehicles that maximize engagement with the advertising message. Four objectives typically guide the development of a media strategy, referred to here as the "4Ms": *matching, monopolizing, moment*, and *mindset*.

Matching

Matching entails selecting media that reach the brand's target efficiently. Historically, matching was a two-step process. First, media that addressed a brand's communication objectives were selected. If a brand required a demonstration of how it performed, TV or a YouTube video might be the most appropriate medium, whereas if the brand sought approval by friends, social media such as Facebook might be chosen. Next identified were vehicles that matched the demographic profile of the target (e.g., age, income, geographic locale) most efficiently—the lowest cost per thousand for target individuals reached. For example, if TV were the medium that best matched the brand's communication needs, the vehicles would be TV time slots (e.g., daytime, prime time, late night) that most efficiently attracted the brand's demographic target.

With the emergence of digital media, a programmatic approach has gained popularity to match consumers and messages. For example, consider a campaign by the state of Tennessee. Consumers' online activity was used to segment prospective visitors by characteristics, including their hometown, interest in outdoor activities, taste in music, and food preferences. When consumers matching the profile of one of these segments went to a web site, the Tennessee tourism site made a real-time bid to present a video clip to that individual. If the tourism site was the highest bid, *pre-roll* creative—video clips developed ahead of time that matched specific consumer interest—would be presented. Consumers interested in music would be shown clips of the Grand Ole Opry, and those interested in outdoor activities were presented scenes of people hiking or boating (https://youtu.be/0t8dla6ltFs). Thus, rather than matching a consumer's profile with that of the audience for a publication, programmatic media serves ads to individuals targeted by the brand at whatever site they happen to be visiting.

Although programmatic media and creative enable the advertiser to tailor the message to an individual consumer's interests, several precautions should be taken when using this approach. Because a programmatic approach presents brand advertising at the site the consumer selects, caution is necessary to exclude web sites that might not fit with the brand's equity. Tide detergent would not want its ads to appear on a web site that featured a story about teens' consumption of Tide pods. In addition, current use of programmatic with pre-roll appears to be most effective when presenting attribute information, as is the case for Tennessee tourism. When a campaign relies on insight about consumer emotions, it is difficult to identify which consumers will be responsive given their online behavior. For example, it is not apparent which consumer online behaviors would predict the target for a Mr. Clean commercial showing a woman's reaction when her husband has cleaned the refrigerator and mopped the floor (https://youtu.be/XkvmUjKz01g).

Whichever media are selected, matching also entails making a decision about the reach and frequency of advertising. *Reach* is the percent of a target exposed at least once during a month to a program containing an advertising message for the brand, and *frequency* is the average number of times these people are exposed to the message during that time. Reach is used to enhance consumers' awareness of a brand, and to provide an occasional reminder when the brand is known but infrequently purchased. Frequency is employed when the goal is to enhance chances that consumers consider a brand when making a category purchase—that is, the likelihood that the brand is in their consideration set. Frequency is also appropriate in cases of repeat purchase, so that exposure to brand advertising occurs close to the moment when consumers are decisional. Finally, frequency is appropriate when consumers' decisions are unplanned, because it enhances the likelihood of exposure to advertising occurring in close proximity to the time they are making a purchase decision.

These considerations imply that reach would be appropriate for brands such as Tide detergent, which have a stable brand position and relatively infrequent purchase. By contrast, substantial frequency would also be required for a quick-serve restaurant such as McDonald's, given how often consumers are decisional about which restaurant to patronize. Finally, tire manufacturers such as Goodyear rely on frequency because purchase in this category is often unplanned.

In deciding on how much reach versus frequency to schedule each month, it is useful to examine the response function related to exposure frequency. Initial exposures to advertising that are relevant to consumers prompt thoughts related to the arguments made in the message. These thoughts are likely to increase recipients' favorableness toward the advocacy, whether measured in terms of brand preference or brand purchase. As ad exposures continue to mount, advertising effectiveness asymptotes and declines. People have learned what they can from advertising, and tedium reduces message processing. If consumers rehearse thoughts about the brand, they are likely to be their own thoughts, which are typically less favorable than thoughts based on content presented in advertising messages, which is designed specifically with the intent to persuade. For example, people might think, "I know this already." The result of not rehearsing the message content—or rehearsing less favorable thoughts than those expressed in the message—is a decline in advertising effectiveness, referred to as "wearout."[16] It occurs most often for media that have loyal audiences and are relatively low in cost, including radio and business-to-business advertising, as well as for online advertising such as display ads, which have an average click-through rate of 0.35 percent across all industries.[17]

In addition to monthly decisions about reach and frequency, matching involves a decision about continuity: that is, when to present advertising over the course of a year. For products that are purchased regularly, such as detergent, advertising is typically placed continuously throughout the year, whereas for seasonal products such as barbeque sauce, most of the advertising weight is placed between Memorial Day and Labor Day, when the majority of category consumption occurs. When a brand has a limited budget, it often uses several flights, which entail presenting advertising for a period (say, two months), followed by a hiatus from advertising, and then another flight. Flighting balances the need for some continuity in advertising throughout the year and a substantial brand presence when advertising is presented. By contrast, using continuity with a relatively small budget often promotes category rather than brand demand.

Monopolizing, Moment, and Mindset

Once there is a match between target and media vehicles, *monopolizing, moment,* and *mindset* serve to enhance consumer engagement. Monopolizing involves driving attention to a brand's advertising by selecting media where a brand can outshout its competition. If larger competitors are using TV to advertise their car dealerships, a smaller dealership might use radio. Even if radio is less efficient in reaching the target than TV, being the dominant advertiser in the category on radio might offset this limitation.

Moment is another means of engaging target consumers by attempting to reach them when the category and brand are salient. Oscar Mayer achieved this goal by having its Wienermobile visit schools at lunchtime to interest kids in its deli meats at a time they would be thinking about lunch. The *Economist* bought space on the tops of buses in major metropolitan areas to catch the attention of executives who might peer out of their office windows and think of the publication's perspective on business issues. Advertising presented at the moment the category is salient to consumers reduces the need for ad frequency to reach people when there is category interest.

Figure 10.4
Absolut Vodka Print Advertising

Finally, mindset enhances consumer engagement by suggesting that the brand and category have a shared interest beyond that directly related to the brand. For example, Absolut Vodka's ad in *ARTnews*, which shows a rendering of the bottle labeled "Absolut Warhol," suggests that the brand and audience have a shared passion for the arts (Figure 10.4).

SUMMARY

A starting point in designing advertising strategy involves considering three types of consumer insight. One entails identifying the fundamental motivations that guide brand preference: competence, community, contentment, or some combination of these. Knowledge of the motivation provides a basis for developing the brand position and evaluating the creative strategy. A second type of insight pertains to how consumers process advertising information in making brand judgments. It entails considering not only the ad content, but also consumers' own thoughts about the content and their feelings about how they arrived at a brand evaluation. A third type pertains to how consumers' brand preferences are shaped by the information they share with others. Typically, consumers only share information with a small number of other people unless there is a community related to a brand. Thus, broadcast advertising is needed for successful diffusion of information.

The execution of advertising strategy involves the design of creative and media strategy. Effective creative requires drawing attention to the message content, selecting a benefit that consumers believe is important, presenting reasons to believe that imply that it dominates competition on this benefit, and including cues to enhance consumers' linkage of the brand to its benefit.

Effective media strategy requires matching the media vehicles to the target, selecting vehicles that enable a brand to dominate its competitors in advertising weight, choosing vehicles that reach people at the moment they are decisional, and identifying vehicles that highlight the interests the brand shares with consumers beyond those related to the product category.

All of these strategies taken together can assist marketers with advertising and brand building in the online age.

Brian Sternthal is the Mondalez Professor (Emeritus) of Marketing and a past chairperson of the Marketing Department at the Kellogg School of Management. He is also a past editor of the Journal of Consumer Research, *an Association for Consumer Research Fellow in Consumer Behavior, and the co-author of* Advertising Strategy *(Copley Custom Textbooks, 2011). He received his BS from McGill University and his PhD from Ohio State University.*

NOTES

1. Statista.com. (2018), "Media Advertising Spending in the United States from 2015 to 2021 (in billion U.S. dollars)."
2. Emarketer.com. https://www.emarketer.com/Report/Worldwide-Ad-Spending-eMarketers-Updated-Estimates-Forecast-20152020/2001916.
3. Statista.com (2018), "Online Advertising Revenue in the United States from 2000 to 2017 (in billion U.S. dollars)."
4. Statista.com (2017), "Digital (Finally) Killed the TV Star" (December 5).

5. https://www.fipp.com/news/insightnews/chart-of-the-week-what-growth-look-digital-arena.

6. Statista.com (2018), "Programmatic Advertising."

7. Analysis of Nielsen data, MarketingCharts.com, 2017.

8. Juniper Research (2017), "Ad Fraud to Cost Advertisers $19 Billion in 2018, Representing 9% of Total Advertising Spend," Juniper Research white paper (September 26). https://www.juniperresearch.com/press/press-releases/ad-fraud-to-cost-advertisers-$19-billion-in-2018.

9. Williams, Henry (2018), "What's an Online Ad Worth? Blockchain Might Help with That," *Wall Street Journal* (June 18). https://www.wsj.com/articles/whats-an-online-ad-worth-blockchain-might-help-with-that-1529326800; Harvey, Campbell (2018), "How Blockchain Technology Changes Marketing," Marketing Science Institute, May 1. http://www.msi.org/video/how-blockchain-technology-changes-marketing; O'Reilly, Lara (2018), "Big Advertisers Embrace Blockchain to Root Out Digital Spending Waste," Williams, Henry (2018), *Wall Street Journal* (June 18). https://www.wsj.com/articles/big-advertisers-embrace-blockchain-to-root-out-digital-spending-waste-1531396800.

10. Neal, Meghan (2012), "Heartbreaking Thai 'Smoking Kids' Anti-Smoking Ad Goes Viral," *New York Daily News* (June 21). http://www.nydailynews.com/news/world/heartbreaking-thai-smoking-kids-anti-smoking-ad-viral-article-1.1100062.

11. Aaker, Jennifer and Angela Lee (2006), "Understanding Regulatory Fit," *Journal of Marketing Research* 43, 15–19.

12. Tybout, Alice M., Brian Sternthal, Prashant Malaviya, Georgios A. Bakamitsos, and Se-Bum Park (2005), "Information Accessibility as a Moderator of Judgments: The Role of Content versus Retrieval Ease," *Journal of Consumer Research* 32, 76–85.

13. Nisen, Max (2013), "This Logo Change Caused Tropicana Sales to Plunge," *Business Insider*, September 3. https://www.businessinsider.com/tropicana-packaging-change-failure-2013-9.

14. See Goel, Sharad, Ashton Anderson, Jake Hofman, and Duncan Watts (2016), "The Structural Virality of Online Diffusion," *Management Science* 62 (January), 1–17.

15. Adforum.com. https://www.adforum.com/creative-work/ad/player/34487550/emma-case-study/le-trefle.

16. Anand, Punam, and Brian Sternthal (1990), "Ease of Message Processing as a Moderator of Repetition Effects in Advertising," *Journal of Marketing Research* 27, 345–353.

17. Volovich, Kristina (2018) "What's a Good Clickthrough Rate? New Benchmark Data for Google Awards," hubspot.com, May 2 (updated). https://blog.hubspot.com/agency/google-adwords-benchmark-data.

CHAPTER 11

DIGITAL BRAND STORYTELLING

MOHANBIR SAWHNEY

In the digital world, consumers are inundated with brand content. With so many brands competing for attention, content that consumers don't find useful or timely is dismissed immediately as noise and easily tuned out. Cutting through the clutter to capture mind and heart share is a very real and pressing challenge for brand marketers today.

And yet, some brand voices are rising above the crowd. Consider the "#LikeAGirl" campaign from Always, the feminine hygiene personal care brand owned by Procter & Gamble (P&G). Instead of talking about its product, Always focused on the negative perceptions associated with what it means to run, throw, or do anything "like a girl." By challenging this stereotype in a multichannel campaign, Always struck a powerful emotional chord with girls and parents worldwide.

The inspiration for this campaign came from research conducted by Always, which found that when girls reach puberty they typically experience a significant drop in self-confidence.[1] Always's response was a cause-related ad campaign that sought to "rewrite the rules" of puberty and bolster the self-confidence of teenage girls. The Always campaign video was one of the top viral ads of 2014, with 54 million views on YouTube alone—and that was before it was shown to the Super Bowl audience.[2]

The success of the Always campaign illustrates the power of digital media to create a conversation between brands and consumers, as well as among communities of consumers. The campaign is also a study in digital brand storytelling best practices. In "#LikeAGirl," Always products are never mentioned. The entire story revolves around addressing the decline in self-esteem among young girls as they mature and providing a narrative that helps make that transition a positive experience rather than a negative one. Always connected its brand to a cause that is very relevant to its brand promise and product category: feminine hygiene products are strongly associated with puberty and the social stigma that comes with transitioning from childhood to womanhood. Always positioned itself as more than a product that offers physical protection—it was able to position itself as a brand that stands for self-confidence and self-esteem. The campaign also associated itself with a cause that consumers care deeply about at an emotional level.

Great brands have always told great stories—think of Starbucks or Harley-Davidson; even when we don't buy the products, we know the stories. These are the timeless truths in branding: success takes great consumer insight, a strong brand promise, and a creative storytelling approach. What has changed is the powerful digital media toolkit that marketers now have at their disposal.

Consider an analogy: Telling a brand story is like painting a landscape. The landscape is the same as before, and so is our judgment of what makes a great painting. However, brand marketers now have the equivalent of a thousand brushes and a million colors to paint a richer landscape. Digital media allows brand stories to be more pervasive, more persistent, and more personalized. But while digital media is a powerful tool, it needs to be used intelligently. A fool with a tool is still a fool, and perhaps even a more dangerous one! In transitioning to new media, we also need to transition to new ways of thinking about content strategy, media strategy, and the role of consumers in brand engagement.

This chapter provides a road map for brand marketers to harness the power of digital media to tell stories that will engage and inspire their customers to drive business results. The chapter begins by making the case for why stories matter and why storytelling is a powerful approach to engage with customers. Next, we discuss what a story looks like and how stories are structured. We then discuss how brands can tell stories by connecting their brand promise and purpose to customer pain and passion points. We present a set of best practices to tell great brand stories. Finally, we discuss digital brand storytelling by presenting the concept of transmedia storytelling—a digital storytelling approach that creates a coordinated story experience that unfolds over multiple media channels.

THE POWER OF STORIES

From the beginning of time, humans have been hard-wired for stories. As Joseph Campbell, the late scholar and writer, observed in *The Hero with a Thousand Faces*, "Throughout the inhabited world, in all times and under every circumstances, the myths of man have flourished; and they have been the living inspiration of whatever else may have appeared out of the activities of the human body and mind. It would not be too much to say that myth is the secret opening through which the inexhaustible energies of the cosmos pour into human cultural manifestation."[3] Brand storytelling draws from this old and venerable tradition.

Stories Are Universal

Indeed, stories are universal. They are a way for people in every culture, religion, and society to talk about themselves, their beliefs, and how they view the world. All the stories that have been written (and will ever be written) can be categorized into basic archetypes. In his voluminous book *The Seven Basic Plots: Why We Tell Stories*, journalist and author Christopher Booker identifies seven archetypical stories that apply equally to ancient mythology, classical literature, and modern fiction. These seven stories are Overcoming the Monster, Rags to Riches, The Quest, Voyage and Return, Comedy, Tragedy, and Rebirth.[4]

These story archetypes are found in digital brand storytelling as well; indeed, in order to resonate, a brand's message must transcend a mere advertisement and become a story that matters to people.

When brands echo one of the story archetypes, they can evoke a visceral reaction. For instance, Nike connects its brand story to Overcoming the Monster. Nike, through its iconic tag line of "Just Do It," urges its customers to overcome their internal limitations (the "monster inside") through fitness and sports. The emotional resonance of the tagline was so strong, though, that people began to adopt it as a "private mantra." *Adweek* observed, "They just did all sorts of things as they strove toward personal goals. These ranged from starting businesses to popping the question, and in some cases extricating themselves from bad relationships."[5] None of these things may have anything to do with athletic wear or running shoes, but by becoming part of people's personal stories, Nike built one of the most powerful brands in the world.

Johnny Walker's "Keep on Walking" campaign, which featured a spoken-word rendition of Woody Guthrie's "This Land Is Your Land" set to a montage of the American experience, is the archetypal hero's Quest. It inspired people by showcasing the cultural diversity that can best be experienced by traveling across America. When done effectively, stories can affect brand perceptions and brand preferences because of how a story makes people *feel*. When people connect emotionally, their guard is down, which allows the message to penetrate more deeply than if only the intellect is engaged. As Maya Angelou famously observed: "I've learned that people will forget what you said, people will forget what you did, but people will never forget how you made them feel."

Stories Inspire

Stories create an emotional connection as opposed to giving a sales pitch or dumping information on customers. General Electric, in its award-winning "Childlike Imagination" campaign, evoked a childlike sense of wonder for its technologies that may otherwise seem unsuited for consumer advertising.[6] This strategy worked because GE wasn't selling its technology; it was selling its story with that all-important emotional connection. "You can't sell if you can't tell," explained Beth Comstock, a former vice chair of GE who also served as its chief marketing and commercial officer. "People don't want to be sold to. They want to be inspired."[7]

By following these principles, GE has been able to employ corporate story-telling to increase its brand awareness across the all its business divisions (from medical equipment to engine turbines) and to create positive associations with its brand. In addition, its story line supported a pipeline of young engineering and business talent that might be otherwise attracted to Google, Facebook, or Apple instead of finding a creative and innovative home at GE. The company was also able to use its story to attract the next generation of shareholders.

Stories Are Sticky

People tend to remember well-crafted stories for a long time; in fact, all great religions and philosophies teach through stories because we remember them. Consider the retailer L.L. Bean, a company with a reputation for standing behind the quality of its products and the ultimate satisfaction of its customers. The company has been making that brand promise and telling that story throughout its entire history. An embodiment of the brand promise was its unlimited, no-questions-asked return policy, which allowed items to be returned regardless of purchase date. This strategy created brand loyalty, but it also opened the door for some to take advantage of the company. (For example, stories have emerged of people buying secondhand L.L. Bean goods at yard sales and returning them years later for a full refund.) When L.L. Bean recently changed its return policy (up to one year, with proof of purchase), customers responded with stories of making returns years later, with the vast majority of them saying the company's new policy was long overdue. The policy may have changed, but the stickiness of the story remains: L.L. Bean stands by the quality of its products and the satisfaction of its customers.[8]

Stories Are Simple

Stories are a wonderful tool for taking complicated concepts and boiling them down to their essence. Timeless storytelling such as the parable is a simplified form. Cisco used its "Circle Story" campaign to show how the Internet of Things, a very complicated idea, could be explained very simply with the content and cadence of a children's story: "This is the cat that drank the milk, that let in the dog, that jumped on the woman, who brewed the coffee, that woke the man, who was late for work . . ." That nursery rhyme-like story continues through the man driving to work, entering the control room, and securing the data, which then directs the turbines that power sprinklers that water the grass, that feed the cows, that make the milk, which is purchased by the man at the grocery store, and finally, to close the circle, is poured by a little girl who loved the cat. Cisco's message about what it called "the Internet of everything" becomes memorable through the simplicity of the story.[9]

BRAND STORYTELLING

So how can brands use stories to engage with stakeholders—customers, employees, analysts, and influencers? The key to effective brand storytelling is to find an intersection between the brand promise or brand purpose and a customer pain point or passion. To be effective storytellers, brand marketers must understand deeply who their customers are and the motivations that drive their behavior.

Connecting with Customer Passions

When a brand intersects with people's passions, it becomes part of their motivation to launch into activities they enjoy or aspire to. Red Bull, a lifestyle brand of beverages, has long been associated with extreme sports, including sponsoring numerous events such as skateboarding, rock climbing, and BASE (building, antenna, span, and earth) jumping. Recently, Red Bull collaborated with Samsung in a new extreme sports video featuring Brazilian celebrity skateboarder Pedro Barros, with the theme of "See the Big Picture." By inviting viewers to experience skateboarding as Barros performs through a set modeled after iconic cityscapes, the video captures the passion of fellow skateboarders and would-be fans of the sport.[10]

Red Bull's tagline, "Red Bull gives you wings," perfectly encompasses the purpose of the brand: do extreme things. By attaching itself to the world of extreme sports, Red Bull is able to connect its brand with customers' passion.

Addressing Customer Pain Points

Brands can also speak to a challenge or obstacle that customers face in achieving their personal or business goals. For example, a business pain point could be low productivity or customer defection, while a personal pain point could be stress or a chronic disease. Take the example of pharmaceutical company AbbVie, makers of the blockbuster Humira rheumatoid arthritis drug. The company began thinking about the drug not in terms of clinical benefits, but in terms of how it improves the quality of lives of arthritis patients. The marketing team took a storytelling approach that began with the pain point (the inciting incident) and unfolded to its conclusion thanks to Humira. The story line went something like this: "John" has been affected by rheumatoid arthritis for years, becoming increasingly debilitated until he is virtually bedridden. When his daughter becomes engaged, walking her down the aisle seems like an impossible dream in his current medical state. John consults with his doctors and begins a therapy regimen using Humira. Six months later, the wedding day arrives. The daughter looks beautiful in her wedding gown and takes her father's arm as John walks her down the aisle.

The moral of the story is, "Don't miss out on life." The story involves a sympathetic protagonist with a very real and relatable pain point (especially for fellow sufferers of rheumatoid arthritis) who faced a "villain" in the story (the debilitating effects of the disease). The "knight in shining armor" that facilitated the rescue was Humira, allowing John to get past the obstacles that stood between him and his life.

Brand as Oxygen: Everywhere yet Invisible

In brand storytelling, the brand should be like oxygen: present everywhere, but invisible. It must be an integral part of the story, yet it cannot enter the story overtly. Typically, a brand enters a story by resolving a conflict or removing an obstacle that the protagonist faces. This concept is demonstrated in the Google brand story "Reunion," which tells of two friends separated suddenly by the India-Pakistan partition of 1947. Seven decades later, a granddaughter searches (thanks to Google) for her grandfather's childhood friend, now living in Pakistan. The search and the story culminate in an emotional reunion.[11] (The YouTube version has 14.5 million views and counting.)

The emotional impact of the story is the heartfelt reunion of two long-separated former childhood friends. Yes, Google is used for Internet searches to locate the long-lost friend and to arrange travel, but it appears in the video seamlessly without any overt commerciality that detracts from the emotional content.

BECOMING A BRAND STORYTELLER

To become a brand storyteller, you must find the great stories to tell, have a process of telling them, and have the right people to tell the stories. The brand is never the protagonist in storytelling; rather, it plays the part of the solution or the vehicle through which the story is told. The story is instead focused on what people care about, which humanizes the story. The effect is often subtle, but impactful; the story is warp and the brand is weft, woven together in an intricate tapestry.

How to Find Brand Stories in Your Own Organization

Where do brand stories come from? The short answer: they come from just about anywhere. Stories can be about the company's origin (e.g., Hewlett-Packard, which started in a garage, or Amazon, which has Jeff Bezos driving across the country to establish the company); the people (the faces of the company); the customers (e.g., Tesla customers sharing stories of their experiences with their cars[12]); a cause the company believes in (e.g., TOMS Shoes and its mission to provide shoes for the poor); or a behind-the-scenes look at the operations of the company.

For example, Microsoft Story Labs captures the behind-the-scenes faces and stories of people who are an integral part of the company and its products. They include gamers who are testing the new Xbox Adaptive Controller that makes gaming accessible to people with disabilities, a researcher who envisions new ways of producing food for urban populations, and a once-unknown salesperson who has become a top Microsoft presenter and now senior program manager in charge of DevOps (software development).[13] By showcasing people, not products, Microsoft puts human faces on a huge corporation.

Similarly, the executive team at Jerónimo Martins, a Portuguese food distributor and specialty grocer, thought carefully about the brand story they wanted to convey. What did their customers and potential customers need to know about them? As the team discussed their strategy, a story emerged about the freshness of their products. This evolved into brand stories such as "A day in the life of a fish," which told the story of the fish being caught, transported, and sold within a day; and "A day in the life of a baker," with the baker entering the bakery at five every morning and producing, just a few hours later, the bread that Jerónimo Martins's customers eagerly await.

Another rich vein to be tapped is customer stories—actual experiences that are shared by the company to highlight the loyalty of customers who use their products. An example is the Toyota "Auto-Biography," a Facebook campaign that asked more than 160,000 people who "liked" the company to post videos and text about why they love their Toyotas. The stories were an invaluable testimony to the brand, which had been faced with a difficult product recall crisis the year before.[14]

A powerful example of stories from customers is Google's Year in Search, a montage of images from the most popular searches. The 2017 list begins with the words: "This year more than ever we asked how . . ." with questions focusing on hurricanes (there were three that year: Harvey, Irma, and Maria), wildfires, North Korea's missile range, helping refugees, the Las Vegas shooting, politics, the solar eclipse, and #MeToo. Through this panorama of storytelling writ large, Google put itself in the center of the biggest questions and events on people's minds as the place to ask "how" and find an answer.[15]

Managing the Story Process

Stories must be well constructed to be told effectively. A classic plot structure, devised by Gustav Freytag, is Freytag's pyramid, which progresses from exposition to inciting incident, rising action, climax, falling action, and resolution. A more modern approach is the three-act structure, which is more commonly used today in many forms, including short stories, novels, movies, and even video games. The basic structure is Act 1: setup; Act 2: confrontation; Act 3: resolution. Within the structure, all the elements of a story are used: setting, characters, a problem (obstacle or challenge), engagement, escalation, loss, and turning point.

In order for an organization to tell brand stories in either the classic or modern structure, you need to have a story process: an editorial team, a content czar, a database, and a distribution process. The storytelling network needs to reach across the organization and beyond the chief marketing officer or corporate communications department to also include sales, customer service, operations—any and every touchpoint where there are opportunities to gather and to tell stories. The stories are out there, among executives, employees, and customers. What's needed is a story dissemination process.

Brands today are like publishers—creating, curating, and disseminating stories. No single ad or story line can capture and convey the multiple aspects of a brand or the expanse of a transformative campaign. Brand journalism is an even greater imperative in the digital age, in which messages must be staged on multiple platforms and shared as part of the effort to spread the word.

Part of that journalism is determining who should tell the story. Leaving it to marketing or PR alone is a mistake. As Comstock notes, some of GE's best storytellers turned out to be engineers, particularly those who were good at translating complex ideas (and huge industrial products) into a message—and who could let their passion for what they did show.[16] Storytellers can be found throughout an organization. They needn't be amazing writers; they just need to be able to tell a great story.

Storytelling begins at the top. It's no surprise that great companies tend to be led by CEOs who could be called "chief evangelist officers." Think of Amazon's Bezos with his annual letter, which is considered by many to be a must read, as he opines not only on Amazon's business, but also principles of business in general. Then, of course, there is the Oracle of Omaha—Warren Buffett, whose Berkshire Hathaway shareholder letters are widely read for their wit and wisdom. Others leaders became synonymous with their brands, as visionaries and keepers of the story—none more powerfully than the late Steve Jobs of Apple. Increasingly, Elon Musk, whose diverse businesses include Tesla, SpaceX, and energy generation, is a spokesman for his brand and for his vision of the future (SpaceX has set plans to colonize Mars).

Powerful Ways to Tell a Great Brand Story

As we've seen thus far, the standout examples of brand storytelling showcase the best practices that should be followed by brand marketers seeking to create a better following for their brands and products. Here are some powerful ways to tell a great brand story.

Be Yourself If you want your customers to love your brand, you have to be authentic—you have to live your brand. You cannot pretend to be somebody else, and you cannot create brand stories that are simply not true. To do this, you have to start with knowing your brand's purpose—a purpose that's not only espoused, but enacted (See Chapter 2 for more on brand purpose). Brands are experienced from the outside in, but they're created from the inside out. Starting within, if a company and its people don't know the story and believe the story, then the customers never will. That's why brand stories must be authentic.

In a recent campaign, Microsoft launched "#MakeWhatsNext," a campaign to encourage young women to stay with STEM (science, technology, engineering, and math). Mary Snapp, corporate vice president and head of Microsoft Philanthropies, wrote in a blog: "It's no surprise . . . that because young girls do not see themselves reflected as scientists, engineers, mathematicians, and technologists in the world around them, many do not believe they can pursue careers in these fields. Closing the gender gap requires us to challenge and shift these cultural norms."[17]

As a company, Microsoft is very passionate about diversity and inclusion. Yes, it's a good business decision, but for Microsoft, it goes further. Staying with STEM is very much a business imperative and passion point for many of the employees. Microsoft employees know that if they don't have women as developers and coders, they will miss out on a large part of the consumer base. This is who they are. In their brand story, they are being themselves.

Be Human   When crafting brand stories, don't think about what works for B2B or B2C. It's always H2H (human to human). Regardless of how or what a company sells, or who uses its products and services, humans are always the decision-makers. That's why stories need to be personalized and emotionally engaging. People don't only think logically; they also want to be entertained.

An H2H approach to brand storytelling emphasizes the people without whom a company could not exist. Such is the case with FedEx's "I Am FedEx," which highlights personal stories of employees and gives customers a better understanding of the corporate culture.[18] The stories are logically organized into categories that include "Who we are," "How we think and work," "What we do," and "Why we matter." These stories allow FedEx to offer a behind-the-scenes look at what makes the organization tick, as well as how the organization is driven by its mission and purpose.

Be Pervasive   The analogy I use here is "surround-sound storytelling." In effective brand storytelling, you have to create the feeling of 360-degree projection. You can't be active in only one channel, such as simply putting out a TV ad. Brand stories need to be pervasive, with multiple consumer touchpoints.

Dove's "Real Beauty" and "Choose Beauty" brand stories are not just an advertising campaign. They are multifaceted initiatives that include education and a scholarship program for women and underprivileged girls. The Dove Self-Esteem Project, for example, focuses on self-esteem education to help young people grow up with greater confidence, overcome body image issues, and achieve their full potential.[19] The lesson is to make sure that your story is told in many different ways across many different channels—physical as well as digital.

Be Persistent   Stories take time to seep into the consciousness. That takes persistence, which means staying with one message—or one theme—and presenting several variations around it. The analogy of variations in jazz music is a good way to think about this type of programmatic storytelling. The theme stays the same, providing a functional base to anchor the messaging, then variations are built around the theme to keep the story fresh and relevant.

A brand story also has to have legs—has to be an idea that will stand the test of time through various story line threads and variations. Brand storytelling is not just one night of Super Bowl ad exposure. It's like a long-running soap opera, with multiple episodes and new characters that keep the interest alive and fresh. P&G began a messaging campaign in 2010 that coincided with its sponsorship of the Vancouver Winter Olympic Games. It was called the "Thank You, Mom" campaign. Typically, P&G stays in the background, while the message focuses on its brands, from Tide to Pampers. But this time the corporate parent was the storyteller, saluting the unheralded and underappreciated moms who have a tremendous interest in the success of their children (who may one day become Olympic athletes!). What's particularly brilliant about this campaign is its longevity: it runs from one Olympics to the next, summer and winter games alike.

The story is as universal as they come: motherhood and apple pie values. Yet, the Olympics tie-in has allowed P&G to keep it fresh and relevant. In advance of the 2018 Winter Olympics in South Korea, P&G paid tribute to love over bias.[20] Motherhood may be iconic, but it plays well, time and again, when the approach is fresh.

Be Visual   The advice given to budding fiction writers applies equally here: show, don't tell. This is especially important given the capacity of digital media to convey images as well as information. One of the most potent and longstanding ads to use this approach is the "This is your brain on drugs" public service campaign, which presents the frying eggs image, complete with sizzle sounds. It is a clear warning to teens about the dangers of drug abuse. As the saying goes, a picture is worth a thousand words. And a video, as a constant stream of pictures, is worth a thousand times a thousand words. With such visual power, why would brand marketers want to do anything else other than show instead of tell information that's too often lost in the overload?

By being authentic, human, pervasive, persistent, and visual, brand marketers go beyond messaging to become storytellers. With a deep understanding of the importance of emotional connection, they put their efforts into discovering and conveying what matters most to their consumers. This approach changes and elevates the story they tell, and takes courage to allow the brand to step back and not be the star of the show. It's counterintuitive but highly effective. Consumers will still notice the brand; in fact, they will probably notice—and remember—it even more.

TRANSMEDIA STORYTELLING

Now we come to the new frontier in brand storytelling. In the world of digital, it's not just about taking a story and repurposing the same content for different channels: that would be a *cross-media* approach.

Instead, each new medium requires new thinking. The idea is to create a coordinated story experience, or *transmedia* storytelling, in which each medium or channel plays a specialized role and does what it does best. This approach requires its own lenses and mental models. With transmedia, one overall story is orchestrated in multiple media, each telling a part of the story. This coordinated, unified story experience encourages customers to go deeper into the story as they are drawn into the experience over a multitude of channels used to create a holistic story world.

Henry Jenkins, the provost professor of communication, journalism, cinematic arts, and education at the University of Southern California, describes transmedia storytelling as a process in which integral elements are dispersed across multiple channels to create a coordinated entertainment experience. When first explaining the concept more than a decade ago, he cited *The Matrix*, which remains a quintessential example of a transmedia story told via three live-action films, a series of animated short features, comic books, and several video games. There is no single source; to grasp the entire Matrix universe, you need to experience them all.[21]

Storytelling as Immersive Experience

Transmedia storytelling allows a story to unfold across multiple media platforms. The "spreadability" of the narrative is an important consideration and is accomplished through viral marketing practices in social media channels. It begins with a core fan base that will share and disseminate the narrative, thus creating more interest in and buzz around the story.

Transmedia storytelling strives for continuity of the narrative as the story expands across multiple channels, thus giving fans an immersive experience. Transmedia storytelling as we know it today emerged in the entertainment industry with films such as *The Blair Witch Project* (1999), whose promotional campaign incorporated televised "documentaries" on the history of the (fictional) Blair Witch and on-the-street personnel who distributed missing-person flyers for the characters who disappear in the film. This technique was adopted by brand marketers across a wide range of industries. The rise of transmedia brand storytelling was fueled by the ability of digital and social media channels to connect with diverse audiences across the world.

A useful case study examines *The Hunger Games* film series, which began in 2012 with the launch of the first movie in the franchise. It was followed in 2013 by the second film, *The Hunger Games: Catching Fire*, which set the record for the biggest opening weekend for any movie ever released in the month of November.

A traditional marketing campaign would have focused on creating brand awareness a few weeks prior to the release of the film, using established media channels such as TV, radio, magazines, and billboards, as well as partnerships, a dedicated web site, and YouTube teasers. Other traditional elements might have included in-person PR (interviews, red carpet), online PR (blogs and social media), and cross-marketing partnerships.

By contrast, the *Catching Fire* transmedia campaign was an elaborate effort that went beyond movie posters and web sites to attract attention and create intrigue in curious fans' minds. Teaser billboards began appearing in April 2013, well in advance of the film's November opening. The story world had many elements that played out over specialized channels. On Tumblr, the studio created an elaborate online fashion magazine called *Capitol Couture*. When curious fans googled *Capitol Couture*, they reached a Tumblr site about the Capitol, which in turn led to the Capitol's links on Facebook, Twitter, YouTube, and Instagram. Fans could experience the strange world of fashion in the Capitol through these sites and links.

Fan engagement could be gauged from the huge amount of fan-created content on the film's social media sites. On the *Capitol Couture* Tumblr, for example, a section called "Citizen Activity" encouraged "citizens" to post their pictures and videos showcasing their fashion creations, thus serving, whether knowingly or unknowingly, as brand ambassadors. Tumblr's focus on images and videos made the site a go-to for fans who loved fashion, design, and creativity. The Tumblr videos were quickly devoured by fans of the film, which provided strong encouragement to other fans to share and participate with their own videos.

How successful was this transmedia storytelling approach? The numbers tell their own compelling story. The Capitol's Facebook page had over 10 million likes and over 850,000 followers on Twitter. *Catching Fire*'s trailer was among YouTube's most-watched videos, and the term "hunger games" was one of the most searched categories on Google. The film was also a top trending topic on Twitter. On its opening weekend the film took in $158.1 million at the box office on the way to a total of $864.9 million globally. *Catching Fire* became the highest-grossing film at the domestic box office for 2013.

Creating Effective Transmedia Campaigns

To create effective transmedia campaigns, brand marketers should understand the four Ps: pervasive, persistent, participatory, and personalized (not surprisingly, two of the four are foundational elements of brand storytelling).

> *Pervasive* As the story evolves and gains more depth, it must remain coherent and connected to the overall story line. In the case of *The Hunger Games*, the campaign was so pervasive in its communication to the target audience via online and offline channels that there was considerable excitement as the movie's release approached.
>
> *Persistent* The campaign must persist through multiple channels—social, digital, and traditional—to foster round-the-clock brand awareness and to stimulate the social participation of the target audience. *The Hunger Games*'s persistence also helped blur the distinction between reality and science fiction, which helped immerse fans in a world that was highly accessible.
>
> *Participatory* The audience must be encouraged to participate actively in the campaign through challenges, content creation (e.g., photos and videos), and active sharing on social media. Active fan participation and real events contributed to shaping *The Hunger Games* story world and adding value to the fans' experience. The interconnection among the media messages ensured that everyone was able to join the storytelling experience on Facebook, YouTube, Twitter, Instagram, and other social media.
>
> *Personalized* Story elements that allow viewers and fans to co-create their experience and help shape the story increase engagement. In *The Hunger Games*, YouTube served as the "official TV broadcast" of the story world. The audience was also given the opportunity to have a personalized experience through such tactics as identity cards, victors' contests, and access to limited information.

Transmedia is the next frontier for digital brand storytelling. The first movers, following the lead of the entertainment industry, will be able to take their brand storytelling to the next level, with the creation of an entire world that's presented holistically and synergistically.

SUMMARY

Good brand storytelling is not easy, but those who do it well will be able to secure share of mind and share of heart in a world where consumer attention has become a very scarce commodity. Stories are powerful, as is the new digital era itself. This is a new frontier, and approaching it begins with the same methods that are foundational to all good storytelling and brand storytelling. But transmedia storytelling places a great deal of emphasis on participation and personalization, to engage the audience even more deeply with a fully immersive experience.

Keep in mind that we are not suffering from a lack of brand storytelling; we are suffering from bland storytelling—crude attempts at storytelling that attempt to sell rather than to tell a story. To become great digital storytellers, brand marketers need to start with customer insights, connect their brands with customer passions and pain points, use a systematic story process, and adopt a transmedia approach to storytelling. Brand marketers who do this well will live happily ever after.

Mohanbir Sawhney is the McCormick Foundation Professor of Technology, clinical professor of marketing, and director of the Center for Research in Technology and Innovation at the Kellogg School of Management, Northwestern University. He has written seven management books as well as dozens of influential articles in leading academic journals and managerial publications. His most recent book, The Sentient Enterprise: The Evolution of Business Decision Making, *was published in October 2017 and was on the* Wall Street Journal *bestseller list.*

NOTES

1. Berman, Jillian (2015), "Why That 'Like a Girl' Super Bowl Ad Was So Groundbreaking," *Huffington Post*, February 3. https://www.huffingtonpost.com/2015/02/02/always-super-bowl-ad_n_6598328.html.
2. Neff, Jeff (2015), "P&G's Always Takes #LikeAGirl Viral Video to the Super Bowl," *Ad Age*, January 29. http://adage.com/article/special-report-super-bowl/p-g-s-takes-likeagirl-super-bowl/296879.
3. Campbell, Joseph (1949), *The Hero with a Thousand Faces*, Princeton, NJ: Bollingen Series, Princeton University Press.
4. Booker, Christopher (2004), *The Seven Basic Plots: Why We Tell Stories*, Continuum Books.
5. Gianatasio, David (2013), "Nike's 'Just Do It,' the Last Great Advertising Slogan, Turns 25," *Adweek*, July 2. https://www.adweek.com/creativity/happy-25th-birthday-nikes-just-do-it-last-great-advertising-slogan-150947.
6. General Electric (n.d.), "Childlike Imagination," General Electric TV commercial. https://www.ispot.tv/ad/7T4v/general-electric-childlike-imagination-what-my-mom-does-at-ge.
7. Comstock, Beth (2014), "The Future of Storytelling," YouTube.com, September 2014. https://www.youtube.com/watch?v=vJ_zQEeU1ag.

8. Troutman, Caitlin (2018), "LL Bean Customers Share Their Stories of Lifetime Guarantee," *Bangor Daily News,* February 15. https://bangordailynews.com/2018/02/15/business/ll-bean-customers-share-their-stories-of-lifetime-guarantee.

9. Cisco Portugal (2014), "Internet of Everything–Circle Story," YouTube.com, August 13. https://www.youtube.com/watch?v=3D8Fkn5fJg0.

10. Red Bull (n.d), "Pedro Barros Takes a Skateboarding World Tour to See the Bigger Picture," https://www.redbull.com/us-en/pedro-barros-the-bigger-picture.

11. Google (2013), "Google Search: Reunion," YouTube.com, November 13. https://www.youtube.com/watch?v=gHGDN9-oFJE.

12. Tesla (n.d.), "Tesla Customer Stories," Tesla.com. https://www.tesla.com/customer-stories.

13. Microsoft (n.d.), "Microsoft Story Labs," Microsoft.com. https://news.microsoft.com/stories.

14. Bannan, Karen J. (2010), "CMOs Explore Digital Domain," *Adweek*, September 13. https://www.adweek.com/brand-marketing/cmos-explore-digital-domain-103250.

15. Google (n.d.), "Year in Search 2017," Google.com. https://trends.google.com/trends/yis/2017/GLOBAL.

16. Comstock (2014), see Note 7.

17. Snapp, Mary (2017), "Inspiring Girls to Stay in STEM and #MakeWhatsNext," Microsoft on the Issues, March 7. https://blogs.microsoft.com/on-the-issues/2017/03/07/inspiring-girls-stay-stem-makewhatsnext.

18. Federal Express (n.d.), "I Am FedEx," iamfedex.com. https://www.iamfedex.com.

19. Dove (n.d.), "The Dove Self-Esteem Project," Dove.com. https://www.dove.com/us/en/dove-self-esteem-project/our-mission.html.

20. Olympic Games (2017), "P&G Promotes Love over Bias, with Latest 'Thank You, Mom,' Campaign," Olympic.org, Nov 2. https://www.olympic.org/news/p-g-promotes-love-over-bias-with-latest-thank-you-mom-campaign-1.

21. Jenkins, Henry (2007), "Transmedia Storytelling 101," Confessions of an Aca-fan (Henry Jenkins weblog), March 21. www.henryjenkins.org/blog/2007/03/transmedia_storytelling_101.html.

CHAPTER 12

BRANDING SERVICES IN THE DIGITAL ERA

TOM O'TOOLE

Eric Smoot Hemphill is an outstanding personal trainer. With his business partner, Silviu Gansca, he founded Redefined Fitness. They provide expert personal fitness training, but providing a great service isn't enough. To be successful, Smoot and Gansca have to build a strong, distinctive brand and be adept in using digital media.

When my exercise physiologist recommended a specialized type of personal trainer, he suggested three potential candidates. Redefined Fitness was one of them. What's the first thing I did before even visiting its location? Googled it. I studied the web site, learned about its approach, and read about Eric and the other trainers. I went to its YouTube channel and watched videos of Eric and others. Then, I went to Yelp to see what others said about Redefined Fitness. After researching Redefined, I did the same for the other two competing trainers. The total impression of what the Redefined brand stands for and the experience it delivers drove my decision to go in and meet Eric.

A strong brand is essential for service providers, given the intangible nature of the product offering and thus the important role of perceptions. However, service branding is a unique challenge, and the task is being transformed as digital technology creates both new opportunities and complexity.

In this chapter, we will discuss the unique characteristics and challenges of service branding, how digital transformation is impacting services branding, and how to build a powerful service brand.

THE UNIQUE DYNAMICS OF BRANDING SERVICES

In services industries, there is enormous value from effective brand building. This is due to several unique characteristics of service brands.

Services Brands Are Intangible

Products are tangible. Services are intangible. Products are physical objects. Services are interactions. As Kellogg professor Philip Kotler wrote, services are "an activity, benefit, or satisfaction offered for sale that is essentially intangible and does not result in ownership of anything."[1]

This dynamic has important implications when it comes to branding. Services typically can't be tried on, felt, weighed, smelled, or otherwise physically judged before purchase. For this reason, it can be difficult for consumers to evaluate services. I can examine and try on a pair of jeans, test drive a car, or see how fresh the fish looks in the case. If I don't like the product, or it isn't as advertised, I can often return it for replacement or a refund. The evaluation process is different when choosing a dentist, hiring an accountant, or choosing a telecommunication provider. This is particularly consequential in the case of big-ticket services: It's inconvenient if I buy a shirt and it's cut too small, because I can always return it. But it's irrecoverable if I spend thousands of dollars on my honeymoon in the South Pacific and the sailboat charter turns out to be a disaster.

There is inherently a higher degree of uncertainty and risk in the selection and purchase of services compared to products. As a result, consumers look for indicators of reliable service quality, making branding particularly important to generate trust and build confidence. Does the hospital look clean? Is the prospective nanny punctual, polite, attentive, and well dressed for her interview? Are the reviews positive? What do my friends and connections say?

The Service Brand and Employee Are Inseparable

A fundamental characteristic of services is that production, delivery, and consumption occur simultaneously and are inseparable. Manufacture of a product occurs at a different time and place than its delivery and consumption. For example, Anheuser-Busch InBev manufactures a can of Budweiser beer at a brewery. The beer is eventually delivered to and consumed by a person in a different location at a later time. I may buy a case of beer a week before taking it to someone's house for a Super Bowl party.

By contrast, the production, delivery, and consumption of a particular service occur at the same time and place. A care worker at a senior-living facility is producing and delivering the service while the resident is receiving and consuming it. Likewise, if a couple hires a chef to prepare dinner at their home for a party, the chef is delivering the service while the customer is consuming it.

In addition, the service provider is interacting directly with the customer—the worker and the service are inseparable. This is true even when the service is delivered through an automated platform.

The Experience Is Variable and Perishable

Services are variable and perishable. Both of these factors increase the branding challenge.

The challenge of variability is clear when you compare two common products: hand sanitizers and hair salons. When the manufacturer of hand sanitizer produces a bottle of the gel, the consumer experience of the product and its marketing are largely under the company's direct control. The manufacturer develops the product, builds it to tight specifications, conducts quality-control checks, and designs the label. Some elements, such as the retail experience and usage conditions, are partly out of the company's control, of course, but the product experience is largely controllable.

The situation is very different for a hair salon. The expertise, experience, and attitude of the hair stylists will vary. A particular stylist may be stressed or enthusiastic. He might be having a bad day or a good day. He might be under pressure to boost productivity, or he might be comfortable financially and therefore unmotivated. The hair salon chain's marketing efforts can get the customer in the door, but the service experience depends on what happens in the moment.

Another critical difference between products and services is perishability. When an airplane pulls away from the gate, any unsold seats on that flight will remain unsold forever—they are perishable. If a resort has unsold rooms in January, it can't sell those rooms to vacationers in February. If a restaurant has empty seats for breakfast on Monday, it can't sell those seats for dinner on Tuesday. This dynamic has practical implications for service brand management, including pricing, demand management, and the resultant customer incentives and customer experiences.

This is quite different from the nature of product marketing. If a candle company produces too many scented candles for this holiday season and some go unsold, it can typically save them and sell them next holiday season. If a manufacturer of commercial ovens sees inventory building, it can reduce future production and let supplies sell down over time. The service marketer can do neither.

Adjusting Supply to Changes in Demand Is Difficult in the Short Term

One of the unique characteristics of some service businesses is that adjusting supply is difficult in the short run. Products are generally not limited to a finite and largely fixed inventory availability—the manufacturer can often make more or less in response to market conditions. If a book is more popular than anticipated, the publisher can print more. If the Eagles win the Super Bowl, the manufacturer can make more Eagles jerseys for fans.

The situation is different for many services providers. If a hotel has 500 rooms and 1,000 people want to stay there for a convention, it still only has 500 rooms to sell. It can't make more. If economic conditions weaken and people cut back on hotel stays, it still has 500 rooms to sell. If a furnace repair company hires and trains five new winter crews, but fewer furnaces break down due to an unseasonably warm winter, it still has the service capacity. If the company finds itself experiencing a record-breaking cold winter and the phone is ringing off the hook for furnace repairs, it can still only fix a certain number of furnaces.

Not only is service inventory generally finite, it is often localized, so it can't be moved easily or quickly in response to regional demand variations. If a healthcare system that operates hospitals in Washington, Oregon, and California is faced with too many beds in Washington and too few beds in California, it can't shift the inventory between states.

The Customer Doesn't Own the Service Asset

With services, the customer doesn't end up as an owner after purchase. When I buy a car, it becomes my car. If I use a ride-share service, however, I don't own the car that picks me up. If I purchase health insurance, I don't own the clinics. With services, I may own the rights to use certain service facilities, but I do not acquire any tangible assets.

In some new digital services, particularly those known as platform businesses, neither the service provider nor the service customer owns or acquires ownership of the assets being used to deliver the service. Airbnb does not own its rental accommodations. Uber does not own the automobiles used for its ride-sharing.

Nonownership of service delivery assets can be financially rewarding for the service provider, but it also introduces much greater potential for service delivery variation and branding problems. Royal Caribbean needs to manage customer service interactions across thousands of points of contact before, during, and after a cruise, but it owns and operates the ship. Uber does neither. Thus, not only might the driver be exceptional or having a bad day, but the car might not be as described to Uber or to the customer.

Franchised services encounter many of the same issues. Holiday Inn Express does not own its hotels. Franchisors focus intensively on consistent delivery of the brand experience through the use of franchise agreements, brand standards, and service delivery metrics.

THE DIGITAL TRANSFORMATION OF SERVICES BRANDING AND MARKETING

While digital transformation is occurring in all industries, categories, and businesses, it is arguably producing the greatest changes in service businesses.

Perhaps the most dramatic shift has been the emergence of cloud-based, digitally enabled, or digitally delivered services. These new service brands include platform businesses (e.g., Uber, Airbnb, eHarmony, eHealth); software as a service (e.g., Microsoft Office, Adobe Photoshop); streaming content (e.g., Netflix, Spotify); and digital content (e.g., Kindle books). Many of these services employ a purely digital business model, eliminating or minimizing any human interaction between the company and its customers, which has traditionally been a hallmark (and challenge) of managing a service brand.

For almost every service brand, digital technology is changing the customer experience. The changes are particularly profound in several areas.

The Rise of Self-Service

It used to be that when a customer wanted to take a flight, she would call the airline and speak to an agent. On the day of travel, she would go to the airport and check in with another agent, then speak to an agent at the gate to ask if the flight was on time. On the plane, she would order a drink from the flight attendant. Later, if the bags didn't arrive, she would talk with an airline agent.

Today, the experience is very different; many of these points of interaction have been supplemented, enabled, or replaced with digital technology. In many cases, the passenger now performs tasks along the customer journey: she searches for a flight, picks a seat, and checks the arrival time.

Self-service delivery can be highly efficient for both the provider and the customer. For many customers, it may be their preferred form of interaction. At the same time, different types of customers in different situations have different service requirements. Service leaders have to carefully think through how digital technology will impact the customer experience, and thus the service brand, for different customer segments and under various usage conditions.

New Opportunities through Informed Contact

Digital technology has opened the window to greater informed contact. For services, informed contact has always been important; I appreciate it when my personal trainer remembers that I had rotator cuff surgery and knows to modify my exercise regimen accordingly. Digital technology has made this vastly easier; the service provider now has access to data that enables more personalized customer interactions.

When an airline flight attendant greets and serves a passenger, for example, he can do so knowing profile and customer history information, such as loyalty program status and recent service experiences. Has she had two flights cancelled in the previous week? Was her last flight delayed by six hours? Marketers can then incorporate this information when providing a service. Front-line providers can even be informed with customer lifetime value and other metrics.

Informed service delivery enables the brand and the front-line service contact to execute differentiated practices, interventions, and enhancements on an individualized customer basis. If a guest arrives at a hotel only to learn that the hotel is oversold, the hotel will typically apologize and perhaps offer some minimal compensation. If the hotel and front desk agent know that the guest is a high-value customer who has had the same experience three times in the last six months, they may upgrade her to a suite and offer free dinner and drinks while she waits for the hotel transfer.

From Product Manufacturing to Service Providers

Digital transformation has upended many business models. In some cases, companies that were primarily product manufacturers have become largely service providers.

Perhaps the best known and prototypical of these transformations from products to services is IBM. After struggling with intense competition from personal computer makers throughout the 1980s and 1990s, IBM successfully transformed itself from manufacturer of computer hardware to provider of software and services. GE is another example; it developed a service offering as an alternative to the physical product of aircraft engines. GE aircraft engines power many of the world's largest airlines, so the company introduced the option for its customers to purchase "power by the hour." In other words, it offers thrust as a service, rather than the conventional model of engine purchases. Some of these product-to-service models work out and some don't, but the shift is steadily impacting a growing range of industries.

More firms will see this transformation in coming years. Consider the automobile industry: it is in the nascent stages of moving from building and selling cars (product) to enabling and providing transportation (service). Bloomberg recently reported on the industry reaching the point of "peak car," with people now shifting in growing numbers to transportation services in lieu of car ownership.[2]

BUILDING A POWERFUL SERVICES BRAND

The fundamentals of building a strong service brand still apply in the digital age, but new tools offer marketers new ways to build a vibrant brand.

Be Clear on the Value Proposition and How to Execute It

Brands create value for services just as they do for products: by creating preference that results in increased demand, premium pricing, and repeat purchase. Marketers must differentiate offerings, set expectations, communicate features and benefits, establish quality level, and reduce purchase risk.

For service brand managers, the brand's value proposition is ultimately created or destroyed at the moments of service interaction. A service brand may have the best-designed marketing strategy, the best advertising, the most robust offering with the best features, the best-targeted promotional campaign, and the most refined pricing strategy. Yet, if the customer service interaction breaks down or doesn't live up to the brand promise, none of the other marketing elements matter. Each time a negative interaction occurs, brand integrity erodes.

So how does a service marketer manage this practical reality? At the most basic level, he or she must understand the service delivery model and processes. This must go beyond a conceptual understanding. It means personally living the experiences of the customer and the person delivering the service in different situations, in different locations, and under different conditions. The challenge is to ensure that the service delivery experience matches the brand platform.

This can only be achieved by getting out into the field. For service marketing leaders, there is no substitute for frequent interaction with front-line service delivery. When I was working at United Airlines, and before that at Hyatt Hotels Corporation, I often reminded myself that the real world is not in the corporate office—it's in the field. The brand doesn't happen at corporate headquarters: it happens in thousands of service interactions in hundreds of locations around the world every day. It's easy for service brand executives to slip into viewing the brand as an abstraction separate from actual service delivery and customers. It is imperative to observe and experience the brand delivery and execution in the field, from both sides of the service interaction and in actual practice under a range of real-world conditions.

The inseparability of the service brand and marketing from service delivery has very practical implications for marketing leadership. Typically, front-line service delivery does not fall under the reporting structure, authority, and control of the marketing function. Often, it lies in the domain of operations management. Thus, the services marketing leader must be adept at working with operations or other service delivery management and staff. Service marketing leaders who try to assert centralized control over service execution without building commitment from both operations leadership and front-line service employees typically fail. In short, effective working relationships with operations leadership are essential for services brand leaders.

Create Standards

To manage the inherent variability of service delivery, *service design* is essential. While a service interaction may seem spontaneous, the best-managed service interactions are carefully structured.

Service delivery should be a carefully *designed experience*. In the airline industry, the timing, presentation, manner, and elements of meal delivery in business class on an international airline is not left entirely to the discretion of the flight attendants. The service is designed and choreographed, based on customer input and operational requirements, to create the desired brand experience. Each step is defined and specified in the operational process.

Digital enablement can be incorporated into the service design and facilitate greater satisfaction, value, utility, and efficiency for both the customer and service provider. Consider the practical example of selecting a meal in business class. The standard procedure is to provide a printed menu for the passenger. Then the flight attendant asks each passenger in succession which meal she would like to select. At the same time, the passenger is still getting settled and the flight attendant is dealing with multiple operational responsibilities, service activities, and passenger inquiries. If the passenger can make her meal selections on an in-seat touchscreen or through a mobile app, it relieves demands on both the passenger and the flight attendant, while still accomplishing a necessary step in the service process. Even better, if the passenger makes her selection before boarding via a mobile phone, the task is accomplished earlier, which also provides the airline with advance information. (There are operational reasons why this is not always feasible.)

It is essential that the designed elements of service delivery be expressed in the form of *service standards*. Service standards tell the delivery organization and front-line service people exactly how the service is to be delivered—the steps, signature features, sequence, descriptions and explanations, options, and so on. In practice, service standards for routine interactions, such as delivering room service at a hotel, can and should be very detailed. What time should be quoted for the guest to expect delivery? How much variance from the quoted time is acceptable? When should the order be checked for accuracy before delivery? How should the guest be greeted? Where should the food be placed? Should the guest-room door remain open or closed? Should the dishes be uncovered or left covered to stay hot? Should the coffee be poured? When and how should the check be presented?

Service standards create brand expectations, brand integrity, and thus, brand value. They can also create brand differentiation for service brands. If I know that Amm's Limousine Service is always going to arrive 15 minutes before my scheduled pickup time, and it reliably does so, I can plan confidently what time to schedule my pickup to go to the airport and have peace of mind that I won't miss my flight. Plus, I know that the Amm's driver is going to be polite and attentive, get out to open the door, take my bags from the door of my house, and ask what route I prefer to the airport. I know exactly what to expect time after time. That experience differentiates Amm's, creates brand preference, reduces risk, and creates customer loyalty. As a customer, it's also worth paying a premium price, rather than trying a different car service that may be a little cheaper but may or may not arrive on time. What makes this all happen are clearly specified, well-executed internal service standards.

At the same time, service design and service standards must allow some flexibility for individual front-line service responsiveness, discretion, and interpretation. Too much room for individual variation can destroy service consistency, but too little can be equally or even more damaging to the branded service experience. Rigid enforcement of service rules by front-line staff without regard for the variance of individual customer situations can alienate customers, undermining the perception of thoughtfulness and resulting in brand-damaging customer service incidents. Too often, service organizations are so driven by the demand for financial performance, productivity, standardization, and efficiency that they limit front-line service discretion to the point that, ironically, it destroys brand value. For many years, Hyatt was known for "the Hyatt Touch." The Hyatt Touch wasn't just a brand tag line. It was the actual expression of an operating culture that called for maintaining very high service standards while allowing for, encouraging, and expecting its front-line staff to be responsive, attentive, and creative in anticipating and serving guest needs.

The art of service delivery and creating service brands depends largely on creating a service culture, operational protocols, and brand standards that allow for the right latitude of personal interpretation, creativity, and expression by the individual interacting with the customer. Finding the right balance between rigorous service standards and individual variation is one of the most difficult, and yet most critical, dimensions of building and executing branded services.

Engage Employees and Communicate, Communicate, Communicate

The most effective, successful, and experienced service marketing leaders know that the brand strategy needs to be shared and understood by the people who will fulfill it. Internal communication is critical.

If the brand wants to be positioned as "professional," "caring," or "helpful," the people who will fulfill that positioning need to understand it, be comfortable with it, and know what delivering it means. Brand communication on the subject should debut inside the company before being launched externally—in other words, the people who deliver the service being advertised should never see the new television campaign for the first time when it airs. They want to be proud of and enthused about the company they work for and the new brand advertising. They want to be in the know and tell their friends and relatives. They want their role to be acknowledged and respected.

For brand initiatives to be effective in a service organization, front-line employees must understand the company's goals and brand positioning strategy. A good practical test is asking front-line staff to explain in simple and practical terms what the brand stands for and what that means for their role. Too often, front-line service employees are asked to fulfill brand claims that don't correspond to their actual daily experience.

A proactive strategy of engaging employees in brand activities engages and energizes the organization. United Airlines' long-time sponsorship of the U.S. Olympic team exemplifies this approach. In its brand advertising before and during the Olympics, the airline closely involves and features United employees who interact with the Olympic athletes. It promotes the brand's relationship with the Olympics in a wide range of employee activities. Doing so greatly magnifies the impact of the sponsorship. The employees love it. The athletes love it. The passengers love it.

Use Metrics to Track Progress

Given the inherent variability of services and reliance on front-line employees to fulfill the brand promise, managing service delivery according to its design and specifications requires clear service metrics. Metrics measure the execution and effectiveness of service initiatives and provide feedback to help the organization improve service delivery. Typically, these include both operational metrics (e.g., on-time flight arrival, completion time for room service delivery, call answering time, waiting time before being seated, response time to pickup request) and customer metrics (e.g., Net Promoter Score, customer satisfaction rating).

Metrics should be shared with and be meaningful to front-line service staff. If service delivery personnel don't know how they're performing, why they are scoring at the reported levels, and how to impact their scores positively, then service metrics will be ineffective as a tool for improvement. It's important that service metrics be meaningful, comprehensible, and make sense in practical terms to the people who deliver the service and are being measured. If they're presented with dozens of service metrics, they won't know which are the most important to focus on. If a service metric is produced through a complicated algorithm, adjusted for multiple factors, or otherwise derived in ways that aren't clear, employees won't know exactly where it came from, what it says, and how it relates to what they actually do and how to improve it. Service metrics such as: "The driver greeted the customer by name," "The coffee was hot when delivered," "The meal came within 10 minutes of being ordered," and "The server was friendly and courteous" are straightforward, meaningful, and practical for the people who need to fulfill them and thus fulfill the brand promise.

Digital technology enables companies to use brand service metrics in new and advantageous ways. Mobile apps can facilitate immediate customer ratings while the service experience is still fresh. Dashboards can provide real-time feedback on service performance. Plus, digital systems enable intensive analytics to understand service performance for specific customer segments, during specific events (e.g., a service outage and subsequent recovery); what is driving service metrics (i.e., what factors are most impactful on the service metric);

and service delivery in specific locations or even by specific service teams or individuals. Additionally, digital information enables companies to compile new types of metrics, such as a customer dissatisfaction score that incorporates multiple specific measures of service performance over time, at the individual customer, segment, or other aggregated level. This output can then be analyzed to correlate it with other outcomes (e.g., customer lifetime value), discover what has the most weight in driving it, and determine how to manage it for optimal service performance and customer value.

Ideally, metrics should enable service recovery efforts before customers are lost or share their disgruntlement on social media. Using predictive analytics, service brand leaders can act proactively to intervene before suffering attrition.

Consider Loyalty Programs

Many services businesses are well suited to loyalty programs. If designed and administered well, these programs can drive customer repeat, build customer lifetime value, and enhance brand perceptions.

Loyalty programs are most effective when designed strategically to achieve defined business objectives. These should be based on customer differentiation and incorporate functional benefits to create a compelling value proposition in an economically sustainable manner.

Historically, loyalty programs have been structured and managed based on fixed tiers of customer value, points earning, redemption pricing, and other features. With the emergence of data-driven digital marketing methods, loyalty programs are increasingly shifting in the direction of what one CMO of a national retailer recently described as "nonprogram loyalty programs," which personalize a wide range of targeted marketing initiatives and promotional offers based on individual purchase history, customer value, and other factors.

Loyalty programs have been and remain a mainstay marketing practice for service brands. Both Uber and Airbnb, megasuccessful service brands in the digital era, introduced new loyalty programs in 2018. Likewise, Starbucks Rewards exemplifies the convergence of loyalty programs, mobile enablement, and payment systems. Finally, Amazon Prime demonstrates the incorporation of delivery services (another feature rapidly growing in importance for loyalty programs) while charging an annual fee and eschewing a loyalty-points mechanism. Loyalty programs are becoming digitally based, mobile-enabled, personalized marketing systems that will remain essential to driving customer value for services brands in the digital era.

SUMMARY

Building strong service brands is more challenging, complicated, interesting, and advantageous than ever before. Virtually no form of service business is untouched by digital applications. Some industries have been restructured and radically changed by digital disruptions. Others will be.

Conventional service brands now must employ digital methods to build their brands. Many—perhaps most—service brands now use a combination of conventional service delivery and digital channels.

While this digital transformation is enormously consequential, the underpinning fundamentals of branding and marketing services continue to apply. Services are characterized by attributes, such as perishability, that guide and structure their marketing. The marketing of services is inseparable from their delivery and execution. The brand value of services is ultimately created or destroyed at the point of service interaction with the customer, sometimes provided by a person and sometimes, increasingly, by a digital interface. There's never been a better, more important, or more interesting time to be responsible for building a services brand.

Tom O'Toole is executive director of the Program for Data Analytics and clinical professor of marketing at Northwestern University's Kellogg School of Management. He teaches courses on data-driven marketing and customer loyalty. Prior to joining Kellogg, he was chief marketing officer for United Airlines, where he was also president of United's MileagePlus loyalty program. Previously, he was chief marketing officer and chief information officer for Hyatt Hotels Corporation. He received his BA and MA from Cleveland State University.

NOTES

1. Kotler, P., and G. Armstrong (2018), *Principles of Marketing*, London, U.K.: Pearson.
2. Nicola, Stefan, and Elisabeth Behrmann (2018), "'Peak Car' and the End of an Industry," Bloomberg, August 16. https://www.bloomberg.com/news/articles/2018-08-17/-peak-car-and-the-end-of-an-industry.

SECTION THREE

Gaining Insight about Your Brand and Quantifying Its Stature

CHAPTER 13

DIGITAL TRANSFORMATION AND THE EVOLUTION OF CUSTOMER INSIGHTS IN BRAND BUILDING

BRIDGETTE BRAIG

Market research has been a core part of brand building for many years, but in a hyper-connected world, marketers have to rethink their approach.

It used to be straightforward. Marketers asked customers about unmet needs and new products they'd like to see. Using cluster and discriminant analysis, marketers then defined target audience segments. By measuring segment demographic characteristics, examining comprehensive print and broadcast media habits, and mapping proximities to various retail outlets and shopping districts, agency partners created media plans and plotted optimal channels of distribution. This process helped companies develop new product offerings and persuade consumers to buy them at local retailers, thereby building powerful brands.

This basic model worked well, given that brands were relatively controllable. At least in the consumer world, there were clear retail channels of distribution. Print and broadcast media markets were both measurable and well defined.

The more complex world in which we now find ourselves is far more variable and democratized. The Amazon-led e-commerce explosion has created do-it-yourself digital marketplaces that include eBay for resellers, chewy.com for pets, etsy.com for small-scale craftspeople, udemy.com for video courses, and so on. Retailers and individual brands also participate in e-commerce, approaching it as a virtual obligation and an opportunity.

Messaging channels have also exponentially increased with the advent of smartphones, mobile apps, streaming content, social media, traditional print and digital-only media platforms, and opt-in or other direct e-mail and push content.

Information on brands and product offerings are now instantly available on web sites, review sites, industry reports, and any number of other digital sources.

As a result, marketers cannot count on traditional market research techniques alone to produce the insights required to develop, grow, and maintain strong brands. Companies must adopt a customer journey mindset to capture the human-centered pain points that can give rise to product innovation. They should also understand the breadth of the more circuitous routes customers can take on their path to purchase and brand adoption. To deliver on brand messages/content and drive customers to sales conversion in the digital era, research needs to provide an in-depth perspective in two contexts: the rich qualitative arena in which customer needs are recognized and experienced, and the quantitative, measurable traits and behaviors that big data provide.

This chapter illustrates the value of the customer journey mindset in executing research and data strategies, explains how traditional qualitative and quantitative methods must adapt to the digital world, and offers advice for holding customer insight teams and partners accountable.

THE VALUE OF THE CUSTOMER JOURNEY MINDSET

Designing and executing customer journey-driven research allows brands and companies to capture the variability in their customers' increasingly fragmented environment. In the digital era, the insights mentality must be more empathy driven and human centered than ever before. In order to find shared points of meaning, brands need this empathy-driven lens to abstract higher-level findings that unify the different paths customers take. What's happening with people physically, emotionally, and intellectually? What are they trying to accomplish and why? How does their current set of needs fit into other aspects of their lives? Successful branding in the digital world requires understanding variability in journeys, but it also requires the ability to extrapolate the findings in order to create brand promises that resonate and solve problems—and ultimately drive sales.

To illustrate the benefit of the customer journey mindset in gathering insights, we discuss in depth the impact of three brand-building application areas:

1. *Exploratory empathy-driven insights* that identify "white spaces" (opportunities for new product or brand innovations)
2. *Persona development* to focus the entire organization on the brand's core customer
3. *Measurement and data collection opportunities* to optimize the customer brand experience

Exploratory Empathy-Driven Insights and Innovation

Ultimately we design products and brands for people, sometimes for individuals (e.g., dads, millennials, amateur athletes, STEM enthusiasts), and other times for customers inside an organization (e.g., systems engineers, procurement managers, heads of surgery, chief data officers). But at the end of the day, brands serve people. Rich, qualitative, and often observational research methods offer a window into people's lives as they experience the customer journey and confront various situations in the course of moving through their world. These empathy-driven insights can prove useful in uncovering white spaces against which to innovate new product and brand ideas.

For example, a cleaning products company spent several weeks talking to women in their homes to understand the context and experience of bathroom cleaning. These women cleaned and spontaneously narrated the experience while the company's insights team watched and generated interpretive hypotheses that resulted in follow-up questions. By the end of the exercise, the consumers and insights team had collectively reached some conclusions about the top friction points that needed a solution. Specifically, the most effective bathroom-cleaning products came at the cost of fumes so intense that women threw windows open and banished kids to the other side of the house to keep them away from the smell. On top of the negative fume experience, the toilet brush and all its germs completely creeped them out. Even wearing gloves, many shuddered and made faces as they pulled the brush from its stand.

As a result of these journey-driven lessons, cleaning products from the KABOOM brand now tout a lack of "obnoxious" fumes alongside the claim of potent efficacy. To address the gross toilet brush experience, KABOOM developed a foaming toilet bowl cleaner that no longer requires a brush. The foam rises up the side of the bowl and cleans as the bubbles go down. The color of the water in the bowl changes once the cleaning process finished. Flushing the residue completes the process. No brush needed (phew!).

Clorox addressed consumers' aversion to the toilet brush a different way. By creating a toilet wand that has disposable one-use scrubbers, it eliminated the need for storing the dreaded brush between cleanings. Note that "the brush grosses me out" insight certainly doesn't propose a clear solution, but it does give a highly resonant problem for product designers to solve and for brand marketers to use in crafting a compelling brand promise. Both Clorox and KABOOM (owned by Church and Dwight) leveraged the same empathy-driven customer experience to drive innovation, albeit arriving at different leap-forward solutions rather than merely trying to develop a less revulsion-inducing brush.

TeamSnap, a mobile and web-based software platform, used a similar journey-driven inquiry into youth sports organizations to develop solutions for managing all their administrative functions (e.g., web site creation, registration, scheduling, team rostering, communication, and so on). A deep dive revealed that these primarily volunteer-run groups had to find workarounds to enter player information from their own registration database into a separate web-based system in order to register kids with the relevant sanctioning association for their sport (e.g., USA Hockey, Little League International). For health insurance and liability reasons, as well as to qualify for certain tournaments and games, registration with these sanctioning organizations was mandatory. As a result, volunteers retyped information or did monstrous cut-and-paste jobs into both systems instead of spending more time on things that had a bigger positive impact on player experience and performance: coaching, conditioning, mentoring, and one-on-one communication with players and parents. From a sports organization perspective, the often-clunky dual registration represented a major friction point, although not all the organizations overtly complained about it.

After learning about these experiences, TeamSnap built application programming interfaces (APIs) with USA Hockey, Hockey Canada, and US Lacrosse. And, it is building more than 20 additional APIs or other semistructured formats (e.g., .CSV files) to enable a sports organization to register its players and collect payment, then use that information and money to seamlessly register with the relevant sanctioning body. This provides another example of how insights based on observing the customer journey identified a problem that spurred innovation and the creation of differentiating features.

Persona Development

As the previous examples illustrate, discovery-oriented customer journey insights can effectively drive innovation and entrepreneurial thinking to generate new ideas. However, once a company uses these insights to identify a white space and direct its innovation, it still has to strategically define its target audience in order to further guide product development and branding activities. Customer journeys as an insight approach have utility in this regard as well.

Traditionally, marketers have identified target audiences in terms of *segments* that describe the demographics of the bulk of the audience (e.g., men 30–64, live in cities of 1MM+, income $75K+, married, white-collar professionals, skilled trades workers). The demographic range captures the variance of the segment. When aligned with brand attitudes and behaviors, segment descriptions are strategically valuable in sizing and reaching an audience for a brand.

By contrast, *personas* go deeper, depicting the prototypical customer in a vivid, in-depth, and often colorful manner. Companies develop personas as a creative expression that consolidates the segment into a single person, often including a photo or visual of the customer along with a written depiction outlining age, specific occupation, skill levels, emotional and functional goals and frustrations, and personality characteristics (e.g., introversion versus extraversion, relative optimism). The persona may also include brands that inspire the customer, their level of technology adoption and integration across devices and platforms, behaviors and habits relative to the category of interest, and behavior-change drivers. This human, journey-fueled lens adds critical empathy to bring demographic clusters to life and put a true heart, head, and face to more sterile variables. In other words, the persona is the average lived experience of a member of the target audience.

Consider the following hypothetical persona example for a typical farm cooperative member. As seen in Figure 13.1, the persona outlines the farmer's goals and concerns, as well as his behaviors around using technology in his work as a producer (farmer). It also depicts app use and brands with which he identifies. This persona could help the co-op design its mobile app and web site to encourage greater patronage and loyalty among co-op members. Keeping the persona in mind, the development teams have a clear picture of the person for whom they are designing, which informs the information architecture, functionalities, user interface, and overall site and app design.

Overall, personas remind organizations that they design products and build brands for people, and help humanize strategic terms such as "customer" and "segments." Personas make it easier to write messaging and design experiences. We *talk to and design for people*, even if we *target segments*.

Persona development also promotes respect for the different players or actors involved in the buying process or overall experience of consuming a given product or brand. For example, in an operating room environment, an electrosurgical and vessel-sealing generator brand must explore the journey of the full cast of characters—surgeon, circulating nurse, scrub nurse, scrub tech—who interact with the device during an operation. This type of customer journey orientation can reveal the unmet and unspoken needs and benefits sought for each actor. Creative expressions of all the players illuminate what is meaningful to them and why, and bring their collective experiences to life.

Picturing how the scrub nurse will stand at the machine next to the surgeon, while the circulating nurse moves around managing the broader surgical case, user interface–user experience designers can effectively design features such as machine button size, placement, color, types of casters and brakes, visual display size, font, location, and so on. Getting into the head of the surgeon helps designers understand what he or she is thinking about during the operation and what

Figure 13.1

Sample Persona: Pete the Millennial Soybean Producer

Age 36
Occupation 3rd generation farmer, former brand manager at General Mills
Status Married, 2 daughters
Location Dighton, Kansas
Education BS Agri-business, minor marketing, Kansas State
Community On church board, baseball coach for daughter's team
Wife Works as home as a digital marketer, on board at Future Farmers of America

Sample Persona: Pete the Millennial Soybean Producer

GOALS AND CONCERNS

Wants full integration across data sources from 3rd party weather data including temperature and precipitation, and own operation data on inputs, yield, past field history, input and crop futures data, and past crop marketing

Data visualizations and comparisons

Worries about technology transition for the farm operation in terms of full capture and integration of data, analysis, and decision making

With his father gone and only one uncle still actively involved, he also worries that he doesn't know what he doesn't know even after being raised on the farm and having a higher ed degree

Responsible for making the farm operation provide for 9 other extended family members

BEHAVIORS

Using multiple apps for weather tracking and forecasts, field management, and grain prices

Excel, Quickbooks, and other desktop software for managing and recording inputs and financial books

Never without his iPhone, also uses tablet (his), and has a desktop shared with his daughters

Believes auto-steer is the best invention in farm equipment. Uses that time for phone calls and other info gathering and transactional needs using both phone and tablet.

APPS AND SOCIAL MEDIA

 Active poster and commenter daily

Primarily follow friends and family, not groups or organizations

 Spectator only

Often forgets to check

 Set up account but never tweets

Checks occasionally but feed not well curated

 Push notifications for multiple weather apps

ESPN K-State football scores and news

BRANDS THAT RESONATE

potential distractions the product design has to eliminate. And, creating messages that appeal to the mindset of each persona represented in the operating room journey makes brand positioning and sales messaging easier to develop and execute. Quite simply, it's much easier to talk to customers in the language they use around your brand if you picture them as, well, people.

In sum, the customer journey lens in creating personas helps build team-level empathy for the human consumer and acts as a guide and filter for brand and product decisions. Personas take targeting to a deeper level and reduce the likelihood that managers will substitute their own personal opinion (or the opinions of friends and family) for the views of the target customer.

Measurement and Data Collection Opportunities

The journey mindset is the driving force behind the current trend of end-to-end customer feedback, which empowers brand marketers, product teams, and operations groups to continually focus on improving the entirety of customer interactions with a brand. If it is true that the totality of people's interpretations of their touchpoints with a brand constitutes the brand's meaning, then experience-driven insights provide the foundation for developing, managing, and maintaining the brand experience. Overall, the customer journey approach uses insights as a tracking tool to understand what is working and what could be improved on both the product side and the brand marketing plan side.

Customer experience platforms such as Medallia[1] and Net Promoter Score programs have become valuable data sources that extend across the full customer journey. They provide the analytics needed for functional groups across all customer touchpoints to find ways to optimize the brand experience while delivering on ROI.

Other quantitative data include search and social media analytics, which offer a data-driven way to target customers based on key words in searches, posts, follows, and likes. Using quantitative data to make inferences about where a person is in the customer journey allows brands to serve up appropriate content. As customers search, post, or engage in social media that indicates they are embarking on a path to purchase in some category, digital analytics allow brands to present their persuasive or informational content to influence that path. As e-commerce continues its exponential growth and each aspect of a customer's journey becomes more measureable, brands can optimize their targeting and content based on real-time results.

Finally, brands can also use customer relationship management (CRM) platforms for journey-related insights. Consider how such data may identify unhappy customers and pinpoint where the customer experience and brand promise failed. A luxury travel company captures every customer's individual stays in its CRM, including e-mails to the company, satisfaction ratings, and account manager notes and observations. This allows the company to not only break down individual stays but also to look for trends by property, account manager, and the like, and to develop operational, product, and communication improvements as needed.

Alternatively, aggregate CRM data on where the sales funnel shows lower conversions or drop-offs may indicate where processes and messaging are failing. For example, high pre-qualification but low subsequent conversion could indicate poor messaging or inadequate product features and benefits. High initial sales or subscriptions and decreasing repeat sales or renewals could indicate product, implementation, or account servicing problems.

ELEVATING RESEARCH METHODS TO LEVERAGE CUSTOMER JOURNEY INSIGHTS

In order to follow customers through their journeys and glean insights from the rich contextual backdrop, brands must go beyond traditional research methods and cast a wider and deeper net around observational, interpretive, and ethnographic approaches. Viewing data collection through the customer journey lens can benefit both qualitative and quantitative approaches.

Qualitative Methods: Relentless Pursuit of the "Why"

On their own, customers can rarely identify, solve, or suggest specific innovations to smooth friction points in their experience with any given brand. Particularly from a technology perspective, most people are generally constrained by what they know versus what might be possible, which is why demanding more from qualitative methods adds unique value.

Methodologically, in-home and in-context interviews, video and real-time diaries, shop-along trips, and the like continue to play a role, but the need to capture the variance in journeys requires researchers to increase their expertise in observing what a customer does or doesn't say or do—and *why* they do or don't. Researchers also must be skilled in generating interpretations, hypotheses, and potential implications on the fly to test with customers. Being able to recognize when tangents are fully veering off course versus heading toward a possible problem to solve or product idea has become more important than adhering strictly to a discussion guide.

Technology has enabled a plethora of mobile and digital data collection and insight-gathering opportunities. The qualitative research company dscout leverages diaries and field studies by giving people missions to capture on their phones.[2] GutCheck was an early pioneer in online focus groups.[3] Both Validately and UserTesting enable moderated and unmoderated online product user testing, and FocusVision developed its Revelation app for insight gathering using a custom-created social media platform specific to the client.[4]

We could devote an entire chapter to outlining the wealth of competitors and technologies in this space. However, their power stems from the *interpretation*, not the *tool* per se. Elevating methods to keep them fresh and relevant in the digital era has less to do with new platforms and allegedly new methods. It's more about constantly pushing observations and hypothetical implications to problems to be solved, which is *not* a task for customers, but *is* an ideal task for engineers and chefs and other creators.

Two examples from entrepreneurs separated by 100 years of history drive this point home. Legendary innovators Henry Ford and Steve Jobs both famously claimed to dislike and distrust customer insight, and focus groups in particular. Ford argued that if he asked consumers what they wanted, they would have asked for a faster horse, and Jobs complained that "people don't know what they want until you show it to them." Brilliant men, but the quotes illustrate why building brands requires qualitative research that does more than try to come up with an answer—it has to produce insight into the true problem customers want solved or the job they want done.

Walter Isaacson's biography of Steve Jobs recounts an executive team meeting at Apple in which everyone tossed their phones on the table and griped about them with annoyance and in highly specific detail. (Sounds a lot like one of those maligned focus groups, doesn't it?) The iPhone ultimately was born out of an innovative design process that sought to "fix" the many things that the Apple team found frustrating about their current phones.

Using qualitative methods to get raw input on frustrations and friction points lets researchers distill the insights into problems to solve, which in turn define the innovation challenges that engineers, entrepreneurs, and designers can use to guide their innovation work. And as the iPhone proves, sometimes those innovations change the world by addressing needs no customer could have articulated directly, but rather by addressing needs derived and interpreted based on the customer experience.

More aggressively exploring the "why" behind insights also helps elevate qualitative insights and renders them more broadly actionable. All qualitative insights experts worth their salt will argue that they have always done this. However, the need to generate implications from a more varied digital world raises the stakes and the importance of translating customer experience insights into product opportunities and angles for ever more critical differentiation.

This challenge is made more difficult in an environment characterized by dense information availability.

For example, consider a premium specialty cheese brand whose makers created a new hard, Italian-style cheese that had crystals dispersed throughout the product. "The crystals set them apart from other cheeses" is a fine start as an insight that might result in a differentiated brand claim. But it needs more probing and definition to find a usable insight for a brand to use in messaging or product implications. "We're the brand with crystals" is clearly too literal and does not help build the brand. If the crystals really do differentiate, how? And *why do they matter*? Is it just a matter of providing a different mouth feel, or is it about a flavor burst that injects a sensorial surprise into what is otherwise a uniformly consistent flavor experience? That ability to add flavor and experiential energy to a cheese could be an emotional benefit to leverage in brand positioning. It could also suggest ideal usage occasions to promote (e.g., transitions throughout the day in which a mental and physical kick are needed). Or, maybe a distinctive, multisensory cheese is more substantive and more like a meal (rather than a topping or a snack), which could open up increased usage volume and inspire different packaging, forms, and flavors from a product development perspective. Relentlessly pursuing the "why" can transform a blunt statement (the crystals are different) into more actionable opportunities.

In addition to even greater attention to the "why," pushing for depth and dimension can offer differentiation insight to even parity-sounding concepts. Consumers and customers now demand innovation from everything from nut butters to automated conveyor systems, and qualitative methods must more meticulously and thoroughly unpack concepts that customers indicate are important to them, in order to characterize them in a way that offers differentiation potential.

For example, in-depth interviews with agricultural engineers and cotton ginners about what they wanted from a ginning equipment partner revealed that (no surprise) innovation mattered. Using an empathy lens, the interviews continued to probe on specifics, proof, and indicators of innovation, and to calibrate incremental versus full-scale invention takes on innovation. The insights gleaned allowed Lummus Ginning to craft a differentiated innovation story for itself, despite innovation claims being widespread in the ginning industry.

The Lummus version of innovation is risk averse and ROI-driven. Lummus uses a strategy of only innovating when it can make the cotton ginning process more profitable and efficient. It never indulges in product changes just for the sake of the new. Its innovation is based on a deep understanding of the trickle-down impacts on ginning of broad shifts in the cotton industry, such as trends in labor, seed oil markets, and technology developments in upstream cotton picking and stripping machinery. Lummus manages to innovate with engineering prowess and ingenuity in a category truly as old as dirt (cotton ginning has existed in some form since 12,000 BCE, give or take) to drive further profitability and improve lint quality for its cotton producer customers.

The elevation of qualitative insights in this example did not result from a new method. It came from leveraging every ounce of potency from traditional depth interviews by crafting follow-up questions, topics, and exercises to pose to customers until they produced new insights that could aid in differentiation.

Quantitative Methods: Harnessing the Power of Big Tech/Big Data

To make quantitative data work for brands in the digital environment, both technical data-science abilities *and* brand-application know-how are needed. Without that combination, companies run the risk of being seduced by tactical ideas that may not align with the longer-term strategic vision for the brand.

In addition, elevating quantitative insights requires ever-growing sophistication in assessing data quality, blending data, and performing analytics and visualizations, all with an eye toward finding leverageable insights that can optimize messaging and distribution channels to build brands.

The digital-era developments that have fueled quantitative insight opportunities stem from the big tech–big data combination. Big tech has provided the devices and apps that customers use to passively and actively generate prolific amounts of data. Neuroscience and cognitive psychology studies that examine attention and behavioral responses to stimuli have provided evidence of users' immersive attention and participation in mobile software. Apps are designed to provide attentional triggers for action (e.g., sounds, notifications, etc.), and they reward and quantify the user's continued engagement with the app, making continued engagement competitive and self-fulfilling. In fact, developers now view sleep as a primary competitor to time spent on apps. With 24 hours a day as the only true limiting factor, the world's collective time spent on apps offers a profound opportunity for data collection relevant to brand building.

With the proliferation of the Internet, mobile devices, and apps, examples of brand-building quantitative data sources in the digital world include:

- Customer/member transactions
- Loyalty information
- Customer experience and customer satisfaction data
- Social media content and comments, likes, dislikes, and shares
- Third-party data (e.g., scanner, Rx prescribing data, government and industry reports)

- Site traffic, including time spent engaging with an app or site
- Geotagged location
- Click-through rates and sales conversions
- E-mails, videos, web site pages
- Salesforce and other CRM data

All of this big tech-enabled big data can provide descriptive data capture, and increasingly, machine-learning opportunities. Machine learning and natural language processing can develop and serve up adaptive and optimized content and experiences to customers, and increase brand adoption (B2C) and opt-in sales prospecting opportunities (B2B)—both of which are clearly a boon for building brands.

It is well beyond the scope of this chapter to assess different data science platforms or provide a guide to predictive analytics and the like. The primary takeaway of the potential of big tech/big data to elevate quantitative insights is this: with big data come big responsibilities in creating a healthy, cross-functional relationship between data/IT and marketing teams. To realize the brand-building potential of quantitative insights, the data wizards and the brand strategy stakeholders must harness their joint ownership of the customer experience to use data-driven insight to propel brands and revenue forward.

IN PRACTICE: HOW TO ENSURE THAT MODERN INSIGHTS CAN DELIVER FOR THE BRAND

We now know that valuable brand insights can be gleaned by integrating the customer journey perspective into traditional research methods. We also know that leveraging the increasing power of big tech/big data can provide powerful insights so long as we are able to interpret these findings from a brand-building perspective. So how do we determine if our outside insight partner or research team will incorporate these perspectives to deliver for the brand, rather than not pushing traditional research approaches far enough?

Below, we offer four strategies:

1. Ask the research team for specific examples of insights that came from inferring what customers *meant* versus what was literally said, and ask for the implications the team generated as a result. Although consultants and agencies often cannot discuss details of past client work, push for unbranded, category-level examples that provide an assessment of the

interpretive skill set. Also look for knowledge of branding and positioning principles that assure that the research team can deliver on smart, fresh action items or decisions.

2. Examine case studies for evidence of broad, wide-net methods. Do past approaches and research designs offer the opportunity to capture the variability of customers' meandering journeys? Do the case studies illustrate skills in using customer insights to define problems and develop hypotheses? Is there evidence of driving to the "why," or root causes and unspoken motivations behind beliefs, behavior, and needs?

3. Determine if the team can coherently discuss brand concepts (e.g., target audience, segments, positioning, brand equities) in addition to data and tactical concepts (e.g., A/B testing, conversion, click-through rate, demographics). More, big, or even ginormous data are not a panacea for anything. Even the most analytically savvy and innovative data scientists still have to connect findings and data visualizations to innovation, go-to-market, and brand-building decisions and actions. You need to be comfortable that you and your insight partner have your eyes on the same brand-building prize.

4. Flesh out whether the research team seems more interested in their method or platform than your insight challenges or market questions. It's important not to fall in love with a potential insight partner's method. As bandwidth and data speeds continue to increase, and mobile devices offer increasingly sophisticated cameras and data-sharing capabilities, digital research platforms will continue to proliferate. Focus instead on the interpretive skills and ability to use data to generate insight relevant to the brand-building activity (idea generation for innovation, positioning-related insight, or messaging and distribution channel prioritization and optimization).

SUMMARY

This chapter argues that the highly varied, democratized digital environment requires brands to demand more from their insights programs. Traditional market research techniques alone are not likely to be sufficient. Adopting an empathy-driven, customer-journey mindset gives the critical insight to fuel new product ideas and the brand building required to launch and grow them.

Although new research technologies have proliferated due to the ubiquity of mobile devices, some things haven't changed. We still have to talk to people in some fashion to understand their experiences, and we still have to measure traits, attitudes, beliefs, and behaviors. What has changed is the need to elevate classic approaches by adopting richer explorations of customer experiences and using machine learning to mine quantitative data. Aggressively pushing to understand the "why" and examine friction points and frustrations, as well as exploiting the ever-greater potential to collect measurable data, provides insights that produce increasingly precise brand-building action items—ultimately making brands more competitive and durable in the digital era.

Bridgette M. Braig is a visiting assistant professor of marketing, College of Business and Economics, Boise State University. Prior to recently re-entering academics, she ran a solo strategy and insights consulting practice, Braig Consulting, for nearly 20 years. She received her PhD in marketing from Northwestern University and has taught at Kellogg as a visiting professor.

NOTES

1. Medallia, https://www.medallia.com; Netpromoter, https://www.netpromoter.com.
2. dscout, https://dscout.com.
3. GutCheck, https://www.gutcheckit.com.
4. Validately, https://validately.com; UserTesting, https://www.usertesting.com; FocusVision, https://www.focusvision.com/products/revelation.

CHAPTER 14

USING NEUROSCIENCE TO ASSESS BRANDS

MORAN CERF

Brands live in the minds of consumers. A brand is the set of associations that come to mind when a particular name or logo is encountered. Traditionally, managers have relied heavily on research techniques, such as focus groups and surveys, that ask consumers to report these associations. Unfortunately, such self-reports often prove to be poor predictors of key metrics of brand success, such as market share and sales volume. Often, consumers claim to love and recognize brands, and have a strong positive set of associations with them, but they do not behave in a manner that reflects such a positive disposition. As a result, managers of a number of major brands are exploring methods for accessing the brain activity and other physiological responses that drives consumers' behavior and decisions in an effort to improve their predictions of behaviors toward brands.

Emerging evidence suggests that neuroscience methods may augment more traditional marketing research techniques in predicting consumer behavior. For example, in 2015 a team of marketing researchers joined with the Advertising Research Foundation to test 37 television ads for 16 unique brands.[1] The goal was to assess the degree to which variation in ad elasticity (the percentage change in sales associated with a 1 percent change in advertising spending) could be accounted for by measures beyond traditional self-reports. Data was collected using a variety of contemporary neurophysiological methods, including eye-tracking, electroencephalography (EEG), and functional magnetic resonance imaging (fMRI). The findings revealed that incremental variance was accounted for by neurophysiological measures, and that those gathered using fMRI explained the most variance in advertising elasticities beyond that accounted for by the baseline traditional measures. This work suggests that neuroscience methods can enhance understanding of how consumers react to brands and brand advertising.

In this chapter, we first describe several neuroscience methods currently in use by marketing researchers. We then outline the type of brand insights that can be obtained using these methods.

THE NEUROSCIENCE TOOL KIT

The neuroscience methods most frequently discussed in brand research currently are EEG and fMRI. These techniques differ in their temporal and spatial resolution, in the time it takes to produce results, in how invasive and uncomfortable they are for participants, and in the ease of interpretation, accuracy of results, and price of the equipment.

EEG

EEG reads the activity of neurons inside the brain using sensors placed on the scalp of participants. EEG signals from various locations on the scalp are captured and analyzed in two standard ways: (1) by looking at an event-related potential (an average of the amplitude of a response after an event) in certain areas in response to brand exposure (i.e., a spike in frontal areas should be observed when a familiar brand is shown, roughly 300 milliseconds after the stimulus onset); and (2) by looking at changes in EEG oscillation frequencies, known as "bands," in response to the presentation of stimuli (i.e., changes in the speed of frequencies in the back of the scalp, where waves increase in their frequency to roughly eight oscillations per second when there is a shift in attention). Neuroscientists are mapping the types of expected outcomes in the brain related to various cognitive functions (e.g., memory activation, emotional response, increase/decrease in attention, etc.), and marketing researchers are then able to use this knowledge to decode the function that is occurring.

Neuroscientists have established some best practices that should be noted by marketing researchers. In addition to a large pool of electrodes (typically more than 32 electrodes covering the entire scalp), a typical EEG study should have a minimum of 25 "good" participants (because of the high noise level in EEG, a pool of approximately 30 subjects is likely to render 25 useable ones). Analysis of EEG data takes a few days, and the results are easy to interpret by a trained neuroscientist. EEG equipment varies in price. A system with high accuracy, multiple electrodes (ideally, in the range of 32 electrodes or more), and a high sampling rate of over 500 Hz costs tens of thousands of dollars.

Aligned with the cost of the equipment, the price of an EEG study testing one condition (e.g., comparison of two ads to determine which drives more attention) is about $20,000, and increases with the number of subjects, conditions (e.g., more ads to compare or more nuanced measures to look into), electrodes, prediction accuracy demanded, and so on.

fMRI

By contrast, fMRI is pricier, slower, and harder to use and interpret, even for experienced neuroscientists. However, in the hands of an expert it provides more precise information than EEG. Typical EEG results would, for example, indicate that "an emotion was evoked by the brand," whereas fMRI data would pinpoint the type of emotion (e.g., "fear") and its interaction with other sites across the brain. However, the price difference is orders of magnitude higher. The equipment (a large magnetic coil that generates fields in the range of 3 tesla) costs millions of dollars and is housed in a special room where a highly trained technician conducts the scan. Thus, study participants must travel to the equipment location. By contrast, EEG data can be collected while consumers shop, watch movies, and engage in other activities in natural settings. A typical fMRI study requires a minimum of 15 subjects, and interpretation of the data can take a few weeks.

In summary, fMRI offers greater precision in readings of the location of activity in the brain but at a substantially higher cost. Not only is EEG less expensive, it also has notably higher temporal resolution. EEG works at a resolution of milliseconds—closer to the brain's actual temporal limitation—whereas the fMRI sampling rate is in orders of seconds. Additionally, neuroscientists have a much better understanding of the drivers of the EEG signal (activity of neurons in the brain) versus the more complex fMRI signal (blood oxygenation, which is a proxy of neuronal activity but not a direct output of those neurons).

Eye-Tracking

Neuroscientists also use tools that offer a proxy of brain activity by measuring the changes in physiological measures that are parasympathetic (changes in the body that cannot be consciously controlled). For example, although individuals typically control the fixations of their eyes and their movement when they encounter new images, they cannot control the first fixation movement. Specifically, if a person views an image of a scene, the first fixation of the eyes is typically happening about 120 milliseconds after the image onset, before the content is consciously perceived, and is entirely driven by salient features in the image that draw attention. Subsequent fixations are driven by our conscious desires. Therefore, neuroscientists often focus on the first or second fixation using eye-tracking devices to assess how a stimulus affects attention covertly. Although looking at an item on a supermarket shelf is no guarantee that it will be purchased, one can be confident that if an item is not seen, it will not be purchased. Thus, eye-tracking is used to inform decisions related to attention (e.g., web site organization and placement of banner ads online, packaging, graphic colors, fonts and sizes, shelf location, and more).

Eye-tracking is typically used by exposing consumers to a visual presentation of the brand while monitoring their eye movements. The metrics used to estimate the attention allocation are the eye movement speed, direction, latency, and dwell time on elements of the stimulus. These measures, which indicate patterns of attention, are then correlated with measures of recall, favorableness of brand evaluation, and intent to purchase.[2] In the last decade, prices of eye-tracking measures have fallen (ranging from hundreds of dollars to tens of thousands at the very high end), leading to a spike in their usage by marketing researchers.

Emerging Tools

In addition to these methods, neuroscientists are pushing the boundaries of tools used in marketing research by proposing techniques traditionally only used for brain research proper. Such techniques include transcranial magnetic stimulation, which can practically shut off a part of the brain momentarily and enable learning about functions of that area by the absence of its activity; and positron emission tomography, the usage of hormones to alter behaviors such as stress and trust. Finally, consumer neuroscience has recently even ventured into the realm of electrophysiology, which records the activity of single neurons in the brains of patients undergoing neurosurgery to learn first-hand about their decisions and behavior predictions—at times before they themselves are aware and with nearly perfect prediction accuracy.[3]

NEUROSCIENCE AND BRAND INSIGHT

The neuroscience methods we've described can deepen marketers' understanding of how consumers respond to their brands. In this section, we review a sample of recent studies using fMRI and EEG to illustrate findings from these techniques.

fMRI Imaging and Brand Associations

The fMRI technique tracks brain activity through voxels (brain VOlume piXELs), which change their oxygenation in response to what a person is thinking at a point in time. A simple way to think about fMRI is that it captures what parts of brain need energy to work at any given moment. Patterns of activity in brain sites that require energy when thinking about a brand can be decoded to make inferences about the attributes associated with a brand, brand personality, and the emotions that a brand evokes. These patterns can also suggest the strength of a brand and the likelihood that it will be confused with another brand.

Specifically, studies by neuroscientists at the University of California at Berkeley[4] and at Erasmus University[5] identified a set of neural signatures that indicate the specific attributes associated with different brands. For example, when a person is thinking of Coke, areas A, B, C, and D may light up, whereas when a person is thinking of Pepsi, areas A, B, C, and E might light up. One can then interpret what these activated areas represent by identifying other stimuli that activate the same areas. Perhaps A, B, C, and D also light up when the person thinks of a friend he likes, whereas A, B, C, and E light up when thinking about an adverse experience.

Neuroscientists also have used fMRI data to classify brands by how emotional they are, as well as the types of emotions they evoke (positive, negative, or more nuanced emotions, such as surprise, anger, disgust, etc.). This is done by first showing subjects stimuli known to elicit an emotion (e.g., a set of frightening images that are used to map the sites in the brain that are active when fear is experienced) and then showing a variety of brand images. Brands that elicit activations resembling those stimulated by frightening images are interpreted as inducing "fear."

Interpreting the meaning of responses to brands may draw upon knowledge of the functions associated with the brain areas activated. Functions such as reward (the feeling of pleasure when an experience occurs), pain, awe, memory, attention, engagement, and more could indicate the experiences evoked by the brand. As an example, Brian Knutson and colleagues have shown that an area in the brain named the nucleus accumbens is activated when people view products they desire. Hence, this area is deemed the "reward" area in the brain, signaling that an item is seen as preferable by a consumer. Another area, the mesial prefrontal cortex, is activated when people view products that they consider to be excessively priced.[6] Similar activity in response to excessive pricing occurs in an area known as the insula, which is typically implicated with the experience of pain, suggesting that high pricing is experienced as subjective pain.

In addition to identifying attributes associated with a brand, the areas that light up offer cues about the brand personality. Chen, Nelson, and Hsu conducted a study in which participants were shown 44 brands and their associated logos.[7] Each brand logo was presented for four to eight seconds, and participants were instructed to think about the characteristics associated with the brand. Following this exposure, each brand was rated on a set of 42 traits (e.g., youthful, competitive). These ratings were compared to neuroimaging voxel signatures to decode the attributes that distinguished the brands from each other. Brands such as Google or Gucci versus McDonald's—polar opposites on key dimensions such as youthfulness and sophistication—were shown to be encoded by nonoverlapping sets of brain patterns, allowing for a decoding of one brand from another. This process generated a list of characteristics associated with each brand and allowed comparisons between brands. Thus, neuroscience provides a complement to the traditional method of assessing brand personality by asking, "If Nike were a person, what would he be like?" (Answer: youthful, competitive, and aggressive). Neuroscience replaces the list of consumer-generated adjectives with neural signatures that code for personality characteristics.

Further, fMRI imaging offers insight into the strength of a brand. Strong brands activate a network of cortical areas involved in positive emotional processing and associated with self-identification and rewards. They also are processed with less effort than weak brands, evidenced by lower levels of activation in areas of working memory. By contrast, weak brands show higher levels of activation in areas associated with negative emotional responses. These activation patterns are independent of the category of the brand.[8]

Finally, fMRI (and even more precisely, the direct recording from neurons in the brain using electrophysiology) can be used to assess the likelihood of brand confusion. Confusion occurs when two brands look alike or evoke similar thoughts or associations. Researchers observe the activity when brand 1 is shown (e.g., Prada) and the activity evoked when brand 2 is shown (e.g., Prado, a knockoff of Prada), and create a *confusion matrix*—a mathematical depiction of the number of elements of the first brand that seemed indistinguishable from the second. If, say, over 90 percent of neural attributes (neurons firing, activation in certain sites) are activated when subjects see both brands, compared to a baseline defined by a third, unrelated brand, a neuroscientist would conclude that consumers' minds may confuse the two brands.

Supplementing the fMRI results, electrophysiology data can also distinguish between brand confusion and brand association by examining the speed of response to the brand in the brain. For example, a high overlap in the activation for brands 1 and 2 could occur because the two brands are perceived to be the same (confusion), or because the knockoff is perceived not identical as such, but it triggers thoughts about the original brand. If the latter is the case, activation for the original brand will be slightly later than the activation pattern for the knockoff. This can be detected through electrophysiology but not fMRI, because of its slow temporal resolution.

For example, if a set of cells in an individual's brain become active when shown a picture of, say, Pepto–Bismol, and the time it takes those cells to become active is precisely 300 milliseconds from the moment the brand image is presented, the latency of those cells is coded as 300 milliseconds. If another brand that shares a similar image, name, or attributes (e.g., Peptol–Bismol) evokes activity in the same cells as Pepto at the same time window (300 milliseconds), the conclusion would be that the brain perceives them as identical. However, if when shown Peptol, the brain cell coding Pepto fires at a delayed time of 350 milliseconds (a 50 milliseconds delay), the interpretation would be that the brands are perceived to be distinct, but that one triggers an association with the other. This application of neuroscience is useful to marketers seeking to quantify the degree to which their brands are confused with competitors (e.g., for trademark infringement reasons). It can also be used to assess the effectiveness of strategies (e.g., changes in packaging) intended to reduce confusion and increase differentiation.

EEG, Brand Emotions, and Engagement

While fMRI enables pinpointing specific associations activated by brands, it is, as noted before, impractical to use on a large scale or in a natural ad-viewing or purchasing setting. In these contexts, EEG is an alternative that also yields valuable insights.

For example, a recent case study by Nielsen evaluated an ad for a pet shelter.[9] The ad, which was 30 seconds long, depicted a dog moving on-screen while a narrator addressed the need for a home for dogs such as the one shown. The stated goal of the pet adoption agency was to evoke a strong positive emotional response with viewers.

First, a focus group viewed the ad and participants reported their emotional responses. Although they were able to identify emotions the ad evoked in its entirety, they were unable to pinpoint emotions evoked by specific moments in the ad or suggest how the ad might be improved in terms of its emotional impact.

However, a test of the ad using EEG provided the missing insight. Assessment of the brains of about 30 viewers revealed that the overall emotional response to the ad was actually below a baseline level, which was established by having the participants sit with their eyes closed before watching the ad and trying to focus on their breathing. Importantly, specific moments in the ad that were expected to evoke a strong positive emotional reaction actually showed the lowest response. A moment-to-moment analysis of participants' responses led to the conclusion that the narration of on-screen text interfered with the desired emotional response to the cute visual of the puppy, resulting in a decrease in emotion. When the ad was revised to separate the text and images of the dog (in the new ad the dog was off screen when the narrator spoke and came back afterwards), a subsequent testing with focus group participants showed the desired emotional response among viewers. Here, EEG data provided insight about emotional responses that consumers themselves were unable to offer, and thereby resulted in the creation of a more powerful ad.

EEG data is also being used to assess consumers' brand engagement—consumers' emotional involvement with a brand and the degree to which the brand connects with the self. A variety of measures can serve as a proxy for consumers' engagement with a brand, including the number of references to the brand in online venues (i.e., tweets, re-tweets, "likes"), the time spent with the brand, and the willingness to endorse the brand.

Neuroscientists argue that heightened engagement with a stimulus leads to increased similarity in the EEG pattern of brain activation across individuals (and conversely, decreased engagement leads to more idiosyncratic responses). The intuition behind this idea is that interesting and engaging experiences make us all look alike and leave very little room for our uniqueness to emerge. By contrast, boring experiences allow our brains to drift, and, in doing so, tap into unique facets of our personalities and experiences. This method of assessing engagement by measuring similarity across brains was established in the context of natural stimuli, but more recently has been employed in marketing settings.[10]

Several studies building on these engagement measures offer evidence that when the brains of many people respond in the same way, a brand is better remembered, evokes a stronger emotional response, is more interesting, and, if the engagement is positive, leads to more favorable outcomes.[11] Additional research has identified features of brand content that are associated with increased engagement: engagement is greater when the visual and semantic elements of the brand stimulus are limited and simple, when people are included and used to direct the viewers' gaze, and when a narrative is presented rapidly.[12] A recent project conducted by the author in collaboration with YouTube serves as an example. YouTube shows ads prior to content viewed on its site. Consumers can elect to skip these ads after five seconds. The goal of the study was to determine whether EEG data from viewers would predict the ads that consumers would skip after five seconds more accurately than consumers' intuitive judgments. The results revealed that the EEG data enabled accurately classifying 70 percent of the ads as skipped versus viewed (compared to actual skip/view data available through YouTube), whereas consumers' predictions based on viewing the ads were only correct 44 percent of the time, which is close to chance level.

fMRI, EEG, and Brand Design

Neuroscience techniques can also offer insight into consumers' responses to elements of brand design (i.e., logos, fonts, colors, symbols, sounds, smells, and other sensory cues). Specifically, EEG and fMRI can detect how rapidly a symbol, such as a brand logo, is processed, and hence, how intrusive and easy it is to recognize the depth of associations it evokes. These techniques also identify in what part of the brain the brand is recognized (is the response semantic, visual, or evoked by memory?), and which modality is involved in what order (Is there an olfactory response that drives the memory, or is the initial response visual? Which is more effective in evoking desired emotions?).

For example, in a study demonstrating the effect of brand symbols on experience, consumers' brains were scanned using fMRI while they tasted what they thought were different wines. The only actual difference between the wines was the price label. However, the *experience* of tasting the wines was dramatically different, with more expensive wines being tastier both subjectively (as reported by subjects) and objectively (as indicated by the activity of pleasure centers in the brain).[13] This finding provides evidence that marketing actions such as pricing not only affect choice but also the internal gustatory experience. It also shows that we can now decode those marketing actions by directly observing the brain, overriding the need to ask participants for their reports.

SUMMARY

Neuroscience methods have enormous potential, and it is likely that market researchers will turn to them with greater frequency to gain insights about brands in the future. The examples and tools mentioned in this review are merely the tip of the iceberg. Many more could be shown; the ones selected here were chosen in order to span a variety of offerings, but are in no way a complete list. The number of studies, examples, and case studies is increasing daily, and efforts by neuroscientists to supplement traditional methods are already showing promising outcomes. This progress is driven by academic works as well as by the corporate world. Many large companies are conducting research using neuroscience methods to promote their business interests in brand management, including Silicon Valley tech giants such as Facebook, Google, and Microsoft; entertainment companies such as Viacom, AMC, Electronic Arts, and Sony; consumer packaged goods companies such as Procter & Gamble and Coca-Cola; and automotive companies such as Ferrari. Research companies such as Nielsen, Millward Brown, and Ipsos are offering services for brand assessment. Together, these efforts grow the field, lower prices, and increase the number of consumers who benefit from the improvements in marketing research.

Still, neuroscience methods currently make up a relatively small part of the branding tool kit, partly because conducting the studies are complex, expensive, and time consuming. As technology advances and we learn more about the brand insights neuroscience can offer, we can imagine that the impact and influence of neuroscience will grow even more, offering not just supplements to traditional methods but also potential replacements for existing offerings.

Moran Cerf is an associate professor of marketing at the Kellogg School of Management and is affiliated with the cognitive neuroscience program at Northwestern University. Dr. Cerf holds a PhD in neuroscience from Caltech, an MA in philosophy and a BS in physics from Tel Aviv University.

NOTES

1. Venkatraman, Vinod, Angelika Dimoka, Paul A. Pavlou, Khoi Vo, William Hampton, Bryan Bollinger, Hal E. Hershfield, Masakazu Ishihara, and Russell S. Winer (2015), "Predicting Advertising Success beyond Traditional Measures: New Insights from Neurophysiological Methods and Market Response Modeling," *Journal of Marketing Research* 52(4), 436–452.
2. Reutskaja, Elena, Rosemarie Nagel, Colin F Camerer, and Antonio Rangel (2011), "Search Dynamics in Consumer Choice under Time Pressure: An Eye-Tracking Study," *American Economic Review* 101(2), 900–926.
3. Cerf, Moran, Eric Greenleaf, Tom Meyvis, and Vicki G. Morwitz (2015), "Using Single-Neuron Recording in Marketing: Opportunities, Challenges, and an Application to Fear Enhancement in Communications," *Journal of Marketing Research* 52(4), 530–545. https://doi.org/10.1509/jmr.13.0606.
4. Chen, Yu-Ping, Leif D. Nelson, and Ming Hsu (2015), "From 'Where' to 'What': Distributed Representations of Brand Associations in the Human Brain," *Journal of Marketing Research* 52(4), 453–466.
5. Chan, Hang-Yee, Maarten Boksem, and Ale Smidts (2018), "Neural Profiling of Brands: Mapping Brand Image in Consumers' Brains with Visual Templates," *Journal of Marketing Research*.

6. Knutson, Brian, Scott Rick, G. Elliott Wimmer, Drazen Prelec, and George Loewenstein (2007), "Neural Predictors of Purchases," *Neuron* 53(1), 147–156.

7. Chen, Nelson, and Hsu (2015), see Note 4.

8. Schaefer, Michael, Harald Berens, Hans-Jochen Heinze, and Michael Rotte (2006), "Neural Correlates of Culturally Familiar Brands of Car Manufacturers," *Neuroimage* 31(2), 861–865.

9. Smith, Michael E. (2016), "Reducing Fear in Advertising Shelter Pets," NMBSA blog, June 14. www.nmsba.com/neuromarketing/news-blog/195-reducing-fear-in-advertising-shelter-pets.

10. Barnett, Samuel B., and Moran Cerf (2017), "A Ticket for Your Thoughts: Method for Predicting Content Recall and Sales Using Neural Similarity of Moviegoers," *Journal of Consumer Research* 44(1), 160–181. https://doi.org/10.1093/jcr/ucw083.

11. Barnett, Samuel Benjamin, and Moran Cerf (2018), "Trust the Polls? Neural and Recall Responses Provide Alternative Predictors of Political Outcomes," *ACR North American Advances in Consumer Research*.

12. Barnett, Samuel B., Hope M. White, and Moran Cerf (2016), "Keep It Simple Stimuli: Brain-Vetted Elements of Movie Trailers Predict Opening Weekend Ticket Sales," *Advances in Consumer Research*.

13. Plassmann, Hilke, John O'Doherty, Baba Shiv, and Antonio Rangel (2008), "Marketing Actions Can Modulate Neural Representations of Experienced Pleasantness," *Proceedings of the National Academy of Sciences* 105(3), 1050–1054.

CHAPTER 15

MEASURING BRAND RELEVANCE AND HEALTH

JULIE HENNESSY

Brands are assets of enormous impact and value. They are the lenses through which consumers see product features and decide whether they are interesting enough for further consideration. Brand stewards, from entrepreneurs to corporate managers, spend enormous effort and resources to support their brands and keep them strong and preferred. So how should we measure the productivity of these efforts? How do you track, tend, and measure the health and vitality of your brand?

Executives have asked this question for years, and the answer is not getting any easier to define. When we thought of brands as logos, trade dress, and intellectual property, the focus was on legal protection of our assets, control over their use, and defense against encroachments on our territory. We fought back when competitors got too close and imitated our brand assets, or even when our brand marks were used incorrectly within the company. To this day, there is swift reaction when a franchisee decides to alter the color of McDonald's Golden Arches, or a dealer gets too creative with the iconic John Deere logo. But the focus of today's efforts to protect the brand has shifted a bit, and digital access to voluminous data will accelerate the changes in how we track brand value.

A story illustrates this point. Over 20 years ago I worked for the packaged food giant Kraft and had responsibility for its iconic Kraft Macaroni and Cheese brand. Within this brand franchise, Kraft earns higher profit margins on the specialty-shaped, macaroni-like spirals and SpongeBob Shapes than the original tube-shaped variety. For years, Kraft has experimented with new shapes for the product. During my tenure, we had the brilliant idea of putting Mickey Mouse-shaped macaroni in the box. After all, mice love cheese, and Kraft has long been deemed the "cheesiest"—a match made in heaven. Out we flew to Southern California to meet with Disney executives and propose a cheesy partnership. Unfortunately, a deal did not result, and no mice ever entered the Kraft Mac and Cheese boxes (at least not on purpose). At the time, Disney was uncomfortable with the idea of people "eating" Mickey Mouse and feared that Mickey would be overexposed as a result of too many licensing deals.

But while at Disney, we caught a glimpse of the voluminous Mickey Mouse "brand standard"—page after page of documentation and guidelines that dictated and delineated the rules for Mickey Mouse. It included what he could wear, what he would say, and even the nature of that oh-so-ambiguous relationship he has with the object of his affection, Minnie Mouse. Clearly, Disney took brand control and protection very seriously.

Then, a year or so ago, I had another opportunity to discuss branding with a Disney executive. I told him about that long-ago meeting, and we laughed about the fact that Mickey Mouse had found himself in many, many food products in the intervening years. Finally, I asked about the old Mickey Mouse brand standard: the document that set the rules and boundaries for the brand that is Mickey Mouse. The executive sighed and commented, "That was a different era." He continued, "Today, in a world of consumer-created content and easy 'cut and paste,' we figure that we control a very small fraction of the images of Mickey Mouse."

While official licensing deals are still plentiful and lucrative, this illustrates the point that the days of controlling an asset and its every use are over. Today, we participate *with* consumers, and even competitors, in the use, interpretation, and protection of the brands we manage. As is true in so much of marketing today, managing brands is as much a conversation as a one-way dictation, where we must spend as much time *asking* consumers what a brand means as *telling* them what to think.

In this chapter, we will talk about today's new definition of the brand, and discuss some cutting-edge techniques for making sure we really hear the voice of the customer in our efforts to track and measure brand value. We will discuss a model for understanding strategies for building a brand, from repositioning to brand extensions. And, we will discuss how the connected digital world impacts the challenges of brand tracking.

BRAND MEASUREMENT TECHNIQUES

If we now think about brands not as logos and trademarks but as sets of associations in the minds and hearts of individuals, the challenge of measuring and tracking the health of brands fundamentally changes. First and foremost, all sorts of entities that we didn't think of as brands before can now be studied. Certainly, companies such as Disney, McDonald's, and Nike are still brands. But locations—such as Las Vegas, Paris, and Dubai—are also brands with rich associations. People are also brands—political figures such as Donald Trump, entertainers such as Beyoncé, and leaders such as Pope Francis. Any entity about which individuals have strong and plentiful associations can be thought of and measured as a brand.

But how do we measure these nebulous and changing sets of associations in a way that is useful to the owners and managers of these brand equities? It is quite a challenge. Traditionally, brand monitoring and measurement has been conducted in two dominant ways: measurement of awareness and tracking of brand attitudes. Both of these methods are still valid today, so it is worth the time to discuss their use and limitations.

Awareness Tracking

Awareness tracking is the most frequently executed measure of brand health and relevance. Many executives think of this metric in a very simple way: they think of high-awareness brands as valuable and low-awareness brands as either troubled or underdeveloped. While awareness is still a relevant metric when considering a brand's strength and health, this simplistic "more awareness is always better" thinking is not particularly accurate or useful. Understanding awareness levels is a piece of the puzzle needed for assessing a brand's health, but it is not enough as a stand-alone measure. In fact, high brand awareness in itself can actually be a challenge or impediment to success.

Think of awareness as the likelihood of consumers knowing or recognizing your brand's name. Certainly, it is impossible for someone who has never heard of you to love or want you. In that way, awareness is a necessary precursor for consideration, trial, purchase, or advocacy. Thus, awareness is the first level of most brand marketing funnels (see Figure 15.1).

However, in some situations, awareness can also be an impediment. If everyone already knows your brand, it is harder to generate growth. And, if you are unfortunate enough to manage a brand that everyone already knows and thinks poorly of, you may be facing the toughest of all brand challenges—changing attitudes about a brand that consumers know well and dislike or distrust. High levels of awareness make the challenge of changing brand attitudes particularly difficult and sometimes even impossible. Thus, awareness can be a friend or foe.

Companies measure brand awareness in two ways—*aided awareness* and *unaided awareness*. In an aided awareness measurement study, the consumer or respondent is presented with a list of brands and asked to check which ones he

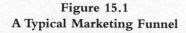

Figure 15.1
A Typical Marketing Funnel

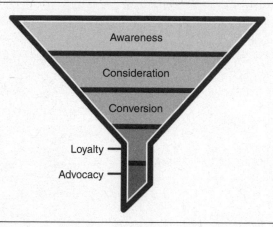

or she is familiar with. This, in effect, is the "aiding" of aided awareness. While aided awareness measures can be useful, the prompting done by showing consumers a list of brands in some ways confounds the testing. Aided awareness measures, for that reason, often overstate actual awareness.

Therefore, the more useful way of measuring awareness is unaided awareness. In an unaided awareness study, a respondent is given a category—such as hotels, athletic shoes, or candidates for president. They are then asked, without any hints or prompting, to list the brands that they can think of in that category. This type of unaided brand awareness is a true measure of actual brand awareness, and the order in which consumers list brands is a reasonable proxy for which are most top of mind (see Figure 15.2).

Attitudinal Brand Tracking

The second form of traditional brand measurement is attitudinal brand tracking. Here the effort moves beyond just understanding whether a consumer knows a brand or not and shifts to assessing what the consumer knows, thinks, or feels. Many companies conduct some sort of attitudinal brand tracking in order to take the pulse of what consumers are thinking about their brands. In these surveys, which may be fielded every few years or as frequently as weekly, consumers are asked to agree or disagree if a predetermined set of attributes is descriptive of a brand. This list of attributes is usually conceived by the managers of the brand and is usually fairly aspirational in nature. They are the brand managers' words, not necessarily the consumers' words (see Figure 15.3).

Figure 15.2
Questions to Measure Awareness

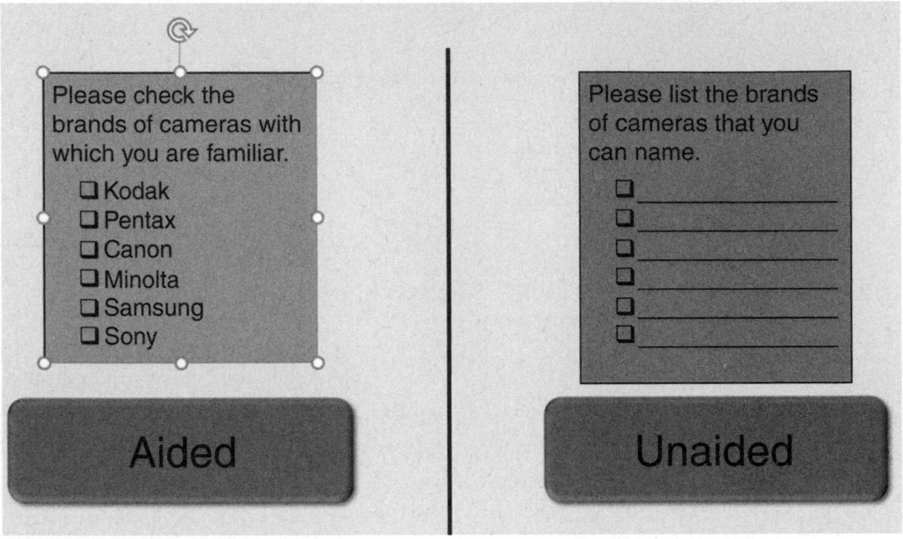

Please check the brands of cameras with which you are familiar.
Kodak
Pentax
Canon
Minolta
Samsung
Sony
Aided
Please list the brands of cameras that you can name.
Unaided

Figure 15.3
Example of Attitudinal Tracking of McDonald's

Fast food restaurants
7.1. Please rate McDonald's on each of the following attributes.
Menu options/variety
Convenience/location
Service quality/speed
Prices
Food healthiness
Food quality/taste
Cleanliness/appearance
NEXT

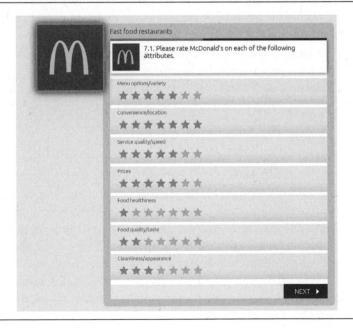

Feedback from this sort of consumer survey can certainly be useful, especially if there is the ability to compare responses to the survey by current users of a brand versus nonusers over time, and if there is data on both the brand and its direct competitors. However, there is one factor that is missing in such a survey. Not unlike the criticism of measures of aided awareness, this sort of survey data does a weak job of capturing the consumers' unvarnished thoughts and feelings. The survey itself suggests some thoughts that the consumer should have and not others. We get no sense of the words that consumers would use on their own to talk about brands.

Asking Open-Ended Questions: A Less-Biased Way To Measure Brand Associations

For these reasons, my research in the past few years has focused on a method for collecting brand associations without this bias. Consumers (or nonconsumers) of a brand are simply asked an open-ended question such as, "What comes to mind when you think of the brand _____?" followed by, "What else _____? What else_____?" Data is tabulated across large enough groups of respondents to be useful and reliable, and yet the data comes in the form of respondents' own words, thoughts, and feelings. Data is frequently collected online, to allow consumers to express themselves freely and without reservation. The recent results of these studies have often been surprising and illuminating.

For instance, surprisingly enough, Toyota drivers' associations of "safety" increased as Toyota experienced problems and garnered bad press about unintended acceleration and recalls. While counterintuitive, consumers needed to believe that their own Toyota cars were safe to justify the daily decision to keep driving it. This enhanced belief in their own Toyota's safety explains why Toyota's repurchase and loyalty measures did not suffer after public scrutiny and multiple recalls.

Similarly, while it was conventional wisdom that 2016 U.S. presidential candidate Hillary Clinton would have a clear advantage with women voters, it was clear that a significant segment of women voters found her to be unlikeable. In fact, women were more likely than men to describe her with negative adjectives. This was a first window into the fact that Clinton would experience a problem with women's support in the election.

Likewise, as the press talked about the likely demise of the Volkswagen brand after the Volkswagen emissions scandal, it was clear that consumers, especially Volkswagen drivers, were just as likely to see the firm's behavior as evidence of the sophistication of German engineering skill. While some consumers undoubtedly thought that the firm had acted in an unethical manner, others focused on how smart and crafty it was to create a "defeat" device in the emissions system.

Uber is another example. Collecting open-ended consumer brand associations provides insight into how the brand was impacted by the behavior of its controversial ex-CEO, Travis Kalanick, who resigned in 2017 over allegations of ignoring sexual harassment at the company. It also sheds light on how the scandal impacted its competitor, Lyft. Open-ended brand association tracking in 2017 and 2018 indicated several interesting findings about the impact that negative stories about Uber and its CEO were having on the Uber brand, competitive brand Lyft, and the category of ride-sharing as a whole. Uber, it turns out, was carrying a sea of negative associations. When asked what came to mind when they thought of the brand Uber, many consumers answered "unsafe," "sketchy," "dangerous," or "be careful." By contrast, Lyft was seen as decidedly more "fun" and "friendly." This was true despite the similarity of the two companies' rider and driver experiences.

As Uber's press turned negative, the former copycat, Lyft, was seen as increasingly differentiated. Instead of the bad press hurting both players and ride-sharing in general, consumers who had fully adopted Uber in their travel routine were quick to switch to the kinder and gentler option, Lyft. While Uber was and is still seen as innovative by many, it is taking on the negative characteristics of being "experimental."

Gender issues also play a role in the comparison of Uber and Lyft brand associations. Some of the negative allegations around Kalanick involved the firm's female-unfriendly culture. As Uber's press focused on sexism and arrogance, Lyft's pink logo (see Figure 15.4) became an inadvertent asset.

Figure 15.4
Lyft and Uber Logos

Lyft is perceived as more playful, more female, and, as a result, for both men and women, more safe. Research conducted at Kellogg showed that females were at least three times more likely to lead with a negative comment when they were asked about Uber than when asked about Lyft. Lyft's longstanding policy of encouraging tipping, which was initially seen as a negative from a rider standpoint, was now seen as being evidence of friendliness and positivity.

Finally, both brands elicited comments from consumers on the subject of alcohol and partying. Once again, the tone of the comments referencing each brand was starkly different. Uber has more associations with drunk, unruly passengers, and the brand even triggers concerns about potential drunk drivers. On the flip side, the perception of Lyft is that it is a way to get home safely and responsibly after drinking. Lyft has the positive associations of being the responsible and safe "designated driver."

In this particular case, consumer association data is particularly important to the challenge of managing these brands. Despite continued growth in revenue and ridership, Uber has significant challenges, which become more obvious when brand associations are tracked in consumers' own words. Meanwhile, Lyft has an opportunity to take advantage of a competitor's problems and to elevate itself as a preferred alternative.

ASSESSING BRAND HEALTH AND DEFINING BRAND-BUILDING STRATEGIES

Beyond the simplistic thinking that says that high-awareness brands are strong assets and low-awareness brands are not valuable, we can combine several factors to assess brand health and recommend a path going forward. We create the awareness/liking/market-share model (see Figure 15.5) by combining (1) an unaided awareness measure, (2) data on "liking," or preference, from brand associations or other measures, and (3) market share or another measure of the brand's size and financial value.

Figure 15.5
Awareness/Liking/Market Share Model

	LEGO	SAMSUNG	Barilla	Old Spice	Microsoft
Awareness	High	High	Low	Low	High
Likeability	High	Low	High	Low	Low
Market Share	High	Low	Low	Low	High

In the following examples, we will rate different levels of awareness, liking/preference, and market-share status (high or low for each category) to define the classic situations that call for a set of different brand-building strategies, including these five:

1. *Category or brand expansion.* This growth strategy is about taking a strong brand into new spaces. These spaces may be new geographic regions, or new product/service categories, or both.

2. *Rebranding.* Rebranding refers to the stripping of a brand name from a product and giving it new consideration through a new brand name. This growth strategy may be employed when an established brand has so many negative associations that it becomes difficult for potential consumers to see positive features when connected with the current brand name.

3. *Awareness building.* This growth strategy is usually executed through some combination of distribution expansion and advertising spending. It is fundamentally about making sure as many relevant purchasers as possible know about the brand.

4. *Repositioning.* Unlike rebranding, which is about changing a name, repositioning is a growth strategy that is fundamentally about altering the dominant associations that consumers connect with a brand name. Interestingly, the higher a brand's awareness rating, the more difficult the challenge of repositioning.

5. *Building relationships.* Almost a subset of repositioning, building relationships acknowledges the difficulty of changing consumers' minds and hearts about well-known, high-awareness brands. Choosing this strategy requires an understanding that changing made-up minds is difficult, and that it is particularly difficult to change consumers' minds when they sense that you are trying to sell something. Therefore, activity behind this strategy focuses away from the transaction itself, where there is more ability to change consumer perceptions.

Lego (High-High-High): The Case for Brand Extension

A brand with high awareness, high likeability, and strong market share (high-high-high in our model) might seem like a no-problem situation. What could be wrong if everyone knows you, everyone likes you, and everyone buys you? But in fact, brands like this do have challenges, especially if they play in categories that are flat or declining. One of the biggest challenges is that you have no one new to tell about your great product, no one new to convince, and no easy way to grow.

Lego is a classic high–high–high brand, and a dominant player in a shrinking category. Unaided awareness is very high, with Lego freely volunteered as a brand name whether consumers are asked to name brands of toys or brands of children's blocks. Almost all consumer associations are positive, with the exception of an occasional mention of how painful it is to step on Lego blocks left on the floor. Lego's share of the block market is dominant. The problem is growth. Lego's efforts over the past 10 years include a series of attempts to expand through licensing into other categories, including movies, video games, and theme parks. While some of these have been more successful than others, this approach makes strategic sense. Lego has also looked at expansion from the perspective of demographic target markets, by introducing products that appeal to girls as well as boys, and also to bring back adult men who are former Lego players and still Lego lovers.

Samsung (High-Low-Low): The Case for Rebranding

As we build our brand strategy matrix, we look at a situation in which a brand has high awareness, low liking, and low market share. In this case, the brand is well known and recognized, but consumers have negative associations about it. For this reason, most consumers choose other brands in the category. This is a challenge faced by many companies, including Spirit Airlines and Ryanair, Kmart and Sears, and Denny's and Burger King. In these situations, sometimes negative associations with the brand overwhelm any efforts to design products and services to give consumers a good experience. Many consumers just cannot like anything these brands would offer. In this case, sometimes even the best product development efforts are for naught, until the brand name itself changes. Consumers need a new *brand lens* to be able to see quality from these providers.

In North America in the 1980s and 1990s, Samsung was a high-low-low brand. Consumers knew it well, but they thought of it as a cheap knockoff of Sony. As such, its market share was not substantial. For this reason, Samsung products were priced substantially below Sony's as the brand fought to be considered by consumers. But this pricing reinforced beliefs that Samsung was a second-rate brand.

Samsung's approach to remedy this issue is interesting because of the path it did not take: when it might have undertaken a rebranding, it did not. Samsung had considerable R&D resources and great ability to design good products. But the brand image and Samsung-branded products were not considered high quality. In a situation like this, the brand appears to have value because of its high awareness, but in reality it is not an asset because of the associations tied to the name. This is the classic situation where a firm must consider using a new brand name, with little or no connection with the first.

While rebranding would have been an obvious answer to Samsung's quality-perception issue, it was a difficult conclusion for Samsung executives to embrace for several reasons. First, these decisions, even for the North American business, were made in South Korea. In Korea, the Samsung brand is strong: it is a very high-awareness, high-liking, high-share asset. In fact, at the time, Samsung was the unofficial national brand of South Korea. Appropriately, Samsung's brand strategy in Korea was one of category expansion. It had taken the Samsung brand successfully into categories as diverse as shipbuilding, insurance, and hospitals. The executives felt that surely this strong, healthy, and valuable brand would be an asset in the United States, just as it was in South Korea. Further, ceding the Samsung name to Japanese rival Sony in the North American market would have been totally unacceptable.

And so the executives stuck with the Samsung brand, even to the point of avoiding any major sub-brands. Eventually, they were able to chip away at the negative perceptions of Samsung—through the passage of time, through entry to new categories like handsets, and as a result of Sony's mistakes and troubles. They did not rebrand; instead they took the longer route of repositioning. But it took nearly 30 years to change the image. Contrast this with the renaming of another Korean electronics firm: from Lucky Goldstar to LG. With no link to the past, LG was able to quickly establish positive equity.

This example demonstrates the power of the rebrand option. Building awareness is expensive, to be sure. But changing perceptions, especially on a high-awareness brand, is not only expensive, it is also very, very, slow. The LG strategy and the Samsung strategy were both successful; it just depends whether you need to get the job done in 3 years or 30.

When a high-awareness brand wants to mean something it doesn't, look for the use of a new moniker. If McDonald's someday wanted to run a chain of super-healthy fast-food restaurants, it might launch under a name with no link to McDonald's. When Toyota wanted to play a significant role in luxury automotive, out came the stand-alone brand, Lexus. And, as Facebook's most committed users became older, the firm focused its youth efforts under a different brand name, Instagram.

Barilla: (Low–High–Low): The Case for Awareness Building

The case of low awareness, high liking, and low share is a clearer, more easily understood problem and solution. Here, most potential targets are unaware of the brand, but those who know it like it a lot. Share is low, but awareness is the clear culprit. In this case, the obvious answer is also the right one: awareness building.

A great example here is Barilla pasta's entry into the U.S. market. In Italy, Barilla is a dominant, mass brand of pasta, perhaps like Prince or Creamette in the United States. It is solid quality but not perceived as anything special. Looking for a way to grow, the firm began importing to the United States, where the brand was an unknown entity, the classic low-awareness situation. However, it was obvious from the packaging that the brand was from Italy. Therefore, in the United States, the product took on all of the positive associations of the "brand of Italy," along with perceptions of authenticity and imported quality. The fact that Barilla was more expensive than domestic pasta didn't hurt. Therefore, though the brand had low awareness, it had high liking among those who saw it. Margins were higher for Barilla than for U.S. brands, and so the brand was given more shelf space by the retailers who stocked it. As it became more visible to consumers, its share rose. Finally, the brand became large enough to afford U.S. advertising, and its managers were smart enough to play on the perceptions of Italian authenticity. Thus, this low-awareness, high-liking, low-share brand became a high-high-high success.

Old Spice (Low-Low-Low): The Case for Repositioning

What do you do if you find yourself in the situation of running a low-awareness, low-liking, and low-market share brand? While this situation might appear to be disheartening, there is a reason to think positively. In fact, the hope in this situation lies in a strange place—the good news is that you have low awareness. Here's why: in a case like this, most potential consumers do not know the brand name, which is a good thing, because those who do know it have negative perceptions. Both the lack of awareness and negative perceptions contribute to low sales. However, in this case, low awareness is the ticket to a potentially brighter future—it provides the opportunity for potential repositioning.

Unlike rebranding, which involves switching to a new brand identity, repositioning is fundamentally about changing the way consumers think and feel about a brand and creating a more positive set of associations around an already existing equity. This is always a challenge, but as we have discussed before, it is even more of a challenge when awareness is high. The more people know a brand, the more difficult it is to tell them something different from what they already believe about it. This is true particularly with political candidates' brands—the more well known a candidate is, the less able he or she is to change positions on issues to please an electorate.

When most potential customers don't know the brand, they become, in a sense, a clean slate where we can start fresh in building positive associations. In fact, when we look at the challenge of repositioning, the greatest success stories often deal not with changing the minds of past customers who have negative perceptions, but with engaging a new group of consumers and building positive associations with this new audience. Sometimes this new audience is a new generation, sometimes it is a new market segment, and sometimes it is in a new country or geographic location. But in all of these cases, marketers are speaking to a fresh target.

A great repositioning example here is the brand Old Spice. When acquired by Procter & Gamble in 1990, this brand was in rough shape. The brand had low awareness and relevancy, especially among young to middle-aged consumers. Among the aware, associations were negative—old men, ships, fish, and the sea—not great associations for a cologne or grooming brand.

As P&G went to work on repositioning and breathing new life into the Old Spice brand, it did many things, including updating product forms, scents, and packaging. But one of the most important things it did was to speak to a new target: both a new generation and a new gender. In "The Man Your Man Could Smell Like," the most famous of all Old Spice television ads (in fact, the 2011 Grand Effie-winning ad), the brand did just that. The spot starts sonorously with, "Hello ladies. Look at your man. Now back to me. Now back to your man. Now back to me. Sadly, he isn't me. But if he stopped using lady-scented body wash and switched to Old Spice, he could smell like he's me."[1] Now Old Spice has a new target—women. And P&G had uncovered a terrifically useful insight: men had started becoming more interested in grooming. The women in their lives were thrilled. However, the men's first steps often involved borrowing the products and scents of a wife or girlfriend. Here was the brand growth opportunity. Get the "lady" to support her man's new interest in grooming by purchasing products just for him. Combine a new target with a great consumer insight, and a brand is reborn.

Many of the most successful brand repositionings of this era, including IBM, Stella Artois, and Havaianas, have one strategic aspect in common. Enabled by low overall awareness, the brand managers changed the brand image largely by speaking to a new target. Instead of convincing the old users that they were wrong, they spoke to a new group to breathe life into a brand again. This is the hope of the low-awareness, low-liking, low-share brand.

Microsoft (High–Low–High): The Case for Building Relationships

And now, the last case, and one of the most challenging ones: the high-awareness, low-liking, high-market share brand. In this situation, everyone knows the brand, no one likes the brand, but they buy it anyway. The last time we examined the high-awareness, low-liking combination, the recommendation was to walk away from the brand through rebranding. However, in this situation, that is probably neither advisable nor possible. The brand has far too much financial value. So how do you convince consumers who know a brand well—and are committed nonfans—to think again? It's not going to be easy, but there is a way.

More brands find themselves in this situation than you would think. Often, these are brands—Microsoft, Commonwealth Edison, and many dominant airlines—whose users feel they have no choice. The brands are well known and have significant negative associations, but consumers buy anyway. Fifteen years ago, Microsoft was in this situation. It was one of the most well-known brands on the planet, but among its top associations in consumers' minds were "evil" and "monopoly." Nevertheless, consumers bought PCs anyway, because computers were important, and the risks of buying a non-Windows PC seemed very high. While Microsoft's image today is hardly beloved, it is far less negative. A look at this transformation will reveal the underpinnings of the interesting "build relationships" strategy.

Once consumers know and dislike a brand, it is hard to change their minds. Ironically, it is most difficult to change their minds when trying to sell something. When someone is selling—whether it's a candidate trying to get a vote or a salesman trying close a deal—consumers know to suspect the messenger. Therefore, efforts to change the mind of a customer who thinks they know best are best placed away from the act of making a sale. To this end, the softening of the image of Microsoft was greatly helped by the halo from publicity around the Bill and Melinda Gates Foundation, the founder's private charitable fundraising arm. Along with the Microsoft associations "evil" and "monopoly" was the association with Bill Gates, the firm's early leader. In the past 15 years, his efforts have shifted from running the firm to other activities, including an active role in the philanthropic foundation that bears his name. Early efforts of the Gates foundation often involved giving away technology to parts of the world that needed it.

Interestingly, at first this charitable activity was seen through the lens of "evil monopoly" as an extended effort to build Microsoft's global dominance. However, more recent efforts of the foundation, focused on global health and the eradication of malaria in the world, have had a positive impact on perceptions of the Gates Foundation, Bill Gates himself, and even Microsoft. Note that getting farther from the act of selling a product or service, and farther from self-interest, was crucial to the progress on moving the brand association to be less negative.

The key to the slow work of changing the image of the high-awareness, low-liking, but high-market share brand is more about making friends than driving sales. To change this brand image, we must focus on building quality relationships away from the act of completing a transaction.

DIGITAL DATA AND THE TRACKING OF BRANDS

How does the digital world change the world of brand tracking? First, it allows quicker, cheaper, and more continuous execution and analysis of existing brand tracking activity. Firms that have historically checked their brand perceptions on an annual basis often field trackers monthly or weekly, especially during times of change. When a new advertising campaign is launched, when a crisis hits a brand, or when competitors introduce a new product, it is useful to keep continual track of consumer perceptions of your brand. Online tracking mechanisms make information turnaround quicker and cheaper, and they also allow continuous versus periodic tracking. Tracking can be done through quick, online fielding of simple surveys, or by analyzing consumer sentiments on social media sites through algorithms. Here, marketers benefit not only from hearing consumer opinions in their own words, but also by capturing sentiments as consumers communicate with each other instead of being asked for their opinions in a survey.

Second, the digital environment has provided marketers with an entirely new set of metrics, with data collected as consumers interact with a brand online. We can track size of audience, how long individuals spend on our images, and how deeply they connect in our content. The cost-per-click metric counts clicks as a measure of depth of engagement. More broadly, firms measure cost per action when the desired action is something other than clicking—often downloading an app or registering interest by leaving an email address. And finally, firms calculate cost per acquired customer (CAC), measuring the cost of all activities attributed to driving a consumer to actually make a purchase.

Increasingly, we also can learn not only about our buyers, but also about those who *don't* buy—consumers who search our categories, investigate our brands, or even place us in a shopping cart, but do not pull the purchase trigger. These hot prospects are in some ways even more useful to identify than the consumers who have already purchased.

In digital environments, the ability to track the activity of consumers and the productivity of our content truly expands. However, this data still begs for interpretation. Whether CAC is high or low, we are challenged to diagnose and explain why. Does lack of customer acquisition stem from an awareness problem? Or are consumers aware of our brand, but just not compelled to buy? If so, why? What do they think and feel, and how should we act to become more compelling? The digital measures are useful, but they do not replace the need to understand how many consumers know us and what they think and feel. Digital measures enhance our decision-making ability, but they must be accompanied by an understanding of awareness and associations.

SUMMARY

Brands are important assets, and so the tracking and measurement of brand health has never been more important. Digital environments make this even more true. It is key to keep a pulse of what users and nonusers think and feel about our brands and to understand these perceptions in an authentic way. As we do so, we must measure consumers' tendency to think of our brands first, their likelihood to consider them a favorite, and the conversion of these thoughts to purchase. Using all of these factors together, we have discussed the awareness/liking/market-share model for determining brand-growth strategy. Building business through awareness building, advertising, repositioning, category expansion, consumer relationship building, and sometimes by even walking away from a brand name, are all useful tools in the brand steward's bag of tricks.

Julie Hennessy is a clinical professor of marketing at Kellogg and associate chair of the Marketing Department. She is one of Kellogg's most recognized teachers, having received more than a dozen teaching awards. She began her career in marketing at General Mills and then spent more than a decade at Kraft Foods. She received her BS from Indiana University and her MBA from Kellogg.

NOTES

1. Old Spice (2010), "The Man Your Man Could Smell Like," YouTube, February 4. https://www.youtube.com/watch?v=owGykVbfgUE.

CHAPTER 16

CONNECTING MARKETING AND FINANCE VIA BRAND VALUE

BOBBY J. CALDER

With an increased emphasis on brand experience and engagement, brands will require ever-higher levels of expenditure in the future. At a Starbucks store in Shanghai, consumers engage with the brand through augmented reality displays on their phones that show (among other things) how the coffees on physical display are roasted. Such cutting-edge efforts, however, are bedeviled by a very twentieth-century problem: the long-standing tension between marketing and finance. Traditionally, it falls to finance to question the contribution of marketing expenditures to the overall performance of the business. Augmented reality at Starbucks may engage consumers, but what does this expenditure contribute to business results? Consumer engagement is very meaningful to marketers,[1] but not to finance executives.

Most often finance plays an adversarial role, adjusting budgets based on the persuasiveness of the marketing case that expenditures strengthen the brand in the minds of consumers as weighed against competing calls on the business's financial resources. Beyond this back-and-forth organizational tussling, CEOs are generally skeptical of branding expenditures, due to their focus on financials. Many a CEO has been known to comment, "I'm pretty sure that part of this money is wasted, but I'm not sure which part." The short job tenure of most CMOs, and the trend to replace them with chief revenue officers or chief growth officers (who often share the financial perspective of CEOs) no doubt reflects this situation.

At the heart of this impasse is a fundamental problem. It is the elephant in the room that neither marketing nor finance is willing to face head-on. Marketing speaks the language of branding (targeting, positioning, engagement, etc.) and has its own consumer-based metrics, but marketers are often unable to translate these metrics into the financial language used for operating the business. Hence, branding comes across as more or less soft, imprecise, and even suspect. As James Meier (p. 151) points out, "Marketing in traditional siloed organizations can be viewed and treated as a cost center, ripe for spending reductions when financial results turn sour."[2]

Thus, there is a long-standing need to bridge the divide between marketing and finance. Fortunately, there is growing recognition of this need. Important institutions such as the International Accounting Standards Board (IASB), the Financial Accounting Standards Board (FASB), the International Standards Organization (ISO), the International Trademark Association (INTA), the Marketing Accountability Standards Board (MASB), and the Licensing Executives Society (LES) have all recently taken an active interest in solutions. (Disclaimer: The author is chair of the ISO Committee on Brand Evaluation [TC 289], a member of the Brand Value Special Task Force of INTA, and MASB advisory board member.)

In this chapter we will closely examine the issues underlying the problem, review some of the existing solutions, and discuss new ideas—such as brand performance evaluation and integrated reporting—that individual companies can use to bring marketing and finance together around a shared approach to brand value.

The Different Worlds of Marketing and Finance

Marketers see their role in the organization as strategic. There is an expanding array of functional activities, including social media, content marketing, sponsorships, activation events, mobile apps, and more, but the overriding strategic goal is brand building. Brands have strategic value because they are valuable to consumers (customers, clients, users). Marketing activities build brands, but brands exist in the mind of the consumer. A brand is the idea or meaning of a product to the consumer.[3] To the extent that the brand is strong, it exerts an influence on consumers' choice of product in the marketplace and ultimately their satisfaction with this choice. Brands add value to the product, making the product worth more to the consumer. Consumers are willing to pay more for this added value, and this price premium over an unbranded product reflects the value of the brand to them. Marketers often refer to this brand value as "brand equity."[4] But because finance may misinterpret this as a financial term (though one that has no meaning), it is probably better to speak of "brand strength," where a strong brand is one that has high brand value to the consumer.

Marketers use a variety of metrics to assess the strength of a brand, from awareness, knowledge, favorability, and loyalty to newer metrics such as engagement.[5] But these metrics belong to the world of marketing. The world of finance, in contrast, is concerned with allocating resources and managing risk from an organizational perspective; accordingly, brand value must be treated in financial terms from this perspective. Much as marketers may try to use techniques such as marketing mix or multi-attribution models to justify activities to finance, there is a disconnect with the way finance thinks about running the business.

With the exception of mergers and acquisitions (M&A), as will be discussed, finance views brand-building expenditures as costs. In the language of financial accounting these expenditures are treated as *expenses*, where an expense is defined as any resource that is used and consumed by the business as part of the process of generating a profit in a period. As expenses, branding expenditures are *subtracted* from profit and viewed, like wages, as part of the costs of doing business. It is therefore perfectly natural for finance to question these expenses and seek cost reduction. Moreover, it is clear to both finance and marketing that spending a lot on branding does not necessarily ensure that a brand will be successful. It is possible to spend a lot and still not have a strong brand. Even a strong brand might be outperformed by another brand in the market, or sales may be affected by business environment forces. From a finance point of view, brand expenses are costs that by definition may or may not enhance the company's bottom line. Given this situation, the often adversarial roles of finance and marketing are to be expected.

The underlying problem is that brand value should not be treated as a cost. Yet this is basically what organizations do.

NONCOST APPROACHES TO THE FINANCIAL VALUE OF BRANDS

For marketing and finance to connect, a different approach to brand value is needed, one that is anchored in the marketer's view that brands represent added value to the consumer as well as in finance's concern with monetary value to the organization. The key is for both finance and marketing to approach brands as assets, not costs.

Brands as Intangible Assets

Both marketing and finance should focus on value creation. Branding creates value for the consumer, which is captured as an asset for the company. A financial asset is defined as a resource controlled by the company from which future economic benefits are expected to flow. As we have seen, brands are typically not treated as assets. But they should be.

Although the brand resides with the consumer, the company does exercise control through its branding activities and the legal rights afforded by trademarks, domain names, and the like. A brand thus functions as a resource, in that future decisions by consumers who value the brand should create an economic flow back to the company. The monetary value of this flow has to be determined, but in principle it is entirely reasonable to view brands as assets that can have a higher or lower valuation (as all assets do). Brands are intangible assets, not tangible assets such as buildings, but this lack of physical substance should not be taken to mean that they are not "real" assets. Brands should have the same status as intellectual property and other intangible assets. Viewing brands as intangible assets goes a long way in bringing marketing and finance into strategic alignment.

We should point out that accountants have long resisted treating any intangible as an asset, because the valuation of intangibles is notoriously difficult. Rather than give a value to a brand that might be overly speculative, accountants have preferred to err on the side of caution by mostly treating brands as expenses, not assets. Their view is that accounting only accounts for the value that its tools allow. This accounting convention, however, leaves marketing and finance stuck with approaching brand value in a counterproductive way. It is far better to acknowledge the difficulties with the valuation of brands and not let this stand in the way of realizing that brands are intangible assets.

Difficulties with Accounting Methods for Valuing Brands

Accountants are more comfortable with treating brands as assets in the case of M&A activity. In this case, brands can be assessed in terms of their *fair value* based on a market transaction. If one company buys a brand from another, or purchases an entire company that owns a brand, the transaction price can be taken as the value of the brand (or it can be derived from the price for the company). The market has determined the brand's value based on what is paid for it.

The market approach can be extended beyond the purchase of a specific brand using the purchase of a comparable brand.[6] The benchmark value is adjusted to reflect any differences in the "comparables," and the value of the brand is equated to some multiple of the comparable purchased brand. The difficulty, of course, lies in identifying comparable brands that have been valued by market transactions.

At least in the case of M&A, accountants have even been willing to put the transaction price (market value) on the acquiring company's balance sheet as an asset. This comes with a significant caveat, however, in that accountants will not allow the value of the brand to increase over time. The brand in effect becomes financially *moribund*.[7] The brand may be tested for *impairment* (declining value), but if not impaired, brand value essentially stays the same over time. Valuing the brand as an asset in this way obviously provides no basis for aligning marketing and finance. The financial value does not increase no matter what marketing does. Beyond this, most brands are developed internally, so market value is considered overly speculative. Thus, finance does not use market values (except for special purposes), as financial accounting considers this too speculative, and brands are treated not as assets but as expenses.

In terms of connecting marketing and finance, the underlying problem with using market value to treat brands as assets is not only that it can be speculative. The basic problem is that market value reflects what an acquiring company paid for the brand. This transaction price may or may not reflect the economic value of the brand based on its value to consumers. In fact, there is evidence that acquiring companies actually pay too much.[8] Many factors can affect the price paid: A company might primarily want to show revenue growth in order to inflate its stock market value. A company might want to buy a brand because the brand is coupled with some new technology. It may not even be planning to use the acquired brand—a company might buy a brand to kill it in order to avoid future competition. Hence, market value may have its uses, but it is inherently unsuited to playing a major role in the interaction of finance and marketing.

More useful is the income method of valuing brands. This approach uses discounted forecasts of income, revenue, or cash flows due to the brand. It is difficult to identify flows that are isolated to the brand, but the excess earnings method (increases when other factors are constant), the revenue premium method (having a higher price than a comparable brand in the category), and the relief from royalty method are options that can be used. Royalty relief, which like revenue premium is actually a hybrid of the income and market methods, is preferred in most cases. It is predicated on the fact that if a company did not own the brand it would have to lease it from another company. This cost of a license is estimated based on the price of actual licensing agreements for comparable brands. The net present value of the royalties saved over time (income) is used to estimate brand value.

The income method provides a basis for treating brand value as an asset. However, it only provides a forecast based on an indirect indicator of the brand's financial contribution, such as royalty relief. It does have the advantage of being more than a lifetime value of the customer estimate, in that it is based on a rationale for why the forecast is credible. Lifetime value, unless there is a contract, just assumes that consumers will keep purchasing for whatever reason at the same rate: it is an extrapolation. With the income method, the value of the brand to the consumer accounts for why the company can expect an economic flow. It assumes, in effect, that the consumer values the brand *and* knows that the brand is an asset the company would not want to lose. The company is sending an economic *signal* to the consumer about future brand performance.[9] The consumer can expect the brand to continue being valuable over time. The brand should thus be treated as an economic resource for the company, an intangible asset, because there is a reasonable basis for the expectation of a continuing economic flow that benefits the company.

Direct Approaches to Brand Value

A shortcoming of the income method is that it is indirect. It requires identifying a specific flow that can be linked to the brand. A more direct approach would base the asset value of the brand on the contribution of the brand to aggregate flows. A number of consulting companies, but not accounting firms, have developed versions of the direct approach. Millward Brown's BrandZ (part of WPP Kantor) attempts to assess a brand's contribution based first on brand strength, which is assessed by consumer responses to survey questions about how meaningful the brand is, how different it is, and how salient it is relative to competitors in the category. Second, realizing that these measures of brand strength do not automatically translate into consumer choice in the marketplace, the strength measures are related to market metrics—the willingness of consumers to pay a premium for the brand, the brand's predicted share power, and the brand's potential for growth. The brand's percentage contribution to aggregate flow is based on its premium, power, and potential. The proportionate share attributable to the brand is its brand value.

Other companies employ different models. Interbrand (part of the Omnicom Group) uses a more straightforward discounted cash-flow income model with the brand's contribution to this flow based on brand demand *drivers*. Sometimes, however, these drivers are based on data and sometimes on expert judgment, introducing a large degree of subjectivity. Gabriela Salinas estimates that consulting companies have developed at least 39 models of this sort.[10] In general these models lack transparency and consistency. Companies have tended to publish league tables of the top brands in order to publicize their work, but the rankings are inconsistent. Interbrand's values, for instance, are consistently lower than those of BrandZ. A big issue is the conflating of consulting services with the reporting of brand values. BrandZ has consulted with the Range Rover brand and its reported rankings show a large increase in the brand's value. While consulting companies should be applauded for attempting to measure brand value more directly, there is a need for simpler, less proprietary-oriented approaches and better reporting.

BRAND PERFORMANCE EVALUATIONS

To connect marketing and finance, companies need to take the lead, with marketing and finance agreeing on a straightforward approach to brand value. This should not preclude experimentation and evolution, yet agreement and trust between marketing and finance depends on transparency. The agreed-upon approach should clearly recognize that marketing metrics of brand strength are important but not sufficient. A test of the brand in a competitive market environment—a brand performance evaluation—is essential. Measures of brand strength only indicate how much consumers value the brand. A brand can be strong but still not perform well because of market forces that negatively affect the choice of the brand. (Conversely, a weak brand may be affected positively.) Brand performance cannot be equated with brand strength. This construct will, and should be, rejected by finance.

Finance is concerned with the value of the brand to the company. Consumers may love the brand, but this translates into financial value only if the brand performs well. Brand performance evaluations are necessary to go beyond only measuring brand strength. A brand performance evaluation provides an objective test of the brand's actual contribution, which can be applied using the income model to determine the asset value of the brand.

The concept of a brand performance evaluation, as distinguished from brand strength metrics, is promulgated in the ISO 20671 standard. A proof of concept has been conducted by MASB's Brand Investment and Valuation (BIV) project.[11] This project related the sales of 33 diverse brands to consumer brand choice and to two other forces—price and distribution levels. Choice was evaluated by asking consumers to choose the brand they truly wanted within each category from a set of competitive brands. The BIV project found that choice explained about 75 percent of variation in the sales data (with the remainder due to price and distribution), thereby demonstrating the logic of using choice as a brand performance evaluation to establish a brand's contribution versus other market forces.

Brand Performance Evaluation Methods

A number of brand performance evaluation methods are available to companies. The BIV method of asking consumers to choose the brand they truly want is one, but finance might argue that this is really a marketing measure of brand strength, in that consumers were not choosing the brand in a setting in which other factors might affect their choice, as would be the case in the marketplace.

In general, two broad types of methods can be used. Actual purchase data available from syndicated data sources is one type. This is what economists call revealed preference (RP), in that actual behavior is used to measure preference. The problem with using RP data for brand performance evaluation is that pricing and distribution levels are not independent of brand choice. This makes separating the effect of brand from other forces statistically difficult. The other type of brand evaluation method is called stated preference (SP). It has a distinct methodological advantage in that brand choices are presented to consumers in a way that does not confound brand choices with price and distribution levels.

SP methods employ consumer surveys that measure preferences based on decisions in simulated choice situations. Again, SP differs from RP methods in that SP methods are designed as experiments in order to avoid the difficulties of analyzing market data. There are two types of SP methods. Self-explication methods explicitly ask consumers to evaluate choice alternatives. For example, consumers could be asked to rate how likely they would be to choose each of the following: (1) the brand at its typical price level, (2) the brand at a lower price level, (3) an unbranded/weak brand at the higher price level of the brand, or (4) an unbranded/weak brand at the lower price. (The unbranded/weak brand serves as a baseline for comparison with the brand being evaluated.) This experiment can be analyzed to reveal the weight placed on the brand relative to factors such as price. The branding firm Siegel+Gale currently uses such a method, based on separating brand and nonbrand attributes to predict choice. Chan Su Park and V. Srinivasan illustrate this approach along with the idea of contrasting the prediction of preferences from brand attributes with prediction from objective values of the attributes, where the values are not affected by brand (such as with expert or lab values).[12]

The downside with SP choice experiments using ratings is that for some product categories consumers may rate all choices highly, obscuring differences between them. In this case, a constant-sum measure where consumers allocate points from a sum of 100 to each choice may be appropriate. Also, for a category where many other market forces need to be evaluated relative to brand, a compositional method may be preferable. Consumers would rate the importance of each choice attribute (brand, price, etc.) using a constant sum and then rate the favorability of each level of the attribute (e.g., for the brand attribute, rate the brand and rate the unbranded or weakly branded product). This can be used to infer consumers' overall preferences for the different choices.

The other type of SP method is decompositional, in that consumers simply make choices among alternatives varying on brand and other attributes, but analytic techniques are used to determine the contribution of brand relative to other forces. The two main techniques are conjoint analysis (CA) and discrete choice experiment (DCE). CA uses the same logic of simulated test marketing in that consumers are given choices that vary on a number of attributes. This allows the estimation of the part-worth contribution of brand and the other attributes.

Take the Starbucks brand. The following is an example of CA using real data from consumers, albeit with a small convenience sample for purposes of illustration. In the brand evaluation of Starbucks, consumers received the following purchase context scenario:

You are visiting another city and want to meet someone at a coffee shop.

Please consider the following eight possible choices that you might see when searching for a coffee shop. The choices differ in the *name* of the coffee shop, the *price* shown for a large regular coffee, and the *distance* from where you presently are. Please rank the choices from 1 (the choice you would *most* prefer) to 8 (the choice you would *least* prefer).

All combinations of brand, price, and distribution are available as choices, and the consumer could be asked to rank them from most to least preferred. Even if brand strength is high, this allows for the possibility that consumers might choose a lower price or more convenient location (distribution) in the market situation.

In this example, CA showed that the Starbucks brand had a part-worth contribution of .276 versus a .470 contribution for price and a .249 for distribution. The brand contribution of .276 would be used as input to the income method of determining brand value.

Marketers are most familiar with CA. DCE is procedurally similar but analytically different. Economists favor this method because the analytics are tied to economic utility theory and allow for a random component in consumers' choices. DCE thus predicts the probability of a choice based on brand and other attributes. This method has the power to accommodate a large number of forces (attributes) besides brand, which is more difficult to do with CA. A disadvantage of DCE, and to some extent CA, is that the analyses require assumptions about how consumers make choices. So, while technically elegant, both methods require more care than the more explicit SP methods.

Although we emphasize the role of brand performance evaluations for determining financial brand value, it should be useful as well to see which brand strength metrics correlate best with the brand choice results. More generally, marketing and finance ideally could experiment with different SP methods and validate them against each other. Also, brand performance evaluations need to be repeated at least on an annual basis, which creates an opportunity to refine selected methods over time.

THE CHAIN OF ACCOUNTABILITY

There is more at stake in connecting marketing and finance via brand value than aligning the two functions. Ultimately what is at stake is accountability for value creation. And value creation reaches all the way from consumers to investors and back to consumers. We can best see the importance of brand value to the process of value creation from the systems perspective shown in Figure 16.1. Each panel in chart represents a link in a chain of accountability for value creation and capture.

The goal of branding is to create added value for the consumer. As shown in Panels A and B, marketing deploys resources to the brand in order to create the associations and experiences in the consumer's mind that make up brand strength and create value for the consumer. Marketers use a variety of metrics to assess the strength of the brand. As emphasized here, there is also a need to conduct brand performance evaluations to demonstrate the brand's actual

Figure 16.1
Systems View of Brand Value Creation

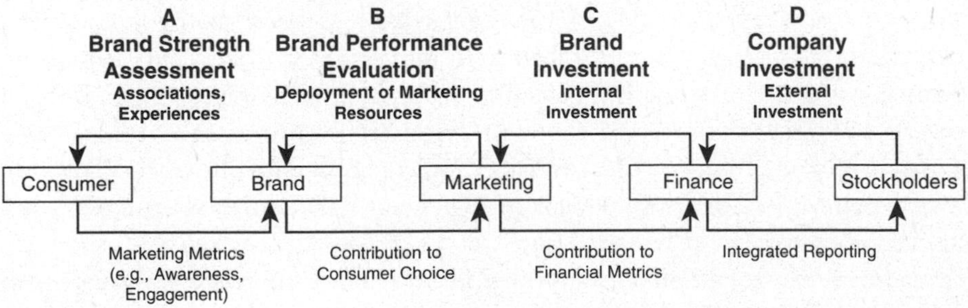

contribution to consumer choice. Finance (Panel C) can then use the brand evaluation to determine the contribution of the brand to financial metrics. This allows finance to make better decisions about investing in the brand and improving corporate governance. In turn, finance (Panel D) can report the asset value of the brand to provide investors with better information, which will allow them to direct funding to companies that are creating brand value. Overall, investors get higher returns by investing in companies that create greater value for consumers.

Viewing brand value in terms of the link to investors is critical. Currently companies may play up their brands in their annual reports, but this is not the same as financial reporting. While reporting the asset value of brands does not have to be part of the conventional financial statement, it should be part of the move to *integrated reporting*. The International Integrated Report Council (IIRC) already promotes reporting annually on a range of different types of capital that are inputs to a company's business model and ultimately create value in the form of capital outputs. Under its social and relationship capital category, the IIRC guidelines specifically include brands. It should be apparent that such reporting is relevant to other stakeholders as well as stockholders.

We have seen that under conventional accounting rules, investors have extremely limited information about the asset value of brands. This problem is greatly magnified by the fact that intangible assets are now more valuable than tangible assets in most developed economies.[13] It directly follows that investors need information about both tangible and intangible assets, such as brand value, in order to make decisions. This fact alone should lead companies to treat brands as assets and report on brand value.

SUMMARY

The time has come for connecting marketing and finance through a shared approach to treating brands as assets rather than expenses. There are complicated issues to be solved. Companies will need to experiment with, and eventually standardize, methods for brand performance evaluation, so that the brand's contribution to financial results can be adequately determined. But the upside potential is enormous. Through better reporting, investors will be able to make better decisions—decisions that assure that capital flows to firms that create more value for consumers. In return, economic benefits to the company and investors will be realized.

Brand value should not be viewed as just a difficult accounting issue. It is an issue of accountability that must be addressed by marketing and finance.

Bobby J. Calder is Charles H. Kellstadt Professor Emeritus of Marketing at the Kellogg School of Management and a professor of journalism, media, and integrated marketing communications at Northwestern University. He has been a consultant to numerous companies, as well as government and not-for-profit organizations. He also served as editor or co-editor for three books published in the Kellogg on book series. He received his BA, MA, and PhD degrees from the University of North Carolina at Chapel Hill.

NOTES

1. Calder, Bobby J., Mathew Isaac, and Edward C. Malthouse (2016), "How To Capture Consumer Experiences: A Context-Specific Approach to Measuring Engagement," *Journal of Advertising Research*, 56(1), 1–14; Calder, Bobby J., Linda D., and Edward C. Malthouse (2018), "Creating Stronger Brands through Consumer Experiences and Engagement." In *Consumer Engagement Marketing*, Eds. R. Palmatier, V. Kumar, and C. Harmeling, New York: Palgrave Macmillian.
2. Meier, James (2016), "Creating a Partnership between Marketing and Finance." In *Accountable Marketing: Linking Marketing Actions to Financial Performance*, Eds. D. Stewart and C. Gugel, New York: Routledge, 149–167.
3. Calder, Bobby J. (2010), "Writing a Brand Positioning Statement and Translating It into Brand Design." In *Kellogg on Marketing*, 2nd edition, Eds. A. Tybout and B. Calder, Hoboken, NJ: Wiley, 92–111.
4. Keller, Kevin L. (1993), "Conceptualizing, Measuring, and Managing Customer-Based Equity," *Journal of Marketing* 57(1), 1–22.
5. Brakus, J. Josko, Bernd H. Schmitt, and Lia Zarantonello (2009), "Brand Experience: What Is It? How Is It Measured? Does It Affect Loyalty?," *Journal of Marketing* 73(3), 52–68; Calder, Bobby J., Mathew Isaac, and Edward Malthouse (2016), "How to Capture Consumer Experiences: A Context-Specific Approach to Measuring Engagement," *Journal of Advertising Research* 56(1), 1–14.
6. ISO 10668: 2010 (2017), "Brand Valuation—Requirements for Monetary Brand Evaluation," ISO standard, www.iso.org/standard/46032.html; Paugam, Luc, Paul Andre, Henri Philippe, and Roula Harfouche (2016), *Brand Valuation*, New York: Routledge.
7. Sinclair, Roger, and Kevin L. Keller, (2017), "Brand Value, Accounting Standards, and Mergers and Acquisitions: 'The Moribund Effect,'" *Journal of Brand Management* 24(2), 171–192; Sinclair, Roger, and Kevin L. Keller, (2014), "A Case for Brands as Assets: Acquired and Internally Developed," *Journal of Brand Management* 21(4), 286–302.
8. Ramanna, Karthik (2015), *Political Standards: Corporate Interest, Ideology, and Leadership in the Shaping of Accounting Rules for the Market Economy*, Chicago: University of Chicago Press; Hayward, Mathew, and Donald Hambrick (1997), Explaining the Premiums Paid for Large Acquisitions: Evidence of CEO Hubris," *Administrative Science Quarterly* 42(1), 103–127.

9. Erdem, Tulin, and Joffre Swait (2016), "The Information Economics Perspective on Brand Equity," *Foundations and Trends in Marketing* 10(1), 1–59.

10. Salinas, Gabriela (2016), "Brand Valuation: Principles, Applications, and Latest Developments." In *The Routledge Companion to Contemporary Brand Management*, Eds. F. Riley, J. Singh, and C. Blankson, New York: Routledge, 48–67.

11. Findley, Frank (2016), "Measuring Return on Brand Investment." In *Accountable Marketing: Linking Marketing Actions to Financial Performance*, Eds. D. Stewart and C. Gugel, New York: Routledge, 52–59.

12. Park, Chan Su, and V. Srinivasan (1994), "A Survey-Based Method for Measuring and Understanding Brand Equity and Its Extendibility," *Journal of Marketing Research* 31(2), 271–288.

13. Haskel, Jonathan, and Stan Westlake (2018), *The Rise of the Intangible Economy*, Princeton, NJ: Princeton University Press.

SECTION FOUR

LESSONS FROM BRAND LEADERS

CHAPTER 17

HAS PURPOSE LOST ITS PURPOSE? McDONALD'S DEFINES ITS STYLE OF MARKETING

SILVIA LAGNADO and COLIN MITCHELL

Purpose has served many brands well. We have both advocated for it in the past. However, today, as purpose has grown in popularity, it risks being disconnected from the product. This makes brands blur together and lack meaning. We must recognize that different brands operate at different altitudes. This will determine both the brand's strategy (the balance between positioning and purpose) and its expression (the balance of "saying" and "doing").

THE RISE OF PURPOSE

Perhaps Jim Collins started it. After conducting a six-year study of successful companies and their less successful competitors in various industries, Collins concluded in his book *Built to Last* (HarperBusiness, 1994) that a sense of vision was the answer: "Visionary companies pursue a cluster of objectives, of which making money is only one—and not necessarily the primary one."

Vision then migrated from the world of general business theory to the world of marketing. In his 1999 book on challenger brands, *Eating the Big Fish* (John Wiley & Sons), Adam Morgan posited that really strong brands were founded on beliefs. Historic campaigns, such as Apple's "Think Different" (1997) and Dove's "Campaign for Real Beauty" (2004) showed the power of this idea.

Gradually, the language of marketing changed. Agencies started producing "brand manifestoes." Campaigns were described as "movements" led by "anthem ads." Around this time, Alex Bogusky, creative director of Crispin Porter Bogusky (arguably the most influential agency of the time), insisted that campaign ideas be presented with the press release as the proof-of-concept.

Purpose quickly entered the mainstream. It became the subject of books, articles, and conferences. In 2011, Jim Stengel, formerly chief marketing officer of Procter & Gamble, revealed the results of a multiyear study conducted with Millward Brown. It argued for the business potential of purpose-driven brands: "Those who center their business on improving people's lives have a growth rate triple that of competitors and outperform the market by a huge margin. They dominate their categories, create new categories, and maximize profit in the long term." The idea quickly won consensus. The Association of National Advertisers announced that "having a societal purpose will be a key competitive advantage in the future, according to 72 percent of Marketing2020 respondents."[1]

Like many big changes in marketing, the purpose-oriented revolution was driven in part by a change in media consumption. Television advertising was beginning to lose its dominance and we entered the era of "paid, owned, and earned," in which companies could no longer rely just on paid advertising. Marketing now extended beyond traditional TV channels, and companies themselves had a social media platform to shape their brand reputations without traditional media as middlemen.

Finally, purpose succeeded because it helped recruitment and retention at a time when the "war for talent" raged—purpose appealed to millennial recruits. In addition, marketers hoped that purpose would enhance corporate reputation in the eyes of influencer elites, such as journalists, analysts, and legislators, as companies came under much greater public scrutiny.

Today, however we are arguably reaching a point of "peak purpose" and we can see difficulties with it.

THE CHALLENGES OF BRAND PURPOSE

Many purposes are very similar. This can lead to the converging of brands. If every airline in the world is bringing people together, then there will be little differentiation.

Much of this is due to "brand laddering"—the practice of pushing a brand's positioning higher and higher up a Maslovian ladder to find higher-order benefits or to "make the brand feel bigger." The difficulty is that the tops of all these ladders reach the same place. This explains the ubiquity of carpe diem advertising and the resulting popularity of taglines using the word "life" or "live," such as "Live Richly," "For Life," "Don't live life without it," and so on.

Another problem with purpose is that customers can lose the connection: the top of these ladders is also a long way from the bottom. Many brand purposes have little direct link to the brand or the product. At times, it seems as if no cause is too far a stretch. Toiletry brands take on police brutality. Fast-food brands battle for net neutrality. Car brands advocate on gender roles. At its worst, this is cynical—using the cause for eyeballs. This leaves the brand vulnerable. For example, after Audi ran a Super Bowl ad advocating for equal pay for women, critics pointed out that Audi's parent company, Volkswagen, had no female board members.

Purpose has suffered from definition creep. It started from a belief that informed the company—often through strong, charismatic founders, such as Nike's Bill Bowerman, who set out to "bring inspiration and innovation to every athlete in the world." But the term is sometimes now conflated with corporate social responsibility goals or political, social, or charitable causes.

Consequently, brand purpose can often be vague and, at worst, insincere.

THE CHALLENGE OF BALANCE

So, what's the solution? Well, it comes in two parts: strategy and execution.

Strategically, we should accept that different brands operate at different altitudes. Some high, some lower. Some may focus on a purpose, others on a good old-fashioned positioning. (The mental space it occupies in the mind of a consumer, relative to its competition.)

In executing, today we have a far richer palette of channels to choose from than before. These include all sorts of exciting entertainments and utilities. Consequently, the brand doesn't have to just "say" something; it can also "do" something. In other words, it can express itself with less rhetoric and more experiences.

This does not, however, mean less emotion. Clearly, emotion drives behavior. But emotion can be found in experience as well as in oratory. (Witness the quiet awe of unboxing an Apple product, the relief at the ease of finding your way with Waze, the bonhomie of bonding with Airbnb hosts, and so on.)

Nor does it mean abandoning guiding beliefs or purpose completely. Clear values force brands to stay authentic, coherent, and on track. While people certainly buy into brands that share their beliefs (such as Nike), they also buy a lot from practical brands that do not shout theirs (such as Uber, Amazon, and—admittedly—McDonald's).

THE MCDONALD'S CULTURE, PRODUCT, AND BRAND

At McDonald's, we are trying to develop a way of marketing that is rooted in the product, the restaurant experience, and the company.

Part of what caused us to reassess the role of purpose was the McDonald's culture. This is a very practical company, averse to pomposity. The key focus is serving hot, tasty food quickly, conveniently, and inexpensively. It is also, as our CEO is fond of saying, the "most democratic brand in the world." Or, as our founder Ray Kroc aptly put it, "We didn't invent the hamburger. We just took it more seriously than anyone else."

At first, we thought this down-to-earth attitude was a weakness, but we now see it as a strength. Others agree. In a recent article on corporate mission statements, the *Economist* noted that, "The danger is that, by aiming to inspire, firms produce pious platitudes instead," and went on to assert, "The best statements are short and describe the business in a way that customers and employees can understand and appreciate. McDonald's is admirably succinct: 'To be our customers' favorite place and way to eat and drink' . . . not the stuff of inspiring oratory. But such clear, direct statements at least create the impression that the company knows what it is doing."[2]

So, while we debated identifying a very high-order purpose, we realized this would not be true to the spirit of the brand or the culture.

That is not to imply a lack of responsibility. We recognize that people care more today about the companies with which they do business. And McDonald's takes its duties seriously. We recently announced our Scale for Good program, which embraces our responsibilities (and opportunities) to act on the most pressing social and environmental challenges in the world today. We do this through our own actions, but also by collaborating with millions of customers, employees, franchisees, suppliers, and other partners (hence, "scale"). The program's pillars are climate action, beef sustainability, packaging and recycling, commitment to families, and youth opportunity.

And McDonald's cares. We give to and facilitate giving to one of the most enduring and well-known philanthropies, the Ronald McDonald House Charities, which keeps the families of sick children together during prolonged hospital treatment.

Trust is also important. Our markets make big efforts to communicate the truth about how our food is sourced and produced. For example, the "Our Food, Your Questions" campaign in our Canadian markets took real consumer questions and made a series of video shorts shot from inside food production facilities to answer them candidly.

While all of these—responsibilities, philanthropy, and trustworthiness—are vital and play specific roles within the marketing, they do not dictate its overall theme and style. What does then?

Feel-Good Marketing

The roots of our brand positioning can be traced to 1971, when legendary copywriter Keith Reinhart wrote the immortal line, "You deserve a break today." Interestingly, this was the same year that Coca-Cola ran its famous "Hilltop" commercial ("I'd like to teach the world to sing") and just before L'Oréal debuted "Because you're worth it." With the advent of the 1970s—the "me decade," as author Tom Wolfe dubbed it—there was a shift in focus from *what the product did* (an early McDonald's ad offered, "Crispy, Tender, Delicious French Fries, only 10 cents") to *how the brand made you feel* (a "break" in your day).

We have defined our positioning as "Making delicious feel-good moments easy for everyone." The word "delicious" anchors the brand in the food. "Feel-good" is the heart of the brand. (McDonald's won't transform your life, but a Big Mac sandwich can make you feel better.) And "easy for everyone" speaks to the democratic nature of the brand, delivered through convenience and sheer reach.

Having defined the brand, we want to envision a form of marketing that expresses it. *How you market is as important as what you say.* For McDonald's, each interaction is an opportunity for a feel-good moment, or a little bubble of happy in its own right. In other words, each moment can be an emotional "free sample" for the brand—hopefully, leaving you feeling a little better than before.

This, we think, is a real opportunity at a time when so much of our lives is consumed by media. American adults spend over half of their days consuming media of one type or another,[3] and much of it could be described as "feel bad."

The Happy Meal Sub-brand

You can see all of this in a microcosm via the Happy Meal sub-brand. This is a balanced kids' meal that meets nutrition criteria with wholesome options such as apple slices and milk. It comes in a fun box with a toy, often tied to a movie release. Depending on the market, some McDonald's locations also offer service elements such as play spaces, games tables, and crew who are trained to talk to kids and make them feel welcome. The communication provides a free sample of the Happy Meal experience. The Happy Studio app provides games and entertainments for parents and kids to enjoy together. The commercials are, effectively, short movies related to the movie tie-in toy offered. These often are developed by the movie studios, such as Illumination or Disney, and are true content that kids engage with.

Is this product, service, or communication? It's all three at once. There is a meal at the core, but it is wrapped in layers of service and communication that enhance the experience. It's certainly not a rhetorical idea. It's an experience.

Little Bubbles of Happy

This brand-building approach works best at some of the most mundane points of contact that the brand has.

Consider the humble job application. Our Australian team had to address the issue of fewer young people applying due to the war for talent. Their solution was to make the application process a feel-good moment in its own right. Rather than filling out tedious forms, people were asked to submit a short video via Snapchat describing why they would be suited to the position. We called it "Snaplications." This was not only more fun, but it ensured that we encouraged those with the right personality to apply.

A simple promotion can turn into a media event that people can enjoy. In Canada, we added bacon to the Big Mac as a limited-time offer—its first change in 50 years. Purists hated it. Others loved it. We turned this difference into a public debate. People could vote on the issue. Teaser posters appeared around Toronto, with deep existential questions such as, "If you're in an empty room, is it still empty?" or "Is a container with a hole still a hole?" (Two-thirds voted for bacon.) It became a major media event and an example of how to elevate an offer into a true "break" in someone's day. It didn't change the world, but it did raise some smiles.

Feel-good marketing manifests itself in restaurants too. Take our kiosks and table service. Instead of standing in line to order (anxious that you may be delaying others), you can now order on a screen, and a crew member will deliver the food to the table. This is clearly a service, but it's also communication, as it allows us to showcase new products. Consequently, the average transaction amount increases. The same applies to McDelivery, mobile ordering through the McDonald's app, curbside check-in (where you can avoid a drive-through line and have the food delivered to your parking spot), and other convenience features.

In all these efforts, the style of McDonald's marketing reflects its brand. It makes people feel good for a moment in their busy lives ("You deserve a break today").

Summary

Brands operate at different altitudes depending on the roles they play in people's lives and the culture of the companies. This should lead to a different balance of purpose and positioning.

Silvia Lagnado is an executive vice president and the global chief marketing officer at McDonald's. Earlier in her career she worked at Bacardi Limited and Unilever, where she led the introduction of Dove's "Real Beauty" campaign.

Colin Mitchell is the global vice president at McDonald's. Prior to joining McDonald's, he was worldwide head of planning at WPP's Ogilvy & Mather.

Notes

1. Marketing2020 (2014), "Brand Purpose Fuels Growth and Brand Consistency," Millward Brown Vermeer, ANA, Spencer Stuart, and Adobe, May 22. www.ana. net/miccontent/show/id/mkting2020-brand-purpose-6.
2. Bartleby (2018), "Mission Implausible: Beware Corporate Expressions of Virtue," *Economist*, August 2.
3. eMarketer (2017), *U.S. Time Spent with Media: eMarketer's Updated Estimates and Forecast for 2014–2019*, eMarketer report.

CHAPTER 18

ULTÀ BEAUTY GETS A BRANDING MAKEOVER

MARY DILLON and DAVE KIMBELL

Should we focus on our brand or theirs? As a multibrand retailer, Ulta Beauty had always answered this question with a resounding "theirs"—putting marketing efforts primarily toward the large assortment of brands the company sold, especially the higher-profile ones. The ongoing pressure to drive sales behind top-selling brands left Ulta Beauty's own brand to languish, and a minimal focus on foundational brand-building discipline had led to low consumer awareness and unclear positioning.

We wanted to change that when we joined Ulta Beauty as CEO (Mary Dillon) and CMO (Dave Kimbell) in 2013 and 2014, respectively. We knew the business could be branded in a bigger, more impactful way that resonated with beauty consumers, making the overall brand a real asset and driving greater financial performance.

To capitalize on that perceived opportunity, we built a multipronged, disciplined new branding strategy based on branding fundamentals. Specific components included identifying and sharpening our core value proposition—"all things beauty, all in one place"—against the competition; enhancing our marketing spending mix well beyond traditional print channels; integrating and aligning the branding stories of products we carried with our own branding; and ensuring that everyone within Ulta Beauty understood our branding elements and was acting consistently with them, especially in our stores.

The results significantly exceeded expectations, with strong annual growth on dimensions including revenue (in store and e-commerce), income (EPS), stock price, loyalty membership, and of course, brand awareness. The growth helped Ulta Beauty enter the Fortune 500 for the first time in May 2018.

Importantly, we also learned best practices for building our brand further, and now we are embarking on a new effort to build on Ulta Beauty's foundational branding to promote more growth in an increasingly competitive market.

In this chapter we provide context for the branding opportunity we faced at Ulta Beauty and then describe in detail how we addressed it, along with results and key lessons learned.

ULTA BEAUTY'S HISTORY

Former Osco Drug executives Terry Hanson and Richard George founded Ulta Beauty in 1990 based on a critical insight: most consumers shop for beauty products across *all* price points, but retailers keep mass-market and prestige brands separate, as evidenced by the beauty sections at Walmart and Nordstrom, respectively. The founders used the insight that women were curating their own mix of beauty products to disrupt the sector by building a retailer that offered *both* mass-market and high-end beauty products under the same roof.

From the start, Ulta Beauty had multiple strong capabilities, including real estate selection (where/when to build new stores), integration of salon services, and merchandising assortment curation, making a broad spectrum of mass to prestige products available to Ulta Beauty shoppers nationwide. The company also created a strong loyalty program, which provided rich data to develop insights into guest behavior.

Yet the retailer faced a significant branding issue. The business sold some of the world's most recognized beauty brands—such as Clinique and Urban Decay—but even well into the new millennium, the company had put minimal effort into building the Ulta Beauty brand itself. Awareness of the brand was low, even in the Chicago suburbs where Ulta Beauty had begun. Moreover, the company hadn't established core differentiating elements to create a consistent brand message that resonated with customers.

Historically, it simply hadn't been an organizational priority to understand and build the Ulta Beauty brand. Real estate and merchandising were the focus, with marketing efforts limited largely to promotion through newspaper inserts and monthly magazines sent to existing guests. The business grew well, largely driven by assortment expansion and new store growth rather than by a unified branding effort.

In 2013 Ulta Beauty's board of directors sought a new CEO. The directors understood the opportunity that elevation of branding efforts represented for the company and wanted someone who shared that view. That's how we became part of the Ulta Beauty story: together we brought brand-building and consumer behavior expertise to lead the transformation.

Below we describe in detail how we led a comprehensive, ultimately successful strategy to build the Ulta Beauty brand.

BUILDING THE ULTA BEAUTY BRAND

In leading Ulta Beauty, we worked hard to strike a much better balance between telling our brands' stories and the story of *our* brand—through multiple, mutually reinforcing initiatives.

First, we turned to classic brand-building fundamentals. Early efforts included a comprehensive segmentation study to understand target consumers better. "Who is our core consumer and what motivates them?" we asked, seeking data-driven answers. We also conducted a detailed competitive analysis to define our unique position in the marketplace, as well as our strongest opportunities to challenge the industry. These in-depth initiatives provided clarity for the first time on Ulta Beauty's most compelling value proposition.

Specifically, the proposition of providing "all things beauty, all in one place," from mass to prestige, still resonated with consumers and provided strong differentiation in the industry based on a functional benefit for consumers. While the founders had recognized the value of this strategy implicitly, the company had not articulated that positioning and branding message clearly in the past. To ensure our branding better reflected that value proposition, we used it as the cornerstone for a five-year vision to set brand direction, with the mission of creating a deeper, more emotional connection to the Ulta Beauty brand over time.

While we wanted to reinvent our marketing approach, we didn't want to abandon existing marketing levers altogether. Rather, the strategy was about expanding the types of media used and increasing the brand's relevance to a broader customer base. We wanted to move beyond our historic reliance on print media to include digital, TV, radio, social, and event formats to reach consumers who wouldn't find us by seeing a Sunday morning newspaper or a direct mail flyer. But the messaging and emotions communicated also had to be consistent across all channels.

As part of the effort, we implemented an ongoing marketing mix analysis for the first time to identify growth opportunities and routes to strong ROI. More specifically, we used the analysis to confirm that our shifts in spending associated with the brand-building initiative were best for the business overall.

As expected, we had to carefully align the promotion of brands sold at Ulta Beauty with the newly articulated Ulta Beauty brand. Here, we took as *integrative* an approach as possible: continuing to carve out opportunities to promote key brands such as Tarte and NYX, but also focusing on linking brand stories to high-priority Ulta Beauty messages wherever possible, including new launches, exclusivity, and featured promotions. Some of it was about ensuring *consistency* across marketing materials, such as making clear that a specific Redken promotion was available at Ulta Beauty. We also tied Ulta Beauty branding elements more clearly to events such as our 21 Days of Beauty, which features prestige products. Again, the focus was on ensuring such events were executed consistently with the overall brand from a creative standpoint, which hadn't always been the case. In general, we wanted consumers to see the specific brands we sell through the broader lens of Ulta Beauty.

Having a clearer sense of our own brand enabled us to specify more clearly how brands in our stores could express their own stories in a manner aligned with our marketing activities. When it was evident that their branding effort might not fit with ours, we took steps to redirect their efforts or, in some cases, exclude them from a specific marketing activity. All our partners are brand builders themselves, so they understand our branding effort's importance and adjusted to it in most cases. In this way, the balance between the brands' influence and ours shifted, and the Ulta Beauty brand became more elevated in priority.

Not surprisingly, internal change management represented a significant element of the brand-building effort—especially with the merchant and store teams. We wanted to excite and align them around the strategy to ensure that they delivered the value proposition daily while negotiating with our brands to manage assortment and creating an engaging in-store experience. Open communication about the branding effort and quick wins (such as increased traffic) based on the branding strategy, along with strong data analytics, assured the merchants we could meet individual brands' needs.

For the store teams, success came from a combination of educating them on the new branding and getting them excited about it. We summarized our brand personality as "fresh, fun, and real" and wanted to make sure these elements characterized the in-store experience, along with a feeling of acceptance, non-judgment, and zero pressure. Importantly, the online shopping experience had to reflect the same brand personality, so we took steps to make sure it complemented the in-store environment through engagement tools that included elevated visuals along with additional richer content, such as product demonstration videos and reviews.

To get everyone on the same page, we created a brand book for the corporate and store teams that communicated the look, feel, and personality of the new brand. It also presented the rationale for needing to understand the consumer more deeply—even to the level of what guests are thinking when they walk in the store. In general, we shared fundamental branding practices company-wide, unifying our efforts to communicate consistently with our customers.

Of course, while building and reinforcing the Ulta Beauty brand, we had to manage the day-to-day issues of running the business and reacting quickly to market dynamics—the daily combat that retail is. For example, competition continued to intensify while we built the Ulta Beauty brand, with players like Sephora, Target, and Amazon all advancing their competitive positions. And from time to time, we had to address slower-than-expected sales for a given week as part of reacting to the relentless retail "report card." This didn't mean abandoning the brand-building process; instead it meant maintaining the flexibility to react to business dynamics and, wherever possible, linking the solution—such as a promotion to increase traffic for the upcoming weekend—back to our broader branding message, as part of a practical approach.

A Successful Makeover

Our brand-building effort succeeded beyond our expectations. Unaided awareness jumped from 28 percent to 52 percent between July 2013 and July 2018; aided awareness rose from 65 to 90 percent during the same period. That placed Ulta Beauty second nationally in unaided awareness among retailers who sell beauty products—behind only Walmart, and gaining.

The branding effort, combined with ongoing strengths such as assortment curation and real estate selection, boosted revenue and stock performance significantly. Overall, sales more than doubled from $2.7 billion in 2013 to $5.9 billion in 2017. Sales increases were supported by growth in the number of stores, from 576 in mid-2013 to more than 1,100 by mid-2018. Comp sales began to accelerate in 2014, with double-digit growth for 2015, 2016, and 2017. The new branding strategy helped to drive exceptional e-commerce growth as well, with increases of 56 percent and 60 percent in 2016 and 2017 alone. In line with these revenue figures, Ulta Beauty's stock price rose 134 percent between 2013 and 2018, with earnings per share nearly tripling between 2013 and 2017. Based on these financial results, Ulta Beauty joined the Fortune 500 for the first time on May 21, 2018.

Loyalty membership also went through the roof, from about 12 million members in 2013 to 28.6 million by the second quarter of 2018. The brand building helped drive traffic to the store, which in turn powered loyalty membership. The program's size continues to enable us to see massive volumes of transaction-level data, significantly more than competitors and standard industry data sources, leading to rich brand-related and other consumer insights.

WHAT WE LEARNED

Building the Ulta Beauty brand provided several key lessons important for leaders of any business. Here are the most compelling ones we learned.

Focus on Fundamentals

Fundamentals are critical, especially when it comes to brand building for retailers. Multibrand retailers may fail to emphasize branding *themselves*, as Ulta Beauty had for decades. Addressing that gap meant returning to the core marketing and branding concepts and tactics, including segmentation and competitive analyses to understand our consumers and positioning.

Make It an "All Play"

Branding isn't an individual sport. As a multibrand retailer, we had to attend very carefully to the balance between branding ourselves and supporting the brands we sell. We did that by creating transparency about our new branding effort and taking an integrative approach to align our products' brand stories with our evolving message. We also took care to align our associates in the field with the branding effort and insights to ensure they became enthusiastic brand ambassadors in the stores with actions consistent with our brand personality. In this way, we brought everyone along.

Adjust, React, Repeat

A branding or rebranding effort never happens in isolation. Always be prepared to respond to issues in your day-to-day business, such as slow traffic or competitive actions. It's not about either building the brand or staying on top of market dynamics, but doing both at once, in an integrative way wherever possible.

GOING FORWARD

We're proud of the success our branding effort has delivered. But, of course, there are new challenges ahead. Like any strong brand, our imperative is to continue to evolve, building our brand by understanding industry shifts and staying close to our guests and store associates.

For our next phase of brand building, we want to elevate the message beyond "all things beauty, all in one place" to create a more emotional, aspirational connection with consumers built around "the possibilities are beautiful." It's the idea of using beauty to unleash your inner self and to express more fully what you stand for to the world.

We'll continue to promote the functional benefit, of course, while emphasizing this emotional connection with our guests. So the assortment remains a strong value proposition for us; but instead of being our exclusive branding focus, it can serve as a foundation and support for the new brand direction. We're laying out the path now, again with focus on branding fundamentals and an integrative approach to bringing along our merchants and teams, such that everyone's aligned around the new messaging. The possibilities are beautiful indeed, as we move toward our ambitious goal: to be the most loved and admired brand in the beauty industry.

SUMMARY

At this chapter's outset we asked, "Should we focus on our brand or theirs?" The answer revealed by our branding journey is *both*. As a multibrand retailer, we built a new branding approach focused on telling our own brand story and aligning it with those of our partners through mutually reinforcing initiatives. It has worked beyond expectations for us, and we hope what we learned resonates with and benefits players within and beyond retail.

Mary Dillon is chief executive officer at Ulta Beauty. The Chicago native has more than 30 years of experience leading consumer-driven brands in a diverse range of industries, leveraging customer and associate insights to build brand engagement and drive results. Mary was number 5 on Fortune's *2017 Business Person of the Year list and was included on* Institutional Investor's *2018 All-American Executive Team: she is the only woman ranked number 1 in her industry. She is a guest lecturer at Northwestern University's Kellogg School of Management.*

Dave Kimbell is chief merchandising and marketing officer at Ulta Beauty. He is a proven marketing and general management leader, with more than 20 years of experience building brands, creating and delivering strategic growth plans, and developing collaborative teams. Dave's multifaceted expertise spans product categories, with a specialized focus on beauty, technology, health and wellness, and environmental sustainability. Dave lives in Evanston with his wife and two high school-aged children.

CHAPTER 19

TRANSFORMING A HISTORIC BRAND FOR A HYPER-CONNECTED WORLD
THE JOHN DEERE STORY

DENNY DOCHERTY and MIKE PORTER

One of the biggest challenges of managing a brand is navigating change. New technology can disrupt market dynamics, change essential capabilities, and create openings for new competitors. A well-crafted brand positioning can become irrelevant when markets shift—the world is full of examples of established brands that stumbled as the market shifted. Kodak, Blockbuster, BlackBerry, and others were great brands that failed to successfully navigate a changing world.

Keeping a brand relevant in a changing market requires a delicate balance: embracing change while maintaining the core of the brand. John Deere is an example of a brand that has successfully responded to fundamental changes in agriculture and construction, and in other complementary industries. The John Deere brand continues to thrive; to this day it remains a powerful brand that delivers remarkable financial results. However, the process has not been easy and has required John Deere to make bold changes to keep the brand relevant and vibrant.

THE JOHN DEERE STORY

The John Deere brand is almost two centuries old and of course has its roots in agriculture. The brand's namesake and founder was a blacksmith in Grand Detour, Illinois. John Deere talked with local farmers, who spoke of their frustrations with their old plows, most of which were designed for the sandy soils common in the eastern United States and were therefore unable to shed the sticky soil of the Midwest. John Deere built a new plow of highly polished steel that was self-scouring, allowing farmers to plow their fields uninterrupted. In 1837 he created the company that bears his name.

The company grew quickly—adding riding cultivators, buggies, grain drills, and hay harvesting equipment—and opened its first semi-independent distributor in 1869. By the firm's 100-year anniversary in 1937, sales had reached $100 million. In 1947 the company expanded horizontally into the construction-equipment business with the introduction of the MC crawler. Operations expanded internationally in 1956 with the opening of a tractor factory in Mexico and the purchase of Heinrich Lanz, a German tractor and harvester manufacturer. By 2017, John Deere had operations in 35 countries, sales in over 130 countries, and revenues of almost $30 billion.

Historically John Deere has focused on helping farmers by building high-quality, reliable equipment and by constantly improving product quality. This focus ultimately built the brand: farmers trusted John Deere and its distinctive green and yellow colors.

In 2010, John Deere's former Commercial and Consumer Equipment Division merged with its Agricultural Equipment Division to form the Worldwide Agriculture & Turf Division. A global operating model reorganization followed, resulting in five independent platform groups: tractors, crop care, crop harvesting, hay and forage, and turf and utility. Each group has functioned as an independent business unit, with engineers driving product development decision-making. They've applied methodical product development processes and partnered closely with customers in testing and quality assurance. Historically, John Deere's customer needs have been able to be addressed by bigger, faster machines. As such, the platform design centers have developed their products accordingly and ensured that farmers worldwide could depend on excellent, uninterrupted performance from their machines. The company's slogan, "Nothing Runs Like a Deere," has encapsulated its focus on quality and commitment to always keep customers' equipment up and running. The company has reached customers through a network of independent dealers, many with just one location. Most dealers have been committed to, and involved in, their local farm communities.

The Changing World of Farming

Getting the most out of a farming operation has always been challenging, but today's farmers face conditions that dictate a new level of effort and concern for their operations. Changes in weather patterns and environmental conditions affect all farms, manifesting in later and earlier growing seasons, storm activity, and drought. Globalization of commodity markets and pricing variability puts pressure on farmers to get their products to market, while labor shortages make it difficult to find the help they need.

To respond to these challenges, many farmers are looking to technology to improve results. Farmers now have the ability to apply in-field and soil-specific insights to determine the best mix of seed and nutrients to ensure a successful harvest, as well as the ability to capture and compare data at key points during the year. Precision, data-driven farming can transform the growing process.

For John Deere, the rise of technology has required dramatic changes. It became clear that twenty-first-century customers needed more than speed and size to address their needs. New agronomic advances required a new approach. The John Deere brand, known for quality and reliability, needed to change. Failure to do so would be a missed opportunity and a major competitive risk.

An immediate issue was clear: John Deere needed to rethink its organizational structure and enterprise processes, because farmers faced problems that required more than a single platform's answer. When a farmer asked how to get a more exact understanding of the farm's optimal seeding and harvest times for a particular crop, no one business unit could offer a solution.

A Plan to Address the Market Opportunity

To seize this moment, John Deere executives wanted to move quickly to answer the questions farmers were asking. They also wanted to get ahead of customers, applying data and system-level thinking to arrive at solutions. This would mean breaking down walls. They knew they needed to take the best of their engineering prowess and manufacturing process orientation, and marry them with agile thinking in order to quickly address the market opportunity.

Importantly, the John Deere team understood that the core essence of its brand was *helping farmers feed a growing world*, not just manufacturing farm equipment. As executives considered organizational changes, they knew that one thing would not change: the company's focus on helping farmers succeed. Farming encompasses many challenging jobs and decisions completed throughout the course of the year, all to support the growing of crops and livestock to market.

John Deere's customers run the gamut from small-scale farmers to large enterprises with tens of thousands of acres. But no matter the scale, farmers share a common set of characteristics. They hold a deep knowledge of the land, which is important to offset the variable conditions in which they work, and they are both artist and scientist. Their revenue is beholden to the grow-ing season and the weather's impact. Depending on the crop and scale of the farm, they might get two chances each year to go from seed to harvest, but it's often just one. They fund their operational costs with debt they take on at the beginning of the season to be paid off after they bring their crop to market at harvest time. This pressure forces them to be cost conscious and to weigh carefully the irreversible decisions they make throughout the course of the season.

The opportunity ahead was clear—the company needed to drive advance-ments in technology to bring new solutions to these evolving customer needs. It meant bringing the farming tech revolution to work in harmony with John Deere machinery to deliver economic impact to the farmer. As such, John Deere created the Intelligent Solutions Group (ISG), a strategic investment that would ensure its role in the technology revolution on the farm. Outside of John Deere's five product platforms and global operations, ISG comprised hundreds of system architects and developers centered on developing advanced farming technologies. ISG helped capitalize on the use of technologies such as GPS, vision, sensors, robotics, and machine learning. Adding this capacity opened up the route to precision agriculture, which provides software and data-based solutions that work with equipment and analyze outcomes to solve complex problems on the farm.

John Deere executives knew that simply developing technology wasn't enough; the company had to be sure the new innovations created real value and supported the John Deere brand. They knew they had to create a trans-formation within the company's organizational structure to support these new initiatives.

INTRODUCING ECAP

To spark this transformation, John Deere's executive team embraced a con-cept they called "enterprise customer acquisition process," or ECAP. Through ECAP, John Deere put customers' needs at the center and then applied all of its capabilities and offerings to develop solutions that created verifiable cus-tomer value. That meant meshing platforms and technologies in new ways and introducing iterative processes to build new behaviors across the company. But most important, it moved John Deere from its historically product-first orien-tation to a customer-first approach.

ECAP was a way to address silos in the organization and more effec-tively involve the company's global regions in product conversations. Previ-ously John Deere had lacked a universal basis for understanding and framing

Figure 19.1
The Farming Process

customers' objectives. With ECAP, the company focused on the individual jobs a farmer has throughout the entire growing season.

John Deere started with the process of growing and harvesting a corn crop, and gathered product leaders, technology experts, and agronomists to isolate the jobs and define the decisions and variables important to each production step. The cross-functional, cross-platform, and tech-centered collaboration teams looked at the four phases of the farming process: field preparation; plant or seed; apply (nurturing and protecting); and harvest, including the analysis and planning that goes into managing each of those phases (see Figure 19.1). This provided an essential orientation for all product development and marketing efforts, and generated a common viewpoint to lay the groundwork for collaboration.

Importantly, the cross-functional ECAP approach created a structure for collaboration between marketing and engineering. Marketing became involved in projects from the beginning, adopting a design-thinking approach to innovation. Marketing leaders conducted cross-functional workshops designed to collaboratively ideate, tasking teams with moving from addressing the customer challenge to creating a solution. These sessions forged partnerships with the engineering team. The data that marketers generated was externally focused, putting market intelligence and customer insights in an anchor position. This allowed John Deere to incubate new ideas and move quickly on opportunities. Thus, ECAP fed into both product development and the entire customer journey.

From ideation, the John Deere team moved to define solutions and validate them with customers. The cross-functional teams—matrixed across job function, platform, and region—identified potential projects and honed the list by considering potential customer value against the potential upside and risk for John Deere.

John Deere opened up these teams to stakeholders from a variety of functional areas—engineering, supply management, operations, finance, and marketing. Projects then evolved into product concepts that stood on validated customer needs and were ready for funding decisions. Engineering validated that the solution would meet customer needs. Marketing documented the value proposition. Funding decisions were made on the basis of knowing that the solution would make a substantial difference for the customer and deliver market advantage for John Deere.

This customer focus helped John Deere teams envision pathways to answer new questions around machine and job optimization. What does it cost for a customer to put seed in the ground? What are the variables? What are the areas we can impact to improve how a farmer plants a field? Importantly, the question was no longer how a particular piece of equipment—such as a planter—performed. Rather, it was how a tractor, planter, and software could work seamlessly to improve the process for the farmer.

With this new approach, anyone involved in R&D across the company had a single view of how John Deere could generate value for the customer: have a tangible impact on the different phases of the farming process. This allowed all players to focus on how John Deere's products could deliver the best possible outcome at each step. It kept the voice of the customer central to granular conversations on how equipment, technology, and data optimize each of the farmer's jobs.

TAKING A MARKETING-FOCUSED APPROACH

Since its founding, John Deere has placed a great value on what it calls "deep customer understanding." Because no two farms are alike, and because each farm comprises fields with often widely varying conditions, this connection to the customer's particular needs has always guided John Deere's sales and product development process. For ECAP, this practice proved invaluable— John Deere had the ability to seamlessly work with farmers to test and vet new ideas.

Listening to the Voice of the Customer

With this history of deep customer understanding, John Deere worked to connect meaningfully with the best guidance it could get: the voice of the customer. The company convened events that allowed John Deere employees to join with customers, agronomists, academics, and other advisors to talk about challenges, discuss solutions at a conceptual level, and gain feedback to fuel product development. These events created an environment to discover customers' unarticulated needs. Historically, customers had been accustomed to weighing in on the relative advantages of a piece of machinery, but now John Deere was addressing how their businesses could run better overall. By linking ECAP with the customer in this way, John Deere could inform a clear view of how to prioritize its portfolios and solution sets, always grounded in how to strengthen the customer's business as a result.

Developing Tactical Marketing Plans

Eventually, teams developed tactical marketing plans. John Deere's marketing teams worked with its dealers on the value proposition development, ensuring that customer insights reflected what customers saw on the ground. Tactical marketing plans for dealers emanated from the company's plans, localizing strategies for individual markets. Staff training for dealers was implemented to ensure that they were equipped to deliver at a solution level. New tools were developed to measure tactics in order to understand potential impact and market-share gain for John Deere. And of course, everything was validated by data. At launch, John Deere's analytics allowed marketing to understand and adjust to ensure maximal impact from the marketing expenditure.

Transforming the Dealer Channel

The transformation at the corporate level also happened in the dealer channel. Historically a John Deere dealership was owned and operated by a local dealer who was the local face of the brand. As John Deere's products became more sophisticated, this method of customer and product support became more of a challenge because dealers needed more capabilities and training.

Over the course of several years, John Deere supported dealer shifts to multilocation ownership as part of its Dealer of Tomorrow strategy. This created stronger businesses that were able to better support farmers. These businesses were equipped to meet customer demand, providing deeper levels of service and support, especially around technology solutions.

Old product sales models were sunset, and dealers shared John Deere's brand effort to shift from a product-first orientation to a solution-selling model. New tools in the form of value-selling guides drew direct lines from personal conversations to tablet screens that dealers could pull up while standing in a farmer's field. Dealers were always able to articulate why John Deere was the better option for the customer, and dealers also addressed customers' need for demonstrated value. Dealers held events for customers that enabled them to witness a result directly on the field, ask questions, and understand how John Deere's solution could make a difference to their work.

SUMMARY: RESULTS AND LOOKING AHEAD

By all measures, John Deere has successfully navigated a notable brand evolution. The John Deere brand continues to stand for integrity, quality, commitment, and innovation, even nearly two centuries after its founding. Throughout its innovation journey, the company has helped farmers understand how new technology can change and strengthen their operations. John Deere has brought a series of innovations to market and has a pipeline with many more projects to come.

Financial results are just one indicator of success, and farming suppliers such as John Deere depend on high grain prices to spark sales. Still, John Deere is performing very well financially, with 2018 revenues of nearly $37.4 billion and a net income of over $2.4 billion. More important, the organization is engaged and energized, and the John Deere brand remains a clear leader in its field.

Looking forward, the John Deere brand will continue to evolve. One thing that won't change: the company's commitment to *helping farmers feed a growing world*. The company's employees will continue to work on smart technologies and develop products that might be unimaginable today. All of this work will focus on maximizing the productivity of its customers' operations.

Dennis Docherty is the director of global marketing for the Worldwide Agriculture & Turf Division at John Deere. He joined the company in 1998. He received his BA from Baldwin-Wallace College and MBA from the UNC Kenan-Flagler Business School.

Michael Porter is a special projects manager at John Deere. He received his BS from Illinois State University.

CHAPTER 20

REBRANDING AN ORGANIZATION: THE NOVANT HEALTH STORY

SCOTT DAVIS and DAVID DUVALL

Sometimes an organization faces so many challenges that small brand-building efforts simply will not be enough to create meaningful results. In these cases the organization may need to undergo a complete rebranding. These shifts are challenging, expensive, and disruptive, but they can provide significant benefits. The story of Novant Health illustrates what is required to successfully complete a rebranding effort.

THE ISSUE: A FRAGMENTED BRAND PORTFOLIO

Novant Health is a nonprofit healthcare provider that traces its history back to 1891, when Twin City Hospital opened in Winston-Salem, North Carolina. The hospital changed names several times over the years until finally it merged in 1997 with Presbyterian Hospital in Charlotte. The combined organization became Novant Health.

Over the next decade, Novant acquired hospitals and medical practices in North Carolina, South Carolina, Virginia, and Delaware. By 2013, the Novant system included 13 hospitals, 500 outpatient clinics, and 1,300 physicians, and was earning over $4 billion in revenue.

While the company grew, its brand portfolio became increasingly complicated. By 2013, Novant was a classic house of brands, operating under 400 different brand names. For example, Hemby Children's Hospital, Huntersville

Medical Center, and Presbyterian Hospital were all part of Novant, but each had completely distinct branding.

The use of multiple names was a challenge. It was inefficient to manage. More important, patients and potential (and some current) employees had no idea that all the different organizations were part of Novant. This was a significant problem as patients became more involved in their healthcare decisions.

REBRANDING A COMPLEX PORTFOLIO

In February 2013, the Novant executive team decided it was time for a sweeping rebranding effort. Led by the CEO and executive team with board support, the organization was clear that it wanted to unify these disparate fragments under one Novant Health brand, reimagining it with a clearer identity, goals, and purpose.

A unified brand would provide multiple benefits, including patient loyalty, easier recruiting, and increased leverage when negotiating with insurance plans. Linking all the elements was the Novant brand and its mission: "To improve the health of communities, one person at a time."

To help shape this reinvention, Novant Health started by identifying the people to lead the change. Novant first brought in the branding firm Prophet, which included chapter author Scott Davis, and then hired chapter author David Duvall as senior vice president of marketing and communications.

Novant created a steering team to guide the efforts. The team knew that simply changing all the brand names wouldn't work—it would just create confusion, conflict, and unhappiness. It would also be a missed opportunity, because the project should include new processes and go far beyond naming and logos.

In order to achieve long-term success, the Novant branding team had three goals: (1) unify the brand portfolio and redefine the Novant brand; (2) redesign the marketing function by borrowing approaches, capabilities, and talent from other leading industries; and (3) engage consumers in new ways to drive growth and relevance of the new brand. It was also important to move quickly, as competitive pressure was building.

The first task was clarifying the Novant brand's positioning and meaning. This was a critical step to identifying the common elements that would unify the portfolio. At the core was Novant's brand purpose: a passion for health care.

Then, the challenge was to develop a new brand design that brought all the disparate brands under one name (Novant), look, and feel. The effort also reviewed key processes, improving some and developing new platforms for others from the ground up.

Perhaps the most important step was engaging employees and explaining the rationale for the change and the new brand guidance. A key event was a massive launch at a stadium in Winston-Salem. The event featured an appearance from Michael Jordan, a new Novant spokesperson; it was a galvanizing time in the organization's history. As thousands of employees stood and cheered, the embrace was palpable. It was as if they were saying, "This is my brand. I'm proud to work here."

Over the past five years, Novant has successfully unified its brand portfolio. The brand is consistently used and embraced across the organization. Brand awareness in the market has tripled, and Net Promoter Score (NPS) has increased. The unified brand has allowed Novant to leverage its scale, making the most of investments in new patient-focused technologies through a broad rollout. There are fewer fragmented efforts with subscale funding. The priority initiatives now have adequate resources and provide benefits across the organization.

LESSONS LEARNED

During the rebranding process, we learned five important lessons.

Executive Alignment and Organizational Buy-In Is Critical

The relaunch couldn't have succeeded without the support of senior leaders: the CEO, the executive committee, and the board of directors. But it was most critical that we were able to achieve buy-in throughout the organization. That meant winning over many disparate groups of skeptical physicians, providers, and administrators.

Change management is difficult, so we held initial conversations with over 30 key leaders of the organization. They were highly accustomed to a style of marketing that was reactive rather than proactive, and they were used to making decisions based on what was best for providers, not consumers. Many believed that providing high-quality health care was enough. But to become relevant with consumers, we had to stand for something more. In early meetings, we had to help the organization's leaders understand marketing from the consumer' point of view, and help them realize that providing quality care, in today's market, is simply table stakes. We had to teach using plenty of real-world examples—even comparing health care to brands such as Starbucks—to help them understand how authenticity, innovation, and relevance build brand equity and affinity.

We also focused on Novant's goals, including the vision of doubling scale in 5 to 10 years. Once the leaders had a better understanding of the region's hyper-competitive healthcare landscape, they realized that meeting the goals required restructuring the brand portfolio to sustain quality and drive down operating costs, while also delivering on the brand promise of "reinventing the healthcare experience to be simpler, more convenient, and more affordable." We knew we were on the right track when some of our most skeptical physicians became early adopters of our thinking.

Invest in Smart Segmentation

Even as the internal branding efforts were underway, we knew we needed a much deeper analysis of the people we wanted to serve. To become the leader in our primary markets—Charlotte, Winston-Salem, Wilmington, and Northern Virginia, which include about nine million adults—we performed an extensive consumer segmentation.

Our starting point came from deep within Novant Health through interviews with important stakeholders, including doctors, clinical leaders, and executives. Our goal was to match emerging consumer demands and preferences with the product and service offering. We used several consumer focus groups, tapping 250 existing and potential patients, to shape our hypotheses. We then surveyed 1,600 additional consumers, including patients and caregivers.

While this type of effort is usually based on demographic characteristics such as age, gender, income, education, location, and ethnicity, we suspected that we needed more. So we added attitudinal dimensions about health, well-being, and lifestyle, as well as questions about caregiving, life stage, and health status. We probed the participants' interest in value-added services that we hypothesized might make a big difference in their lives, such as financial navigators, online scheduling, and same-day appointments.

This deliberate and interactive process took nearly nine months. Using statistical analyses rooted in the social sciences, such as factor analysis, latent class modeling, and migration tables, we identified six unique population segments:

1. *Eager and Engaged Stewards* are actively involved with health care, and many are in the "sandwich generation."
2. *Savvy and Connected Patients* enjoy taking care of their health and are looking to maintain and increase their involvement in health care.
3. *Healthy and Unconcerned Individuals* want as few interactions as possible and engage with healthcare providers only when necessary.

4. *Cost-Conscious Guidance Seekers* are generally frugal but will pay for access to services that they value.
5. *Responsible and Resolute Boomers* prefer one-on-one care interactions with their providers and are averse to alternative and digital care.
6. *Uninterested and Unengaged Individuals* attribute minimal value to an improved care experience.

One of the most exciting moments of our rebranding effort happened when we introduced these six segments to key stakeholders at an internal event where we brought the segments to life on stage using actors. The dramatization made it very clear that different people required a different care experience. Importantly, the segments were not meant to replace understanding and empathy at the individual level; instead, they allowed us to focus our efforts and investments with more confidence than ever before.

Of these six segments, we identified two—the Eager and Engaged Consumer and the Savvy and Connected Consumer—as our top priorities; they accounted for close to 50 percent of the target market, or approximately four million people. And these groups contained a higher proportion of women, who are more likely to be healthcare purchasers, caregivers, and decision makers. While our highest priority was to increase engagement and loyalty with these two groups, we could also begin building familiarity and affinity with the other segments.

Focus on Changes That Are Data Backed and Strategy Led

The segmentation work also began to fuel new ways of thinking and acting. We learned a great deal about customers' price sensitivities within health care, about smart-phone penetration, and about how much time consumers spent online and on social media, for example. We got insights into how they saw Novant Health's competitors in terms of value, technology, trust, and quality.

Three central issues emerged as critical in all the segments: *cost clarity*, *access to care*, and *digital integration*. To help translate those insights into initiatives, we sat down with over 40 cross-functional team members from across the health system. Our task was to generate an inventory of all ongoing activities, identify gaps, and ideate to generate new products and services to go to market.

A tangible result of these early meetings was a new online tool, Your Healthcare Costs, which was designed to help patients better understand the healthcare landscape by providing content and video that explained premiums, deductibles, co-pays, and out-of-pocket maximums. We also strengthened the financial navigator program for patients who needed help estimating healthcare expenses. Since the program's launch in 2015, Novant Health's 75 financial counselors have created more than 10,000 personalized price estimates for both inpatients and ambulatory-care patients using this new cost-assessment tool.

Our strategy to *expand access* came directly from understanding how much consumers wanted to see their provider of choice at times that fit into their busy lives. Care Connections, Novant Health's 24-hour virtual care hub, is staffed by more than 100 administrative and clinical professionals and includes nurse triage, scheduling, wellness coaching, discharge follow-ups, medication management, psychosocial consults, and class registration. Same-day appointment availability also was expanded through extended walk-in clinics and physician office hours, new care locations, and increased use of e-visits and video visits. The Care Connections team provides services for more than 800 Novant Health employees and independent providers in 150 locations across North Carolina, South Carolina, and Virginia. In 2016 alone, approximately 10,900 patients were "seen" by clinicians through electronic visits. According to Epic, the organization's patient portal vendor, Novant Health ranks number two in the nation among its 125 clients who have turned on the e-visit module.

Make Sure That Brand and Experience Are Synonymous

Today, meaningful customer engagement and experiences are essential if you hope to build a strong brand. If you can't provide them, consumers will fire you, no matter how good the advertising or how compelling the brand promise. At Novant Health, experiences must genuinely and consistently bring the brand to life, giving people precisely what they need, when they need it, and in a format that's easy for them.

Watching Novant Health insiders come alive with this realization—the radical notion that they need to think first about what is most helpful for the consumer, not the hospital or the physician—was and continues to be truly exciting and game changing.

Perhaps the best illustration of this new thinking is Novant Health's *digital integration* plan, which focuses on improving how the organization connects with patients through their computers, smartphones, and tablets. In 2015, Novant Health introduced online appointment scheduling. Since the launch of Open Schedule, which provides online visibility into physician and clinic schedules, about 180,000 patients have made appointments through the web or the MyChart patient portal. Novant Health currently ranks in the top 5 percent of the 245 Epic clients that use the patient portal for direct scheduling. The organization is also integrating fitness trackers with care plans, and the online caregiver resource now includes recommendations from primary care providers. Today, more than 800,000 patients currently use the MyChart patient portal, pushing Novant Health into the top 5 percent of 330 organizations based on the absolute number of active patients. In fact, Novant Health was the first health system worldwide to receive the prestigious Health Information and Management Systems Society's Analytics Stage 7 Ambulatory Award for the implementation and advanced use of the electronic health record.

To Manage Well, Measure Well

Amid all these changes, Novant Health also committed to making sure it was measuring consumer preference in an ongoing and dynamic way. Currently, the organization monitors over 50 brand-equity metrics with key elements tracked on dashboards, including NPS at the system, market, and service-line levels.

Novant Health developed a marketing model mix that has the powerful ability to discern base volume from marketing-driven volume. The model performs simultaneous regressions of time-series data, which enables it to decompose and attribute total patient volume based on correlations with each pre-specified, independent variable.

These metrics also provide the evidence to invest further: based on initial success, the CEO felt confident about devoting an additional $7 million to an out-of-cycle ad campaign that further drove results and won a Cannes top 100 advertising award in 2016.

SUMMARY

There is no doubt that Novant's bold branding strategy is working. In a five-year period, from April 2011 to April 2016, Novant Health tripled rates of brand awareness and interest.

The organization has never stopped monitoring the health and relevance of its newly built brand. For Novant Health, brand building is a two-step process. First, marketing decisions must be understood and fully supported by the entire organization. Then, fostering close relationships with clinical and administrative leaders is essential. When key leaders embed themselves in the clinician's world to understand the front lines of serving patients, the organization can have new and frequent conversations about redesigning care delivery and patient experience.

The hard work and rewarding experience of unifying the Novant brand portfolio continues. Having unified a collection of more than 300 small brands, Novant is now becoming one of the most relevant brands in health care.

Scott Davis, Prophet's chief growth officer, has over 20 years of brand, marketing strategy, and new product development experience. He is the author of Building the Brand-Driven Business: Operationalize Your Brand to Drive Profitable Growth *and* The Shift: The Transformation of Today's Marketers into Tomorrow's Growth Drivers. *He is an adjunct professor at Kellogg, where he received his MM.*

David Duvall is Novant Health's senior vice president of marketing and communications. He has more than 25 years of experience in healthcare strategy, branding, life-cycle management, and consulting. He's held executive leadership roles at WPP/CommonHealth and Publicis Healthcare Communications Group. He received his MPH from University of Illinois at Chicago and his MBA from Kellogg.

CHAPTER 21

REPOSITIONING A COUNTRY BRAND: CHANGING THE CONVERSATION ABOUT MEXICO

GLORIA GUEVARA

When people think about brands, what typically comes to mind are classic consumer brands such as Coke, Starbucks, and Apple. However, branding is a factor across many different parts of the economy.

In recent years, the country of Mexico has faced a series of branding challenges. A campaign to reposition the brand of Mexico successfully addressed these challenges, and the experience highlights why branding is so important and how leaders can change brand perceptions.

THE CHALLENGE

In 2009 Mexico faced what experts described as a "perfect storm," which resulted in a significant economic downturn for the economy. Several factors contributed to the storm: the H1N1 flu outbreak; fighting among drug cartel gangs (which led to violence in certain areas of the country); and the financial and economic crisis in the United States, whose economy is intertwined with Mexico's. Tourism and travel, a critical economic sector for Mexico, was particularly hard hit: the country saw a decline of four million people in international visitors. Despite efforts to reverse the decline, the negative trend continued into the first half of 2010.

Travel and tourism is the third-largest contributor to the Mexican economy after oil and remittances, accounting for 16 percent of the Mexican GDP and employing around eight million people.[1] However, this important sector lacked the strong foundation needed to withstand the perfect storm it faced.

In March 2010, the president of Mexico, Felipe Calderón, invited me to join his cabinet as the secretary of tourism. My team and I needed to find a way to reverse the decline by growing Mexican tourism and thereby boosting the economy.

THE INSIGHT: WE NEEDED TO CHANGE THE CONVERSATION

Mexico has an amazing history, a unique culture, and a diverse geography. It has more than 3,000 years of recorded history and over 40,000 archaeological sites. There are 62 ethnic groups that maintain distinct cultures, languages, and culinary traditions. And, the country is home to 35 tangible sites on UNESCO's World Heritage List as well as 9 intangible offerings, such as cuisine. According to Virtuoso, the leading luxury travel network, Mexico has the world's second-largest offering of hotels, tours, and experiences for high-end travelers.

However, most international travelers have limited knowledge of the diversity in geography and culture in Mexico. For example, few know of Mexico's enchanting colonial and cultural towns, such as San Miguel de Allende in Guanajuato, which has festivals and unique traditions and was named one of the top destinations in the world by *Travel + Leisure* following our campaign. Another little-known destination is Puebla, a city with unique cuisine and beverages that features a Baroque museum and a church built atop the largest pyramid in the world.

From 2009 to 2010, stories of drug violence in Mexico captured the headlines and created the impression that Mexico was a dangerous place to visit, even though the violence was concentrated in only a few areas of the vast country. Presenting data that countered these impressions only served to continue the conversation about drug violence and failed to provide a compelling reason for prospective tourists to visit Mexico. U.S. travelers were weary of Cancún and Cabo, but they were not willing to push their boundaries and consider unfamiliar destinations within the country. International travelers from countries beyond the United States were simply not coming in large numbers because they held images of Mexico that were limited to "sun, sand, and burritos," and because, for some nationalities, the need to obtain a visa seemed like too much red tape.

To grow tourism in Mexico, we needed a fresh approach—one that would paint Mexico in a positive light and expand travelers' views of what a vacation in Mexico could offer. We also needed to attract more visitors from countries beyond the United States and Canada.

THE PLAN: A HOLISTIC APPROACH

In order to achieve our goals, we took a holistic approach to engaging both public and private stakeholders and developed a four-step plan. First, we made an inventory of tourism assets and aligned stakeholders around the goal of growing tourism through a strategy of diversification. Second, we identified the need to diversify both the tourism experiences we offered and segments we targeted, and developed a strategic plan around this goal. Third, we persuaded government officials and the private sector to increase their investment in tourism. Finally, we launched an aggressive rebranding campaign to position Mexico as a tourist destination.

Step 1: Assessing the Opportunity and Aligning Players around a Shared Goal

We knew we had been missing opportunities by only promoting sun and beach destinations targeted to U.S. and Canadian travelers. So we assembled a task force of government officials and representatives from the private sector and charged it with exploring the possibilities for tourism related to Mexico's history, traditions, gastronomy, and cultural variety within its 32 different states and federal entities.

President Calderón made tourism a national priority, declaring 2011 the "Year of Tourism." Following his lead, members of the cabinet embraced our initiative, as did all 32 governors and the country's senators and congress. Our initiative also received support from leaders in the private sector, trade associations, academia, unions, the chamber of commerce, and international organizations such as the United Nation's World Tourism Organization and the World Travel & Tourism Council. These diverse stakeholders formalized their commitment to tourism in a national agreement (see https://cedocvirtual. sectur.gob.mx/janium/Documentos/11252.pdf).

Step 2: Building a Strategic Plan Based on Diversification

The image of Mexico as the destination for tourists seeking a beach vacation had been fueled over the years in the United States by classic movies such as those featuring Elvis Presley in Acapulco and Elizabeth Taylor in Puerto Vallarta. Although such destinations remained popular and important to tourism, we recognized the need to attract travelers from a broader range of countries who were seeking more varied experiences.

We began by identifying additional tourism segments we could target. We expanded our historic focus on the United States and Canada to include international travelers. Then we parsed through demographics and spending power to develop a clear picture of each segment (e.g., singles, couples, families, and groups).

Our next step entailed creating distinct travel experiences around the pillars of culture, adventure, gastronomy, luxury, and so on. Specifically, we developed the "Routes of Mexico" campaign, which provided tourists with 10 detailed itineraries, each of which was organized around one of the pillars (see www.weareonetravel.com/trip-ideas/10-routes-of-mexico and www.youtube.com/watch?v=6A6OYNFKJBg).

One of these, the Maya route, evolved into a major, multiyear initiative. It capitalized on the 5,000-year cycle on the Maya calendar that ended on December 21, 2012. The Maya culture is an ancient civilization known for its advanced knowledge of topics such as astronomy and math. The Mayas still live in the southeast of Mexico and maintain their traditions and language. The Ruta Maya covers the five Mexican states of Chiapas, Oaxaca, Yucatán, Quintana Roo, and Tabasco. Two archaeological sites in each state were included on the route, as were museums and other experiences. In addition, Mexico spearheaded a regional initiative that involved four other countries in which Mayan sites and culture exist: Guatemala, Belize, El Salvador, and Honduras. This culturally rich, multicountry offering appealed to tourists who sought an experience that went beyond a simple sun-and-fun vacation.

We also knew that in order to grow and diversify the number of tourists coming from both the United States and international markets, we would need to make it easier to enter the country. A policy change allowed all citizens with a valid U.S. visa to visit Mexico without a Mexican visa. In addition, an online system was instituted to provide 24-hour approval of visa applications from those in emerging tourist markets such as Russia and China. Within our own region, visa requirements were removed for citizens of countries such as Peru, Brazil, and Colombia.

Step 3: Increase Both Public and Private Investment in Tourism

Achieving both public and private investment in the tourism initiative was essential to our success. The buy-in and full support of the Mexican government mentioned earlier was just the start. The administration assigned and redirected resources for improving infrastructure, upgrading destinations, and creating the unique experiences for tourists described above. In addition, the government allocated significant funding for a public relations strategy that helped us reset the tone of the new Mexican "brand."

Private sector investment followed public investment. Companies invested in new hotels near cultural sites and in magical towns. They developed products and experiences linked to the new routes. They also worked to train travel agencies in promoting the new vision of tourism in Mexico and ran promotional campaigns that were aligned with the government ads. The result was a comprehensive and cohesive approach that led to an energized rebranding of Mexican tourism.

Step 4: Rebranding Mexico

Once we had our "product" (a diverse mix of tourism offerings) and the buy-in of all the necessary stakeholders, we turned our attention to rebranding Mexico as a tourist destination for both U.S. and international travelers.

U.S. and Canadian tourists believed they knew what Mexico had to offer . . . sun and fun. We tackled this belief head-on with our campaign, "Mexico, the place you thought you knew," and then described the new routes. Prospective tourists in Europe and elsewhere had different perceptions. Often they were familiar with "old" Mexico through artists (Frida Kahlo) or history and culture (Maya), but were not aware of the range of experiences that modern Mexico offers. Our campaign for the European market presented a contemporary view with a "Mexico Today" campaign. Although the two campaigns spoke to different targets and prior beliefs, they were complementary at an abstract level.

We supported these efforts in both the United States and Europe with aggressive public relations and social media strategies. Working with the public and private sectors, we conducted more than 800 interviews with U.S. and international media in 12 months. In addition, we held road shows in the United States, Canada, and Europe with local, regional, and national media to tell our Mexico story.

We significantly increased our presence on Facebook and Twitter, and launched the web site www.Mexicotoday.org. With the belief that first-person testimonials are always a powerful way to influence people, we focused our online and media efforts on voices and stories from travelers and hired bloggers to write about their first-person experiences.

Live feeds of travelers enjoying their time in Mexico were shown in New York City's Times Square and other locations. We also developed the "Mexico Taxi Project" campaign, which featured a hidden camera recording tourists' conversations with taxi drivers as they traveled to the airport after their Mexican holiday. Excerpts of these conversations were featured on the web site Mexicotoday.org (with the tourists' permission, of course). Finally, recognizing that Mexico is a popular destination for celebrities, we invited more than 30 high-impact individuals from the music, entertainment, and sports industries to visit the country and share their experiences. Some celebrities filmed content within the country that helped promote Mexico to their followers.

THE RESULTS: CLOSING THE GAP BETWEEN PERCEPTION AND REALITY

Mexico's rebranding efforts delivered clear and positive results. Mexico broke a new record for international arrivals and domestic travelers in 2011 and each subsequent year, with the number of tourists from 143 nations around the world increasing significantly in just 12 months. The number of tourists from Russia increased by 85 percent, while those from Brazil increased by 51 percent and from Peru by 30 percent. Canadian tourists also increased and accounted for 15 percent of total travelers. Tourists from the United States continued to visit in large numbers that increased by 5 percent, but Mexico became less dependent on them. After the campaign, the United States accounted for 50 percent of the total volume of tourists, down from 70 percent.

Our campaign achieved 12.5 billion impressions in traditional media, due to interviews, road shows, and participation with editorial boards. We also achieved 13 billion media impressions of celebrities endorsing Mexico and sharing their experiences. Most important, we were able to dispel some of the negative perceptions and build positive associations with the brand of Mexico.

SUMMARY: FIVE LESSONS LEARNED

Our experience taught us several important lessons.

Lesson 1: Control Your Narrative

Negative stories will always appear, and sometimes it is necessary to counter them directly. However, countering a negative story just brings you back to neutral ground. You need to have a positive story to shift the narrative to your advantage. This was the single most important aspect of our strategy. We created a compelling positive story about all that Mexico has to offer and focused on telling that story.

Lesson 2: Embrace Brand Management Principles

While countries, destinations, and tourism boards are not products per se, they benefit immensely when they embrace the same principles of enterprise brand management. We drew upon basic marketing and branding concepts of segmentation, product development (creating experiences), and targeting to create a diverse mix of travel offerings for different types of tourists. We also employed branding principles to present clear, packaged offerings so that consumers knew what to expect (i.e., mapping the routes). Finally, we ensured a positive experience by coordinating with the entire channel of distribution, which required aligning both public and private players. And we supported the entire effort with a compelling brand and marketing campaign. Too often, countries have great strategy and promotion, but the execution falls short.

Lesson 3: Diversification Is Crucial

Mexico's dependency on one product (sun and beach) and one tourist market (the United States) was a recipe for disaster. It made the country's tourism business highly vulnerable to economic fluctuations in a single market. Diversification in both product offering and target markets is crucial. And, diversification requires customizing campaigns to different target segments, as we did by using separate campaigns in the United States and Canada versus Europe.

Lesson 4: Personal Voices (Testimonials) Are Powerful

People love to hear what others think. The taxi confessions campaign had great impact. The celebrity endorsement of Mexico was also very powerful, as it provided not only testimonials, but also helped change the conversation and allowed Mexico to become an aspirational destination of the "rich and famous."

Lesson 5: Be Prepared

In today's world things change quickly. It's not a matter of *if*, but *where* or *when* a crisis that can derail your efforts will occur. A country is no different from a corporation in terms of the need for preparation. Having a clear brand strategy in place and a good understanding of your audience through careful segmentation and targeting allows you to communicate the appropriate messages during a crisis.

In the end, the tourism rebranding initiative closed the gap between perception and reality. Before we began, 70 percent of media mentions about Mexico were negative. After the initiative, 77 percent of media mentions were positive or neutral. We had succeeded in changing the conversation.

Gloria Guevara is CEO of the World Travel & Tourism Council. She was secretary of tourism for Mexico and CEO of the Mexican Tourism Board from 2010 to 2012. She is a G20 pioneer with vast experience in the private sector. She holds a BS from Anahuac University and an MBA (2009) from Northwestern University's Kellogg School of Management.

NOTES

1. World Travel & Tourism Council (2017), *Travel & Tourism Economic Impact 2017: World*, WTTC. https://www.wttc.org/-/media/files/reports/economic-impact-research/regions-2017/world2017.pdf.

CHAPTER 22

MANAGING BRAND COMMUNICATIONS IN A DIGITAL WORLD

CINDY HALVORSEN

Today, consumers often check their mobile phones before they roll out of bed—and then check them an average of 150 more times throughout the day. At work, many consumers spend the majority of their days staring at a computer screen. When they're not at work, many view entertainment on demand across multiple screens ranging from a mobile device to a TV.

Long gone are the days when the family gathered around the TV, captivated by Lucille Ball and Desi Arnaz in *I Love Lucy*, which garnered a 71.7 rating at its peak in 1953.[1] In 2018, the top scripted show, *This Is Us*, only achieved a 9.3 rating during its most-watched episode.[2] Back in the 1950s, there were few options for both consumers and advertisers, so fewer ads would provide mass reach with high consumer attention. Even as recently as the late 1990s, TV shows such as *Seinfeld* and *Friends* drew large audiences. But TV no longer dominates consumer attention. Viewers are in control of when, where, and how they consume content, and are no longer reliant on TV schedules set by networks or on sharing a single TV with everyone in the home.

In today's world, marketers must not only define how digital has changed consumer behavior and what it means for their branding efforts, but also choose digital partners to support consumer communications. Digital technology has spawned myriad companies whose mission is to help marketers build brands and navigate this new digital world. The advertising and ad technology landscape has become incredibly complex and fragmented, as is depicted in various LUMAscapes (see https://lumapartners.com/luma-content).

287

There are giant tech companies, such as Google, Amazon, Microsoft, and Facebook, as well as smaller players, such as Pinterest and Snapchat. Sprouting up across this new ecosystem are thousands of new companies with business models fully dependent on extracting value in the digital supply chain.

The sheer number of technology options and service providers can be overwhelming. How do marketers keep up? One thing is very clear: marketers must embrace the notion of modern brand building in a digital world rather than viewing digital as simply another communications channel.

As an industry leader at Google, I've seen and helped hundreds of brands transition their marketing efforts with varying degrees of success. Traditional media and digital media require different skills and activities, and organizations with the right talent structure and mindset for change enjoy a smoother ride on this journey.

Traditional media campaigns—especially TV campaigns—often require companies to commit to a creative and media strategy far in advance of when consumers actually see the campaign. Then data on campaign effectiveness can take months to obtain and analyze. By contrast, digital campaigns provide some immediate metrics about their effectiveness in driving consumer action, such as clicks or even sales, which fosters an approach that allows for continual improvement and optimization. The nature of more active campaign management requires focused efforts and agility, and an appetite for taking risks, trying new approaches, and learning continually.

There isn't one perfect organizational structure to accommodate all business models or transformation stages. At the early stages of embracing digital, a devoted digital team may be appropriate for determining how digital media fits into the larger company strategy. Changing an organizational structure can be difficult, but it can vastly impact your ability to reap the rewards of the new digital environment.

In this chapter I provide three recommendations for senior leaders seeking to align their marketing, branding, and communication strategies to reach consumers in a digital world.

RECOMMENDATION 1: CHOOSE FEWER DIGITAL MEDIA PARTNERS AND DEVELOP DEEP RELATIONSHIPS WITH THEM

Digital marketing is incredibly fragmented and prolific. There are dozens of platforms to use and partners to work with. Choosing the right partners can help marketers stay focused on the most impactful business outcomes and keep their companies at the forefront of innovation. Fewer partnerships can also save time for marketers and agencies.

When transforming digital marketing capabilities, it's important to make the transition from a transactional media partnership to a true business partnership. Start by developing a joint business plan and/or partnership strategy, and engage your partners in helping to solve your business problems. You should ask for thought leadership on data strategy, industry expertise, organizational talent and structure, and processes that will help to achieve your goals. As part of the dialogue, establish common goals and agree on performance indicators.

The key here is to think of your digital partners as more than just media. Your partners have a wealth of data about your consumers that will allow you to leverage insights to shape your total business strategy and activation, not just digital communications.

For example, Google search data enabled a bourbon brand to uncover a strong positive correlation between search query volume and brand bottle sales.[3] The data also offered the company insight about consumers' interests and concerns related to the category. The top three questions consumers asked Google related to bourbon are "What is bourbon?," "How do I drink bourbon?," and "What is the difference between whiskey and bourbon?" Google analytics also revealed that most queries about bourbon take place between 5:00 and 7:00 p.m.[4] For this spirits advertiser, insights from Google's data helped illuminate opportunities for brand communications to be relevant and useful to their consumers, with the right message at the right time. Insights such as this resulted in new advertising creative strategies that generated breakout ad recall and brand-awareness lifts on YouTube, far surpassing industry benchmarks.

The takeaway is that if your digital partners are only bringing you media plans, you should ask whether they are the right partners, and/or whether you can leverage them more effectively.

RECOMMENDATION 2: CREATIVE CONTENT MUST WORK IN A MOBILE ENVIRONMENT

Consumers today often view ads on very tiny screens, and all ads can be skipped no matter how they are delivered. Distracted viewing behavior has only grown over time, and innovations in digital ad formats have heightened the need for advertisers to earn viewer retention. Although YouTube is viewed on all screen types, more than half of YouTube viewing is on a mobile device, and for some brands up to 85 percent of viewing occurs on mobile devices.

Both TV and online video ads are built with sight, sound, and motion, but the viewing environment differs significantly. As an analogy, think about an ad placed on a billboard on the side of highway, a print ad in a magazine, and a bus wrap. These are all still images, but the context and consumer engagement with each medium differs greatly. Would you put the same version of an ad in these three locations? Probably not—you would tailor it to the medium.

Similarly, to improve creative effectiveness in the digital environment, advertisers should build creative strategy with a mobile screen in mind. Creative content and execution is half to two-thirds of advertising effectiveness, according to Dynamic Logic[5] and Nielsen.[6] The old three-step story arc of a commercial spot—establishing the accepted consumer belief, delivering brand benefit, and giving a reason to believe—has changed. Today, grabbing attention in the first five seconds of an ad by starting with the peak of the story arc is the preferred method to engage consumers. Use the initial interaction to establish your brand and earn the next 10, 20, or 30+ seconds of viewer attention.

What can help create better video ads for mobile? Consider that the screen size of a TV is at least 10 times larger than that of mobile. Mobile is an intimate, one-to-one experience on a small, handheld screen. These tips can help your creative be more effective:

- Talent speaking directly to the consumer creates a more personal connection.
- Tight framing focuses the viewer's attention by more clearly conveying facial expressions and emotions to better highlight the brand benefit.
- Quick pacing and multiple story arc peaks keep consumers engaged and away from the "skip" button.
- High contrast and/or bright lighting improve the viewing experience on mobile, whose users may dim lighting to preserve battery life.
- Clear calls to action or next steps take advantage of the interactive nature of mobile.

It's critical to review rough cuts and final spots on a mobile device before viewing them on a larger screen. Are the sponsoring brand and the main message clear? Can you see the talent's facial expression? Can you read the text? If the message isn't conveyed on a mobile screen, hit the edit button.

RECOMMENDATION 3: TIE YOUR METRICS FOR SUCCESS TO THE MEDIUM AND TO YOUR BUSINESS GOALS

Using the right metrics to understand the performance of a campaign allows the advertiser to adjust the media mix and optimize advertising spending.

The ultimate goal of any marketing or advertising campaign is to increase sales efficiently. Thus, in an ideal world, the effectiveness of a campaign (with either traditional or digital media) would be judged by its impact on sales. However, disentangling the effect of a campaign from numerous other factors that also affect sales can be challenging, and it is also difficult to calculate the impact on long-term metrics, such as brand equity. Further, just knowing the impact on brand sales in the near term offers limited insight into *why* the campaign succeeded or failed. Therefore, metrics tied to the media presentation (who saw the ad, how many times people saw the ad, whether they clicked on the ad and/or visited the brand's web site) and intermediate marketing goals (new customer acquisition, customer retention, revenue per user) are both valuable. No one metric is sufficient; insight comes from laddering media outcomes to marketing to business (sales) outcomes.

Below are three things to keep in mind when evaluating communications in digital versus traditional media.

Link Media Outcomes to Business Outcomes

Often, media managers evaluate campaigns on media metrics rather than on business goals. This is natural and especially likely to occur when the communication function has media silos. To ensure that advertising dollars are spent wisely, insist that media outcomes be linked to marketing *and* business outcomes, such as brand equity and sales.

Traditional and Digital Media Impressions Need To Be Evaluated Differently

When evaluating a campaign involving both traditional and digital media, be sensitive to the fact that the metrics are sometimes not comparable.

Impressions, for example, comprise a common unit of measure in traditional media. Ad impressions are computed by multiplying the reach (the number of people who are exposed to an ad) by the frequency (the number of times an individual sees the ad). When buying traditional media, such as TV, advertisers pay for the placement of an ad during a show; the people viewing the ad are a function of the TV show audience. These viewers may fit the profile of the target customer, but they may or may not be in the market for the advertised product; their goal is to watch a particular show.

With digital media, an ad can be targeted and shown to consumers whose online behavior (search behavior, videos watched, sites visited and brick and mortar locations visited) suggests they are good prospects for purchasing the advertised product, often referred to as a "qualified audience." And often, the advertiser only pays for the viewing if the prospect takes action, such as clicking on the ad. So, while the term "impressions" refers to both traditional and digital media, the calculation is based on a different base of viewers. Be careful not to equate impressions for traditional and digital media when evaluating a plan that includes both types.

Digital Offers Methods for Making Stronger Inferences about the Link between Ad Exposure and Sales

Historically, marketing mix analysis (MMA) has been conducted to link advertising in different media channels to sales. MMAs use statistical regression to model the relationship between media impressions for different channels and sales. While such models offer some insight, the results are correlational and based on aggregate rather than individual-level data. Further, as noted earlier, impressions computed for traditional and digital media are very different, which can confound interpretation of the relative effectiveness of each medium.

Digital media can allow for stronger inferences about campaign effectiveness by tracking consumers' online (and, in some situations, offline) behaviors following ad exposure. And the results are quickly available, so that corrective action can be taken if a campaign fails to show the desired effect. For example, YouTube's brand-lift results are available within two weeks of a new video launch. Using this information, the brand manager can optimize decisions about creative, audience targeting, and viewership—an advantage that's not possible when using TV. Having a continuous improvement approach to media borrows a chapter from business operations to drive more sales, more efficiently.

SUMMARY

The digital world enables you to build stronger brands by being present with the right message at each stage in the customer's path to purchase. Doing so requires you to identify the right partners and forge deep, meaningful relationships with them. In addition, creative content must be built for an online, mobile, and connected world in order to maximize effectiveness. It is also important to have clear business, marketing, and media objectives, and to measure outcomes that allow for real-time assessment of where a communication plan may be falling short. The pace of change in our digital world has accelerated, so building strong brands means marketers have to be as agile and adaptive as the platforms in the market.

Cindy Halvorsen is the head of industry, home, and fashion brands at Google. She previously worked in brand management and consumer insights positions at Kraft Heinz, Wm. Wrigley Jr., and Procter & Gamble. She received her MBA from Northwestern University's Kellogg School of Management in 2010.

NOTES

1. *Hollywood Reporter* (2011), "How 'I Love Lucy' Dominated Ratings from the Start," *The Hollywood Reporter*, August 15, 2011. https://www.hollywoodreporter.com/news/how-i-love-lucy-dominated-222960.
2. Nielsen Answers on Demand 2017 and Google internal search query data.
3. www.google.com/trends.
4. www.google.com/trends/correlate.
5. Patel, Kunur (2009), "Online Ads Not Working for You? Blame the Creative," adage.com, October 20,. http://adage.com/article/digital/digital-online-ads-working-blame-creative/139795.
6. Nielsen (2017), "When It Comes to Advertising Effectiveness, What Is the Key?" Nielsen Insights, October 9. http://www.nielsen.com/us/en/insights/news/2017/when-it-comes-to-advertising-effectiveness-what-is-key.html.

CHAPTER 23

CUSTOMER EXPERIENCE: THE NEW FRONTIER OF BRANDING

SERGIO PEREIRA

When the iPhone launched in 2007, no one knew the extent to which the world was about to change. The music industry would never be the same. The retail industry would never be the same. And taxis certainly had no idea the fate that would befall them once Uber came on the scene.

Indeed, the lightning-fast mass adoption of smartphones dramatically changed the world of consumer habits, which in turn changed the world of branding. Traditional brand-building models were upended, which allowed small, innovative companies to build powerful direct-to-consumer brands by cutting out the middleman (this process is called "disintermediation").

Before digital, customers who wanted a product would simply drive to the store, find the desired section, and shop the shelf. Their first experience with the brand itself was at the point of purchase, and awareness was the key driver, built through mass media and packaging aesthetics. From there the product would be taken home and used or consumed. It was a linear journey, and one that allowed manufacturers to build a business model that revolved around the power of retailers. This chapter explores how the new digital environment has created experience brands that are turning the world of marketing upside down.

EXPERIENCE: THE HEART OF A BRAND

The advent of the smartphone and apps broke down barriers for new products and brands. With access to millions of shoppers via an app store, retailers were bypassed as new brands promised delivery directly to the home.

As a result, brand experiences have now evolved to be more complete customer experiences that rely on more customer touchpoints. There are more so-called moments of truth for a brand to delight or fail. Several examples illustrate this point.

Blue Apron Meal Kits

Meal kits from Blue Apron and its competitors (such as HelloFresh) provide busy people with meal solutions that compete with takeout or food prepared from scratch. At a cost of $8.99 per serving, they offer a viable alternative to fast-casual dining and a reasonable upcharge to made-from-scratch meals.

Each meal kit arrives in a sturdy box packed with ice and containing all necessary ingredients. A detailed recipe is printed on heavy stock with simple instructions. But the customer experience actually begins at the web site, where you create an account, choose your meal plan, and customize your dietary requirements. This is the first moment of truth. A good, intuitive user experience (UX) design is critical, because losing people at the beginning of the process guarantees a "skinny" customer base at the end.

The next critical moment for Blue Apron occurs when the product arrives at the doorstep after traveling through the supply and delivery chain. The shipping and handling process is fraught with risks for this brand, given the perishable nature of the ingredients: a box left outside too long or dented by conveyors in the sorting facility can lead to perceptions that harm the brand.

Finally, the process of prepping and cooking shapes a whole new set of brand perceptions: easy prep is good, but long, complex prep is bad. Clear instructions are a delight, while unclear instructions will frustrate. Ultimately, the finished product will provide the final block in building the brand perception. And then it begins anew with the next shipment.

This model offers great opportunity to create a rich, immersive, and satisfying brand experience, but every element of the product design and delivery must be perfect. Any breakage in the chain will dent the brand perception (such as meat leakage in the packaging). And indeed, Blue Apron has been struggling with customer retention, a sign that somewhere the customer experience is suboptimal. Its customers are not sticking, imperiling the viability of the model.

Harry's Razors

Online delivery has also disrupted the razor business. Harry's provides an easy online buying experience, and the package arrives in a clever but simple box with good brand messaging. The blades are neatly packaged in well-designed pods that are easy to store, and the blades are good enough (not quite at Mach3 quality, but good enough) and the price per blade is lower. Replenishment e-mails provide you with the flexibility to delay the order, add items, or cancel altogether.

The customer experience is owned by Harry's throughout the process and feels personal. By contrast, Gillette surrenders the customer experience when the product leaves the factory. Harry's has very few points of potential dissatisfaction, due to its "set it and forget it" replenishment option. It also has low shipping and distribution costs due to compact packaging.

While Harry's remains a predominantly online model, it's interesting to note that it has sought retail partnerships in Target's brick-and-mortar stores. Starter kits and blade refills can now be found in-store, increasing the ubiquity of the brand and expanding its presence and awareness. There seems to be a pattern emerging of online brands looking for incremental business in the physical retail world, an encouraging sign for brick-and-mortar retailers.

Indochino

The men's suit business is dominated by chains, specialty stores, and high-end tailor businesses. Indochino seizes on the labor arbitrage of manufacturing in China and the lower cost of global commerce logistics to deliver a custom suit experience for the cost of an off-the-rack suit at a department store.

Here is how it works: You shop on Indochino's online store for a suit, then submit your measurements or choose to have them taken at an Indochino store (currently there are fewer than 30 in the United States). The in-store measurement process is elaborate (taking about an hour) and allows for customization of lining and monograms. From that point, the measurements are sent to China, where the suit is tailored and then mailed directly to the customer. As a customer, you feel special and catered to. However, having to trek 30 or more miles to find a store adds a level of inconvenience that may limit the brand's appeal.

The Indochino suit arrives nicely folded with a nice hanger in a well-presented box. A great moment of truth. However, this moment of truth can come tumbling down if something has gone wrong in the tailoring process, which results in having to send the suit back for alterations (this happened to me).

Contributing positively to the Indochino customer journey are the simple online experience, the one-on-one attention at the measurement appointment, the high-quality feel of the materials, and the good look of the finished product. Detracting from the customer experience is the lack of physical points of sale and the need to possibly rework the item, as well as the extra time involved.

As we can see, the key to the success or failure of an online retail experience rests on the brand's ability to deliver a great customer experience. It begins with the simple step of navigating a web site with ease. Then delivery must be seamless, and the product must meet or exceed expectations. One misstep and the customer will be lost to someone else that can deliver to perfection on the next purchase.

IMPACT ON THE FOUR PS

In the new direct-to-consumer age, the fundamentals of marketing (Kotler's Four Ps of *product, pricing, place*, and *promotion*) are still important, but technology is forcing brand builders to consider the entire customer experience in the shopping, buying, and delivery process. Let's consider each of the Four Ps and how they have been impacted.

Product

Today, emerging companies are no longer being developed for the masses but instead for microsegments that are likely to be more loyal to products that fit their lifestyle and values.

For example, the UNTUCKit brand of shirts targets people who prefer an informal look, while the Magnetuck brand of accessories makes sure your shirts remain tightly tucked. Allbirds shoes targets environmentally conscious customers with highly comfortable footwear made from wool and sugar cane instead of petroleum to create the foamy sole. This brand is gaining traction with very little spending on mass advertising, driven by its sustainability positioning.

In this hyper-segmented world, customers will reward brands that "get" them. This is a high hurdle.

Pricing

The upside in a world of precisely targeted brands is that customers will reach deeper into their pockets. If customers value the brand and brand experience, they are willing to pay.

Consider Blue Apron. It is unquestionably cheaper to purchase all your groceries at the supermarket and prepare meals from scratch. However, Blue

Apron's customers will gladly pay a premium per meal for curated recipes, clear and specific instructions, high-quality ingredients, and family involvement in the preparation, not to mention avoiding the grocery store.

Similarly, Indochino's customers are paying more out of pocket than they would at Macy's, but they are getting a great perceived value—a custom suit for $400 or less. Finally, a pair of Allbirds costs about $100, only a slight premium compared to other casual shoes such as Skechers and TOMS. These brands will be able to hold these premium price points if they can deliver flawlessly.

Place

Distribution is far and away the most changed of the Four Ps in today's brand environment. Having direct customer contact provides an opportunity to create delight, but it also raises challenges.

Blue Apron might have very good internal processes and standards for how it packages its items, but failure can easily occur during the shipping process. If its corrugated cartons, plastic packaging (to contain the meat juice), or ice packs fail, a subpar consumer experience results.

In addition, many large manufacturers of consumable products have failed to update their products for the e-commerce world. As an example, disinfecting wipes come in rounded canisters that are shipped in cases of a dozen to supermarkets and mass merchants. However, when they are sent to an e-commerce company, they must be broken down to ship as a single unit and commingled with other items in a box, creating the possibility of a dented plastic canister and the resulting liquid leak.

Promotion

In terms of promotion, the most significant brand risk exists in social media, where customer experiences—particularly failures—are often shared with networks of like-minded people. A failure in customer experience, be it a custom suit that rips during the wedding ceremony or a dinner that's ruined because of a missing key ingredient, will likely result in a Yelp post, an emotional tweet, or a Facebook share that can sink the image of the brand gradually and steadily.

Social listening as a mechanism to identify potential customer experience issues and trends is critical, and creating a channel for direct communication with customers to hear their suggestions is also of great value.

Finally, instituting formal channels to funnel customer comments and complaints from customer service teams is critical. Customer service teams are among the first to identify patterns, a first line of awareness for any brand.

Gone are the days when customer service was a function dedicated to dealing with small and seemingly unrelated complaints, operating in a silo and disconnected from the brand leaders.

HIRING FOR A CUSTOMER-CENTRIC WORLD

The people angle of a brand-focused customer experience deserves special mention. A company that truly wants to delight the customer must look at its culture and honestly assess how customer focus stacks up on the list of company values.

For companies that rely on online channels, the path to a great experience starts with great UX or CX (customer experience) talent. These are people who design the customer flow on the web site or app and work closely with the engineers who write the code, and the creatives and merchants who populate the content. They are the creatives and merchants who populate the content. This talent must be highly collaborative, externally focused, and capable of representing the voice of the customer within the organization. They combine graphic and creative talent with an affinity for research and understanding the human experience as well as the friction points that customers encounter.

Small changes in the customer experience can have a large impact. When signing up for Blue Apron, for example, I was asked to input payment information before I was able to look at the menu choices. This created uncertainty and doubt in my mind. What if I didn't like the choices? Am I now committed to a first delivery? This slight amount of unnecessary friction will lose prospects early in the journey and reduce the appeal of the brand. By contrast, the Allbirds site is clean, simple, and provides a quick transaction. No unnecessary friction there.

CX people need to be surrounded by an agile research team that can develop new tools and conduct research to better understand the customer in a digital environment. Researchers and CX developers need to operate in a nonterritorial and non-siloed manner, as the development of hypotheses for CX improvement should flow from both of them.

Merchants and marketers must abandon old paradigms. Retail stores design their floor plans to drive customer traffic in an attempt to influence behavior. Many web sites used this same principle, frustrating customers with irrelevant suggestions and carousels, long checkout paths intended to increase the ring, and never-ending add-on suggestions. This mindset believes the seller is in control, but the reality today is that the buyer is in control. Get customers to the product they want to buy first, then surround them with suggestions and options that are valuable to them, not just self-serving to you as the seller.

Finally, in this customer-driven world, a company's supply chain has to evolve from a narrow mindset of efficiency to one centered on customer delight. The existing paradigm of packaging and shipping items for stocking and redistributing from a wholesaler or regional warehouse to a retail store has been altered forever, because new brands have the ability to reach the customer directly. Customers now have high expectations for the delivery experience. As a result, the brand must be represented by someone in the supply chain who is actively anticipating the likely issues that will arise, and pressing for solutions that will ensure an excellent customer experience.

SUMMARY

Technology has fundamentally changed the world of branding. Large brands have lost the competitive advantage of dominating through mass channel distribution, and small brands are disintermediating them by going directly to the consumer. Some of these insurgent brands are succeeding, albeit also learning about the great power in brick-and-mortar stores. Other brands are still struggling to build the right experience, and could run out of time and money if they don't quickly cure major customer issues. Those struggling brands will present an opportunity for large companies to acquire and refine the model with operational excellence.

The new world of e-commerce provides great opportunity to both small and large players. There is great willingness to try new brands and new products, and even pay more for what is considered a brand that fits "my lifestyle." But the more demanding nature of today's consumers does not afford many second chances. Bad customer experiences will not only taint the user but likely be shared socially, magnifying the damage to the brand.

There is enormous money to be made when you connect with a customer and fulfill their tangible and emotional needs. Thus, brand and business leaders today will succeed when they refocus and place the customer and customer insight at the center of their work. This may require reorganization, a reshaping of company values, and hiring new talent that has experience in customer-centric organizations. Brands and marketers who understand and champion the customer experience from end to end will be the winners in this brave new world.

Sergio Pereira is president of Quill.com, a $1.2-billion division of Staples. He was previously general manager of dairy products at Conagra Brands and vice president of marketing at Barilla. He received his BS from Syracuse University and his MBA from Kellogg School of Management.

CHAPTER 24

BRAND NEW: CREATING A BRAND FROM SCRATCH

PAUL EARLE

No new product or service can launch anonymously—even, ironically, the global hacker collective Anonymous. Its cheeky name and iconic Guy Fawkes mask visual identity are as good as any new brand created by a professional, and Anonymous is now famous.

Similarly, Brandless—a new company that purports to be the antihero in a postapocalyptic brand world run amok—is of course itself a brand, and has now trademarked its name in nearly 70 categories.

The truth is that brands are omnipresent and inescapable. They impact everything: not just products and services, but people and places. Brands have impact, and great new ones can quickly take hold. Especially now.

Why now? I believe we are in the early stages of a full-fledged revolution in the consumer sector: within the next five years, practically every category will face radical change brought on by a new brand created from scratch. The big incumbent brands don't have the cachet and consumer hold that they once did, and marketplace conditions—starting with the rise of e-commerce—are making it easier than ever for upstarts to get a new alternative commercialized.

As I often preach, a superb brand wrapped around an average product will outperform the inverse every time. If you're interested in creating an instantly resonant and relevant brand that develops relationships with people, secures a real competitive advantage, and ultimately materially improves your company's financial value, read on.

FOUR STEPS TO CREATING A BRAND THAT WINS

Here are the four steps to creating a powerful new brand, based on my decades of experience as a practitioner, academician, and writer.

Step 1: Look for a Hook: Finding Sparks

When creating a new brand, it must absolutely be rooted in, well . . . *something*. You just need some sort of hook, a spark, a way in. Great new brands are never arbitrary.

So what defines the "something" in which a brand must be rooted, and how do you uncover it? My partners and I explore *product*, *story*, and *purpose*.

Product   Deeply ponder the product or service that you're looking to brand. What is unique about it? What's special? What's . . . a little weird, even? Any nuances or eccentricities of the product should be celebrated, not dismissed; this is the magic that can make a difference.

You can deploy what I'll call the "Altoids convention." Altoids is the confection that became a sensation in the 1990s when it was touted as "Curiously Strong," a line that survives to this day. As you consider how to breathe life into your own new product or service, ask yourself, what is *curiously strong* about it? The answer to this question should spark a great brand idea or two (and if there simply isn't anything, you have a product problem and had better solve that first).

Story   We're innately narrative creatures: simply look at the petroglyphs on caves dating back thousands of years. Does your brand have an inspiring story construct? I was part of the team that created a successful new brand called High Noon vodka, inspired directly by a story about people enjoying each other's company outside, under blue skies; imagining and capturing this moment far preceded landing on the name itself. Founder origin stories are also compelling . . . and even better, real! There is a great new brand of oatmeal called Mush, inspired by the product for sure, but also by a story that goes back to co-founder Ashley Thompson's childhood and her unusual practice of soaking her breakfast cereal in milk overnight (see Figure 24.1).

Purpose   The principles for which you stand make for great brand sparks, so your brand purpose should be articulated at the beginning of the process,

Figure 24.1
Oatmeal Brand Mush

not at the end. Consumers today want brands they can *join*, not simply buy. You should also consider the timeliness of your brand's purpose. Nike is an example of a brand that is evergreen but also inextricably linked to the time of its birth. Coming of age in the 1960s and early 1970s, the Nike brand still has not completely lost its counterculture attitude. What is happening *right now* that moves people's hearts and minds? The answer might lead to a powerful brand idea.

Step 2: The Name Game: Proving Shakespeare Wrong

In *Romeo and Juliet*, Shakespeare wrote: "What's in a name? that which we call a rose / By any other name would smell as sweet."

The Bard was one heck of a writer, but he was *way* off on this one. And apparently the big rose companies agree: the international rose grower David Austin, for example, owns over 60 active trademarks (including "Juliet"). And none of its branded roses have names such as "Sewer Gas" or "Donkey Vomit," for obvious reasons. Do you think those handles would affect your perception of smell and your experience with the rose overall?

Names, of course, matter. Here are some markers for a great name.

Product Relevance   The name should tell a story that directly or at least indirectly ties to the product itself, its reason for being, and consumer needs/wants. A great example is Peloton, the new home exercise equipment company best known for its digitally connected stationary bike. In cycling parlance, a "peloton" is a group of cyclists at the front of the pack. This name is obviously relevant to cycling and leadership, but also speaks to the fact that via the online community, home cyclists are connected to each other—a "virtual pack" (see Figure 24.2).

Figure 24.2
Home Exercise Equipment Brand Peloton

Another great example is the name for New England's football team: the Patriots, which honors the region's key role in the American Revolution. You may not like the team or Tom Brady, but it's a great name. I shake my head when I see new sports franchises pick names that have nothing to do with their home cities. Exhibit A: Las Vegas's recent selection of "Golden Knights" as the name for its new pro hockey team, pushed through by the owner because he was formerly in the U.S. Army and that was the name of its parachute team. Huh?!? Wouldn't a moniker such as "Aces" or "Blackjack" be more of a fit, and more engaging?

A few years ago, I was part of the team that created Angel's Envy, a brown spirits brand that was eventually acquired by Bacardi for over $100 million. The name tells a compelling and useful story about the product: our master distiller figured out how to reduce the amount of distillate that would evaporate inside the barrel during aging, making the flavor more intense (the lost spirit is called the "angel's share," so we created heavenly envy, of course). The name highlights this innovation and enhanced experience in an interesting and memorable way.

The importance of product and consumer relevance is why I typically don't care for names that are portmanteaus (new composites of existing words, or elements of words). What the heck is an "Accenture," and what adds up to "Xfinity"? Again, these brands may work now, but only thanks to massive resources, a lot of time, and frankly, some luck. Of course, there are exceptions. Procter & Gamble's "Swiffer" is an effective name, and it previously had no meaning at all. And one benefit of portmanteaus is that they can skirt trademark challenges, because by definition the composite word is unlikely to have previously existed.

Emotion   "Form follows function, but both report to emotion," said Willie Davidson, superstar designer and grandson of the founder of a certain motorcycle company. Emotion is the king of the jungle in marketing and innovation, and it certainly wins in naming. A great name is essentially a short ad for the product, evoking feeling and inspiring some kind of action (consciously or unconsciously). If the name is met with indifference, it is by my definition a lousy name. Even slightly polarizing names are better than those bereft of all feeling (the previously mentioned oatmeal brand "Mush" is a great example; most love the name, but some really hate it. Nobody is indifferent, however, and that means the company is on to something!). The bottom line is that names must *engage*.

One reason Angel's Envy is so engaging is that the name is rife with creative tension. "Envy" is one of the seven deadly sins in Roman Catholic theology, and certainly not what you'd expect from a divine figure such as an angel. The feminine associations with "angel" also clash with the overwhelmingly male skew of a bourbon's consumer base. All this prompts intrigue, discovery, and dialogue—simply from the marriage of two words.

Ease of Use   Generally speaking, names should be as short as possible and roll off the tongue. Brevity is important not just because short names tend to be more memorable, but also because they make it easier for your design team, which has precious limited real estate to work with when creating packaging labels and other elements. Procter & Gamble has mastered the art of short, snappy names: Tide, Gain, Cheer, Scope, Bold, Crest, Joy, and so on. Again, there are exceptions to these unofficial rules. I think a name *can* be long, provided it is intentionally so and not because of sloppiness. I Can't Believe It's Not Butter is an example, as is the great old 1970s brand Gee, Your Hair Smells Terrific.

Regarding the important role of sound in branding, it's best if your name is mellifluous (mellow or sweet sounding)—or at least not the antithesis. Avoid tongue twisters or names that might be confusing to pronounce. Try saying the name out loud a few times; if it sounds like you're clearing your throat in the late stages of a cold, it's time for plan B.

Names that are vaguely feminine are among my favorites, mainly because the abundant use of vowels just makes them nice to say and hear. Some of the great new names today hit this mark: Hello (oral care), Olly (vitamins), and Mio (water enhancers).

Marketability   Identifying a brand name that is inherently marketable reminds me of Supreme Court justice Potter Stewart's comment on recognizing pornography: that it was impossible to define, but you know it when you see it. However it is defined, marketability is an important consideration in today's world of hyper-connectedness. Put simply, the idea has to be hardwired for multidimensional engagement from the beginning. Run a few internal tests for what we call "campaignability": What is a potential tagline? What about a launch act? Or a social campaign? If you find that it feels unnatural to market your name idea, it's probably not a very good name. In the Angel's Envy example, we knew early on that playing off the juxtaposition between an angel and a cardinal sin would be a winner in the marketplace.

When I'm deep into a naming dive, my internal name finder is at a very high state of alert practically around the clock. Once I'm "on," every word I see or hear might be repurposed into a winning name. It might be in print or in online media, on television, in conversation with a Lyft driver, on street signs, or on a bumper sticker. Or it might be on a menu at a restaurant, a lyric of a song on the radio, a paper flyer stapled to a telephone pole, the air safety manual on a 737—anything, anywhere. And if it's interesting to me, I'll write it down. Some collect stamps, or coins, or antiques: I collect words.

I have heard lots of chatter about technology-based solutions to name creation, but I'm dubious that naming can be done well without a really intense and really analog, old-fashioned human touch.

Step 3: A Click and a Prayer: Searching the Trademark Office

As with all other functions of the innovation game, an idea that is never implemented has essentially no value. In context: you will need to properly clear your name of all trademark issues if you want to comfortably (and responsibly) use it.

In the United States alone, there are over 400,000 new trademark applications *every year*. This inventory of potential land mines and roadblocks is massive, and chances are that name you love has already been conceived of by someone else. Anxiety, for me, is that couple of seconds waiting for the return from a search for a name I love on the trademark office web site. Usually, the results are disappointing.

To improve your odds of success, it's helpful to know how trademark law actually works. With a few exceptions, rights to a mark are specific to a predefined class of goods. For example, the mark "Acme" may be in use in beverages but available in laundry detergent. Where things can get tricky is the standard of "confusingly similar," which is ultimately a matter of judgment. If there is a valid Acme trademark for beverages and you file for Acme-1 in the same category, the U.S. Patent and Trademark Office examiner might argue that your mark would be confusingly similar and refuse it. Even if you did get your application through, the Acme brand owner could still litigate if you persist. In this instance, the plaintiff would probably win.

At their essence, trademarks are indications of source—the roots of this idea go back to the mark or "brand" used to identify cattle. I would argue that, indeed, Acme-1 might confuse consumers into thinking that the product is related to the original Acme. However, you can certainly try altering your trademark through unusual spellings or other forms of modification. For example, Yoplait named its latest yogurt "Plenti," not the more common "Plenty," and passed the trademark test.

The strongest rights to a trademark that you can have still come from actually using it. In trademarks, use reigns. A trademark owner can even lose rights to a brand if usage stops; in trademark parlance we often say, "use it or lose it." If you desire a trademark in a particular category, and you think that a trademark that is blocking you has not been in bona fide use within the past three years, you can actually move to cancel that mark and take it as your own. This happens all the time.

Indeed, much of trademark management is an art, not a science. With a few extreme and obvious exceptions (I would *not* recommend that you file a trademark application for "Coca-Cola"), practically everything lives in a gray area. You have to be smart and try to find creative work-arounds to problems. Experience and judgment are key (and so is a good trademark lawyer).

Step 4: Say It with Pictures: Developing Brand Design

Once you have your name, you still need to take the final step toward creating your great new brand. You have to animate it—bring life to it—through great design. If done well, design has nearly magical qualities. Design can work at a very powerful psychological level and provide incredible depth and breadth of meaning to an otherwise lifeless word.

Design can be as simple as a logo and preliminary color scheme, or it can be as complex as full packaging concepts. When he was first starting out, my friend Craig Dubitsky was able to generate substantial interest in his Hello oral-care brand with many sophisticated retail buyers simply by using the name and its backstory along with beautifully designed packaging: while he had a smart point of view on formulation, he didn't even have a finished product yet! (See Figure 24.3.) This interest helped him raise capital and sign up retailers—and the rest is history. When combined with design, names make for very valuable brands, right from the beginning. Design can also be a real asset financially (it is categorized most often under copyrights, one of the four pillars of intellectual property assets).

As an example, the Angel's Envy design was instantly one of the enterprise's most important elements (see Figure 24.4). The angel's wings painted on the back of the bottle took on the illusion of glowing and nearly taking flight when backlit on a bar shelf. This design treatment instantly made the new brand intriguing and engaging. It also helped with investor and customer pitches, long before the first case of bourbon was finished. A well-developed brand design is a great selling tool.

Figure 24.3
Toothpaste Brand Hello

Figure 24.4
Bourbon Brand Angel's Envy

SUMMARY

Creating a new brand is an incredibly challenging process. It can also be thrilling, should you go all the way from a blank piece of paper to a gleaming, purposeful, beautiful new brand that is out in the world.

It's a contact sport, for sure. But if you follow the guidance here, you might just find yourself still standing when the whistle blows at the end . . . a winner.

Paul Earle is principal of Earle & Company, an innovation, branding, and design collective, an adjunct lecturer of innovation and entrepreneurship at Northwestern University's Kellogg School of Management, and a monthly contributor to Forbes. *He previously served as founder and president of the brand acquirer River West Brands, and executive director of Farmhouse, the innovation center at the global creative agency Leo Burnett. He received his BA from Hamilton College and his MBA from Kellogg.*

INDEX

Page references followed by *fig* indicate an illustration.

A

AB InBev, 42

A/B testing, 205

AbbVie
Humira (rheumatoid arthritis drug) of, 166
"moments of meaning" strategy used by, 75

Abrams, D., 139

Absolut Vodka's ad (*ARTnews*), 158*fig*

"Absolut Warhol" ad, 158*fig*

AC Hotels by Marriott, 40

Accenture brand, 305

Accounting methods for valuing brands, 237–239

Acem trademark, 307

Advertising. *See also individual ads;* Motivation
brand building through, 143–159
managing brand communications in a digital world, 287–292
messages and judgments communicated in, 146–148
for seasonal products, 157
statistics on corporate investment in, 143

Advertising messages
diffusion, community, and sharing of information on, 148–150
4Ms media strategy for, 155–158*fig*
Hanes boxer brief ad, 146*fig*–147
processing messages and brand judgments, 146–148
using insight to design persuasive, 150–154*fig*

Advertising Research Foundation, 22

Advertising strategies
consumer insights informing, 4, 146*fig*–150
digital brand storytelling, 161–175
the 4Ms media strategy transmitting message content, 155–158*fig*
using insight to design persuasive messaging, 150–154*fig*

Advocacy and leadership sharing, 28

Agency motive, 132–133, 134*fig*

Ahrendts, Angela, 16

Air France–KLM Flying Blue rewards program, 40

Airbnb
"belong anywhere" purpose of, 33–34
decentralization strategy of, 81
as disrupter, 113
loyalty program of, 188
nonownership of service by, 180
overly rapid global expansion of, 86
purpose path to growth model in, 32–34
two-minute purpose video at, 32

Aleve, 15–16, 18

Alibaba, 24

All-Clad pressure cookers, 8

Allbirds shoes brand, 297

Allstate
  ice-skating ad, 151
  "Mayhem" commercials, 154
Alta Vista, 62
Altoids' "Curiously Strong" catch-line,
  302
Always brand
  "#LikeAGirl" campaign by, 161–162
  as one of Procter & Gamble's
    brands, 45
  points of difference of, 13–14, 45
Amazon
  as disrupter, 113
  do-it-yourself digital marketplace
    explosion led by, 193
  innovation of, 61, 62
  similarities between P&G CEO and
    Jeff Bezos of, 20
  technological disruptions used by,
    53–54
  U.S. grocery store strategies to
    compete with, 119
Amgen, 48
Amplification (or elaboration) strategy,
  151, 152
Analogy strategy
  to illustrate brand performance, 153
  jazz music analogy, 170–171
  telling a brand story as like painting a
    landscape, 162
Angelou, Maya, 163–164
Angel's Envy brand, 304, 305, 308–309*fig*
Anheuser-Busch InBev, 178
Anonymous, 301
Apple. *See also* iPhone (Apple)
  as both a brand and a company, 26
  brand positioning statement of, 4
  challenging IBM, 62
  complex and varied brand images
    of, 130
  consumer insight in positioning
    statement of, 5
  focus on the core brand by, 48

iCloud of, 60
initial and revised positioning of Apple
  Watch, 16, 17*fig*, 18
innovation of, 61
as a primary brand, 38
reasons to believe benefits of
  products, 7
Steve Jobs of, 57, 169, 201
"Think Different" campaign (1997),
  139–140, 249
Apple brand community (1980s and
  1990s), 139
Apps
  immediate customer ratings through,
    187
  incentivize brand usage through, 140
  incentivize brand usage through apps,
    140
  McDelivery (McDonald's), 254
Aquaphor, 6
Association of National Advertisers, 250
Aston Martin, 41
Athleta, 13
Atkin, Douglas, 32
Attitudinal brand tracking, 221–223
Attribute(s)
  of brand used as reasons to believe,
    8–9, 152
  switching to image reasons to believe
    from, 12
Aural brand design, 98*fig*, 103–104
"Auto–Biography" Facebook campaign
  (Toyota), 167–168
Awareness
  awareness/liking/market-share model
    on, 225*fig*–226
  Barilla case for building up, 228–229
  tracking, 220–231*fig*, 222*fig*
Awareness/liking/market-share model,
  225*fig*–226
Axe brand
  common thread of sex in marketing,
    78, 79

educating new markets to launch internationally, 84–85

success story of, 86–88

tapping into three principles for building global brand, 78

B

B2B (business-to-business)

consideration and evaluation stage strategies by, 118

focusing on customer expectations, 113

keeping up with consumer digital tools and channels, 110

pre-need stage strategies by, 116

prioritizing most important target customers, 121–122

trigger stage strategies by, 117–118

B2B buyer data, 125

B2C (business-to-consumers)

consideration and evaluation stage strategies by, 118

focusing on customer expectations, 113

keeping up with consumer digital tools and channels, 110

pre-need stage strategies by, 116–117

trigger stage strategies by, 117–118

Babson College, 34

Baily, Christopher, 16

Banca Monte dei Paschi di Siena (1472), 23

Barilla brand health, 228–229

Barra, Mary, 24

Barros, Pedro, 165

Barry, Laura, 75

BCG, 112

Bear Ears National Monument (Utah), 14

Ben & Jerry's, 145

Benefit(s). See Brand benefit(s)

Benioff, Marc, 24

Berkshire Hathaway, 26, 169

Berluti brand, 45

Best Buy, 85

Bezos, Jeff, 20, 62, 169

Big tech–big data, 203–204

Bill and Melinda Gates Foundation, 231–232

Bird, Larry, 153

BlackBerry brand, 99, 263

BlackRock, 23, 34

The Blair Witch Project (film), 172

Blockbuster, 263

Bloomingdale's, 50

Blue Apron

brand positioning of, 3–4, 18

challenges faced by other meal kit category brands, 15

customer experience with, 295

"dinner in a box" concept of, 3

frame of reference used by, 6

user experience (UX) design of, 295

Bogusky, Alex, 250

Booker, Christopher, 163

"Born of Fire" ad (Chrysler, 2011), 135, 140

The Boston by Steinway, 39

Bottom-down engagement, 28–29

Bounty paper, 10, 45

Boutelle, Jeff, 31

Bowerman, Bill, 251

Brady, Tom, 304

Braig, Bridgette, 193, 206

Brand awareness

awareness/liking/market-share model on, 225*fig*–226

Barilla case for building up, 228–229

tracking, 220–231*fig*, 222*fig*

Brand benefit(s)

amplifying the, 151, 152

analogy used to illustrate, 153

announcing the, 151–152

as part of conceptual equation expressing value, 9

points of differences related to, 7

reasons to believe, 7–9, 12, 152, 153

Brand category
  frame of reference conveying the, 6–7
  late identification (ID) of the, 154
  naming, 98*fig*, 102–103*fig*
  a pioneer sets the standards for, 56–57
  "points of parity" features of a, 6
  VIPP's stretching its brand to new, 41
Brand communication
  how the digital world has changed,
    287–288
  recommendations for digital media,
    288–292
Brand communication recommendations
  1. choose fewer digital media
    partnership, 288–289
  2. creative content must work in a
    mobile environment, 289–290
  3. tie metrics for success to medium
    and business goals, 290–292
Brand communities, 138–139
Brand council, 74
Brand design. *See also* Design thinking;
    Logo(s)
  Coca-Cola, 95–97
  components of, 97–107
  description and growing interest in, 94
  design thinking for developing a,
    95–97
  fMRI and EEG used for detecting
    consumer response to, 215
  holistic, 108
  illustrative perceptual mind map for
    Coca-Cola, 96*fig*, 97
  for a new brand, 307–309*fig*
  template for, 98*fig*
Brand design component(s)
  brand lexicon, 98*fig*, 103
  brand naming, 98–100, 303–306
  category naming, 98*fig*, 102–103*fig*
  color palette, 98*fig*, 106–107
  corporate identity, 98*fig*, 100–101*fig*
  corporate symbols, 98*fig*, 106
  illustration, 98*fig*, 104–106

  scent, 98*fig*, 107
  shape, 98*fig*, 107
  signature lines, 98*fig*, 101–102
  sound, 98*fig*, 103–104
Brand governance system
  brand implementation role of the,
    71*fig*, 73–74
  global versus local, 74
Brand health
  awareness/liking/market-share model
    used to assess, 225*fig*–226
  Barilla (low-high-low), 228–229
  Lego (high-high-high), 226–227
  Microsoft (high-low-high), 231–232
  Old Spice (low-low-low), 229–230
  Samsung (high-low-low), 227–228
Brand identity
  Cadbury brand's, 93–94*fig*
  of Guy Fawkes mask, 301
  increasing product's market success
    with a, 93
Brand image(s)
  description and use of, 130
  how it constraints the choice of
    target, 6
  witching from attribute to reasons to
    believe image, 12
Brand Investment and Valuation (BIV)
    project, 240, 241
Brand leader(s)
  critical brand strategy implementation
    role of, 76
  tools used by, 71*fig*, 74–75
Brand lexicon, 98*fig*, 103
Brand linkage, 153–154
Brand marketing funnels, 220–221*fig*
Brand measurement techniques
  asking open-ended questions, 223–225
  attitudinal brand tracking, 221*fig*–223
  awareness tracking, 220–221*fig*, 222*fig*
Brand naming, 98*fig*–100, 303–306
Brand performance
  analogy used to illustrate, 153

evaluations of, 240–243
story grammar used to demonstrate, 153
Brand performance evaluations. *See also*
Metrics
conjoint analysis (CA), 242–243
discrete choice experiment (DCE),
242–243
MASB's Brand Investment and
Valuation (BIV) project, 240, 241
revealed preference (RP), 241
stated preference (SP), 241, 242
Brand personality study, 212
Brand portfolio keys to success
1. build and extend core brands, 47–48
2. add brands to the portfolio to
address major opportunities, 48–49
3. proactively prune weak and
redundant brands, 49–50
4. keep things simple, 51
5. involve senior management, 51
Brand portfolio model(s)
branded house, 46–47
house of brands, 45–46
Brand portfolio strategy
definitions of, 38–40
Marcus brand (Goldman Sachs)
example of, 37
Brand portfolio(s)
characteristics of strong, 42–43
expanding the brand portfolio
through, 42
keys to successful, 47–51
making decisions on the, 44–45, 51
the power of, 40–44
problems of, 43–44
stretching the brand through, 41–42
types of brands associated with, 38–40
Brand position
See also Repositioning brand(s)
laddering strategies to sustain, 12–13,
250–251
modern instantiation sustaining, 11–12
sustaining a, 11–15

switching from attribute to image
reasons to believe, 12
Brand positioning statement(s)
answers the brand purpose question,
13–15
Apple, 4
frame of reference element of, 6–7
Miller Lite Beer, 4
points of difference, 7–10
target element of a, 5–6
testing for clarity, credibility, and
distinctiveness, 11
Brand purchase. *See also* Consumer
behavior
coherence, agency, and communion
motives for, 132–133, 134*fig*
ModCloth shirt, 133
motivation for, 132–133, 135, 140,
144–146
Brand purpose
Always (feminine hygiene products),
13–14
brand positioning statement answers
the question of, 13–15
the business case for, 22–23
business context of, 21–22
the challenge of balance, 251
the challenges of brand, 250–251
implementation through three activity
systems, 27
McDonald's culture, product, and
brand, 252–254
the motive matrix of, 133–134*fig*
POP (product, oratory, and purpose), 302
purpose sea-change events, 23–24
the rise of, 249–250
Title Nine's, 13
Brand storyteller(s)
finding brand stories in your
organization, 167–168
managing the story process, 168–169
powerful ways to tell a great brand
story, 169–171

Brand storytelling
  addressing customer pain points, 166
  connecting with customer passions
    through, 165
  everywhere yet invisible, 165
  sending message through, 139–140
  story grammar used to demonstrate
    performance, 153
Brand strategy implementation
  a framework for orchestration and,
    70–76
  implementation-friendly brand
    strategy with cross-functional
    collaboration, 67–68, 72
  pitfalls in, 69–70
  senior management communicating
    the, 67–68
Brand strategy implementation model
  brand governance system, 71fig, 73–74
  brand platform, 71fig, 72
  company strategy, 71fig–72
  culture, 71fig, 72–73
  illustrated diagram of, 71fig
  momentum, 71fig, 75–76
  tools, 71fig, 74–75
  two critical roles in branding journey,
    76
Brand symbol(s), 98fig, 106
Brand tracking
  attitudinal, 221–223
  awareness, 220–231fig, 222fig
  of brand association in the brain using,
    fMRI, 211–213
  of brand emotions and engagement
    using fMRI, 213–215
  digital data and, 232–233
  metrics for progress of service brand,
    187–188
Brand value
  different approaches to, 236–240
  systems view of creating, 243fig–244
Brand value approaches
  brands as intangible assets, 236–237

difficulties with accounting methods
  for valuing brands, 237–239
direct approaches to brand value,
  239–240
Brand Z database, 22
Branded house model
  description of the, 46
  examples of companies using the,
    46–47
Brand(s). See also Evaluation; Products
  creating a new one from scratch,
    301–309fig
  diffusion, community, and sharing of
    information on, 148–150
  incentivize usage of, 140
  as intangible assets, 236–237
  linking the self to the, 131–133
  repositioning a, 15–18
  service, 40, 177–189
Brand–self connection(s)
  self-concept aspect of the, 130
  self-concept clarity and, 131
  understanding the self in, 129–130
Brand–self linking motive(s)
  1. coherence, 132
  2. agency, 132
  3. communion, 132
Branson, Richard, 46, 47
"Brisk drinker" self-concept, 131
Bubbly (PepsiCo), 46
Bud Light brand, 15
Buffett, Warren, 169
Buick brand, 43, 44
Built to Last (Collins and Porras), 22, 249
Burberry brand repositioning, 16
Burger King's
  creative and persuasive messaging, 150
  "Have it your way" campaign, 145
Burn brand, 56
Business goal(s)
  during each customer journey stage,
    124fig
  mapping KPI(s) and, 124fig

tying brand communication metrics to medium and, 290–292

Business Insider leader ranking(s), 24

Buying stage
of the customer journey, 116*fig*, 119
illustrative vacation planning customer journey, 123*fig*
key questions to ask during, 123*fig*
mapping business goals and KPI(s), 124*fig*
typical customer path including, 122*fig*

C

Cadbury brand, 93–94*fig*

Cadillac brand, 43, 44

Calder, Bobby J., 93, 108–109, 234, 245

Calderón, Felipe, 280, 281

Calkins, Tim, 37, 52

Camp, Garrett, 46

"Campaign for Real Beauty" (Dove, 2004), 135, 170, 249

"Campaignability" tagline(s), 306

Campbell, Joseph, 162–163

Campbell's "Chunky" soup, 104, 105*fig*

Capability KPI(s), 75

Capitol Couture (online magazine), 173

Carcieri, Matt, 20, 25, 35–36

Carpenter, Gregory S., 53, 58–59, 65

Cascades of information sharing, 148

Case, Steve, 59

Catching Fire campaign, 173

Category. *See* Brand category

Category naming, 98*fig*, 102–103*fig*

Cayenne SUV (Porsche), 41

Cerf, Moran, 207, 216

Chandron brand, 45

Change
identifying your motivation for, 27
what are the business drivers for, 28

Change management
focused on data backed and strategy led change, 275–276

Novant Health's lesson learned on, 273–274

Channel(s)
See also Media; Social media
B2B and B2C need to keep up with new, 110
John Deere's marketing-focused approach and transforming dealer, 269–270
omni-channel commerce, 119
tying business goals, brand communication metrics, to medium or, 290–292

Charmin brand, 45, 50

Chen, Yu-Ping, 212

Chesebrough-Pond's, 88

Chesky, Brian, 32, 33

Chevrolet brand, 43, 44

Chicago Cubs, 130, 134

Chief executive officer (CEO). *See also* Senior management
branding expenditure skepticism by many, 234
critical brand strategy implementation role of, 76

Chief marketing officer (CMO), multiple roles and narrow span of control by, 76

Child napping image, 7, 8*fig*

"Childlike Imagination" campaign (General Electric), 164

Chobani Greek yogurt, 102

"Choose Beauty" campaign (Dove), 170

Chouinard, Yvon, 14

Chrysler
"Born of Fire" ad (2011) of, 135, 140
Hemi brand of, 40

Cialis, 59

Cinnabon, 107

Cisco's "Circle Story" campaign, 165

"Citizen Activity" (*Capitol Couture*), 173

Click–through rate, 205

Clinton, Hillary, 223

Clorox brand, 48, 195
Coca-Cola Corporation
  battle between PepsiCo and, 57
  brand design and System 1 thinking
    used by, 95–97
  brand portfolio of, 42
  challenges to, 54
  Coke Zero Sugar brand of, 6–7
  competitive advantage of, 63
  "Hilltop" commercial (1971) of, 253
  lemon-lime version of Hanssens
    lemon-lime drink by, 61
  as prototypical brand, 57
Coherence motive, 132–133, 134fig
Cohn, Dustin, 37
Coke Zero Sugar, 6–7
Collins, Jim, 22, 249
Color Hunt app, 107
Color palette, 98fig, 106–107
Commonwealth Edison brand, 231
Communion motive, 132–133, 134fig
Communities (brand), 138–139
Community of consumer, 145
Comparison. See Differentiation
Competence of consumer(s), 144–145
Comstock, Beth, 164, 168–169
Confusion matrix, 212
Conjoint analysis (CA), 242–243
Consideration and evaluation stage
  of the customer journey, 116fig, 118
  key questions to ask during, 123fig
  mapping business goals and KPI(s), 124fig
  typical customer path including, 122fig
Consumer behavior. See also Brand
    purchase
  crafting customer journey by using
    data on, 125–126
  persona development to better
    understand, 194, 196–199
  pioneers' opportunity to influence, 57
Consumer data. See also Metrics
  big tech–big data to harness power of,
    203–204

brand communication management
    using, 289
CPG company segmentation process
    based on past buyers,' 120–121
crafting customer journey from,
    125–126
customer relationship management
    (CRM) contributing to, 199–200,
    204
journey mindset driving collection of,
    194, 199–200
neuroscience tool kit for collecting,
    208–210
for segmenting across habits and
    needs, 79
Consumer insight(s). See also
    Customer(s)
  in Apple's brand positioning statement
    of, 4
  diffusion, community, and sharing of
    information, 148–150
  elevating research methods to leverage,
    200–204
  how to ensure delivery for the brand
    from, 204–205
  processing advertising messages and
    brand judgments, 146fig–148
  types of analysis required for, 144
  understanding fundamental
    motivations, 144–146
  used to design persuasive messaging,
    150–154fig
Consumer journey methodology, 70
Consumer packaged goods (CPG), 112
Consumer pain point, 5
Consumer preference(s)
  pioneer influence on, 57
  segment across habits and needs, 79
Consumer segmentation. See Marketing
    segmentation
Consumer(s)
  in Apple's brand positioning statement
    on insight by, 4

B2C (business-to-consumers) and, 110, 113

brand overcoming pain point of, 5

competence to achieve their goals, 144–145

diffusion, community, and sharing of information on brands by, 148–150

remember pioneers, 56

System 1 thinking by, 95–96

System 2 thinking by, 95

Contentment of consumers, 145

Corporate identity, 98*fig*, 100–101

Corporate symbols, 98*fig*, 106

Cost per acquired customer (CAC), 232–233

Cost(s)

cost per acquired customer (CAC), 232–233

determined by the price charged, 10

marketing traditionally viewed as center of, 235

as part of conceptual equation expressing value, 9

Courtyard by Marriott, 40, 101

CPG companies, 120–121

CPG shopper data, 125

Creamette brand, 229

Crest brand, 45

Crispin Porter Bogusky, 250

Cristal champagne, 53, 54

CRM (customer relationship management) data, 199–200, 204

Culture

educate new markets for new countries or, 84–85

how business metrics are affected by company, 85

McDonald's product, brand, and, 252–254

start small and scale thoughtfully in new, 85–86

supporting brand building, 71*fig*, 72–73

"Curiously Strong" (Altoids), 302

Curry, Stephen, 7, 153

Customer experience. *See also* User experience (UX)

Blue Apron, 295

empathy-driven, 194, 195–196

Harry's Razors, 295–296

as the heart of a brand, 294–297

hiring to support brand-focused, 299–300

impact on the four Ps (product, pricing, place, promotion), 297–299

Indochino, 296–297

Customer experience (CX) talent, 299

Customer feedback

dashboards providing real-time, 187

John Deere's marketing-focused approach and listening to, 268–269

McKinsey on customer loyalty loop and, 114, 120

mobile apps providing immediate, 187

Yelp reviews, 298

Customer journey

creating a, 121–126

elevating research methods to leverage insights in the, 200–204

finding the data to craft the, 125–126

how to best leverage, 126*fig*–127

typical customer path during the, 122*fig*

Customer journey mindset

exploratory empathy-driven insights and innovation, 194, 195–196

measurement and data collection opportunities, 194, 199–200

persona development, 194, 196–199

the value of the, 194

The customer journey model

AIDA (awareness, interest, desire, and action) of the, 113

illustration of the, 115*fig*

McKinsey's evolution of, 114

moving from company–centric to consumer–centric, 114

a touchpoint-specific approach, 114–121

The customer journey steps
1. pre-need, 115*fig*–117, 122*fig*–124*fig*
2. trigger, 116*fig*, 117–118, 122*fig*–124*fig*
3. consideration and evaluation, 116*fig*, 118, 122*fig*–124*fig*
4. buying, 116*fig*, 119, 122*fig*–124*fig*
5. usage, 116*fig*, 119, 122*fig*–124*fig*
6. post-usage evaluation, 116*fig*, 120*fig*–121, 122*fig*–124*fig*
Customer loyalty
the loop of, 114, 120
service brand loyalty programs, 188
Starbucks' digital applications to increase, 140
Ulta Beauty's brand makeover and increased, 260–261
Customer loyalty loop, 114, 120
Customer pain points, 166
Customer passions, 165
Customer relationship management (CRM) platforms, 199–200, 204
Customer satisfaction metrics, 75
Customer(s). *See also* Brand purchase; Consumer insight(s); Motivation
cost per acquired customer (CAC), 232–233
nonownership of the service brand by, 180–181
touchpoints for interacting with, 110–113

D

da Vinci Surgical System (Intuitive Surgical), 54, 57
Data. *See* Consumer data
Davidson, Willie, 305
Davis, Scott, 271, 272, 278
Dawn brand, 45
Dayton's, 50
De Beers
signature line used by, 102
social influence used by, 54
Decentralization strategy, 81
Deere, John, 263–264
Deft brands, 136
Deloitte's purpose-driven study, 23
Design thinking
See also Brand design
Blue Apron's user experience (UX) design, 295
to design distinct and exclusive brand communities, 138–139
"making mode" of, 94
"show, don't tell" focus of, 94
System 1 thinking, 95–96, 102
System 2 thinking, 95, 102
DevOps (Microsoft), 167
DeWalt tools, 134
Diet Coke brand, 6
Differentiate or Die (Trout), 47
Differentiation
clarify superiority of brand benefit through, 152
just different enough strategy, 61
points of difference, 6–10, 15, 40, 152
Diffusion of brand message, 148–150
Digital brand storytelling
Always'"#LikeAGirl" campaign, 161–162
the power of stories used in, 162–165
Digital technology. *See also* Innovation
brand storytelling, 161–165
digital data the tracking of brands, 232–233
harnessing the power of big tech–big data, 203–204
how it has changed market research, 193–194
managing brand communications with, 287–292
new opportunities through informed contact, 182
rise of self-service, 181–182
transformation of product manufacturing to service providers by, 182–183

Dillon, Mary, 256, 262

Discrete choice experiment (DCE), 242–243

Disintermediation process, 294

Disney
created to "bring happiness," 22
failed deal between Kraft Foods and, 218–219
Mickey Mouse "brand standard" of, 219

Disney, Walt, 22

Docherty, Denny, 263, 270

Dollar Shave Club's (DSC) initial YouTube video, 149

Domino's, 68

Dos Equis beer, 8–9

Double RL, 42

Dove
"Campaign for Real Beauty" (2004) of, 135, 170, 249
"Choose Beauty" campaign of, 170
Dove Self-Esteem Project of, 170

Dropbox, 60

Dubitsky, Craig, 308

Dukesmith, Frank, 113

Dunkin' Donuts, 9

Dunn, Renée, 20, 25, 36

Duvall, David, 271, 272, 278

Dynamic Logic, 290

E

Earle, Paul, 301, 309

Easy names to use, 305–306

Eating the Big Fish (Morgan), 249

eBay
ad showing man breaking antique vase by, 7
challenges to, 54
as do-it-yourself digital marketplace, 193

ECAP (enterprise customer acquisition process) [John Deeere], 266–268

Economist magazine, 252

EEG (electroencephalography), 207, 208–209, 215

Egelund, Kasper, 41

EMI, 58

Emotion
Angel's Envy and associated, 305
customer experience driven by empathy and, 194, 195–196
fMRI used for tracking brand, 213–215
growth model principle on branding, 29

Empathy-driven customer experience, 194, 195–196

Employees. *See also* Local manager(s)
hiring in customer-centric world, 299–300
UX or CX (customer experience) talent, 299
"war for talent," 250, 254

Endorser brand(s)
definition of, 39–40
examples of, 40

Enterprise customer acquisition process (ECAP) [John Deeere], 266–268

Erasmus University, 211

Evaluation. *See also* Brand(s)
brand advertising creating positive feeling transferred to, 147–148
customer consideration and, 116*fig*, 118, 122*fig*–124*fig*
customer post-usage, 116*fig*, 120*fig*– 121, 122*fig*–124*fig*
customer's perceptual processing to make an, 148
different approaches required for traditional and digital media, 291–292

Execution KPIs, 75

Experience. *See* Customer experience

Extra gum, 12

Extreme sports, 165

Eye-tracking, 207, 209–210

F

Facebook. *See also* Social media
  advertising through, 144
  Axe brand page on, 87
  brands posted on, 110
  Capitol Coutures on, 173
  as fast follower to MySpace and
    Friendster, 58
  as part of the new mobile platform,
    112
  portfolio of brands by, 42
  as a primary brand, 38
  Tough Mudder's obstacle–course
    events on, 150
  Toyota's "Auto–Biography" campaign,
    167–168
Fast follower(s)
  ability to overtake pioneers, 58
  the fast-follower advantage, 58–59
  growth-stage entrants, 59
FedEx brand (Federal Express),
  100–101, 170
Feedback
  dashboards providing real-time, 187
  John Deere's marketing-focused
    approach and listening to customer,
    268–269
  McKinsey on customer loyalty loop
    and, 114, 120
  mobile apps providing immediate
    customer, 187
Feel-good marketing (McDonald's),
  253, 254
Financing
  differences between marketing and,
    235–236
  noncost approaches to brand value,
    236–240
  skepticism over brand expenditures
    and, 234–235
"Finding the Data to Craft the Journey,"
  122
Fink, Larry, 23, 34

Firms of Endearment (Wolfe, Sheth, and
  Sisodia), 22
Floral–delivery company's usage stage,
  119
fMRI (functional magnetic resonance
  imaging)
  description as data collection tool,
    207, 209
  detecting consumer responses to brand
    design, 215
  tracking brand association in the brain
    using, 211–213
  tracking brand emotions and
    engagement, 213–215
Folgers brand, 63
Ford, Henry, 60, 201
Ford Motor Company, 106
Forrester report (2017), 118
Fortune magazine, 33
Four Ps (product, pricing, place,
  promotion), 297–299
Four Seasons Hotel print ad, 154*fig*
4Ms media strategy
  Absolute Vodka print advertising,
    158*fig*
  matching component of, 155–157
  monopolizing, moment, and mindset
    components of, 155, 157–158
Frame of reference
  brain positioning statement element
    of, 6–7
  Coke Zero Sugar's, 6–7
  communicated by showing goal of
    brand use, 7
  informing consumers about the goal
    in brand use, 6
  orchestrating point of difference and,
    10
Franchised services, 181
Fresh brand, 45
Freytag, Gustav, 168
Freytag's plot structure pyramid, 168
Friendster, 58

G

GAAP (generally accepted accounting principles), 35
Gaining attention strategy, 151
"Gangnam Styles" video (2012), 149
Gansca, Silviu, 177
Gardner, Wendi L., 129, 141
Gates, Bill, 24, 232
Gates Foundation, 231–232
Gates, Melina, 24
Gebbia, Joe, 32
GEICO, 9
Gelbart, Tony, 50
Gender issues
  negative stories on Travis Kalanick and Uber related to, 224
  STEM gender gap, 169–170
  Uber and Lyfit brand comparisons related to, 224–225
General Electric (GE)
  "Childlike Imagination" campaign of, 164
  overtaking EMI in CT scanners, 58
  storytellers among engineers of, 168–169
  transformation from aircraft engine manufacturer to services by, 183
General Mills
  Oui by Yoplait brand by, 103
  Yoplait Greek brand by, 102–103
General Motors Corporation (GM)
  Mary Barra's leadership of, 24
  overlooked value strategy of, 60
  poor brand portfolio management, 43–44
Gerber brand, 47, 104–106
Gibbons, Euell, 11
Gillette Fusion brand, 5, 45, 87–88
Glad OrdorShield, 40
Global brand success storie(s)
  Axe brand, 86–88

Gillette and Chesebrough-Pond's, 87–88
  McDonald's, 88–89
Global brand(s)
  finding global–local balance, 81–84
  insights necessary to expand, 79–80
  orchestrating a global rollout, 84–86
  success stories and challenges of, 86–89
  understanding the core essence of the brand, 82–84
Global insight(s)
  enlist local managers, 80
  find the common thread, 79
  segment across habits and needs, 79
  test and adjust, 80
Global rollout
  educate new markets, 84–85
  start small and scale thoughtfully, 85–86
  stay nimble and create agility, 84
Global–local balance
  decentralize to find the right, 81
  draw clear lines of responsibility among collaborative networks, 81–82
  understand the core essence of the brand, 82–84
Goals
  competence of consumers' ability to achieve their, 144–145
  during each stage of the customer journey, 124fig
  illustrative vacation planning journey with KPIs and, 125fig
  mapping KPI(s) and business, 124fig
  tying brand communication metrics to medium and business, 290–292
"Golden Knights" pro hockey team, 304
Golder, Peter N., 58
GoldieBlox advertising strategy, 145
Goldman Sachs, 37, 39

Google
  advertising through, 144
  brand communication management
    using data from, 289
  dominant market share of, 53
  following Netscape, 59
  innovation of, 61, 62, 63
  as prototypical brand, 57
  "Reunion" brand story of, 166
  touchpoints for interacting with
    customers through, 110
  Year in Search story montage of, 168
  "ZMOT" (zero moment of truth),
    117
Grand Ole Opry, 155
Grape-Nuts cereal, 11–12
Great Places to Work Institute, 22
Great Recession, 135, 140
Grocery Marketers, 112
*Grow: How Ideals Power Growth and Profit
  at the World's Greatest Companies*
  (Stengel), 22
Growth model
  Airbnb example of the, 32–34
  five underlying principles of, 27–29
  illustration of the, 25*fig*
  Pharmavite example of the, 29–32
  purpose path to, 25–27
Growth model phase(s)
  1. discover (or rediscover) their
    purpose, 25–26
  2. involves mining brand's heritage
    and building purpose framework,
    25–26*fig*
Growth model principle(s)
  common understanding of the case for
    purpose, 27
  integrate, 29
  remember that it is emotional, 29
  shared leadership and advocacy, 28
  top-down and bottom-up
    engagement, 28–29
Growth-stage entrant(s), 59

Guevara, Gloria, 279, 285
GutCheck, 201
Guthrie, Woody, 163
Guy Fawkes mask visual identity, 301

H

H2H (human to human) stories, 170
Häagen-Dazs, 58, 145–146
Halvorsen, Cindy, 287, 293
Hanes boxer brief ad, 146*fig*–147, 153
Hanes brand analogy YouTube video,
  153
Hanssens, 60, 61
Happy Meal sub-brand (McDonald's),
  253–254
Harley–Davidson, 130, 135, 137, 305
Harry's bread brand, 7, 8*fig*
Harry's Razors, 295–296
Harvard Business Review Press, 69
Harvard Business School, 35
Haus, Shelley, 72
Havaianas repositioning, 230
Health Information and Management
  Systems Society's Analytics Stage 7
  Ambulatory Award, 277
Heavenly Bed brand (Westin), 40
Hello toothpaste brand, 308*fig*
HelloFresh, 4
Hemphill, Eric Smoot, 177
Hennessy brand, 45
Hennessy, Julie, 218, 233
Herman Miller, 34
The Hero with a Thousand Faces
  (Campbell), 162–163
Hershey's Kisses advertising, 144
Hewlett Packard brand, 47
The Highlander SUV, 39
Hillary, Sir Edmund, 11–12
"Hilltop" commercial (Coca-Cola,
  1971), 253
Hiring in customer-centric world,
  299–300
Holiday Inns, 107

Holistic brand design, 108
Honda Civic compact car, 39
Honey Maid graham cracker(s), 14–15
House of brands model
  advantages and downsides of, 46
  description and examples of, 45
Hsu, Ming, 212
Hublot brand, 45
Huffington, Arianna, 85
Humira (rheumatoid arthritis drug), 166
Hummer brand, 44
Humor
  eBay ad showing man breaking
    antique vase, 7
  gaining attention through, 151
  Le Trèfle campaign videos, 151
The Hunger Games film series, 173, 174
Hyatt Centric, 39
Hyatt Hotel Corporation, 39, 184
Hyatt Place, 107
Hyper-targeting, 136

I

"I Am FedEx" story (FedEx), 170
I Love Lucy (TV show), 287
IBM
  Apple's challenge to, 62
  repositioning success of, 230
  transformation from manufacturer to
    services by, 182–183
iCloud (Apple), 60
Illustration (visual cues), 98*fig*, 104–106
Implementation-friendly strategy
  communicated by senior management,
    67–68
  three guidelines for, 72
Income accounting method, 238–239
India–Pakistan partition (1947), 166
Indochino customer experience, 296–297
Information
  brand, 148–150
  cascades of sharing, 148
  diffusion of, 148

Informed contact, 182
Ingredient branding, 40
Innovation. *See also* Digital technology
  the challenge of, 62–63
  empathy-driven customer experience
    driving, 194, 195–196
  of late movers, 61–64
  the Lummus Ginning version of,
    202–203
  of pioneers, 54–57
Inside-out brand metrics, 70
Insights2020 study, 22
Instagram, 42, 112
Instant Pot, 8
Integrated reporting, 244
Intel, 54
International Integrated Report Council
  (IIRC), 244
Internet of Things, 165
Interpublic, 143
Intuitive Surgical's da Vinci Surgical
  System, 54, 57
iPhone (Apple). *See also* Apple
  designed to make imitation
    difficult, 58
  failure to penetrate the Indian
    market, 83
  frame of reference used in launch
    of, 6
  launched 34 years after first mobile
    phone, 53
  world-wide impact of 2007
    introduction of, 23
IRI, 112
Isaacson, Walter, 201

J

Jazz music analogy, 170–171
JC Penney, 18
Jeep's Jeepster sports car, 61
Jenkins, Henry, 172
Jif brand, 20–21
Jobs, Steve, 57, 169, 201

John Deere brand
Dealer of Tomorrow strategy by, 269–270
Intelligent Solution Group (ISG) created at, 266
introducing ECAP (enterprise customer acquisition process), 266–268
making a plan to address the market opportunity, 265–266
origins of the, 263–264
responding to the changing world of farming, 264–265
taking a marketing-focused approach, 268–270
Johnny Walker's "Keep on Walking" campaign, 163
Johnson & Johnson
corporate plus brand name identity, 101fig
robotic systems interest by, 54
"to alleviate pain and disease" purpose of, 22
Johnson, Robert Wood, 22
Jordan, Michael, 153, 273
"Just Do It" slogan (Nike), 83

K

KABOOM brand, 195
Kalanick, Travis, 46, 85, 98, 224
"Keep on Walking" campaign (Johnny Walker), 163
Key performance indicators (KPIs)
description of, 74
illustrative vacation planning journey with goals and, 125fig
mapping business goals and, 124fig
three types of, 75
Khan Academy, 24
Khan, Salman, 24
Khosla, Sanjay, 78, 89–90
Kiddon, Joan, 74
Kikkoman brand, 48

Kimbell, Dave, 256, 262
Kiva Han (sixteenth century), 63
Knowledge structures
description of, 130
the self as a, 129–130
Knutson, Brian, 211
Kodak, 263
Korn Ferry purpose-driven study, 22
Kotler, Philip, 34–35
Kotler's Four Ps, 297–299
Kraft Foods
failed deal between Disney and, 218–219
international launching of Oreo by, 81–82
Tang testing and adjusting by, 80, 83
Krishnamurthi, Lakshman, 58–59
Kroc, Ray, 252
Krug brand, 45

L

LaCroix sparkling water, 46
Laddering-down strategy, 12–13
Laddering strategy
brand's point of difference sustained by, 12
as challenge of brand purpose, 250–251
description of, 12
Laddering-up strategy, 12–13
Lafley, A. G., 73
Lagnado, Silvia, 249, 255
Lands' End, 18
Lanz, Heinrich, 264
Late identification (ID) of category, 154
Late mover(s)
innovation by and examples of, 61–62
the innovation challenge of, 62–63
strategic innovation of, 63–64
Later entrant(s)
description of, 58
examples of, 59–60
just different enough strategy by, 61
overlooked value strategy by, 60–61

Lauren, Ralph, 41

Lazarus, 50

Le Trèfle brand, 151

Leader(s). *See also* Senior management
  critical brand strategy implementation
    role of brand, 76
  tools used by brand, 71*fig*, 74–75

Leadership and advocacy sharing, 28

Legend, John, 78

Lego brand health, 226–227

Leininger, Eric, 67, 77

Lever Brothers, 22

Lever, William Hesketh, 22

Levi Strauss & Company, 54, 67

Lexus brand, 61, 228

LG (formerly Lucky Goldstar), 228

LGBTQ community, 14–15

Licensing deals
  changing level of control in modern,
    219
  Disney's old Mickey Mouse brand
    standard used in, 219

Life transitions, 135–136

LifePaint (Volvo), 13

Light, Larry, 74

"#LikeAGirl" campaign (Always),
  161–162

Lincoln Motor Company, 101

Line, 112

LinkedIn, 110

Lite beer (Miller), 4, 15, 18

L.L. Bean's return policy, 164

Local manager(s). *See also* Employees
  Chinese NBA star Yao Ming used to
    see by, 82
  enlisting the, 80
  test and adjust as, 80

Logo(s). *See also* Brand design
  designing for new brands, 308*fig*
  first Cadbury, 93–94*fig*
  of Lyft and Uber, 224*fig*
  original Uber, 98*fig*–99
  repositional Uber, 99*fig*

L'Oréal, 79, 253

Louis Roederer, 53

Louis Vuitton, 7, 45

Loyalty programs
  service brand, 188
  Starbucks' digital applications of, 140

Lucky Goldstar (later LG), 228

Lufthansa, 38, 40

Lululemon, 13

LUMAscapes, 287

Lummus Ginning, 202–203

LVMH's house of brands, 45

Lyft
  differentiation strategy used by, 60
  gender issues related to comparison of
    Uber and, 224–225
  logo of, 224*fig*

M

Ma, Jack, 24

MacBook Air, 152

Macy's, 50

Magetuck brand, 297

Magnum brand, 58

"#MakeWhatsNext" campaign
  (Microsoft), 169–170

"Making mode," 94

Marc Jacobs brand, 45

Marcus brand (Goldman Sachs), 37, 39

Marineau, Phil, 67

Market pioneer. *See* Pioneering
  advantages

Market research
  data from existing, 125
  data from primary, 125–126
  data from secondary, 125
  how digital technology has changed,
    193–194
  for leveraging customer journey
    insights, 200–204
  traditional approach to, 193

Market share by brand entry order,
  54–55*fig*

Marketability of brand name, 306
Marketing
  brand marketing funnels, 220–221*fig*
  brand value connecting finance and,
    234–244
  comparing services and product,
    179–180
  differences between finance and,
    235–236
  digital transformation of services
    branding and, 181–183
  John Deere brand's approach to,
    268–270
  McDonald's culture, product, and
    brand approach to, 252–254
  prioritizing allocation of resources
    principle of, 121–122
  traditional viewed as cost center, 235
Marketing mix analysis (MMA), 292
Marketing segmentation
  consumer habits and needs, 79
  creating a customer journey by
    beginning with, 121–122
  identifying primary path for selected
    segment, 122
  Novant Health's investment in smart,
    274–275
  persona development replacing
    traditional, 194, 196–199
Marriott Corporation
  corporate identity of, 101
  Courtyard by Marriott, 40, 101
  endorser brands by, 40
  portfolio of brands by, 42
Marshall Fields, 50
Martins, Jerónimo, 167
MASB's Brand Investment and Valuation
  (BIV) project, 240, 241
Matching (4Ms media strategy), 155–157
Maxwell House brand, 63
Maya-based tourism (Mexico), 282
"Mayhem" commercials (Allstate), 154
McDelivery (McDonald's app), 254

McDonald's
  attitudinal tracking of, 222*fig*
  brand lexicon of, 103
  bringing brand implementation
    strategy to life in context of, 73
  competing in terms of quick and
    inexpensive, 9
  feel-good marketing used by, 253, 254
  French fries container shape used by,
    107
  global brand success of, 88–89
  the Happy Meal sub-brand of, 253–254
  "I'm loving it" signature line of,
    101–102
  matching strategy used to advertise,
    156
  "Our Food, Your Questions"
    campaign by, 252
  as a primary brand followed by
    product description, 38
  targeting multiple segments, 121
McKensey & Company, 114, 120
McTigue, Kevin, 110, 127
"Me decade" (1970s), 253
Medallia, 199
Media. *See also* Channel(s); Social media
  different evaluations required for
    traditional and digital, 291–292
  link outcomes of both business and,
    291
Medtronic, 54
Meier, James, 235
Mercedes-Benz, 60, 61
Mercedes snow-driving ad, 153
Mergers and acquisitions (M&As), 236,
  237, 238
Messages. *See* Advertising messages
Messenger, 112
#MeToo, 168
Metrics. *See also* Brand performance
  evaluations; Consumer data
  brand measurement techniques,
    220–225

for EEG data on consumer engagement, 214–215
journey mindset driving collection of data and, 194, 199–200
Net Promoter Score (NPS), 75, 124, 125*fig*, 199
for tracking service brand progress, 187–188
tying business goals, medium, and brand communication, 290–292
Mexico
amazing historic and geographic features of, 280
economic downturn (2009) and other challenges faced by, 279–280
five lessons learned during repositioning brand of, 284–285
holistic plan for repositioning, 281–283
"Mexico Taxi Project" campaign to increase tourism in, 283
"Routes of Mexico" campaign to increase tourism, 282
San Miguel de Allende (Guanajuato) of, 280
Mickey Mouse "brand standard," 219
Microsoft
Bing search engine of, 63
high-low-high brand health of, 231–232
"#MakeWhatsNext" campaign of, 169–170
Microsoft Philanthropies, 169
Microsoft Story Labs, 167
Miller Lite beer
brand positioning statement of, 4
repositioning by, 15, 18
Millward Brown BrandZ, 239, 240
Millward Brown Optimor, 22
Millward Brown's purpose study, 250
Mindset (4Ms media strategy), 158*fig*
Mitchell, Colin, 249, 255
Mitsubishi, 60–61

Mobile environment
brand communication must work in a, 289–290
immediate customer ratings through apps, 187
McDelivery (McDonald's), 254
ModCloth brand, 133, 135
Moment (4Ms media strategy), 157
Momentum
brand strategy implementation role of, 71*fig*, 75–76
quick wins to keep up the, 76
Monopolizing (4Ms media strategy), 157
Monster, 56
Montblanc, 130
Morgan, Adam, 249
Moss, Kate, 16
"The most interesting man in the world" ads, 8–9
Motivation. *See also* Advertising; Customer(s); Self-brand connections
for brand purchase, 132–133, 134*fig*
incentivize brand usage, 140
self–brand connection principle on targeting one motive, 134–135
understanding fundamental customer, 144–146
Motivation fundamentals
community, 145
competence, 144–145
contentment, 145
Motive matrix, 133–134*fig*
Motorola, 53
Motorola's "Telematics" brand, 103
Mr. Clean commercials, 156
Mush (oatmeal brand), 303*fig*, 305
Musk, Elon, 169
MySpace, 58

N

Nakamoto, Kent, 53, 65
Naming brands, 98*fig*–100, 303–306

Nelson, Leif D., 212
Nestlé, 50
Net Promoter Score (NPS), 75, 124, 125*fig*, 199
Netflix, 54
Neuroscience
  brand insights from, 210–215
  tool kit for collecting consumer data using, 207–210
Neuroscience tool kit
  EEG (electroencephalography), 207, 208–209, 213–215
  emerging tools, 210
  eye-tracking, 207, 209–210
  fMRI (functional magnetic resonance imaging), 207, 209, 211–213, 215
New brand creation steps
  1. look for a hook, 302–303*fig*
  2. the name game, 303–306
  3. obtaining a trademark, 306–307
  4. developing brand design, 307–309*fig*
New Brand Leadership (Light and Kiddon), 74
New brands
  challenges of creating from scratch, 301
  the four steps to creating a successful, 302–309*fig*
Nielsen, 290
Nike
  capitalizing on "everyone wants to be an athlete," 79
  "Just Do It" slogan of, 83
  Nike Pro Hijab project by, 83
  self-concept clarity of customers of, 131
  spokespeople used by, 153
  struggling to overcome impressions of child labor, 86
Ninja pressure cooker(s), 8
"No name" brand, 98
Nontargeted consumer(s), 5–6
Noodles & Company, 76

Nooyi, Indra, 34
NorthShore University HealthSystem, 99
Northwestern University's Kellogg School of Management, 34–35
"Nova" car brand, 99
Novant Health
  background information on, 271
  Care Connections (virtual care hub) of, 276
  digital integration plan of, 276–277
  increasingly fragmented brand portfolio of, 271–272
  lessons learned on rebranding by, 273–277
  rebranding a complex portfolio, 272–273
NYX brand, 259

O

Oatmeal brand Mush, 303*fig*
Old Navy, 16–18
Old Spice brand health, 229–230
Oldsmobile brand, 43, 44
Olfaction (scent), 98*fig*, 107
Olympics
  2018 Winter Olympics at South Korea, 171
  United Airlines' long-time sponsorship of, 186–187
  Vancouver Winter Olympic Games tie-in with P&G ads, 171
Omega brand, 135
Omni-channel commerce, 119
Omnicom, 143
Omnicom Group, 239
Online customer data, 126
Oracle of Omaha, 169
Oratory (POP–product, oratory, purpose), 302
OrdorShield (Glad), 40
Oreo cookie brand, 81–82
O'Toole, Tom, 177, 189

Oui by Yoplait brand, 103
"Our Food, Your Questions" campaign
    (McDonald's), 252
Outside-in brand metric(s), 70
Overlooked value strategy, 60–61

P

Packaging (Tropicana orange juice), 148,
    149*fig*
Pain points (customer), 166
Palmer, Andy, 41
Park, Chan Su, 241
Park, Missy, 13
Parker, Warby, 119
Patagonia branded briefcase, 137
Patgonia, 14
Peloton home equipment brand, 304*fig*
PepsiCo
    battle between Coca-Cola and, 57
    Bubbly brand of, 46
    in cola category, 102
    color palette used by, 106–107
Pepto-Bismol brand, 213
Perceptual processing, 148
Pereira, Sergio, 294, 300
Perrier brand, 7, 60
Persona development, 194, 196–199
Persuasive messaging
    Burger King's creative and, 150
    print ads for Ritz-Carlton and Four
        Seasons Hotels, 154*fig*
    strategies for creating a, 151–154
Pet shelter ad study, 213
Pete the Millennial Soybean Producer,
    198*fig*
Pharmavite
    the growth model in action at, 29–32
    key beliefs and worldview at, 30
    "We exist to bring the gift of health
        to life" purpose activated at, 30–32
Phillips pressure cooker(s), 8
Pink, Daniel, 23
Pinterest, 112

Pioneering advantage(s)
    consumers remember pioneers, 56
    description and examples of, 54–55
    estimated market share based on brand
        entry order relative to pioneer,
        54–55*fig*
    pioneer is a low-risk choice, 55–56
    a pioneer sets category standards, 56–57
Place (Four Ps), 298
Plated, 4, 6
Platform businesses, 181
"PocketLink" (BlackBerry candidate
    name), 99
Points of difference
    Bud Light's differentiating its brand, 15
    clarify superiority of brand benefit
        through, 152
    ingredient and service brands as, 40
    orchestrating the frame of reference
        and, 10
    point of difference in terms of value,
        9–10
    reasons to believe, 6–9
    reasons to believe that support, 7–9
    specifying benefits that serve as, 7
    in terms of value, 9–10
"Points of parity" features, 6
Polo Ralph Lauren, 42
Pontiac brand, 43, 44
POP (product, oratory, and purpose), 302
Porras, Jerry, 22
Porsche Cayenne SUV, 41
Porter, Michael, 35
Porter, Mike, 263, 270
Post-usage evaluation stage
    of the customer journey, 116*fig*,
        120*fig*–121
    illustrative vacation planning customer
        journey, 123*fig*
    key questions to ask during, 123*fig*
    mapping business goals and KPI(s),
        124*fig*
    typical customer path including, 122*fig*

Pre-need stage
 of the customer journey, 115*fig*–117
 illustrative vacation planning customer journey, 123*fig*
 illustrative vacation planning journey with goals and KPIs, 125*fig*
 key questions to ask during, 123*fig*
 mapping business goals and KPI(s), 124*fig*
 typical customer path including, 122*fig*
PricewaterhouseCoopers' *Putting Purpose to Work* report (2016), 23
Pricing (Four Ps), 297–298
Primary brand(s), 38
Primary path of target segment, 122
Primary research, 125–126
Prince brand, 229
Procter & Gamble (P&G)
 Always (feminine hygiene products) of, 13–14
 brand leader position created by, 76
 copy strategy of, 20–21
 as enterprise comprised of multiple brands, 26
 house of brands model used by, 45
 Old Spice acquired and repositioned by, 229–230
 once an innovative market leader (1980s), 20
 short snappy names for brands of, 305
 Swiffer brand of, 305
 "Thank You, Mom" campaign of, 171
 three moments of truth for all brands of, 73
 White Cloud trademark lost by, 50
Product relevance, 303–305
Products. *See also* Brand(s)
 creating a new brand from scratch, 301–309*fig*
 as one of the Four Ps, 297
 POP (product, oratory, and purpose), 302
 relevance of, 303–305

"white space" opportunities for new, 194, 195–196
Prolia brand, 48
Promotion (Four Ps), 298–299
Protea Hotels by Marriott, 40
Prototypical brand(s), 57
Pruning brand portfolio(s), 49–50
PTA moms and Jif, 21
Publicis, 143
Purple Carrot, 4
Purpose-centered approach
 description of, 21
 purpose path to growth model, 25*fig*–27
Purpose framework, 25–26*fig*
Purpose implementation
 captaining activity system, 27
 telegraphing activity system, 27
 walking the talk activity system, 27
Purpose. *See* Brand purpose
Putting Purpose to Work report (2016), 23

Q

Quelch, John, 49
Questions
 McDonald's "Our Food, Your Questions" campaign, 252
 to measure brand awareness, 222*fig*
 measuring brand associations using open-ended, 223–225

R

Racial inclusivity ad message, 14–15
Ralph by Ralph Lauren, 42
Ralph Lauren Corporation, 41–42
Ralph's Coffee Shop, 42
Ram brand (Dodge), 39
RCA, 58
"Real Beauty" campaign (Dove), 135, 170, 249
"Real Beauty Sketches" (Dove's "Real Beauty" entry, 2013), 135

Reasons to believe
  attributes important to consumers
    used as, 8–9, 152
  featuring an attribute as a, 7
  Harry's bread delivers "nice and soft,"
    7, 8*fig*
  points of difference supported by, 7–9
  spokespeople used as, 153
  spokesperson of brand as type of, 7
  switching from attribute to image, 12
  that Apple's products make consumers
    smarter, 7
Rebranding
  Novant Health, 271–277
  Ulta Beauty, 72, 256–262
Red Bull
  competitive advantage of, 63
  pioneering advantage of, 54, 56, 57
  "See the Big Picture" brand
    storytelling by, 165
Red Cross, 134
Reddit's DSC video visitors, 149
Redefined Fitness, 177
Redundant brand(s), 49–50
Reese's advertising, 144
Reinhart, Keith, 253
Repositioning brand(s). *See also* Brand
    position
  Aleve's need to undergo, 15–16, 18
  Apple Watch's initial and revised, 16,
    17*fig*, 18
  Blue Apron's approach to, 3–4
  Burberry's approach to, 16
  cautionary tale of Old Navy's, 15–18
  the country brand of Mexico, 279–285
  Miller Lite's approach to, 15
  Old Spice case for, 229–230
Research. *See* Market research
Residence Inn by Marriott, 40
"Reunion" story (Google), 166
Revealed preference (RP), 241
Rio de Janeiro Summer Olympics
  (2016), 81

Ritz-Carlton Hotel print ad, 154*fig*
RJMetrics, 106
RL Restaurant, 42
Robinson's, 50
Roese, Neal, 129, 141
Romeo and Juliet (Shakespeare), 303
Rose, Kristine, 39
Rust–Oleum, 102
Ryanair, 227

S

Saab brand, 44
Sainsbury's, 119
Salesforce, 24
Salinas, Gabriela, 239
Samsung
  brand health of, 227–228
  as fast follower, 58
  leading global sales of smartphones, 58
San Miguel de Allende (Guanajuato,
  Mexico), 280
San Pellegrino brand, 60
Sansom, Will, 113
Saturn brand, 44
Saunders, Neil, 42
Sawhney, Mohanbir, 161, 175
Scent (olfaction), 98*fig*, 107
Scent (product), 98*fig*, 107
Schultz, Howard, 64
Scotch-Brite paper, 10
Seasonal product advertising, 157
Secondary research, 125
See Jane Work brand, 137
"See the Big Picture" (Red Bull), 165
Segmentation. *See* Marketing segmentation
Seinfeld and Friends (TV show), 287
The self
  linking the brand to, 131–133
  as one knowledge structure among the
    ones in human memory, 129–130
  psychological conceptualization of, 129
  working self-concept describing
    aspects of, 130

Self-brand connection principles
  1. target one motive, 134–135
  2. target life transitions for powerful self-brand connections, 135–136
  3. use the brand to bridge self-concept conflicts, 136–137
  4. use the brand to compensate for threats to self-concept, 137–138
  5. design distinct and exclusive brand communities, 138–139
  6. use multifaceted brand storytelling, 139–140
  7. incentivize brand usage, 140
Self-brand connections. *See also* Motivation; Targeted customer(s)
  description of, 130
  the motive matrix for brand purchase and, 133–134*fig*
  motives for linking the brand to the self, 131–133
  the self aspect of, 129–130
  the self-concept aspect of, 130
  the self-concept clarity aspect of, 131
  seven principles for building strong, 134–140
The self-concept
  brand–self connections and role of, 130
  clarity of, 131
  definition of, 130
  self-brand connections that target life transitions of, 135–136
  use the brand to compensate for threats to, 137–138
  working, 130
Self-concept clarity, 131
Self-Esteem Project (Dove), 170
Self-service delivery, 181–182
Senior management. *See also* Chief executive officer (CEO); Leader(s)
  brand portfolio involvement by, 51
  communicating implementation-friendly strategy, 67–68
Sephora brand, 45

Service asset ownership, 180–181
Service brand building
  be clear on value proposition, 183–184
  create standards and digital enablement for, 184–186
  engage employees and communicate for, 186–187
  loyalty programs for, 140, 188
  use metrics to track progress, 187–188
Service brand(s)
  building a powerful, 183–188
  description of, 40
  digital transformation of services marketing and, 181–183
  franchised, 181
  of platform businesses, 181
  rise of self-service delivery impacting, 181–182
  unique dynamics related to, 178–181
Service delivery standard(s), 184–186
The Seven Basic Plots: Why We Tell Stories (Booker), 163
7 Up, 102
Sex commonality, 79
Shakespeare, William, 303
Shankar, Venkatesh, 58–59
Shape (product), 98*fig*, 107
Sheth, Jagdish, 22
Siegel+Gale, 241
Signature line(s), 98*fig*, 101–102
Simple principle
  global rollout by creating agility of the, 84
  as key to successful brand portfolio, 51
Sisodia, Rajendra, 22, 34
Skinner, Jim, 73
Snapp, Mary, 169
Snickers bar advertising, 144
Social influence, 54
Social media. *See also* Channel(s); Facebook; Media
  advertising through, 144

Capitol Couture (online magazine)
  on, 173
  Instagram, 42, 112
  managing brand communication
    through, 287–292
      Pinterest, 112
  transmedia storytelling on, 172–174
  Twitter, 26, 110
Sound (aural brand design), 98*fig*,
  103–104
South Korea 2018 Winter Olympics, 171
SpaceX, 169
Spirit Airlines, 227
Spokespeople, 153
Spotify, 112
Srinivasan, V., 241
Standards
  Mickey Mouse "brand standard," 219
  pioneer advantage of setting category,
    56–57
  of service brand, 184–186
Stanford d.school, 94
Starbucks
  competing on value differences, 9
  consumer engagement strategy used
    by, 234
  digital applications of loyalty programs
    of, 140
  leadership management of racial bias
    incident, 68
  racial bias expressed by Philadelphia
    manager damaging, 15, 68
  social influence used by, 54
  strategic innovation of, 63–64
  touchpoints used by, 111–112
Starwood, 117
State of Tennessee campaign, 155
State of the Global Workplace study, 23
Stated preference (SP), 241, 242
Steinway Corporation, 39
Stella Artois repositioning, 230
STEM gender gap, 169–170
Stengel, Jim, 20, 22, 35, 250

Sternthal, Brian, 143, 159
Stewart, Potter, 306
Storytelling
  brand, 139–140, 153, 165–171
  digital brand, 161–175
  the power of stories used in, 162–165
  transmedia, 172–174
Sub-brand(s)
  definition of, 38–39
  examples of, 39
SunTrust bank, 26
Super Bowl
  ad exposure during, 171
  adjusting supply in case of Eagles win
    of, 180
  criticism of Audi's ad during the, 251
Supply and demand changes, 180
Surface Pro 3 table, 152
Swiffer brand, 305
Symbols
  brand, 98*fig*, 106
  corporate, 98*fig*, 106
System 1 thinking, 95–97
System 2 thinking, 95, 102
Systems view of brand value creation,
  243*fig*

T

Tampax tampons commercials, 147
Tang brand, 80, 83
Targeted customer(s)
  See also Self-brand connections
  considerations for selecting a, 5
  deciding who they are, 121–122
  description in the positioning
    statement, 5
  how brand image constraints the
    choice of, 6
  hyper-targeting of, 136
  target one motive of, 134–135
Tarte brand, 259
TeamSnap, 195–196
Technology. *See* Digital technology

Tellis, Gerard J., 58

Tesla, 169

Test and adjust, 80

"Thank You, Mom" campaign (Procter & Gamble), 171

"Think Different" campaign (Apple, 1997), 139–140, 249

This Is Us (TV show), 287

"This is your brain on drugs" public service campaign, 171

"This Land is Your Land" (Guthrie), 163

Threat appeal(s), 151

Tide detergent advertising, 156

Tiffany brand name, 100

Time-Fortune conference (2017), 85

Title IX legislation (1972), 13

Title Nine, 13

TOMS Shoes, 21, 167

Top-down engagement, 28–29

Touchpoint(s)
  description of, 110, 111–112
  exponential growth of, 112–113

Tough Mudder, 145, 150

Tourism
  Mexico's Maya-based, 282
  repositioning Mexico's country brand to increase, 279–285

Toyota
  "Auto–Biography" Facebook campaign of, 167–168
  Highlander SUV brand of, 39
  as late mover, 59
  Lexus brand of, 61, 228
  open-ended questions to measure brand association, 223

Trademark applications, 306–307

Transmedia storytelling, 172–174

Trigger stage
  of the customer journey, 116*fig*, 117–118
  illustrative vacation planning customer journey, 123*fig*
  key questions to ask during the, 123*fig*

mapping business goals and KPI(s), 124*fig*

typical customer path including, 122*fig*

Tropicana orange juice packaging, 148, 149*fig*

Trout, Jack, 47

Trump, Donald, 33

23andMe, 24

"Twist, lick, dunk" Oreo tradition, 82

Twitter
  as both a brand and a company, 26
  brands posted on, 110

Tybout, Alice M., 3, 19

U

Uber
  brand leader position created by, 76
  branded house approach of, 46
  as disrupter, 113
  failure to start small and scale thoughtfully strategy of, 85
  gender issues related to comparison of Lyft and, 224–225
  impact of negative associations with, 224
  logo of, 224*fig*
  loyalty program of, 188
  Lyft strategy differentiating from, 60
  nonownership of service asset by, 180, 181
  original logo of, 98*fig*–99
  as prototypical brand, 57
  repositional logo of, 99*fig*
  ride-sharing category of, 102
  successfully segmenting across countries, 83
  taxi frame of reference used by, 6

"UberCab," 98

Ulta Beauty
  branding makeover of, 256, 260–261
  building the brand of, 258–260
  challenges and future directions of, 261–262

having a clear brand strategy, 72
history of, 257–258
rebranding lessons learned at, 261
Under Armour basketball shoe(s), 7
UNESCO's World Heritage List, 280
Unilever
Axe brand of, 78–79, 84–85, 86–88
Chesebrough-Pond's of, 88
Magnum brand launched by, 58
United Airlines, 68, 184, 186–187
United Nation's World Tourism
Organization, 281
University of California at Berkeley, 211
University of Southern California, 172
UNTUCKit brand, 297
UPS, 106
U.S. Patent and Trademark Office, 307
Usage stage
of the customer journey, 116*fig*, 119
illustrative vacation planning customer
journey, 123*fig*
key questions to ask during, 123*fig*
mapping business goals and KPI(s),
124*fig*
typical customer path including, 122*fig*
User experience (UX). *See also*
Customer experience
designing, 295
hiring talent for, 299
UserTesting, 201

V

Vacation planning
illustration complete with analysis,
126*fig*
illustration of customer journey, 123*fig*
illustration with goals and KPIs,
125*fig*
Validately, 201
Value
conceptual equation expressing, 9
connecting marketing and finance vis,
234–244

noncost approaches to brand,
236–240
representing a point of difference in
terms of, 9–10
Value proposition of services brand,
183–184
Vancouver Winter Olympic Games, 171
Verb Surgical, 54
Viagra, 59
VIPP, 41
Virgin Group, 46–47
Volkswagen emissions scandal, 223–224
Volvo
laddering-up strategy used by,
12–13
LifePaint product used by, 13

W

Waitrose, 119
Walker, Brian, 34
Walmart
brand symbols used by, 106
charges of bribery against, 86
White Cloud relaunched as premium
brand at, 50
"War for talent," 250, 254
Watkinson, Matt, 113
WeChat, 81, 112
Westin Heavenly Bed brand, 40
White Cloud brand, 50
Wojcicki, Anne, 24
Wolfe, David, 22
Wolfe, Tom, 253
"Working mother" identity, 137
Working self-concept, 130
World Travel & Tourism Council, 281
WPP, 143
WPP Kantor, 239

X

Xfinity brand, 305
Xgeva brand, 48

Y

Yahoo!, 62, 63
Yao Ming, 82
Year in Search story montage (Google),
    168
Yelp reviews, 298
Yoplait Greek brand, 102–103, 307
YouTube
    brand-life results from, 292
    Dollar Shave Club's (DSC) initial
        video on, 149
    EEG study on consumer engagement
        with videos on, 214–215
    Google's "Reunion" story, 166

Grand Ole Opry, 155
Hanes brand analogy video on, 153
as *The Hunger Games* film series'
    "official TV broadcast," 174
Le Trèfle campaign videos on, 151
as part of the new mobile platform, 112
primarily viewed on mobile devices,
    289

Z

Zajac, Ed, 70
Zenith brand, 45
Zevia brand, 56
"ZMOT" (zero moment of truth), 117